GW01375091

Nelles Guides

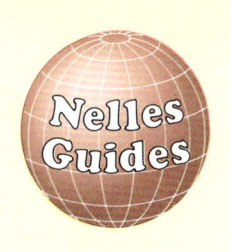

INDONESIA
WEST

Sumatra, Java, Bali, Lombok

First Edition
1990

TABLE OF CONTENTS

Imprint 240
List of Maps 7

HISTORY AND CULTURE

Indonesia - the Greatest Archipelago 9
- by David Henley
A Portrait of Java 37
- by James Fox
A Portrait of Bali 49
- by Putu Davies
A Portrait of Sumatra 61
- by Anthony Reid

TRAVELING IN INDONESIA

- by David Henley

SPRAWLING METROPOLIS
Jakarta 79

WEST JAVA 87
Banten 89
Sundalands 90
Bandung 93
Cirebon 95

CENTRAL JAVA 101
The Mountains 101
Borobudur 103
Prambanan 105
Yogyakarta 109
Solo 112
North Coast 114

EAST JAVA 123
North Coast 123
Surabaya 124
Madura 128
Malang 130
Penataran 136
Bromo 138

BALI / LOMBOK 145
Denpasar 145
Sanur and Kuta 147
Balinese Heartland 149

TABLE OF CONTENTS

Ubud 152
The Mountains 156
North Coast 158
Karangasem 160
Lombok 161

ACEH 169

NORTH SUMATRA 179
Medan 179
Bataklands 182
Padang Lawas 187
Nias 189

MALAY SUMATRA 195
Island Riau 197
Mainland Riau 199
South Sumatra Province 200
Jambi 204

WEST SUMATRA 207
Minangkabau Highlands 207
Bukittinggi 210
Padang 212
Mentawai Islands 214

SOUTH SUMATRA 217
Bengkulu 217
Lampung 219

FEATURES

Indonesian Cuisine 224
- by Yohanni Johns
Traditional Arts and Crafts 228
- by Robyn Maxwell and Adrian Horridge
Wildlife and Environment 235
- by Colin Groves
Islam 238
- by David Henley

GUIDELINES

Travel Tips 242
Indonesian Language 250
Credits 251
Index 252

WESTERN INDONESIA

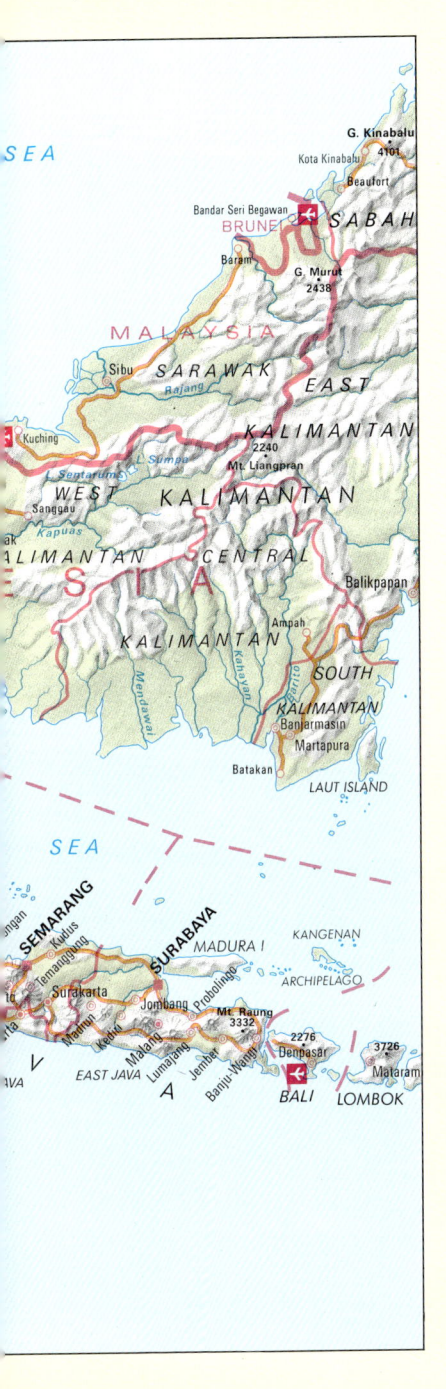

LIST OF MAPS

Western Indonesia	6
Jakarta	78
West Java	88
Bandung	92
Cirebon	95
Central Java	102
Yogyakarta	108
Surakarta	113
Semarang	115
East Java	124
Surabaya	126
Malang	134
Bali	147
Lombok	163
Aceh	171
North Sumatra	178
Medan	180
Nias Island	190
Malay Sumatra	196
Palembang	201
West Sumatra	208
Lampung / Bengkulu	219

Please note: in some cases the spelling of the place names on the maps is not the same as in the text, because the spelling on the maps is according to UN guidelines, whereas the usual English spelling is used in the text.

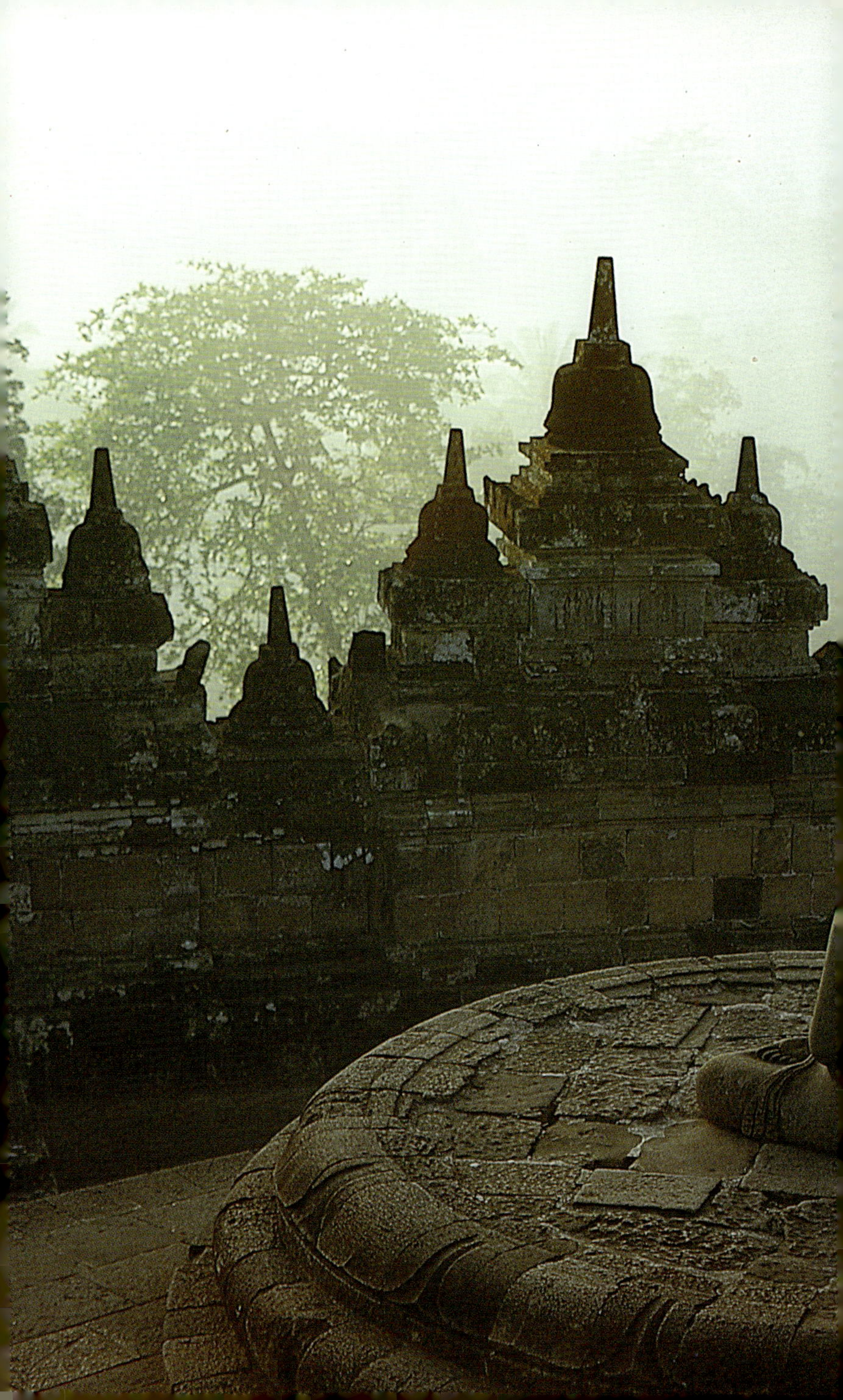

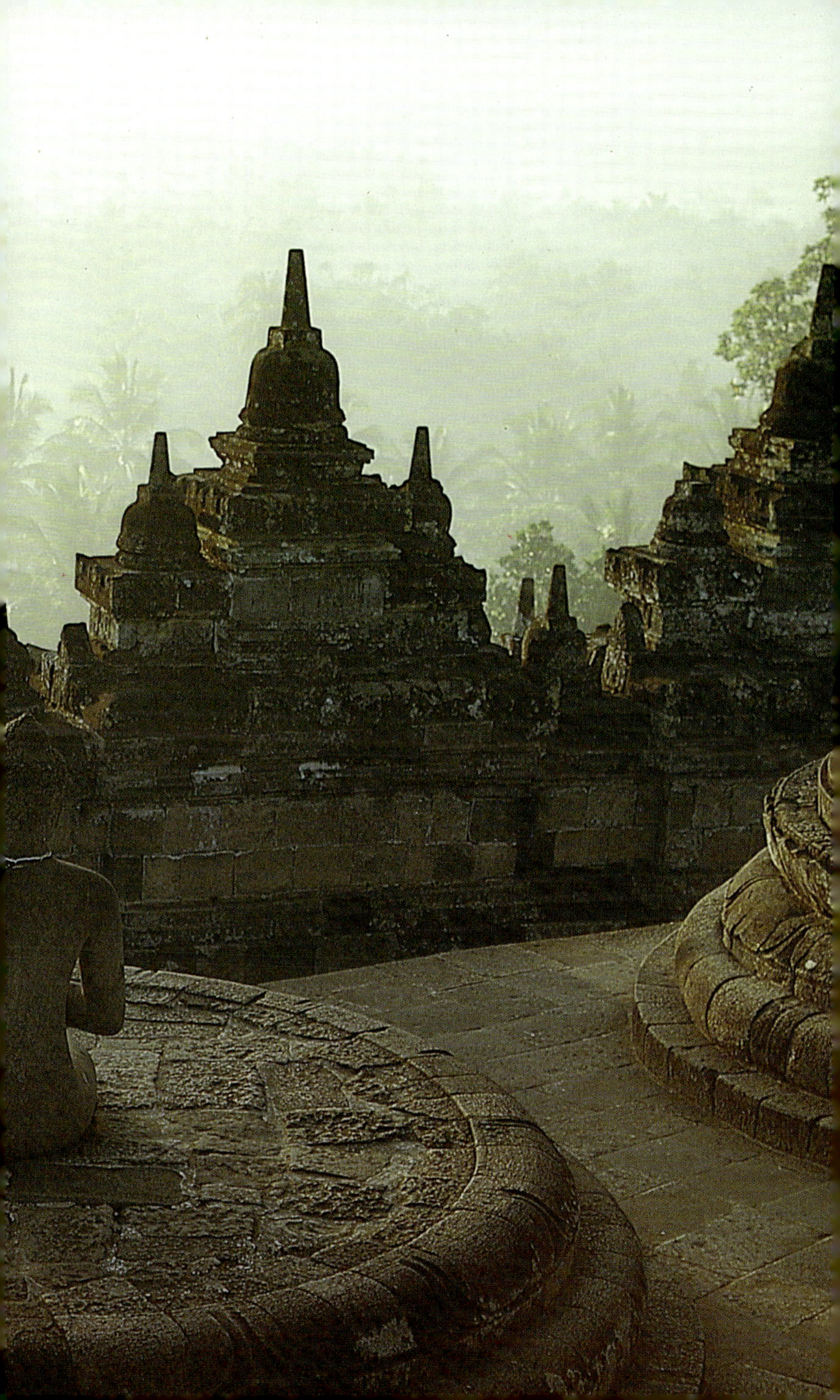

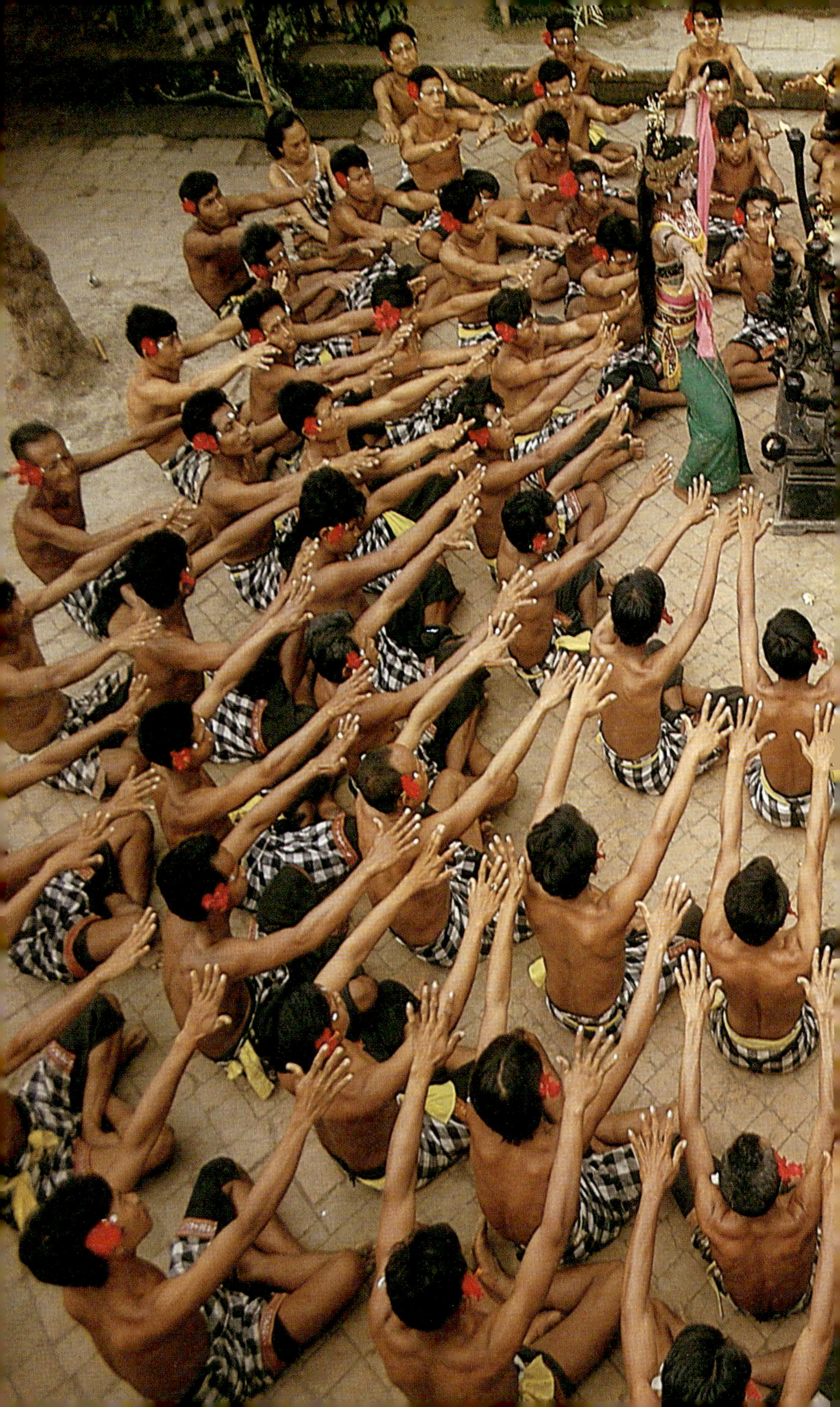

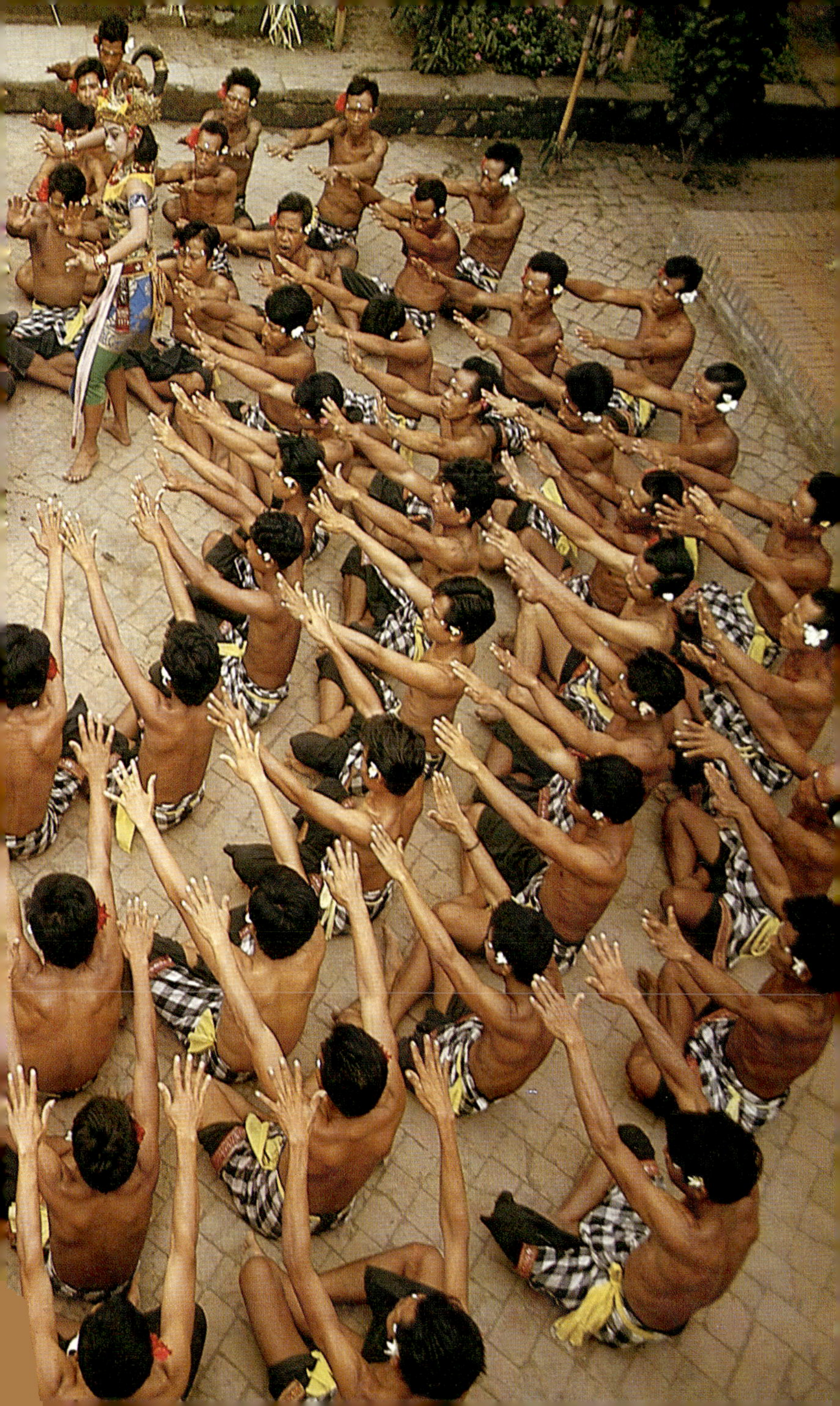

INDONESIA – THE GREATEST ARCHIPELAGO

INDONESIA THE GREATEST ARCHIPELAGO

Indonesia is a strange blank in the modern world's imagination. Other Asian nations – Japan, China, India, Pakistan – have widespread popular stereotypes. But is there a stereotypical Indonesian? What does he or she look like? A barefoot peasant in a coolie hat? A tatooed tribesman with blowpipe and jungle knife? A poised dancer in batik and gold? A braided general? The images are too many, too disparate and too vague. The landscapes which could stand for Indonesia are just as ambiguous. On a postcard, the fabled beaches of Bali look indistinguishable from those of Jamaica or Tahiti, while temples, ricefields and rain forests seem to the layman to blur with the backdrops of tropical Asia as a whole.

Why is it that foreign images of this great and beautiful archipelago are so confused? After all, Indonesia is a major nation by any standards. Its 13,600 islands span fully one-eighth of the circumference of the earth, and its 175 million citizens make it the fifth most populous of all countries, after China, India, the USSR and the USA. And Indonesia has an impressive and surprising history. Parts of it have been civilised for longer than England, and ruled by Europeans since the time of Oliver Cromwell. Indonesians were also the very first Asians to rid themselves of colonial rule through national revolution.

Yet some of the major reasons for the country's present obscurity are also historical. Indonesia was not part of the great global empires of Portugal, Spain,

Preceding pages: Balinese temple decoration. Woman from West Java. The magic of Borobudur. Kecak dance on Bali. Left: A detail from Borobudur.

Britain and France, but the sole substantial jewel in the colonial crown of the tiny Netherlands. Between the seventeenth century and the Second World War, it was remote from the mainstream of world history, a strange remnant both of old Asia and of Dutch overseas power, contributing little to the world except the sugar, coffee, rubber and other tropical crops upon which the diet and industry of Europe and America came to depend. The Japanese occupation released a tide of revolution which swept away the placid old Dutch East Indies and proclaimed in their place a volatile new nation calling itself Indonesia, a term then familiar only to a few oriental scholars. For two brief decades, the infant state projected itself into the international spotlight, confronting the superpowers and posturing as the leader of world anti-colonialism. Then in 1965, the assertive order fell victim to the tension and chaos which its own romantic radicalism had produced at home. A military regime picked up the pieces and has ruled ever since, committed to stability and economic development above either bombast or human rights. For the last quarter of a century, Indonesia has once more been waiting in the wings of history, a distant presence remembered only in fleeting press reports of reconstruction and repression. Of the developed countries, only Australia, the southern neighbour, retains a slightly fuller picture of the enigmatic archipelago.

There are other, equally important reasons why single images and stereotypes of Indonesia refuse to come into sharp focus. One is the country's vast and profound complexity. Of all today's states, only India, the Soviet Union and perhaps China can match Indonesia either in the number of cultural influences which it has undergone through the centuries or in the diversity of distinct traditions still present in its various regions. Every one of the major world religions, for example,

Traveling by bemo – a popular means of transportation.

has found its way here, and each is still represented by living communities as well as dead monuments. In the present century, every ideology and every shade of political idea from the nation-state to the Islamic state, has had its Indonesian exponents.

The final difficulty of trying to find universal symbols for Indonesia is that many of those symbols which mean most to Indonesians themselves are impenetrable to outsiders. At first encounter, some seem so alien as to defy memory itself. Few untrained westerners, for instance, can recall a passage of the aimless, haunting music of the Javanese *gamelan* orchestra. Its rippling gongs run scales to which their minds are not attuned, its interlocking rhythms find no echo in their hearts. And to someone familiar neither with the Indian gods and heroes nor with their Indonesian mutations, the filigreed, double-jointed puppets of the *wayang kulit* shadow play, good and evil alike, may be too strange to evoke any reaction other than curiosity.

Even when the outsider has learned to love such things for reasons other than their mystery, they retain an elusive quality which makes them difficult to recall or appreciate outside their native Indonesian context.

Pinned to the wall of a European living room, the shadow puppet is an absurdity; reduced to a deathless cassette and activated at the touch of a button, the *gamelan* loses all its life. But put them together in the hot Javanese night, with the buzz of the audience and the rich, sharp smell of clove cigarettes, and they generate the kind of magic which all travel guides celebrate but none can begin to evoke. A startling number of visitors agree that Indonesia, more than any other land, is an experience which cannot be wrapped up and taken home. This sensual, transient quality, this powerful and obscure spirit of place, is absolutely intrinsic to Indonesia, and cannot be taught

Women replanting seedlings in a Lombok rice paddy.

by any book. It is perhaps the strongest reason for going there.

A Pattern of Islands

On a map, Indonesia's composite geography seems to mirror its cultural complexity. The pattern of contorted islands is as intricate and strange as a shadow puppet. Some of the island names – Java, Sumatra, Ambon, Timor – are half-familiar from yellowed text books, vague notes on the margins of European history, the stuff of forgotten trade disputes and diplomatic wrangles. Others, victims of the nationalist passion for renaming, no longer carry any international associations. Squat Kalimantan, the largest member of the archipelago, is what Joseph Conrad and Somerset Maugham knew as Borneo. Spidery Sulawesi, in the centre, was the melodious Celebes. Nusa Tenggara was the Lesser Sundas, the small islands east of Bali from Lombok to Timor. Maluku was the Moluccas, the legendary spice islands. Irian Jaya is the western half of remote New Guinea, where Melanesia and the Pacific begin; Britain and Holland divided New Guinea between them by a gentleman's agreement, with the result that while the east is now independent as Papua New Guinea, the west is part of Jakarta's Dutch inheritance. The full extent of that inheritance, as every Indonesian schoolchild knows, stretches "from Sabang to Merauke", from the northern tip of Sumatra to the Papuan border, a span much greater than America's "sea to shining sea". Superimposed upon Europe, Indonesia would reach from Ireland to the Caspian. Indonesians call their country *tanah air*, "earth and water", and most of its vastness is sea. Yet even the dry land amounts to some 2,000,000 sq km, an area larger than Tibet or Mexico.

The most striking regular feature of the archipelago is the graceful curve of its southern margin, a smooth and almost

Trying to escape the heavy monsoon rainfall on Java.

continuous arc formed by Sumatra, Java and Nusa Tenggara. This barrier marks a geological battleground upon which two vast continental plates converge. Away to the northwest, a different section of the same front has thrown up the mighty Himalayas; its continuation can be seen sweeping down from Tibet to Sumatra through Burma and the Andaman islands. At the margin of the Indian ocean, the granite raft upon which both India and Australia float is forced downwards beneath the stronger Asian plate of which most of Indonesia is a half-drowned extension. The edge of Asia rucks and buckles into the mountain range which is the backbone of both Sumatra and Java; beneath it, the sunken edge of Indo-Australia melts in the burning depths, spewing up magma to feed dozens of great volcanoes. The volcanic highlands of Indonesia's southwestern rim stand like some giant dyke, shielding the gentle, shallow seas around Malaysia and Kalimantan from the storms of the Indian Ocean, which stretches deep and empty from the equator to Antarctica. East of Java, the archipelago crumbles gradually away into a confetti pattern of tiny islands.

Sun and Rain

Nature has generally smiled upon Indonesia, though not everywhere with equal sweetness. Straddling the equator, the archipelago is perpetually hot; except for Timor and adjacent parts of Nusa Tenggara, which parch under the rain-shadow of the Australian desert during the southern hemisphere summer, it is also reliably wet. Everywhere there are two fairly distinct seasons. Between November and April, cold, heavy winter air spilling out of the distant Asian steppes sets up a wind system which brings a wet monsoon sweeping down across the South China Sea. Veering left to blow from the north-west as it crosses the equator, the monsoon unleashes drenching rain wherever it touches land. The rest of the year is hotter and drier, but west of Bali a full rainless month is a rarity even in the so-called dry season. The seasonal distinction increases from west to east and from north to south. In general, local factors like topography and altitude tend to make as much difference as season to the weather. At sea level, temperatures seldom stray outside a range of 22-32°C, day or night, the whole year round. This is actually not as hot as, say, an Australian summer; but because air humidity never falls below 50 per cent and often approaches total saturation, it feels much hotter. However, the heat eases rapidly with altitude, and Indonesia has plenty of mountains. On a windswept pass in upland Java, the temperature may fall almost to freezing point in the early hours, while the summits of Irian Jaya are cold enough to cradle the only permanent icecap in the eastern tropics.

Heavy rainfall means heavy cloud cover. In many areas, the average day follows a predictable weather cycle. After a bright start, clouds build up steadily all morning before emptying themselves in an ineluctable afternoon downpour.

Especially in highland areas, the typical Indonesian skyscape is not the luminescent blue which many newcomers expect, but an overcast sky more menacing than ever glowered upon Manchester or Boston. Under such skies, vivid tropical colours shine with a dark, suppressed intensity. And at night, it is not unusual for electrical storms to flicker almost continuously on the horizon. Weather is largely responsible for the unexpectedly dark, almost gothic, aspect of Indonesia's beauty.

Man and Nature

Of the hundreds of volcanoes in Indonesia, 61 are officially regarded as dangerous to human life. When the infamous island-mountain of Krakatau exploded in the Sunda Strait in 1883, it destroyed 165 villages and killed more than 36,000 people. But the volcanoes are bringers of life as well as death. Their ash and lava often supply vital minerals which can render soils lastingly fertile even in the teeth of 3000 mm of leaching, draining rainfall per year. This is why the greatest concentrations of population in Indonesia cluster at the very feet of the deadly mountains.

In its virgin state, virtually all of Indonesia looks fertile enough. In most areas the natural vegetation is, or would be, lush 40 m tropical rain forest. Though it shrinks daily, Indonesia's rain forest area amounts to one-tenth of the world total. The presence of rain forest, however, reflects only heat and rainfall, never the suitability of the underlying land for sustained agriculture.

Often the green cathedral is founded upon an acidic wreck of a soil, and survives only by its highly evolved ability to recycle nutrients before they can be washed down into the lifeless earth. Over vast tracts of Sumatra, Kalimantan and the eastern islands, agriculture has traditionally been possible only by the technique based on the *ladang*. A *ladang* is a crude clearing slashed and burned out of the forest. It can be planted with subsistence crops, but within two or three years the unprotected soil has been depleted of nutrients and the farmer must open a new *ladang* elsewhere. The Dutch called this *roofbouw*, or "robber-farming". Constrained by the forest's own ability to regenerate itself after the nutrient theft, it could support only a sparse population.

The fertile volcanic soils of Java and Bali, on the other hand, combined with a happy climatic mean between the droughts of Nusa Tenggara and the perpetual rain of the equatorial islands, made possible not only much longer cultivation periods on dry fields but also a com-

17

INDONESIA – THE GREATEST ARCHIPELAGO

Still an impressive and frightening scene an eruption on Krakatau.

pletely different and much more intensive agricultural technique: the *sawah* or irrigated ricefield. This ecological contrast is the foundation for the classic distinction which has been drawn between "Inner Indonesia" – Java and Bali – and the "Outer Islands" – the rest of the archipelago. The dichotomy is far from perfect, as there are many ancient outposts of irrigated farming in the Outer Islands. But it does identify a crucial bifurcation in Indonesian history. Java and Bali have become teeming agrarian islands, more densely populated than Holland or Japan but incomparably poorer; on the other hand Sumatra and Kalimantan have remained rich, empty frontiers for the planter, the logger and the miner. To examine just how this bifurcation occurred is to leave the realm of natural history and enter that of human history.

There have probably been people in Indonesia for as long as there have been people at all. More than half a million years ago, members of the near-human species *Homo erectus*, which ranged from Africa to China, lived in Java. The discovery of their skulls in 1890 threw Indonesia into the center of the then bitter debate over human evolution and the "missing link".

We still do not know whether the Javanese *Homo erectus* contributed any of his genes to *Homo sapiens*, of whom the first Indonesian evidence dates from some 40,000 years ago. The earliest *Homo sapiens* population was a sparse one of hunting and gathering communities, scattered across the forests and beaches of islands which fused and parted as the sea level oscillated to the slow rhythm of the ice age. These people were probably small, dark-skinned and fuzzy-haired, and remnants of their race survive as the "Negrito" populations of remote parts of the Philippines and the Malay peninsula. But in Indonesia proper, except for Irian Jaya and the far eastern islands, all previous populations

INDONESIA – THE GREATEST ARCHIPELAGO

Taking a shower. Right: This man has clear Melanesian traits.

have been obliterated by newcomers, whom scholars call Austronesians.

The Austronesian Story

As a physical type, the Austronesian group is characterized by the faces which we associate with Malays, Filipinos and Polynesians: brown skin, thick black hair, round eyes. They must have originated on the mainland of China, but there is no trace of them there now; they have become an archipelagic race. Their great odyssey probably began around 7000 years ago – a very short time by the standards of prehistory – with the colonization of Taiwan island. Until recently it was believed that the immigrants entered Indonesia from the Malay peninsula, but now it seems that their progress was seaborne from the beginning: from China via Taiwan to the Philippines and beyond. Over the millennia, ever-improving sailcraft dispersed them across the warm oceans like floating mangrove seeds, and by about 1000 AD Austronesian colonists had occupied tropical islands and coasts over more than half the circumference of the earth, from Madagascar to Easter Island. Indonesia lay at the center of this vast distribution.

Besides their nautical skills, the Austronesian migrants had another secret of success: agriculture. The peoples which they displaced were slaves of nature; the newcomers could control and modify it. It used to be thought that the immigrants were dry *ladang* farmers, and that they had no rice at first. Recent research, however, suggests that the Austronesians not only brought rice with them, but also grew it in wet fields, perhaps on the naturally irrigated flood plains of major rivers – not true *sawah*, but certainly its ancestor. The need to seek out such special environments may help explain the extraordinary speed of the expansion. If this is so, then today's *ladang* is not an ancient survival, but a recent adaptation.

INDONESIA – THE GREATEST ARCHIPELAGO

What kind of people were these distant ancestors of the modern Indonesians? Their societies were of the sort usually described as "tribal". They had no organized states, and lived in small communities held together by custom rather than law. They were very conscious of individual status, but took charisma and achievement as well as descent and kinship into account when according it; purely hereditary offices were rare. Slavery was then universally practised, though of a milder type than that of Europe. The position of women was relatively fortunate; in particular, women were often credited with magical and religious authority. Untouched by the great religions, the Austronesians adhered to a complex variety of beliefs based upon the souls of living and dead people, plants and objects, upon the stages of the life cycle and the agricultural cycle, and upon such paired concepts as male-female, old-young, and earth-sky, interpreted as cosmic dichotomies. Life was heavily spiced with ritual. Some rituals demanded human sacrifice and led to internecine war. Another very Austronesian ritual practice was the "secondary mortuary rite" in which a long-dead body, as cremated ashes or as a decomposed corpse, was recovered for a second "send-off" to ensure the safe departure of its soul.

The Austronesians generally fashioned their clothes, their homes and many of their tools from plant material: wood, bamboo, rattan, palm leaves, pounded bark, cotton and hemp. Even their shrines and temples were usually wooden, although monolithic monuments were occasionally carved in stone. The material culture had a throw-away quality: since even houses were relatively cheaply built and easily replaced, people tended to spend more time decorating their own bodies – tattooing, tooth filing – than beautifying their environment. However, many Austronesian groups became accomplished weavers, producing superb textiles for use in ritual and trade. Metalwork was introduced around the time of Christ, and skilled blacksmiths were soon found in the remotest villages. But Indonesia is not rich in ore deposits and the high price of iron restricted its use to essentials. For recreation, the ancestral Indonesians gambled on cockfights, chewed the mild stimulant based upon the betel-nut, and played music on metal gongs. "Gong" is in fact an Austronesian word, which later entered English.

This, then, was the cultural basis upon which subsequent influences would build. But it was far from being a uniform foundation. Beyond Sulawesi in the east, the Austronesian expansion had mysteriously halted on the threshold of New Guinea, the few pioneers there intermarrying with black-skinned Melanesians to produce strange hybrid races and cultures. Even in the purely Austronesian west of the archipelago, the diversity was, and is, huge. Nowhere is this clearer than in the field of languages. During the long expansion of the Austronesians, their lost ancestral tongue splintered into a Babel of more than 700 related but mutually unintelligible languages, of which about 200 are spoken in Indonesia. Parallel to the linguistic divisions ran countless other local differences. There were patrilineal societies and matrilineal ones, warrior-leaders and matriarchs, mountain farmers and boat-dwelling sea-gypsies, gold miners and palm tappers.

Some of the detail of this diversity was to be softened by later centuries, as groups of previously independent communities were brought under the influence of single states, single religions, single trading systems. On a larger scale, however, different chunks of the archipelago would be pulled in different social and economic directions, creating broad divisions which had not existed before. One such division to emerge was that between Inner and Outer Indonesia.

Monks celebrating Buddhist New Year in Candi Mendut, Java.

Another, less decisive but almost as pronounced division, distinguished a historically crucial western segment – Sumatra, Java, Bali and to some extent Lombok – from the eastern islands and Borneo, which participated only fitfully in major historical developments. After the coming of the Austronesians, almost all of the important external influences upon Indonesia were to arrive from the west – from India, from the Middle East, from Europe. Most strongly and uniformly affected were always Sumatra, the immediate window on the west, and Inner Indonesia, almost as accessible and with its natural fecundity a perennial magnet for traders, missionaries and conquerors.

The Spirit of India

The first important foreign ingredients came in from India, on a cultural current which washed the shores of all Southeast Asia from the beginning of the Christian era until the European Renaissance. From Burma to Bali and from Vietnam to Sumatra, so many Hindu and Buddhist kingdoms appeared during these centuries that Indian nationalists would later talk of a "Greater India" in the far east.

In Hinduism, the accumulated wisdom of the Sanskrit-speaking Aryan people, India had a world-view more philosophically and aesthetically advanced than the folk religions of Southeast Asia. Hinduism boasted a plethora of striking gods and goddesses, of which the central triad were Brahma, the creator, Vishnu, the preserver, and Shiva, the destroyer. This baroque pantheon must have appealed strongly to existing Indonesian sensibilities. However, it was also combined with elegant doctrines of moral law, of the immortality of the soul, of ultimate liberation from earthly suffering, and of an absolute reality behind the phenomenal world. Buddhism, founded by a prince of Hindu India in the fifth century BC, took the philosophical tendency of Hinduism still further, doubting even the existence of gods. The first of the universal salvation religions, Buddhism identified desire itself, rather than frustration of desire, as the source of human sorrow, and proposed a set of techniques to free the individual from both desire and sorrow. India also had more down-to-earth cultural goods to offer. One was the useful skill of writing, then unknown in Southeast Asia; others included new architectural techniques, new artistic styles, and new draught animals and crops.

Some hearts and minds were won over more quickly and completely than others. The upper social strata were most strongly affected by Indianization; indeed, they may have owed their existence to it. Just as caste, kingship, royal ritual, scribes and bureaucracy had helped the nomadic, warring tribes of northern India become the great Asokan empire, so Indian influence in Indonesia made chiefs and strongmen into *raja*, warriors into *ksatria* knights, and tribal federations into theocratic kingdoms. According to the Indian political model, the *raja* was an incarnation of one of the gods, and his kingdom a miniature of the universe with the capital at its navel.

The early Hindu-Buddhist period in Southeast Asia is known only from fragmentary inscriptions and from sparse, cryptic references in Chinese travelogues and diplomatic sources. There was an Indianized polity in Indochina in the second century A.D., but the earliest sure evidence for Indonesia is from the early fifth century, by which time there were Hindu rulers in West Java, where the state was called Tarumanegara, and at a now obscure place called Muara Kaman on the Mahakam river in East Kalimantan. Over the following centuries, Indian cultural influence in Kalimantan gradually faded into insignificance, and the zone of intense Indianization in the archipelago became restricted to western Indonesia. Today, Indian culture in Indonesia is most strongly associated with Bali and Lombok, where a form of Hinduism is still practiced, and with Java, where the most spectacular Hindu and Buddhist monuments are found. It was Sumatra, however, which produced the archipelago's first really important Indianized state. This was Srivijaya, a maritime power which rose in the seventh century and dominated the western seas of Indonesia for more than 400 years. Apparently based upon oceanic trade, Srivijaya comprised a number of dispersed harbor cities of which the most important was probably Palembang. Its élite was Buddhist, and its capital a major center for Buddhist learning.

In Java, meanwhile, the focus of activity moved from the west to the center. The first temples of the eerie Hindu sanctuary on the Dieng Plateau date from the end of the seventh century, and the eighth and ninth centuries saw in Central Java a spate of monument-building unparalleled in Indonesian history. Celebrated Borobudur, the largest Buddhist stupa in the world, dates from this period, as does the matchless Hindu temple complex of Prambanan.

In the first half of the tenth century, Java's political center of gravity shifted abruptly eastwards again, coming to rest in the valleys around the Arjuna-Kawi-Kelud mountain group in East Java. The eastern period of Javanese history is characterized by the blending of the two Indian religions with each other and with indigenous beliefs, and by great political flux. After a long period of division, East Java was reunited in the thirteenth century by the ruthless Singosari dynasty. In 1294 Singosari's successor Majapahit, the last and greatest of the Indianized states, was founded on the Brantas delta, upstream of Surabaya. Majapahit combined a bountiful rice-producing hinterland with the maritime power which Srivijaya had now lost. Under King Hayam Wuruk and his vizier Gajah

Wayang kulit puppets ready for a Ramayana play.

Mada, it was able in its fourteenth-century heyday to become a Southeast Asian superpower, claiming tribute from the coastal kingdoms throughout the archipelago and beyond. After 1389, however, Majapahit fell victim to internal decay and external competition, declining until finally overrun by Muslim enemies in about 1527. Much of its élite is said to have fled to Bali, bringing new cultural life and prestige to an island which, like Java, had already been at least partly Hindu for more than six centuries.

India inspired not only Indonesia's temples, but also many other areas of the arts, popular as well as courtly. The beloved shadow-puppets, for instance, came from the south of India, where their prototypes are still in use today. And their classical repertoire, like the raw material for much of traditional literature, comes from the *Ramayana* and *Mahabharata* Sanskrit epics.

Without the Indian period, the cultural heritage of western Indonesia would have been very different and much poorer. Nevertheless, what happened was no simple transfusion of Indian ideas and styles in their original forms. The Indonesian temples, for instance, combine Indian motifs from different periods in novel ways, and blend them with entirely indigenous elements. And through the Indonesian distorting lens, the statues and puppets of India became subtler, lither and weirder. The Indian influence is perhaps best understood as an inspirational spirit, infusing Indonesia as the spirit of Greece once infused Europe. The classic judgement on the result is that of the Indian poet Rabindranath Tagore, on a visit to Java in 1927: "I see India everywhere, but I do not recognize it."

New Forces: Islam and Europe

Whether it was Indians or Indonesians, priests or traders who introduced the archipelago to the cultural wealth of India,

Veiled Muslim girls from Sumbawa.

they did so by sea. One reason why long-distance shipping was already well established was the material wealth of Indonesia – gold, aromatics and spices. But even if Indonesia had not produced any valuable commodities of its own, the western islands would still have become major foci of commerce, for they lie at the meeting place of the two Asian monsoons. Each year, wind blows from the west for just long enough to take sailing vessels from India to Indonesia, or from Indonesia to China, before it reverses, blowing the sailors back home.

Moreover, all through-shipping, unless it follows some wildly circuitous route, must pass through one of two narrow valves: the Sunda Strait, between Java and Sumatra, or the Malacca Strait, between Sumatra and the Malay peninsula. At the beginning of the fifteenth century, a new gatekeeper state, Malacca, appeared on the peninsular side of the strait which still bears its name. The new city quickly became so central to the global trade in spices and oriental luxuries that it was said that whoever controlled Malacca had "his hand on the throat of Venice." Malacca lies in present-day Malaysia, but has played an important role in the history of western Indonesia as a focus of the two portentous changes which spelled the end of the Hindu-Buddhist period: the coming of Islam and the arrival of the Europeans.

The youngest and most dynamic of the great religions, Islam was founded in Arabia by Mohammed, six centuries after Christ. Within a century of the prophet's death in 632, Islamic caliphs had conquered a huge arid swathe of the Old World from Spain to the threshold of India. From the mid-thirteenth century onwards, Islam began to dominate the cosmopolitan culture of the trading system between India and China, and it was possibly with business in mind that the far-sighted ruler of Malacca decided in about 1436 to become a follower of Mohammed. Malacca was not the first outpost of Islam in the area: the kingdoms of Perlak and Samudra on the coast of present-day Aceh in northern Sumatra were apparently Muslim as early as the 1290s, and even in Java there are a few Islamic tombstones from the fourteenth century. But the conversion of the greatest trading port in Southeast Asia gave Islam a powerful new core from which it radiated to the numerous Indonesian port kingdoms now freeing themselves from the slackening grip of Majapahit and other residual Hindu-Buddhist powers. The most important of the new states was Demak, which conquered and Islamized the whole north coast of Java between 1505 and 1546, administering the final death-blow to Majapahit in the process.

Islam in Indonesia was spread partly by economic calculation, partly by the sword. Enduring conversion, however, is seldom a simple matter of greed or fear, and many have speculated on what intrinsic aspects of the religion may have attracted Indonesians.

Islam in its purest form – austere, demanding, egalitarian and uncompromisingly monotheistic – seems so discordant with the tenor of the existing culture that some have seen its acceptance as a symptom of social revolution, accompanying the rise of a new merchant class. Most of the sparse evidence, however, suggests that the first converts were made among the old Hindu-Buddhist aristocracy itself. Another possibility is that Islam arrived in an unorthodox mystical form which made it more digestible for Indonesians. In either case, the early impact of the new religion upon the popular consciousness was very uneven. In some areas, including Aceh, it put down strong roots which would deepen with the centuries. Elsewhere it lay dormant: selected Islamic rituals were incorporated into existing lifestyles, but there would be little sense of Islam as a self-contained worldview, nor as a redeeming faith, until the nineteenth or twentieth centuries. A few areas, including the mountains of north-central Sumatra, were simply untouched. Nevertheless, in the long run Islam has proven by far the most successful religion in Indonesia. Today it claims 87 per cent of the population as adherents, giving Indonesia, on paper at least, the largest Islamic population of any country on earth.

The rise of Islam in Indonesia heralded no great artistic revival like that experienced in India under the Mughals. Many temples, particularly in Sumatra, were vandalized, yet in their place came mosques differing little from Hindu shrines, later giving way in turn to simple copies of Arab designs. The Islamic taboo on representation of human and animal forms cramped the visual arts, although it possibly contributed to the unique stylistic motifs of some textile designs. Music was only slightly affected, for instance by the adoption of the two-string Middle Eastern lute or *rebab.* The Arabic alphabet, however, supplanted older Sanskrit-based scripts in many Islamized areas and remained a common method of writing Indonesian languages until superseded by Roman characters in the present century.

It was not by a wide margin that Islam outran Europe to Indonesia. In 1509, when much of Sumatra and most of Java were still under Hindu-Buddhist kings, the first ships of distant Portugal appeared in the Strait of Malacca. The world's greatest states, industries and even technologies were still in Asia, but the tiny kingdoms of Europe had already begun to cast giant shadows across the globe. Unable to break into the close-knit Islamic trading network, the Portuguese quickly resorted to violence. In 1511, about 1200 ragged soldiers, their greed matched only by their fanatical courage and faith in a merciless God, successfully stormed Malacca, the most important port in Southeast Asia. The sultan retired to the hills, expecting the marauders to plunder the city and leave, as a local enemy would have done. Instead, the Portuguese rebuilt the defenses and settled in for a 130-year stay. From Malacca they quickly reached Maluku, where the most valuable spices, clove and nutmeg, were grown, and where a decade later they came face to face with the first of their Spanish rivals to accomplish the almost incredible feat of sailing to the East Indies the long way, via Cape Horn and the vast Pacific. Europe had encompassed the world.

In Indonesia, however, it was not immediately apparent that a new age had begun. Unable to sustain the momentum of their initial expansion, the Portuguese gradually became a peculiar but perennial fixture of the Indonesian trading world, while the Spaniards restricted their activities to Maluku and Sulawesi, and ultimately retreated to the present-day Philippines. A pidgin Portuguese was established for a time as a lingua franca of the archipelago, and Jesuit missionaries founded some Christian communities in eastern Indonesia, but there were no substantial territorial conquests. After its capture by the infidel, Malacca prospered as a waystation for Portuguese ships sailing to and from China, Japan and Maluku, but lost much of its former native trade to Johor, at the tip of the Malay peninsula, and to Aceh, which became one of the most powerful states in Southeast Asia. By the middle of the seventeenth century the only remnants of Portuguese power were a few outposts in the Lesser Sundas.

In the Shadow of the VOC

Malacca itself was lost in 1641, not to an Asian monarchy, nor to a European one, but to a commercial consortium - the Dutch *Vereenigde Oost-Indische Compagnie* or United East India Company. The VOC, as it was mercifully known, was formed in 1602 to pool the resources of several Netherlands ports for the great venture of displacing Portugal in the Indonesian spice trade. A pioneer Dutch expedition of 1596 had already proved that, with the aid of leaked Portuguese maps, the voyage was possible. The VOC was a landmark in the history of capitalism, one of the first global corporations. In Asia it was also a state in its own right, minting money, fighting wars and concluding treaties. It formed the thread linking Indonesian history for almost two centuries, and laid the foundations of the colonial Netherlands East Indies which succeeded it.

Like their Portuguese predecessors, the Dutch were only interested in profit, not in conquest for its own sake. But the greater resources and organizational skills of the VOC did make it capable of succeeding where the Portuguese had failed in enforcing monopoly trading conditions, at least for certain zones and commodities. In Maluku, it went so far as to organize annual naval expeditions to locate and burn all unauthorized clove

Christ painting on a World War II pillbox. Left: A reminder of the VOC era.

plantations. Even in Java, where its influence was more tenuous, the constant endeavour to determine the very conditions of trade led to ever-deepening political involvements which eventually made the VOC a territorial power.

The rise of the VOC was a more critical turning point in Indonesian history than the arrival of the Portuguese. In the sixteenth century, most of the wealthy commerce of Indonesia was still in indigenous hands. With vast tracts of forest still uninhabited, it is even possible that there were more Indonesians in the cities than in the countryside; certainly the archipelago was more urbanized, in relation to its total population, than Europe. The Javanese, hardly known today as a seafaring race, were then great shipbuilders; the name of one of their traditional vessels, the *jong*, is misapplied in English to the Chinese "junk". By 1700, however, almost all Java trade was controlled by the Dutch. And when in need of middlemen, the VOC promoted the growth of Chinese enclaves, creating a pariah business class which survives to this day. Marginalized in the towns, indigenous Indonesia turned back to the fields, where it was encouraged or forced to produce crops like coffee and tobacco for the European market. The new Indonesian was to be neither tribesman nor urbanite, but peasant. These changes were most pronounced in Java, where the VOC had its Asian capital, Batavia (now Jakarta), and where Dutch commercial operations came to be concentrated. In Sumatra, where VOC interest was intermittent, more of the old order survived, although trade suffered badly from Dutch competition.

Indigenous states could resist Dutch pressure only by imitating the armaments, the organization, the discipline and the grim rationality of the intruders. The power which came closest to success was the Javanese kingdom of Mataram, which appeared in the late sixteenth cen-

Detail from a painting in the Palace of Justice, Klungkung, Bali.

tury near modern Yogyakarta in Central Java. Under the rule of Sultan Agung (1613-46), Mataram became a powerful centralized state. Agung conquered almost the whole of Java and came within an ace of sacking Batavia. But the pace of change proved too much for Java's political traditions; Agung's son Amangkurat lost control of his vassals and was deposed, upon which the VOC regained the initiative by backing Amangkurat's son in the ensuing civil war. The VOC-Amangkurat II victory brought Mataram effectively under Dutch suzereinty. Internal problems continued, partly as a result of ambiguous Javanese conceptions of royal succession and legitimacy, and the empire finally disintegrated in 1755.

The Imperial Indies

Constant involvement in Javanese wars ultimately weakened the company finances, while rampant corruption and a shift in European demand away from spices and coffee towards Chinese tea and Indian textiles made the effort less and less worthwhile. In 1799, the VOC collapsed into bankruptcy and its Asian possessions passed to the Dutch state. The truly colonial phase of Indonesian history had begun. Holland, however, was now caught up in the Napoleonic wars, thus bringing confusion to the new colony.

A French-backed regime in the occupied Netherlands dispatched a soldier, Herman Willem Daendals, to fortify Java against British attack; his most lasting achievement was the island's first arterial highway, the Great Post Road, of which the British made grateful use when they took Java anyway in 1811. The legendary Thomas Stamford Raffles – naturalist, linguist, diplomat and visionary – now took over the reins of government at the age of 30, promulgating so many enlightened reforms that the short-term result was administrative chaos. Raffles planned for an Indonesia permanently under the Union Jack, but five years later the dream was shattered by the news that the peace settlement in Europe left no room for a British Batavia. Java was returned to the Dutch, Raffles consoled himself by founding Singapore, and in 1824 remaining British outposts in Sumatra were swapped for Dutch Malacca, fixing what has now become the Malaysia-Indonesia border. The turmoil of the period had deeply disturbed the Indonesian status quo, and in 1825 large parts of Java erupted in rebellion under a disaffected aristocrat, Diponegoro. It took five years for the Dutch to bring this Java War to an end, by which time they were determined to extract a profit from Indonesia at last.

Farmland, it was decided, would be taxed, but since the peasants had little cash they were to pay the tax in the form of export crops – sugar, coffee, indigo. This was the infamous *cultuurstelsel* or "cultivation system". As a source of finance for Holland it was hugely successful, but in Java it caused misery and hardship. Assessed crop values were unrealistically low, profit over and above the tax rate was not repaid, abuses and excesses among officials were commonplace.

The iniquities of the system are the subject of the classic Dutch novel *Max Havelaar,* published by a disillusioned colonial official in 1860. As much because of changed economic conditions as for ethical reasons, the *cultuurstelsel* was ultimately dismantled in a series of piecemeal reforms beginning in 1870. The new strategy was to open Indonesia to private investment; once more, it was to prove more advantageous to Dutchmen than to Indonesians.

Ironically, it was during the privations of the *cultuurstelsel* period that Java's population boom got underway. In 1815 there were perhaps 4 million people on the island, but by 1870 the figure had almost quadrupled. By 1930 it would reach 41 million. The full range of factors behind this explosion is not understood, but Dutch innoculation and irrigation programs must have played a part, as must the deep peace which settled over Java from 1830 until 1942. Demography crystallized the divergence between Inner and Outer Indonesia: 62 per cent of today's 175 million Indonesians live in Java or Bali, which together make up only 7 per cent of the country's land area.

The Indonesian Dream

Modernity came suddenly to Indonesia. In 1900, Java was still in the grip of a sort of supercharged feudalism in which the barons had become bureaucrats but the peasants showed no sign of becoming citizens. Sumatra was a patchwork of tribal anachronisms, antique Muslim ports and sultanates, and plantations worked by opium-enslaved coolies. Bali was a Hindu lost world, virtually unknown to Europeans. Few Indonesians lived in sizeable cities, and almost none had enjoyed a secular education.

Moreover, there was still no sense of solidarity or shared identity among them. Those who had resisted the expansion of Dutch power over the years had fought for many things – gods, kings, pride, honour, wealth, renown, even perhaps loyalty to an ethnic people – but nationalism was not among their motives. It is a myth that Dutch rule was founded upon a principle of 'divide and rule'. Until the very last years, there was nothing to divide: the archipelago had never known any sort of political unity since Majapahit, and perhaps not even then.

The year 1908 saw both the death of the old idiom of anticolonial resistance and the birth of the new. In Bali, the last defiant Hindu dynasty committed mass suicide before Dutch rifles at Klungkung; in Batavia, the first modern nationalist organization, Budi Utomo, was formed. Budi Utomo was novel in that it was a voluntary, secular association devoted in the first place to the very Western ideal of "progress" – for its members, but also for the Javanese people as a whole. In the coming years, the successors of Budi Utomo would add two more ideals to complete the classic triad of nationalist aspirations: progress, unity, freedom. There were many strands in the emerging nationalist movement, some of which were never satisfactorily spun together. Some drew their inspiration from the great current of Islamic renewal flowing from Cairo and Istanbul, others from the communism of the Russian revolution. But by 1927, when the Indonesian National Party was founded under the charismatic leadership of a Javanese engineer called Sukarno, many of those involved had reached a minimal consensus: "progress" was economic and mental; "unity" was that of all the peoples of Indonesia; and "freedom" meant to be rid of colonial rule.

Two factors contributing most to the rise of nationalism were Western education and the press. The former was initially a gift of the new "ethical" colonial policy proclaimed by the young Queen Wilhelmina in 1901; later it was widely imitated by Indonesian-run schools, Islamic as well as secular. Directly or indirectly, Western schooling taught criticism both of traditional Indonesian society and of the iniquities of the colonial situation.

The growing native press, meanwhile, sustained a new sense of national community. Its medium was Malay, the language of the Malacca Strait, long a lingua franca in the trading ports of the archipelago and the official language of the lower colonial administration. Few spoke it as a mother tongue, but it was a good leveller: renamed Indonesian, it was adopted in 1928 as the "national language" – a hopeful gesture at the time, but a momentous reality today. Although an authentic Austronesian language, Indonesian has incorporated huge numbers of words borrowed from Sanskrit, Arabic, Portuguese, Dutch and English, making it a veritable dictionary of the archipelago's history.

At first, the Dutch were inclined to look indulgently upon the Indonesian political awakening as proof of the success of their own "civilizing mission". A degree of limited democracy was introduced in 1916 in the form of a *Volksraad* or People's Council. Then an abortive communist uprising in 1926 shocked the authorities into a harder line. Radical leaders were exiled to remote islands and a mild form of police state created to deny urban nationalism access to the rural masses. The principle of independence was not really conceded even as a long-term target.

The Price of Freedom

The Dutch would certainly have been there for a lot longer if the catastrophe of the Pacific War had not intervened. The speed with which the Dutch East Indies fell to the Japanese invaders in the first weeks of 1942 was a shock and a revelation to all Indonesians. Like the Dutch, the Japanese were determined to rule Indonesia to their own advantage, but their methods were quite new: spectacle, indoctrination, mass mobilization, arbitrary violence. While their former masters starved in prison camps, Indonesians were drilled, marched, worked, robbed and lectured by the nation which styled itself the "Light of Asia". The only consistent message was hatred of the West. Where the Indonesian nationalists could help, they were used by the Japanese, who gave them the mass audiences and radio broadcasts they had always been denied by the Dutch. Only a brave few refused to collaborate, but many nevertheless kept their heads, realizing that the Japanese were losing the war and that their chance to be more than tools would soon come. On 17 August 1945, two days after

INDONESIA – THE GREATEST ARCHIPELAGO

A street poster for Independence Day in Jakarta.

the surrender of Japan but with Japanese forces still in occupation, Sukarno and Mohammed Hatta proclaimed national independence "in the name of the people of Indonesia". The Indonesian revolution had begun.

The revolution was a time of extreme disorder, in which Indonesians fought their own countrymen as often as foreign troops. Aristocrats too slow to move with the times were swept away; ideological, religious and personal factions among the revolutionaries battled with each other. Nevertheless, in the end enough Indonesians did rally to the red and white national banner to make the dream of independence a reality. It was achieved by a strange combination of bitter military struggle and cool-headed international diplomacy. Thousands of armed youths, mostly trained in Japanese militias, provided the former; a handful of Dutch-educated politicians were responsible for the latter. During the revolution Holland was able physically to reconquer much of its former colony, but, not understanding why so many Indonesians valued a chaotic freedom above the colonial *rust en orde* ("peace and order"), the Dutch won back few hearts. World opinion, too, turned against them. The crux came when the United States, impressed by the ability of the Indonesian Republic to put down a communist uprising on its own territory in 1948, threatened to cut reconstruction aid to the war-torn Netherlands. In December 1949 the Dutch recognized the independence of all parts of Indonesia except West New Guinea (Irian Jaya).

The first 15 years of independence produced just two significant achievements: in education, where the expansion of primary schooling more than kept pace with renewed population growth, and in nation-building in the mental sense, where the magical oratory of President Sukarno strengthened the patriotism and national pride forged during the revolution. The physical nation, on the other hand, came

President Suharto and his wife at a ceremony in Bali.

close to breakdown, and the parliamentary democracy introduced during the revolution collapsed.

After a short boom during the Korean War, the economy went into decline. The Dutch had developed what was in some respects a model colonial economy, but they had done it by themselves, with some Chinese help: Indonesians had not been trained for management and were ill-prepared for the huge task of development. Yet politicians placed the blame for economic failure at the feet of the remaining foreign businesses, almost the only ones still operating efficiently. The nationalization of all Dutch enterprises at the end of 1957 heralded a spiral of hyperinflation and chaos. The machinery of government also began to break down.

The formation of political parties sharpened old ethnic, religious and economic rivalries and created new ideological ones. The most ominous tensions were set up by the success of the Indonesian Communist Party, reconstructed since the failed revolt of 1948, in winning support among the underdogs of rural Java and Bali. Communist cadres and development programmes gave self-respect and ambition to the landless and powerless of the villages, destroying the symmetry of old hierarchies and generating simmering hatreds. The anger of devout Muslims and Hindus at the atheism of the Left heightened the danger of an explosion. In parliament, meanwhile, no party or stable coalition could hold power for long enough to pursue policies instead of tactics. The election of 1955, the only free one in Indonesia's history, gave seats to 28 parties, none with more than a quarter of the total vote. The president and the army grew sick of the bickering ineffectiveness of the civilian politicians. A series of regional rebellions gave Sukarno his excuse to declare martial law in 1957 and introduce "guided democracy", a nebulous concept according to which the elected parliament was replaced by an appointed council deemed to represent social groups – youth, peasants, workers, women, regions, religions and so on – rather than political parties. In 1958 the most serious regional challenge, a rebel government called PRRI in West Sumatra, was firmly suppressed by troops loyal to Sukarno.

A New Order

As the 1960s began, Sukarno became progressively less realistic, commissioning ever more grandiose prestige projects and monuments, governing by slogans, flinging insults at the superpowers, and embarking upon military adventures against "neo-colonial" Malaysia and Dutch New Guinea. The outside world was still fooled: in 1962, the USA pressured Holland into surrendering the last remnant of its empire. But at home, prices were rising at 30-50 per cent per month, the country had a foreign debt of $2.5 billion, blackouts darkened the cities, and Sukarno had moved the Greenwich meridian to Jakarta.

On 30 September 1965, a bungled coup attempt was blamed upon the communists, to whom Sukarno had become very close in the last years. The army gave the signal for a purge of communists, which quickly snowballed into a horrific communal massacre as pent-up tensions erupted in the villages. Half a million or more, mostly in Java and Bali, are thought to have died. Sukarno, father of the nation, was discredited; over the next two years he was discreetly eased out of power. Suharto, the army officer who had thwarted the coup, became president, founding the military-dominated New Order regime which has governed Indonesia under his leadership ever since.

The New Order is notoriously difficult to characterize. More thoroughly committed to the welfare of its subjects than most Third World governments, it has nevertheless perpetuated major human rights abuses against them. Not democratic in any conventional sense, it nonetheless represents a clear consensus among the majority of Indonesians.

Many have compared it to the old colonial state: it has the same concern for stability over politics, the same vast, loyal, paternal bureaucracy, the same positive attitude to foreign capital, the same internal security role for its army. In some respects – pervasive corruption, contempt for the rule of law – the New Order compares very badly with the prewar regime. But there are also positive differences. As soon as Suharto's Berkeley-trained economists had got inflation back under control in 1969, they instituted the first of a continuing series of Five Year Development Plans *(Repelita)* designed not only to revitalize the export economy but also to bring greater prosperity and welfare to the masses.

Success on both counts has been substantial, even considering generous aid from the West. The world's biggest rice importer in the 1960s, Indonesia was self-sufficient in rice by 1985. Per capita income increased from $80 in 1971 to $450 in 1987. Life expectancy at birth rose from 44 in 1965 to 60 in 1987. A massive family planning campaign has made promising early advances against the insidious enemy of overpopulation. Some have benefited much more than others from these achievements, but the majority has certainly benefited.

However benign when the going is good, the New Order has been merciless with its enemies, real and imagined. Born in an anticommunist bloodbath, it reacts violently to anything which smells of the left. In 1975, when an organization modelled on Mozambique's Frelimo took power in the Portuguese enclave of East Timor, the prospect of a leftist beachhead within the archipelago prompted an Indonesian invasion which ultimately cost tens of thousands of civilian lives. At home, those domestic communists who survived the massacres and the prison camps, and even their children, are still regarded as pariahs.

In the 1970s and early 1980s, the New Order was fortunate enough to have at its disposal a huge income from oil and gas exports. This could be poured into development or dispensed as patronage without making any great demands upon the recipients. The best of the oil boom, however, is now past, and Indonesia must find new sources of income. The government is set upon a diversified industrial future and proclaims the free-market values of enterprise, efficiency and deregulation as the keys to progress. These are hardly traditional Indonesian virtues. Whether they can be cultivated, and whether a new entrepreneurial Indonesia will continue to tolerate a political system of rigid hierarchy and institutionalized graft, remains to be seen.

Living History

Viewed panoramically, the whole human geography of western Indonesia is itself a sort of dateless cross-section of the past. In the east, Bali and its cultural offshoot in Lombok are like living cuttings of glorious Majapahit, saved from the mother tree before its fall: not quite a changeless museum of the Hindu middle ages, but the next best thing.

The very interior of Java is a memory of Agung's Mataram: proud, feudal-minded, nominally Islamic but unrepentant in its guardianship of older, mystical traditions. The north coast of Java gives us the half-traditional, half-proletarian peasantry of colonial times, tied to the international economy by the sugar cane and other cash crops among its ricefields.

Sumatra is more complex, a chronological core-sample in its own right. In the mountains of the north are weakly Indianized tribal peoples, as close an approximation to virgin Austronesians as western Indonesia has to offer, despite their gradual conversion to Islam and Christianity over the last two centuries.

The Acehnese and Malays of the coastlands are orphans of the great Muslim trading centers which colonialism destroyed; the plantation coolies around Medan are children of the tropical agrobusiness which colonialism created.

Take a Javanese village. Its cluster of red-roofed, white-walled houses is set like an island amid *sawah* alternately silver with water, black with volcanic earth and green with the hallucinatory green unique to growing rice. In the foreground, a farmer drives a plough team of unhurried water buffalo. A timeless scene: the Dutch called it "de eeuwige rijstvelden", the eternal ricefields.

Indonesian cityscapes have a timelessness of a different kind – a sense of living for today, in an eternal, frantic, gimcrack present. Flimsy pedal-taxis jostle with growling buses, sounding little bells and horns in quixotic faith that they will be heard above the din and make it through the day intact. At the roadside, the informal economy – Indonesia's most efficient money-maker – is in full swing under umbrellas and canvas awnings. Vendors of cigarets, comic books, medicines and myriad different meals, snacks and drinks are all anxious to reach the turnover they need to feed themselves today and perhaps to send a tiny sum back to their families in the villages; at dusk, they will have to pack up and make way for a different shift of nighttime stallholders. Professional beggars hold out crippled hands with equal urgency. Behind the stalls are the dark caverns of open shop-fronts, blaring forth deafening Indonesian pop music from worn cassettes. Between the shops, narrow alleys lead off to the kampong beyond, the labyrinthine urban villages where most city-dwellers live. The air is hot and muggy, laden with traffic fumes and the pungent scent of the *kretek,* clove cigarettes.

INDONESIA – THE GREATEST ARCHIPELAGO

Transport in modern Yogyakarta.

The big cities of modern Indonesia were essentially built by Europeans. The road and its flanking storm-drains were laid following Dutch textbooks of tropical engineering. Well within living memory it will have had a Dutch name – Lindelaan or Molenstraat, perhaps – instead of the name of a revolutionary hero or a Hindu king. Stamford Raffles, on the other hand, is responsible for the fact that the traffic drives on the left, not on the right as in Holland.

The shop-fronts may be Dutch-colonial, with gaudy new façades, or they may be shoddy post-war creations of international concrete. But rural Indonesia has invaded Europe's tropical other self, and battles with it for the city's soul. Herbal remedies, augury manuals, and cartoon excerpts from the *Ramayana* and *Mahabharata* are on sale in the stalls; *dukun* or witch-doctors, lineal descendants of pagan priests, practice in the *kampung*. Even the streetside demi-monde embodies an incredible diversity of foreign influences.

Of the foodstall staples, the noodle soup and fried soybean products are as Chinese as the owners of the prosperous shops behind. And chilli pepper, the flavoring without which Indonesian food seems virtually inconceivable, was brought on Spanish or Portuguese ships from its native Central America. An even more unlikely Hispanic flavor comes from the *kroncong* melody at the heart of the sugary, amplified pop music, a distorted echo of the lutes of sixteenth-century Portugal.

Some things seem deceptively new, others deceptively old. The ubiquitous *becak* or man-powered tricycle taxi is more recent than the motor car, appearing in Indonesia only during the Japanese occupation. The dwindling horsecarts are older, but nevertheless of European rather than native design: their most common Indonesian name, *dokar*, is probably a corruption of the English "dog-cart".

PORTRAIT OF JAVA

A PORTRAIT OF JAVA

Before he was named Susuhunan Paku Buwana V, Crown Prince Adipati Anom of the court of Surakarta commissioned court poets to compile a compendium of all that was known of Java. He sent each poet on a journey – one to East Java, one to West Java and the third to Mecca because Java's history was, by that time, inextricably connected with Islam.

On their return, these poets composed a twelve-volume encyclopedia of Javanese culture and history, known as the *Seluk Tambanglaras* or *Serat Centhini*. The literary device that the poets used to convey all that they considered worth recording was a series of interconnected journeys conducted by different characters in search of knowledge. Visiting the important places on Java involved a string of adventures. Every place had its tales and always some local figure was called upon to reveal new knowledge. Thus, in recounting a history of Java, the *Serat Centhini* compendium covers everything from the significance of the shape of the Javanese *kris* to the many ways of making love, and ranges from the highest forms of religious knowledge to the basest techniques of thievery.

The *Serat Centhini* is a marvelous source of knowledge about Java, but unfortunately the whole of this work comes to some 6000 manuscript pages, all written in Javanese verse. Although it could still be used as a traveller's guide, one would hardly wish to recommend all its adventures. The modern traveller needs something a little more accessible, perhaps somewhat less detailed, and certainly more contemporary. It is best therefore to begin with some basic features of Java that make it one of the most remarkable and fascinating islands on earth.

Java is the site of the oldest and most important fossil remains of early man. Various sites – such as Trinil, Ngandong, and Sangiran – located along the Solo river as it extends into East Java, have yielded a large collection of prehistoric human remains. These remarkable fossil finds and their association with artifacts suggest a continuity of habitation of over 800,000 years with the development of populations of early man over this period. That these populations lived in small nomadic bands, that they were hunters and gatherers; and that they sheltered in caves and exploited the rich shellfish resources of Java can be deduced from the archaeological evidence. But beyond this one can only speculate on the nature of their social and cultural life.

The Austronesian Heritage

The beginnings of the Neolithic era on Java are generally associated with the arrival of Austronesian-speaking populations. To have spread as they did in so short a period, the early Austronesians must have been reasonably skilful sailors. They relied not just on hunting, fishing and gathering but had begun to cultivate rice, millet, and certain tree crops. They also brought with them domesticated chickens and pigs. Early Austronesian sites reveal the use of pottery and suggest the beginnings of weaving and the use of bark cloth. More important still, the presence of related and relatively mobile island populations led to a more rapid diffusion of cultural ideas and goods.

Five related Austronesian languages are of historical importance to an understanding of Java. The first of these is Javanese itself – the language of the majority of the population of Central and East Java. In West Java, the majority of the population speak Sundanese. There is

Left: A court official, grown old in service, at the kraton in Yogyakarta.

Ploughing a rice paddy in Central Java.

no rigid border dividing speakers of Sundanese and Javanese, and in the adjoining areas between West and Central Java, the local population speaks both languages in a fashion that shows the strong influences they have had on each other. A dialect of Javanese is also spoken in two historically important former court centers, Banten and Ceribon, on the north coast of West Java.

A third language of importance on Java is Madurese. This is the language of the population of the island on the north coast of the eastern end of Java. The island of Madura has for centuries been part of the cultural sphere of Java and Madurese have played a critical role in Java's history, moving in large numbers from their island to Java. Now over twenty per cent of the population of East Java speak Madurese as their first language. In large parts of Pasuruan, Probolinggo, and Jember in East Java, a Madurese population predominates.

Another language of historical importance on Java is Malay, which formed the basis for modern Bahasa Indonesia. Today all schoolchildren learn Indonesian. It is the only medium of education from class three onwards in elementary schools and this language serves as the chief vehicle for national communication. However, this use of Malay on Java is not a recent phenomenon. One of the oldest inscriptions found on Java, dating from 832 AD, is written in a form of old Malay. Malay was the *lingua franca* for trade throughout the Indonesian archipelago and was vital in the northern coastal cities of Java.

Yet another language of importance for Java is Balinese. Java's culture has exerted a strong influence on Bali, but some influence has also gone the other way. As Java was transformed by Islam, Balinese rulers sent military expeditions to support the final struggles of the Hindu rulers at the far eastern end of Java. As a result of these struggles, the populations at the easternmost end of Java have often been oriented more to Bali than to the rulers of central Java.

Non-Austronesian Languages

Four other languages have figured prominently in Java's history. The first of these is Sanskrit, which was used as a religious and literary language by the rulers of Java. Trading contact with India began far earlier. The first inscriptions in Sanskrit are those by a ruler using the Sanskrit name Purnavarman, from a kingdom called Taruma in the western part of West Java. In Sanskrit, Java was known as the great *Yawadwipa*, a designation that occurs on an inscription of the early eighth century found in Central Java and again on a later inscription from the eleventh century found in East Java. The eighth to fifteenth centuries saw a great flowering of Hindu and Buddhist civilization on Java and the building of some of the most remarkable temple complexes in the world. The central idea behind virtually all of these edifices was to create a dwelling place for the gods. In the course of this Hindu-Buddhist period, the use of Old Javanese came to predominate over Sanskrit in texts and inscriptions just as the temples themselves began to show an increasingly distinctive Javanese style.

With the coming of Islam, Arabic began to exert a profound influence on Java. From the thirteenth century onward this influence was notable and has continued to the present day. The chief institution of Islamic learning on Java has been the *pesantren*. The *pesantren* is based on a relationship between a learned teacher who is respectfully referred to as a *kyai* and a group of pupils called *santri*, who support themselves and their *kyai* while they learn.

The foundation of Islam on Java is now popularly associated with nine saints known as the *Wali Songo* whose tombs, scattered along the north coast of Java, are places of special reverence. The mystic powers of these saints suggest a strong Sufi background to the establishment of Islam and the *pesantren* have maintained this tradition in teaching *tasawwuf*, mystic knowledge, as the highest form of Islamic learning. The most important of the Islamic *tarekat* orders ("Muslim brotherhoods", although on Java they are not confined to men) have firm links to the *pesantren* and *Nahdatul Ulama* (Indonesia's most important Islamic organization) as well and these organizations foster Sufi religious practices. All of this makes Islam a complex and potent force that has penetrated all aspects of Javanese life.

Dutch is yet another language that has had an important influence on Java. Initially its use was confined to merchants and officials of the Dutch East India Company at the beginning of the seventeenth century. Malay was used as a more general language of communication and in many of the early Dutch settlements, including Batavia, which was the center of the Company's trading network in Asia. Portuguese was for a long time a more important language of common use than Dutch. As a result, Dutch had to be promoted but always remained the language of a small elite. When, in the nineteenth century, Java's nobility were admitted to this elite level and were given access to a Dutch education, Dutch began to exert a considerable influence. Many leaders of the Nationalist movement in the twentieth century were educated in the Dutch language. The previous Sultan of Yogyakarta, Hamengku Buwana IX, was summoned back from Holland in 1939 to replace his father and went on to become one of Indonesia's most respected Nationalist leaders.

After the struggle for independence from the Dutch, English replaced Dutch as Indonesia's first foreign language in the national education system. English is now taught widely in schools throughout the country; three English-language newspapers are published in Jakarta, and various English-language programmes, including the news, are regularly broadcast on television.

Social Geography of Java

The Javanese classify the different areas of Java in terms of historical and linguistic criteria. At the far western end of Java is Banten; moving eastward is the large area known as Sunda, whose mountain heartland is referred to as Priangan; the north coast from Cirebon to Gresik (near Surabaya) is called the Pasisir. The rest of Java takes its orientation from the court centers of Central Java – Surakarta (Solo) and Yogyakarta (Yogya). The territory surrounding these centres, which once formed the main area of jurisdiction of the kingdom of Mataram, is known as the Negara Agung. To the west are the areas of Bagelen and Banyumas; to the east as far as Malang is the Mancanegara. This area came under the strong but less direct cultural influence of the courts.

An ornate Javanese kris. Right: Dieng Plateau landscape.

The eastern land beyond this area of influence is described as the Tanah Sebarang Wetan; and at the far eastern end of Java is Blambangan. Jakarta, which was founded in 1619 by the Dutch East India Company as its trading center, Batavia, and Surabaya, which has a long and often independent history, are generally considered as separate entities in this native geography. This social geography embodies a Mataram-centered view of Java, so the history of Mataram provides a key to an understanding of Java.

The Rise of Mataram

Sunan Agung reigned from 1613 to 1646, and is accorded a pre-eminent role in the creation of the kingdom of Mataram. His grandfather, Senopati, had already advanced the dynasty and overthrown the kingdom of Pajang to which Mataram had been subordinate. His father had ruled for twelve years. Despite this, it is Sunan Agung, not Senopati nor his father, Panembahan Seda Ing Krapyak, who is considered as the symbolic pinnacle of the kingdom of Mataram.

From the fourteenth century onward, the ports of Java's north-coast Pasisir adopted and developed distinct Islamic traditions while remaining open to Chinese and, later, European influences. Complex and cosmopolitan, the Pasisir opened gateways to the rest of Java. By contrast, although occupying an area of previous Hindu-Buddhist culture, Mataram was then a backwater, better known for its military organization than for its art and learning. It was during the reign of Sunan Agung that Mataram began the task of making itself not just the political center of Java but also the center of Javanese culture and refinement.

Sunan Agung's efforts involved incorporation and synthesis. After his conquest of the north coast, he brought the crown prince of the royal house of Surabaya, Raden Mas Pekik, to his court and allowed him to develop the arts and literature of the Surabaya court in Mataram. At the time, Surabaya was a center of artistic culture and Islamic learning and Raden Mas Pekik claimed descent from one of the most important Islamic saints in the Javanese tradition. Later Sunan Agung gave his sister in marriage to Raden Mas Pekik and some years later he arranged the marriage of his son to the daughter of Raden Mas Pekik, thus binding the dynasty of Surabaya to that of Mataram.

Austronesian languages, such as Balinese and Sundanese and even the language of Tonga in the Pacific, recognize different speech levels but no Austronesian language has elaborated them to the extent that Javanese has. These levels, reffered to as *unggah-ungguhing*, form the basis of social politeness. It is clear that the Mataram court in its quest for refinement gave impetus to the development of ever-increasing forms of linguistic elaboration. There are distinct speech levels in Javanese marking social strata: *ngoko* (low), *madya* (middle) and *krama* (high), with a number of special vocabularies to bridge such cases as when a person of high status addresses an elder of lower status.

Besides developing linguistic etiquette, the Mataram court has also been responsible for preserving some of Java's ancient traditions. Like his grandfather before him, Sunan Agung was believed to be capable of consorting with the powerful Queen of the Seas. This relationship has always provided one of the traditional underpinnings of the Mataram dynasty and to this day is still commemorated in various court rituals. One of the most important of these is called *Labuan* when an offering representing the ruler is carried in procession to the shores of the south coast and then cast into the sea.

At the height of his power, although recognized as a Muslim ruler, Sunan

Agung had not yet reconciled his reign with the forces of Islam. By one account, this reconciliation came in a dream, while Agung was in Blambangan in East Java.

Sultan Agung's Dream

In this dream, the figure of an old man, resplendent as the moon, appeared to him and identified himself as the lord of an important tomb-site at a place called Tembayat, or simply Bayat, in the center of Mataram's territory. The tomb is said to be the resting place of an Islamic saint known as Ki Pandhan Arang who originally came from Semarang on the north coast of Java. Popular folk tradition, however, which still survives today, identifies Ki Pandhan Arang as the last Hindu ruler of the kingdom of Majapahit who disappeared from his palace rather than face a struggle with his Muslim son and who wandered through Java until he became himself a Muslim saint.

The old man who appeared to Sunan Agung in his dream held a staff in his

This Yogyakarta palace retainer explains a painted relief.

hand, a symbol of authority. He extended it to Sunan Agung who took hold of it and was miraculously thrust back to his own court.

As with all events on Java, there is more than one interpretation of this mystic occurrence. Clearly a spiritual relationship with the Islamic personage at Bayat was of importance to Sunan Agung and this relationship is associated with some of the most far-reaching acts of Sunan Agung's reign. We know specifically about some of these events, which can be dated to the year 1633, because by this time there were Dutch observers at the court of Mataram.

In the *Bataviaasch Daghregister* for 29 May 1633, a brief report relates that Sunan Agung had departed the Mataram court to make a special pilgrimage to Tembayat. According to popular tradition, on this visit Sunan Agung slept and dreamed. The significance of this event for Javanese history can be judged by what followed immediately. On his return to Mataram, Sunan Agung ordered the rebuilding of the tomb complex at Tembayat. No horses were to be used to haul the stones for the wall and gates at Tembayat. Instead, it is reported that Sunan Agung commanded 300,000 of his subjects to form a human line stretching some forty kilometers between the Mataram court and Tembayat and, respectfully seated, to pass the materials needed to build the structures to honor the religious lord of Bayat.

At this same time – dated by Western reckoning as Friday, 8 July 1633 – Sunan Agung ordered into existence a restructured Javanese calendar, thus changing the way in which time was calculated on Java. This new calendar was perhaps Sunan Agung's greatest effort at cultural synthesis since it attempts to combine quasi-solar and lunar cycles, an Islamic time sequence with a prior Hindu system of reckoning while still preserving critical elements of a five-, six- and seven-day week.

Immensely complex, this elaborate system of time reckoning consists of a series of interrelated cycles, whose different points of coincidence mark periods of special significance. This means that different activities may follow separate cycles and events become identified by their conjunction amid a number of cycles. Thus the legendary figure of Watugunung presides over a *wuku* cycle of thirty seven-day weeks while the holy days of the Muslim year follow an Arabic cycle of twelve lunar months with either twenty-nine or thirty days.

After honoring the lord of Bayat and reordering the calendar, Sunan Agung celebrated the marriage of his son, who was to succeed him and later become Amangkurat I, to the daughter of Raden Mas Pekik. At about this same time, Sunan Agung also appears to have initiated overtures to officials of the Dutch East India Company in Batavia in an attempt to achieve reconciliation.

All of these events occurred in the same Javanese year. The named gates at Bayat, 30 km east of Yogyakarta, still bear witness to this moment in Javanese history. One of these gates still bears an inscription whose numerical interpretation designates the year 1555 as the year of the reordered Javanese calendar. The power of Mataram after Sultan Agung was continuously encroached upon by the Dutch East India Company and internal dissension among members of the Mataram dynasty led to bitter disputes and the eventual loss and fragmentation of Mataram's territory. In the end, what remained of Sultan Agung's kingdom was divided among four courts: a major and a minor court in Yogyakarta and another major and lesser court in Surakarta. As Mataram's power declined, however, its quest increased for cultural refinement based on ideals of the past. This gave rise to an elaboration of standards of linguistic appropriateness, of rules of etiquette and moral conduct, and of subtlety of artistic expression - in short, an entire code of forms of social and cultural life.

Java Today

In 1990, Java's population passed 106 million. This population, and in particular the Javanese who are the inheritors of Mataram, still value the pleasures of sociability; show deference to seniors, superiors and strangers; endeavor to control strong emotions; tolerate individual idiosyncracies as intrinsic to human nature; and preserve a sense of a superior civilization. Yet the people of Java are in great haste for development with all its attendant consequences.

Java today could perhaps be considered one single vast settlement – neither urban nor rural. Villages are set close to one another and most rural settlements have population densities greater than the suburbs of Western cities. By one authoritative account, there are 170 towns on Java ranging in size from 25,000 to over 500,000 inhabitants. There are the major cities: Bandung and Semarang with populations of over one million; Surabaya with a population over two million and, finally, there is Jakarta.

In 1945, Jakarta had a population of barely one million; now it is approaching seven million. But if one includes the Greater Jakarta area, where in recent years an enormous amount of industrial and housing development has been located, it is over twelve million.

What makes Java a single settlement is its incredible flow of traffic. The Dutch left the island with a peasant population very much tied to the land in separate subsistence-oriented villages. But within the past twenty years, Mitsubishi and Mercedes-Benz have managed to open up the villages: Mitsubishi with its Colt mini-van that could reach the most isolated villages and then Mercedes with

Lava flows near Bromo volcano.

huge buses that could take loads of passengers across the island in less than a day.

For villagers throughout Java, there is work to be found in the towns and cities and these are the places they go – for short periods or between peak seasons of the agricultural cycle. The local differences that make Java so varied are transported to the large cities. Villagers from all the regions of Java reassemble to work in Jakarta's so-called informal sector. The Madurese are there selling *saté*; the *bakso* noodle peddlers with their pushcarts come from Wonogiri. Pemalang seems to have a strong hold on the lucrative recycling and disposal industry. A joke says that there will soon be no one left in Tegal: the men are all working in the construction industry, building Jakarta while their wives and daughters have set up food stalls to feed them and anyone else who wants a good, cheap meal.

Javanese rice-farmer at work in the evening.

Cities and towns on Java, despite their urban trappings, are still composed of village-like local neighborhoods. One result of the Japanese occupation of Indonesia has been the adoption of the Japanese system of residential wards. Whether in a city or a village, everyone is officially assigned residence in one of these neighborhood wards.

But it is not only in the cities that one meets the villagers of Java. Over ten per cent of Indonesia's Javanese-speaking population now live outside of Java. In Sumatra alone, there are over six million Javanese. The new-found mobility of the Javanese has provided a safety-valve for developments on the island. It is not just poor villagers who leave to seek employment; it is also the ambitious, the frustrated and those in trouble. If a villager has had a quarrel or is suddenly divorced or pregnant, then often the bus offers an escape to new possibilities.

To travel in this new Javanese world, one must speak Indonesian. Previously, it was possible to live in a large self-contained world of Javanese speakers. Literacy in Indonesian for Javanese was among the lowest of all the different populations of Indonesia. Although many of the older generation can claim only a "passive" knowledge of Indonesian, the younger generation uses Indonesian without hesitation. Government pressure, parental pressure and peer pressure keep children in elementary school and prompt many to go on to further schooling. As villagers have become better educated, they have also become more mobile.

The Indonesian language is also the means by which the outside world reaches the villages of Java. In the 1970s, Indonesia set up its own satellite called *Palapa* to create a modern telecommunications system for the country. (At the time, this decision was criticized as an extravagant folly, although now it looks like a brilliant bargain). With this satellite and local transmitter stations, it was

PORTRAIT OF JAVA

Mother and children out for a day trip.

possible to beam television broadcasts throughout the country. Java's villages were among the first to get television in a big way.

Television is used to communicate a great deal of government instruction, particularly about development. This includes a farmers' hour with video clips of local farmers from all over Indonesia talking about specific farm problems and their solution. Besides this, there are Indonesian dramas and programs of both popular and traditional singing. Also broadcast to the villages are American serials like *Kojak*, *Dynasty*, *Lost in Space*, and *Little House on the Prairie*.

Both radio and tape recorder play an important part in village life. Turning up the volume of a broadcast shares listening pleasures with one's neighbors, creating a desired sense of lively sociability. Cassette recordings of both popular and traditional music are cheap and widely available throughout all of Java.

Traditional entertainment has taken on new media forms. The master puppeteers of the court centers of Yogya and Solo are still revered. Recordings of their performances are sold on cassettes and on one Saturday night in every month, a famous puppeteer is given the opportunity to broadcast an entire *wayang* drama on national radio. But now there are competing interests to those of the shadow plays. Most village families would rather spend money on the education of their children than on major performances at times of family ritual.

Village life has its own rhythms. The new "day" begins at dusk, and mid-day, when it is too hot to work, offers a break in which to nap. Villagers rarely sleep in full eight-hour stints, which means that there is always someone with whom to chat at all hours of the night. In fact, the night, especially the hours from midnight to three in the morning, is the time most propitious for traditional religious activities. The recent introduction of electricity to many villages and the desire to watch television have begun to change these rhythms fundamentally.

Many houses serve double households. Different households under the same roof are distinguished as separate "hearths". Married children reside with parents before eventually building another house squeezed in on some vacant spot belonging to a parent or near relative. In most households, it is difficult to keep track of young children who spend their time in the homes of different relatives. Visiting relatives is a way of life and no matter how crowded they may appear, houses always seem to be able to accommodate visitors. This crowded Javanese conviviality makes a place lively and thus worth living in.

Land is at a premium and residential areas have become increasingly densely settled. These residential areas consist of several interconnected hamlets surrounded by fields. Village populations live crowded together on a fraction of their land in order to be able to maintain as much land as possible in active cultivation. Even the land reserved for settlement is heavily committed to fruit growing – bananas, coconuts and papaya. Nevertheless, on Java a great deal of prime cultivated land has been encroached upon for residential and industrial purposes and continuing loss of valuable irrigated land threatens future rice production.

In the villages of Java it is rice that matters most of all. With an ever growing population, Java's task has been to increase its production of rice to keep ahead of the needs of its population. Java has more than doubled its rice production in less than two decades. The effort to do this has changed every rice-producing village on the island.

The government's role has been to provide new high-yielding quick-growing varieties of rice, a guaranteed support price for the crop and subsidized fertilizer to grow it. Irrigation works on Java were rehabilitated and extended to permit multiple cropping. In Dutch times, a large proportion of irrigated land was communal property held by the village and apportioned in fixed lots among households. Since land has been scarce in most parts of Java since the nineteenth century, communal holdings were often informally subdivided into even smaller, Lilliputian-sized plots.

At the beginning of the 1960s, Indonesia passed new agrarian laws that granted individual title to communal landholders. These fortunate landholders, most of them with plots of less than a hectare or two, profited greatly from the government's effort to stimulate rice production. With some of the richest and most fertile land on earth, even farmers with only one hectare of land are capable of remarkable production.

Farmers now harvest an average of over five tonnes of rice per hectare and often plant two crops each year, followed by a third of soybeans or maize. In the village context, these farmers are an elite and increasingly in Javanese villages this elite represents a shrinking minority of the total population. In intensive rice growing villages, a majority of villagers are now agricultural labourers, petty traders, or workers employed outside the village.

The enormous productivity of these lowland rice-growing areas of Java depends on preserving the critical watersheds that support the island's irrigation system. In the mountains of Java, where the rush of human activity is less apparent, are the precarious forests that protect the integrity of the island's ecology. In Javanese eyes, these mountains have always been the abode of the gods and spirits that safeguard life on Java. Their protective role will be even more important in future, for by the year 2000, Java may well have a population of more than 120 million.

PORTRAIT OF BALI

A PORTRAIT OF BALI

The island of Bali has been much photographed, discussed, and described. Guidebooks and photo albums have dubbed it "Island of the Gods", "Island of a Thousand Temples", "Morning of the World", "Last Paradise". At the same time, scholars have attempted to fathom its "unique" religion, to describe its social organization, and to understand its history. At least since the 1930s, and with increasing volume and fervor in the last decade, Bali has been romanticized by Westerners seeking an idyllic, unspoiled, pristine paradise to set against their own disillusionment with the emptiness and materialism of modern life. Bali came to represent that paradise, as did Tahiti, Jamaica, and the Seychelles.

The island was conceived of as unique and unchanging. It was a last outpost of ancient Indonesian Hinduism in a Muslim country, and a museum of traditional life and thought. While the rest of the world developed, it was thought that Bali remained suspended in the sixteenth century, endlessly elaborating the beauties of its singular culture with virtually no disturbance from outside. The coming of the Dutch to North Bali in 1849 and to South Bali in 1906-8 was said to have disturbed little. The Dutch were reverent about the "Bali-museum" concept, and sought only to "restore" cultural elements which had become decadent, and to "rationalize" a few organizational muddles, while leaving the whole "untouched".

This view of Bali has dominated the majority of writing about it, both scholarly and popular, to the extent that the modern visitor, who will be jostled by thousands of his/her fellows, is still invited to partake of the purity, romance, and uniqueness of the Bali experience. The writers, scholars, artists, and photographers who have created the prevailing image of Bali are not wrong. The island does strike most visitors as physically beautiful, exotic, and special.

For the present short introduction, I will explore this legendary place in terms of its relationship to other places and peoples, and show that it is not a timeless museum faithfully preserving vanished ages. Bali does not exist in a vacuum; it probably never has. Throughout its long history, visitors have landed on its shores bringing goods and/or cultural influences, and many Balinese have traveled overseas, as slaves, traders, and occasionally as conquerors.

Balinese culture is a three-dimensional jigsaw puzzle, whose pieces and layers have been shaped by a variety of intersecting factors. Not all the pieces fit perfectly; some are duplicated, others are missing, still others fit loosely, or must be jammed into place by the earnest scholar. All the pieces come from a variety of sources, the Austronesian substratum, India, Indianized Southeast Asia, Java, Lombok and the Lesser Sundas, China, and the West. Over time, and with significant local variation, the pieces have interacted, colliding, retreating, rubbing, crumbling, and merging along their interfaces. The result is Balinese culture as we experience it today - very much in flux, but nevertheless founded on tenacious beliefs and cultural patterns which are widespread and ancient.

Bali has possibly been occupied by man for as long as nearby Java, where human remains have been found which date from 500,000 to 1.7 million years ago. The very early prehistory of Bali is all speculation, as no remains of early man have yet been found there. With the coming of the Austronesians evidence becomes abundant.

Left: Boy during an initiation rite on Bali.

A cremation ceremony at Legian, Bali.

Balinese Language

The Austronesian world, whose boundaries are based on linguistic and cultural affinities, extends discontinuously from Taiwan in the north to New Zealand in the south, and from Madagascar, off the coast of Africa, to Easter Island, which is closer to South America than it is to Asia. The peoples of this enormous area speak more than 700 different languages, yet a large number of words are identical, and close cognates abound.

The Balinese language is most closely related to those of East and Central Java, Lombok, and Sumba, but it shares some of its vocabulary with languages spread across the Austronesian world. The word *lima*, for instance, means "five" in Balinese, and the same in languages spoken from Taiwan to Fiji and Samoa. Balinese is an extremely difficult language which features several "levels" of speech.

The importance of language levels in Balinese signals the presence of another crucial element of the Austronesian substratum. That element is hierarchy; the concern with social ranking and its meticulous observance in all aspects of daily life. Although not all Austronesian languages have elaborated the notion of hierarchy as Balinese has, many words indicate its importance. The term *datu*, or *ratu*, for instance, which means "lord", "king", or "chief", is found in various forms over a wide area. Some Austronesian languages have special ceremonial vocabularies or speech styles which can be used only on ritual occasions.

The notion of hierarchy is also elaborated across Austronesia in spatial terms. Height is important, as is relative closeness to the mountains or the sea. Higher is better. Temples and great houses are built on pedestals, or in stepped designs; and the world, including heaven, is conceived of as a layered structure. Ranks of divinities and human ancestors inhabit the upper levels. Humans, in their own carefully graded society, occupy the middle. Demons and powers of the earth exist below. In Bali, megalithic stepped temples have been found in the village of Sembiran, in the north, about 30 kilometers east of Singaraja. Sembiran has been occupied since Paleolithic times. It boasts a number of megalithic temples which are still in use. They resemble structures found in Java and Cambodia and as far away as Polynesia. Their lineal descendants can be seen in terraced temples like Besakih (the Mother Temple of all Bali), Pura Kehen (the old state temple of Bangli), and Pura Penulisan, built on a high point of the rim of the ancient Batur volcano.

Along with height, closeness to the mountains denotes power, purity, and status. The Balinese words for the cardinal directions, *kaja*, *kelod*, *kangin*, *kauh*, which are usually mis-translated as "north", "south", "east", and "west", actually mean: "towards the mountains", "away from the mountains or towards the sea", "where the sun rises", and "where the sun sets".

Direction is thus variable according to topography and the season. Other Austronesian cultures share this peculiarity. The Malay/Indonesian word *selatan*, "south", may once have meant "towards the sea", in this case the straits (*selat*) of Malacca, Sunda, and Riau.

Birth and Death Rites

Balinese houses are oriented in terms of the mountains and the sea. The domestic altars for the gods and ancestors are placed in the mountain-eastward part of the compound, followed by the dwelling pavilion of the head of the family, rice storehouses, lesser dwelling pavilions, the kitchen, and so on, down to the pigsties and latrines in the furthest seaward-westward corner of the yard. Stepped pavilions and the tell-tale position of altars and formal sitting places will enable the observant guest to witness Balinese etiquette in action. Polite Balinese keep the head lower than those of higher status at all times, and in a gathering one should be careful not to take a seat too close to the east-mountain side of the space!

Another Austronesian cultural trait, which is shared with China, is the preoccupation with ancestors. Many Austronesians remember long and detailed lineages of their forebears, but the Balinese do not: only some royal and high priestly families keep genealogical records. Instead, the link with the ancestors is perceived as a connection between an non-individualized original clearer-of-the-land, and his/her descendants, the people who continue to occupy that territory. Each village has a *pura puseh*, or "navel" temple, where this pioneer/ancestor is venerated. Similarly, families possess a *sanggah*, or domestic shrine, for their own forebears, and clans commemorate clan progenitors in a *pura kawitan*, or "origin" temple.

Ancestors are given offerings. This ensures their continuing progress through the graded ranks of heaven, and therefore their increasing power. Offerings also encourage the ancestors to intercede beneficently in the affairs of their descendants. Ancestors are not quite gods; they are not exactly worshipped; yet they become semi-divine with the passage of time until they merge with the local God of the Soil. In the meantime, ancestors must be remembered for they constitute a definite link between a given social group and the world of the gods.

Austronesian involvement with the ancestors is expressed in a curious array of mortuary customs which occur in different forms in mainland Southeast Asia, and throughout Indonesia and the Philippines. These practices are known as "secondary burial", or "secondary mortuary rites". They involve initial disposal of the corpse (by burial, cremation, or exposure), followed by its recovery after decomposition for the performance of additional rites, followed by a second disposal. This series of rites expresses the continuing and changing tie between the living and the recently dead. Family ties cannot be broken once and for all by a single ceremony; they require a gradual and formal letting go. The ceremonial sequence encompasses the ritual expression of the soul's assimilation into the Other World. Gifts (offerings) ensure its ascent into the higher, more pleasant regions of the Hereafter. Some Austronesians placed their secondary burials in jars, carved tree trunks, or stone sarcophagi. Others put them in niches hewn in high cliff faces, or burned them, or painted the bones and left them in caves.

In Bali, burial jars have been found at Gilimanuk, and stone sarcophagi abound in the Pejeng-Bedulu area. Today, the preferred method is burning, and the colorful "Hindu"-Balinese cremation ceremony has been made world-famous by thousands of photographs. Despite Hindu overtones, Balinese funerary practices are clearly Austronesian. Cremation

Balinese musicians at a cremation ceremony.

is not immediate, as in India, but follows initial burial, sometimes many years later. Cremation is accompanied and succeeded by a series of ceremonies in Bali. The rich or important may hold as many as seven. These are designed to free the soul from human ties, launch it into heaven, and establish it in its proper place in the divine hierarchy. Like many other Austronesians, the Balinese visualize the journey of the soul to the Other World as a voyage in a boat.

Birth, like death, is understood to be a gradual process, each stage of which must be ceremonially marked. In Bali, rituals for the baby begin as soon as it is known that conception has taken place. They continue throughout pregnancy, during and after the birth, and at regular intervals until the baby is a Balinese year (210 days) old. Thereafter, rites recur at birthdays, at puberty, and when the teeth are filed, and again at marriage.

Young Balinese women are harvesting rice.

Balinese Women

Gender roles are remarkable in Austronesia. Despite widespread beliefs and customs relating to female pollution such as the segregation of menstruating women, women enjoy relative equality. Descent is commonly reckoned bilaterally, so that the mother's kin are as important as the father's in determining inheritance. Women can administer property and hold political and religious power. Women have ruled various Southeast Asian and Polynesian societies, the most notorious in Bali being the eleventh century Queen Mahendradatta, possibly the original of the *Rangda*, the Balinese wicked witch. In Bali and elsewhere, women generally manage the family finances, and they have many ways of making money in their own right, the most visible and common being the ubiquitous *warung*, or coffee stall.

The influences of Hinduism and Islam have somewhat undermined the traditional equality of the Austronesian woman. Patrilineal inheritance is often preferred in Muslim societies, and even in Bali the divorce laws distinctly favor the man, who, in a dispute, can take all the children as well as the house, leaving the woman to survive alone or return to her natal family. Polygamy was and still is common in Bali. The limitation to the four wives allowed to Muslims, and the ruling – in the 1978 Indonesian marriage law - that the husband must have the written permission of his first wife before he can marry again, has progressively reduced the practice. The tendency among young people is to marry once only.

Women visiting Bali can move about easily without any of all the restrictions common in Muslim or conservative Christian societies. Men and women mix freely and happily, but Balinese ways are generally more conservative and modest than Western mores. To avoid offense, it is wise for both men and women to cover

Ulun Danu temple on Lake Bratan, Bali.

the torso, including the upper arms, and the legs at least to the knee. Shorts and plunging necklines or backs should be avoided, unless one wishes to be labelled *kurang sopan*, "impolite, immodest". In heavily Westernized enclaves (Kuta, Sanur) anything goes, but Western visitors who wish to make contact with village Balinese are advised not to make social interactions uncomfortable by improper dress. When entering any temple, domestic or public, both men and women should wear a sarong, a clean shirt or blouse with sleeves, and a sash, the Balinese *selendang*, around the waist. It is very important that women visiting Bali respect the pollution laws. It is a serious infraction of religious law for a menstruating woman to enter a temple or the home of a high priest.

Indianization

The second great complex of ideas and influences which contributed to the shaping of Balinese culture is "Indic". It includes elements brought to Bali directly from India, as well as others transmitted via other "Indianized" states, especially Java and Sumatra, but also possibly Champa (Vietnam), and Cambodia (the Khmers).

Scholars have argued much over the "Indianiaztion" of Southeast Asia. Was it brought about by colonists, traders, missionaries, or conquerors? Did it represent a wholesale re-modeling of the pre-existing cultures, or was it more a case of informal, widespread influences, percolating through already well-established societies in a myriad subtle ways? There is no definitive answer, but probably active trade brought many types of Indians to Southeast Asia, as well as spurring traffic in the opposite direction. Trade goods and ideas, images for conceiving of the divine, patterns for social organization, and a wealth of Sanskrit words and concepts entered Southeast Asia with this commercial traffic over a period lasting several centuries. In Bali, a very recent find on the north coast near the village of Sembiran has disclosed pieces of South Indian rouletted ware which date from between 200 BC and 200 AD. This pottery provides a strong indication that there was a nearly direct contact between Bali and India.

When Indian traders and learned men began to arrive in Southeast Asia they certainly did not find a cultural vacuum. Local cultures possessed sophisticated rice agriculture, metal technologies, religious ideas centered on a Lord of the Soil or a local deified ancestor, stepped temple structures, and a preference for mountains as particularly holy places. Indians probably never conquered territories in Southeast Asia; the extensive spread of obvious Indic ideas and symbols was facilitated by the nature of indigenous Southeast Asian culture. Indian mythology and imagery could be grafted easily onto locally accepted religious ideas and social structures. The Lord of the Soil became Shiva (Siwa in Bali) or Buddha; the Indian *varna* were added to local hierarchies; the holy mountain became Mahameru, the cosmic mountain, pillar of the world in Indian mythology; Indian ideas about a statecraft influenced the idiom of local chieftainship; Indian gods and goddesses were assimilated to the pantheon of deified tree, ground, and water spirits. In each instance, the "genius loci" refashioned and adapted the Indian elements so that Hinduism in Bali became vastly different from the parent religions in India.

In Bali, Indic influences are legion. The religion of Bali is an eclectic mixture of Hinduism, Buddhism, and indigenous forms of Austronesian animism. Balinese call their religion the *Agama Tirtha*, the "Holy Water Religion", because all its rites involve the liberal sprinkling of water consecrated by a priest. The most important Hindu gods worshipped in Balinese temples are Siwa (Shiva), Wisnu (Vishnu), Iswara (Isvara) and Brahma. They are accompanied by numerous ancestors and Soil-Lord gods and goddesses as well as the rice goddess, Dewi Sri; the god of the sun, Bhatara Surya; and Bhatari Durga, the goddess of death who is the malevolent form of Siwa's wife, Parvati. Above and beyond this plethora of divinities, the Balinese conceive of a unitary divine principle, Sang Hyang Widhi Wasa, who is the sum and source of all the lesser deities. Citing this belief in Wasa, some modern rationalist Balinese claim to be monotheists!

Sharing religion and mythology with India, Bali has absorbed a multiplicity of related concepts and symbols from the religious homeland. Gunung Agung, Bali's holiest mountain, is said to have been fashioned by the Hindu gods from a piece of the Indian Mount Mahameru. The Balinese temple towers (*meru*) mirror the shape of both the cosmic mountain and the layers of heaven. Hindu gods and goddesses are painted or sculpted as they are in India, bearing the same attributes.

Bali preserves much of the literary and linguistic heritage of pre-Islamic Java, to which it was closely related culturally and politically for several centuries. Hermits' caves hewn into rock faces at Goa Gajah (the Elephant Cave, Bedulu) and Tampaksiring are similar to the cave sanctuaries in East Java and India. These indicate the presence of monasteries in tenth and eleventh century Bali. Imposing rock-cut mortuary *candi* (death shrines) at Gunung Kawi (Tampaksiring) date from the eleventh century, and are clearly the formal prototypes of modern Balinese temple towers.

Not all of Bali became Indianized. The famous Bali-Aga villages (Trunyan, Tenganan, Sembiran, the villages around Mount Batur) did not absorb Indic influences. These villages are still characterized by the ancient worship of stone megaliths, strict endogamy (marriage

Colorful fighting roosters in the village of Tenganan, Bali.

only within the village), and exposure of the dead, rather than burial and cremation. They are traditionally divided into two parts, and ruled by village elders chosen in equal numbers from both sides. Even in so-called "Hindu" villages, where Indian and Javanese elements are strongest, it is unwise to assume a too close relationship between the two islands. Balinese culture (especially its music, dance, drama, and etiquette) is livelier and less consciously refined than Javanese, and it includes a large number of discrete local components.

Traces of cultural influences from China and Vietnam are much fainter, yet it is evident that they have also been penetrating Bali for a long time. Bronze drums and other implements closely related in form and decoration to those made by the Dong-Son culture of ancient North Vietnam (commencing c. 2000 BC) have been found in Gilimanuk, Manuaba, and Pejeng. In Pejeng, which was the central territory of an early Balinese kingdom, the finest of these specimens, the "Moon of Pejeng", can be viewed in the Pura Penataran Sasih. It is a large (almost two metres high) bronze drum of a distinct Dong-Son derived type.

Chinese influence is demonstrated in an old Balinese story and by the frequent mention of Chinese trading vessels in the Balinese *babad* (traditional histories). Miscellaneous pieces of Chinese porcelain are still available for sale today, some of them possibly the remnants of past trading ventures. Chinese brass coins, round with a square hole, are plentiful in Bali, and are used in many kinds of offerings. The *Barong*, personification of the forces of good, who battles the wicked *Rangda* in a popular Balinese dance drama, has much in common with the Chinese dragon, bearer of good fortune. Chinese influence seems to have been exerted mainly through trade.

Evidence of significant Chinese-Balinese contact is provided by the tale of

King Sri Adi Jayapangus, who controlled the area around Mount Batur some time before the rise of the kingdom of Bedulu-Pejeng, which was ruled by his descendants. Unable to wed any local princess as all were inferior to him, he sought out and wooed a Chinese maiden, the owner of a rich vessel which had called at one of his harbors. Enamored of the maiden, the king proposed; but she demurred, reminding him that he was a Hindu, whereas she followed the Buddhist faith. The king swore that both religions would be equal in his kingdom, married the girl, and erected statues of himself and his Chinese spouse in a local temple. Later the couple proved to be childless, so the king dallied with Bhatari Dewi Danu, the goddess of the Batur lake, and founded the dynasty which culminated in the kings of Bedulu-Pejeng. Jayapangus' adultery with Dewi Danu aroused her father's divine wrath, and both the king and his wife were consumed by supernatural fire in the grounds of the Batur temple. The statues honoring the makers of this Balinese mixed marriage can still be seen in Pura Batur. Their love story lives on in the *Barong Landung*, a dance-drama performed by men wearing giant dummies, one Chinese and female, the other Balinese and male. The Barong Landung is danced in the streets of some villages during the celebrations for Galungan, the Balinese Feast of the Gods. At this time, all the ancestors and divinities descend to Bali for a ten-day period of festivities and offerings, provided by their Balinese hosts.

Ties between Bali and its closest neighbors have existed intermittently from the dawn of Balinese history. The connection with Java has been touched on, and is the most important constant and long-lasting of Bali's foreign relations. There are indications that Balinese Buddhism may have come from the Sumatran kingdom of Srivijaya, which flourished from the seventh to the twelfth centuries AD. At different times Balinese kingdoms controlled East Java and parts of Lombok and Sumba. There are a few small Muslim communities in Bali, descendants of traders, soldiers, and retainers of Balinese rulers, who have stayed where they first settled, and clung to their divergent faith. Balinese literature and history show that there were occasional relations between Balinese rulers and Islamic kingdoms, and that the elite, if not the mass of the people, were aware of the need to defend and maintain the Balinese religion as the last bastion of Hinduism in an Islamic world. Modern Balinese, despite their easy tolerance of other religions, show a happy sense of the superiority of their own, especially in comparison to Islam.

Western Influence

Balinese exposure to Europeans occurred sporadically over several centuries, and climaxed in bloodshed in 1906-8. The flood of modern European visitors poses some new cultural options, both positive and negative, for the Indonesian government and the modern Balinese. Early visitors to Bali may have included Sir Francis Drake, or some of Magellan's men. English and American whalers hunted near there during the eighteenth century. Alfred Russel Wallace, discoverer of the Wallace Line, spent a few days there in 1856. The Wallace Line follows a deep-sea trough which runs between Sulawesi and Borneo, and then comes down through the narrow strait which divides Bali and Lombok. Wallace opined that it marked the point of division between the tigers, monkeys, and jungle trees of Asia, and the marsupials and eucalypts of Australia.

Mads Lange, a Dane, was the most interesting of the early Westerners to experience Bali. He traded first in Lombok, and then came to Bali in 1839. He remained until his death in 1856, marrying two wives, one Chinese, one Balinese, trading with the Balinese kings, and occasionally dabbling in diplomacy on behalf of the slowly encroaching Dutch. He adapted himself happily to Balinese life and was able to function as a mediator, or cultural broker, between the bewildered Balinese *rajas* and the smoothly determined minions of the Dutch colonial government. The Dutch, installed as colonial overlords in north Bali from 1849, began to encourage organized research into Balinese culture. At the same time, they set about trying to subdue the rest of the island. In 1906, the pretext of a looted ship was used by the Dutch to land an armed force on the coast of Bali near the capital of the kingdom of Badung (modern Denpasar). The Balinese king and royal family, faced with their defeat, committed ritual suicide.

By 1908 the whole island had capitulated, and the Dutch began to settle themselves in as the new, "enlightened" rulers of Bali. The colonial officials believed that they were changing very little in their

Tourists waiting for sunset near the temple of Tanah Lot.

new dominion. Misunderstanding much of what they saw, and generalizing from conditions in other places, they attempted to "reform", "tidy up", and "rationalize" the apparent confusion of Balinese ranks, rulership, village and territorial boundaries, *adat* (customary law), and so on. They made substantial changes. The Dutch noticed only the Hindu *varna* ranks, and gave preference to members of the upper three *varna* (the *Triwangsa*) in choosing "native" deputy rulers, soldiers, and other functionaries. In this way, the Dutch alienated the holders of non-*varna* ranks, barring them from educational advancement or power-holding, and simultaneously driving a wedge between them and the *Triwangsa*. In order to "rationalize" village boundaries, the Dutch split big villages, combined parts of others to make artificial communities, and often established new borders which took no account of village or clan temple mem-

This fisherman is casting his net near Tanah Lot, Bali.

bership. This meant that many families found themselves owing money, labor, and produce to temples in both their traditional *adat* village and a new government administrative village. The Indonesian government has left most of these colonial arrangements in place.

Positive consequences of the Dutch colonization of Bali centered around the bringing of Western scholars and artists to the island. Balinese manuscripts were collected and stored in a library in Singaraja (the Gedong Kirtya), where scholars began to translate and discuss them. During the 1930s, a colony of Europeans were living and working in Bali. Walter Spies, Theo Meier, and Rudolf Bonnet painted, and encouraged Balinese artists. The Puri Lukisan, the art museum in Ubud, provides fine examples of their influence. Margaret Mead, Jane Belo, Gregory Bateson, Katherine Mershon, and Miguel Covarrubias all undertook anthropological studies of Bali. Vicki Baum wrote a delightful novel, *A Tale from Bali*, set on the island, Ketut Tantri had adventures with the Indonesian freedom fighters, while Colin McPhee studied Balinese music.

Bali's romantic image was largely created by these expatriates of the 1930s. Consideration should be given to the impact of their depiction of Bali as a miraculous, uniquely beautiful and harmonious place. Tourism has attained extraordinary levels in the last twenty years, and is still increasing by leaps and bounds. In relative scale and impact, the modern invasion of pleasure-seekers is probably comparable to that of Majapahit, and it may ultimately have the same kind of long-term effects on Balinese culture. Tourism cannot be labeled good or bad: it brings in money and new opportunities. It also exposes the Balinese to unsettling ideas and influences. So far, the Balinese are adapting creatively and with success to the presence of tourists on their island.

PORTRAIT OF SUMATRA

A PORTRAIT OF SUMATRA

Sumatra is a frontier. For the ancient civilizations surrounding the Indian Ocean it was always a mysterious eastern island of riches – *Suvarna-dvipa*, the gold-land, guarding the entrance to all the wealth of Southeast Asia. For Indonesia it is the land of opportunity, of vast natural resources and economic dynamism. For the foreign visitor it offers natural beauty, cultural diversity, untamed forests still home to elephants, tapirs, tigers and rhinoceros, and rapidly developing facilities which still offer surprises. Having spent much less of their history under the tutelage of powerful states, Sumatrans frequently admit that they are less cultivated than upper-class Javanese, but they quickly add that they are far more egalitarian, enterprising, and self-reliant.

The world's sixth largest island, more than twice the size of Britain or Honshu, Sumatra has been separated from the mainland of Asia (and Java and Borneo) only for the last 10,000 years. It is dominated by its westerly spine of mountains, the Bukit Barisan, formed by the collision of the northward-moving Indian plate with the Asian continent from 60 million years ago. The uneasy conjunction of plates continues to cause geological instability along this range, including earthquakes and volcanic eruptions. 75,000 years ago Lake Toba was formed in the ruins of a massive eruption which deposited a thick layer of ash still readily discernible all over Sumatra and Malaya and as far away as Sri Lanka. At the other end of the island, in 1883, Krakatau erupted to give the modern world's biggest blast, claiming 36,000 lives.

Left: A Nias islander with ornate headgear.

The vastness and physical variety of Sumatra give it a wild, open quality in striking contrast to Java and Bali. Both those islands long ago tamed their vast forests, established efficient internal lines of communication, and unified their densely settled people into a few large linguistic-political units. Sumatra, by contrast, never approached political unification until the Dutch conquest at the beginning of this century. Although its strategic location, its great rivers and its prized exports supplied the basis for a succession of powerful kingdoms, the eastern marshes and western mountains provided protection for interior peoples who developed their own civilizations very little influenced by the outside world. Despite giving Indonesia its national language, its dominant religion (Islam) and its modern literature, Sumatra therefore retained a dozen mutually unintelligible languages and divergent religious and cultural systems of its own.

Srivijaya

Sumatra may have been the Taprobana of Ptolemy; it certainly formed a crucial (though not very distinct) part of the "gold-land" of early Indian epics and the "Jawah" of Muslim travellers. Most seafarers from outside, like the inhabitants themselves, had little sense of the separate unity of this island of many kings so narrowly divided from Java and Malaya. They were however aware in early times of the kings who controlled the export of gold and dominated the vital straits of Sunda and Malacca. Chinese records tell of successive shadowy kingdoms in the southeast Sumatran area, but these were all eclipsed by the rise of Srivijaya in the seventh century AD.

Several Srivijaya inscriptions, found within a few kilometers of modern Palembang, provide the earliest record of the use of the Malay language, in the period 683-6 AD. They tell of a Buddhist

61

king responsible for the spiritual and material welfare of his subjects, and extracting from them solemn oaths of loyalty. His capital was a major Buddhist center. Although it continued to dominate the Straits of Malacca until the eleventh century, Srivijaya left no great monuments to rival the Borobudur in Java. What temples it built in stone fell victim to the greater militance of Sumatran than of Javan Islam. Moreover, the empire sat lightly upon the scattered interior populations, concentrating on dominating the various international ports of eastern Sumatra and the Malayan Peninsula, in many of which inscriptions and buried Buddhist statuary have been found. Its capital at Palembang was plundered in a south Indian raid in 1025, and during the next century independent trade centers grew up in Java, northern Sumatra and Malaya. By 1080 the principal center of what may always have been a multi-centred polity was near modern Jambi.

The chief heir of Srivijaya's glory was Minangkabau, the heavily populated rice

Famous Batak-style houses at Lake Toba.

and gold producing area in the central mountains. After the thirteenth-century Javanese conquest of the major ports of Sumatra's eastern seaboard, a prince claiming descent from both Majapahit and Srivijaya established his own kingdom near the headwaters of the Indragiri and Batang Hari Rivers, controlling the gold of Minangkabau. This (Tantric) Buddhist king, Adityavarman (1356-75), left numerous statues and inscriptions suggesting he controlled most of central Sumatra.

Islam

The north and west coasts of Sumatra long remained a political low-pressure area. Its rivers were not navigable, its ports were exposed to the northwest monsoon, its peoples reportedly stateless, barbarous cannibals. The major attractions of the northwest were its location

Solemn Toba Bataks during a ceremony.

for Indian Ocean traders and the camphor which was collected as resin from trees in the hills above Barus and Sibolga.

Along the lengthy coast between Barus and present-day Medan were numerous other small river-ports. At one of them Marco Polo waited for the monsoon in 1292, as part of the expedition carrying a princess from the Mongol Emperor of China to Persia. He relates that his expedition disembarked there and "for fear of these nasty and brutish folk who kill men for food we dug a big trench round our encampment ... and within these fortifications we lived for five months". Despite his distaste, Polo and his colleagues lived and traded sufficiently with them to give Europe its first account of sago, of palm-wine, of rhinoceros and of cannibalism itself. This was at the port of Samudra (Sanskrit for "sea"), or Sumatra (near modern Lhokseumawe), which during the ensuing two centuries became sufficiently important to give its name to the whole island, at least for Arabs and Europeans coming from the West. In Polo's time it was still a small kingdom practicing shamanistic animism. He reported however that already the neighboring kingdom of Perlak (near modern Langsa) had become already Muslim, "owing to contact with Saracen merchants, who continually resort here in their ships".

Samudra itself was Muslim by 1297, to judge from the earliest of the tombstones in the ancient cemetery at Geudong. When it was visited by the greatest of Arab travel-writers, Ibn Battuta, in 1323 it was a sophisticated sultanate with international relations around the Indian Ocean and to China. Under its preferred Muslim name of Pasai, it issued gold coins, sent ships to the major ports of Asia, and developed a Malay system of writing in Arabic script. For subsequent sultanates Pasai represented the great Southeast Asian center of Islamic scholarship. Pasai was a producer of silk, and

63

in the fifteenth century grew much pepper for the Chinese market.

Despite its commercial and religious eminence, Samudar/Pasai never united northern Sumatra politically. On the arrival of the Portuguese (1509), there were still separate Muslim port-states at (west to east) Barus, Daya, Lamri, Pidië, Pasai and Aru. After conquering Melaka (Malacca) in 1511, and driving out many of its Muslim merchants, the Portuguese attempted to gain influence in Pasai and Pidië by supporting one side of their numerous succession disputes. The effect was to drive all the anti-Portuguese elements, who included the wealthy Muslim merchant community, to unite under the banner of Aceh, a new sultanate formed around 1500 on the ruins of ancient Lamri at the northwestern tip of Sumatra. Between 1519 and 1524 Sultan Ali Mughayat Syah of Aceh drove the Portuguese out of northern Sumatra and began what was to be a century of bitter conflict with the Christian intruders.

On the Portuguese arrival the important ports of Sumatra were all under Islamic authority, and Islam had begun to make inroads on the major interior population centre of Minangkabau. Most of these gains can be attributed to the wealth and status of Muslim traders, and the need of an increasingliy commercialized people for a portable, universally valid, faith. The Portuguese onslaught against Muslim trade, and Aceh's counter-crusade against the Portuguese, introduced a new element of holy war. In the period from 1540 to 1630, Aceh fought a number of wars against interior peoples called Bataks, in which the acceptance of Islam was a major Acehnese aim. In northern Sumatra a clear line developed between those who accepted Aceh authority, Islam, and the Arabic script, and those who withdrew to mountain fastnesses, accepted the designation Batak, continued to eat pork, use their ancient Indic script and practice the old spirit worship. The Gayo people around Lake Tawar (in modern Aceh) were in the former group, the Toba and Karo in the latter. In south and central Sumatra, by contrast, Islam spread very gradually from the coastal centers to the interior, with no major center of resistance to it ever developing.

The Aceh Sultanate

Initially the Portuguese succeeded in disrupting Muslim shipments of Indian pepper to Egypt and the West. It was the achievement of Aceh to expand greatly the growing of pepper in Sumatra, and to find a way of shipping it directly to the Muslim ports in the Red Sea, avoiding the areas of Portuguese strength on the Indian west coast. By the 1550s Aceh was supplying Europe with about half of its pepper through this route.

Since Turkey was then the master of Egypt, this brought the Sultan of Aceh into contact with the Ottomans. In the 1560s Sultan Ala'ad-din al-Kahar ("the conqueror") sent envoys with gifts of pepper to Sulaiman the Magnificent, appealing for help against the accursed infidels who had seized Melaka and terrorized Muslim traders and pilgrims in the Indian Ocean.

The Ottomans responded by sending gunsmiths and artillerymen, who contributed much to Aceh's holy wars against the Bataks and the Portuguese. The memory of this assistance from the Caliph of Islam was kept alive by a great Turkish cannon which guarded the palace, by a Turkish-style red flag, and by various popular stories. Economic rivalry with the Portuguese over the pepper trade reinforced the religious and political hostility. Portuguese Melaka had to endure a dozen attacks from Acehnese fleets between 1537 and 1629.

For the Dutch (in 1598), English (in 1600) and French (in 1602), Aceh was one of the first Asian targets because of

Worshipping Allah in the Grand Mosque of Banda Aceh.

its abundant pepper and its own aversion to the Portuguese enemy. These northern Europeans were welcomed, mounted on elephants for their official reception at the palace, and honored with gifts of *sarung* and *kris*.

They found the Acehnese difficult bargaining partners, but continued to visit the busy port. They confirm the Acehnese popular memory that the peak of power and wealth of the sultanate was reached under Sultan Iskandar Muda ("the young Alexander", 1607-36).

In this period Aceh was one of the important powers of Asia, with its authority stretching as far as Tiku and Priaman (near modern Padang) in west Sumatra, Asahan in east Sumatra, Pahang, Johor and Kedah in the Malay Peninsula. Thousands of captives were brought back from its victorious naval expeditions to populate the city, man the war galleys, and conduct the heavy construction work in the sultan's buildings. Yet warfare and the impermanence of wooden buildings have left little trace of its former splendor.

The last years of Iskandar Muda were marred by his 1629 defeat before Melaka and signs of paranoia in which he killed many of those closest to him, including his son. His son-in-law succeded him as Iskandar Thani, but in turn died in 1641. Anxious to avoid such autocratic extremes the leading men then put four successive women on the throne. Foreign traders were gratified by more predictable conditions, and local Acehnese chiefs were able to demand greater autonomy. But Aceh was no longer able to counter persistent Dutch attempts to prise loose the pepper-growing regions and the tin-producing areas of the Malay Peninsula. Aceh remained a great Southeast Asian port, and the only major Indonesian state to retain full freedom of action vis-à-vis the Dutch. But its major exports were now non-renewable items formerly monopolized by the king – gold and elephants.

A Muslim trader disembarks from his sailing vessel.

Decline of the Harbor Sultanates

While Aceh dominated the coasts of northern Sumatra, sultanates arose on the southern rivers for similar reasons. Pepper-growing spread to almost every suitable part of Sumatra during the boom caused by the exceptional European demand in the sixteenth and seventeenth centuries. Much of this was grown by Minangkabau on the higher ground of central Sumatra. When they found Aceh's attempted monopoly on the west coast oppressive, they sought other outlets down the Musi and Batang Hari rivers. At Palembang and Jambi the English and Dutch competed vigorously for this pepper, though the Dutch got the upper hand by the middle of the century.

The dominance of these port-cities over the vast and varied hinterland of Sumatra was in sharp decline by 1700. The European demand for pepper dropped after 1650, and the Dutch and English companies drove ever harder bargains for guaranteed delivery at fixed low prices. Both companies ended by relying on pepper suppliers over whom they had monopoly control. Female rule was overthrown in Aceh in 1699 on the grounds of being non-Islamic, but this only initiated a period of dynastic conflict in which the autonomy of the many local chiefs (*uleebalang*) was confirmed.

During the late seventeenth and eighteenth centuries the weight of state authority was even less felt by the majority of Sumatrans, who organized themselves in the highlands around kinship-based communities, and in the coastal areas around entrepreneurial chiefs who could open up an area to cultivation or trade. Such conditions made it easy for enterprising outsiders to play a role. Bugis from south Sulawesi, Arabs from Hadhramaut, and Minangkabau adventurers from Sumatra itself formed many new dynasties.

The biggest players in this league of foreigners were the British and Dutch companies, but for them pepper had become a marginal trade item by the eighteenth century, and therefore Sumatra was something of a backwater. The Dutch established their own permanent Sumatran headquarters at Padang in 1663, as a result of the Painan Treaty agreeing to protect local pepper-growing principalities from Aceh in exchange for their produce. The British established theirs at Fort Marlborough, Bengkulu, in 1685. Each became a center of rival networks of trade along the west coast, but they remained small and vulnerable colonies.

Revival of Commerce and Islam

A new phase of commercial expansion affected Sumatra from the 1780s, as private traders broke the fading monopolies of the Dutch and English companies. Private British and Tamil traders came from India, British and Chinese from the new free British port at Penang (1786), French pepper-buyers and Nias slavers from the Mauritius and later Réunion, and Americans from the maritime centers of New England. American attention focused on the west coast between Sibolga and Meulaboh, where Acehnese river-chiefs created the world's biggest center of pepper production in the early decades of the nineteenth century. In the Minangkabau area cassia (a substitute for cinnamon), gambir (for tanning), and from 1790 coffee, became new crops attractive to Americans and others. In the eighteenth century the tin lodes of Bangka began to be exploited, initially by Chinese.

Since the decline of the powerful Islamic sultans, the chief bearers of Muslim influence had been brotherhoods of Sufis known in Indonesia as *tarikat*, under whose auspices the young men of a village would live and study together in a *surau* (prayer hall). Such *tarikat* schools were especially popular among young Minangkabau men, for whom there was little place in the household or in agriculture according to the matrilineal inheritance system. These schools provided the basis for a powerful movement of Islamic reform.

The new commercialism had increased the social ills this movement attacked, but also the number of Sumatrans able to make the pilgrimage to Mecca. In 1803 three such pilgrims returned after having witnessed the victory in Mecca of the fundamentalist Wahhabis, and set about trying to reform Minangkabau in a similar direction. Society was quickly polarized, as the reformers (known as Padris) tried to ban such beloved traditional pastimes as cock-fighting and betel-chewing, as well as tobacco and opium, and at the same time forced the people to pray and to adopt Arab dress. In 1815 the movement struck at the remnants of the old Minangkabau kingdom centered at Pararuyung, killing several princes and burning the palace.

Young couple decorated in traditional Aceh dress.

The Dutch Conquest

Despite all their seventeenth-century treaties with most of the coastal states of Sumatra (notably excluding Aceh), the Dutch had to start almost from scratch when Britain returned to its prewar possessions after the Napoleonic Wars, in 1816. They were in no position to prevent the dominance over Sumatran trade of the British ports of Penang and Singapore, which continued well into the twentieth century. Dutch military advances were slow, and usually provoked by the need to exclude other Europeans. Almost nowhere did Sumatrans accept the extension of Dutch authority without a fight.

The basis of the present Malaysia-Indonesia border is the 1824 Anglo-Dutch Treaty, whereby the British withdrew all their claims and possessions in Sumatra, and the Dutch in the Malayan Peninsula. Melaka therefore became British, Bengkulu became Dutch, and the Sultanate of Riau-Johor was divided between British-protected Johor and Dutch-protected Riau. Palembang was considered vital to Dutch interests because of its claim over Bangka tin and its proximity to Singapore, but it required two military expeditions, many casualties and repeated attempts to find a pliable sultan before the Dutch finally abolished the sultanate and ruled Palembang directly from 1825. Rebellions were frequent throughout the nineteenth century both here and in neighboring Jambi, where the Dutch established a garrison in 1834.

But in Padang the returning Dutch inherited the Padri headache from the British. Despite their weakness, they were drawn into supporting the opponents of the Padris in a series of protracted operations from 1820 to 1841 which became known as the Padri War. This made the most densely populated region of Sumatra also the principal Dutch stronghold. The expenses of the garrison were met by the forced delivery of coffee at fixed prices. Enterprisig Minangkabau also took advantage of improved communications and markets to grow their own coffee, as well as tobacco, sugar, cassia and gambir, providing a prosperous commercially oriented middle class in many areas of Minangkabau. The same group responded enthusiastically to modern-style education, funding their own secular schools from the 1840s. By 1872 there were almost 1200 Minangkabau children in such schools – a proportion several times higher than in Java, where education was limited to the aristocracy. This first generation to be literate in Malay in Latin launched Minangkabau into its role of providing Sumatra with a high proportion of clerks, schoolteachers, journalists and political activists.

On the east coast of Sumatra the Dutch advanced slowly, opposed by Singapore merchants as well as local *rajas*. The most valuable Dutch acquisition proved to be the hitherto insignificant Malay states of Langkat, Deli, Serdang and Asahan in 1865. Jacob Nienhuys began to grow tobacco in Deli with labor brought from Penang, and within a decade this was acknowledged as the finest leaf tobacco for wrapping cigars. British objections were quickly overcome by the opportunities of supplying the burgeoning new "plantation district" from the Straits settlements. 20,000 Chinese laborers each year were brought in to cut down the forests and tend the tobacco plants, until the 1890s when cheaper and more tractable Javanese took their place - there were 260,000 contract workers there in the 1920s. Rubber, tea and oil palm estates followed the tobacco. Prosperous modern towns grew up at Medan, Binjei, Pematang Siantar and Tanjung Balei, and the Malay *rajas* who were held to own the valuable land grew unprecedentedly wealthy on the royalties from it.

Aceh was by far the biggest challenge to Dutch arms and diplomacy. Proud and free, it had wealth and foreign contacts from its pepper and betelnut trade, a self-image as "the verandah of Mecca", and deep suspicion of Dutch advances on both east and west coasts of Sumatra. In deference to Britain's relations with Aceh, including a treaty of mutual defence in 1819, the Dutch had undertaken to respect the sultanate's continued independence, in a note appended to the 1824 treaty. This was annulled by another Anglo-Dutch Treaty in 1871.

The Dutch attack was hastened by energetic Acehnese attempts to form defensive alliances with Turkey, France and the United States. A force of 3,000 men attacked Banda Aceh in April 1873, but withdrew after losing its commander and 80 men. This proved, however, only the first chapter of a war which was to last until 1903, exhausting all Dutch resources of men, money and morale, and leaving a terrible legacy of bitterness in Aceh. By the mid-1880s resistance

Brimming with life – night market at Tanjung Pinang.

leadership had passed to *ulama* (religious scholars) who preached the necessity of a holy war at any cost. The Dutch graveyard in Banda Aceh remains as a monument to more than 10,000 who died on the Dutch side. For the Acehnese, who lost five times as many, the monument is the crop of war heroes who continued to inspire them, some of whom are now officially recognized as Indonesia's national heroes. At the approach of the Japanese in 1942 the province rebelled and drove out the remaining Dutch presence.

Much of the credit for the eventual Dutch success in imposing their authority was given to Colonel J.B. van Heutsz, Military Governor of Aceh from 1898 to 1904. His policy of relentless pursuit and emphatic assertion of Dutch power was endorsed by a government, which made him Governor-General (1904-9). In that capacity he sent Dutch troops to every corner of the archipelago where independent *rajas* and villages continued to exist. By 1910 the whole of Sumatra was for the first time under a single authority, albeit a much resented foreign one.

Christian Sumatrans

Though Christian missionaries occasionally visited the ports of Sumatra as early as the fourteenth century, it was only the isolated peoples who had firmly resisted Islam – Bataks and the islanders off the west coast – who offered any real prospect of conversion.

The history of Christian conversion in Sumatra really began with the decision of the German Rhenisch Mission Society to work there in 1861, and the arrival the following year of their dominating figure, Ludwig Nommenson. Winning confidence as a doctor, mediator and teacher, he extended the mission's work northward from Silindung to Lake Toba, always in advance of Dutch control. Protestant Christianity was melded onto Toba Batak identity with great skill, and the reward was the acceptance of Christianity by virtually the whole Batak people in the period 1880-1900. Responding to nationalist movements against Western control in the 1920s, an autonomous Batak church was established in 1930 which helped to maintain the identity of Toba Bataks as they began their successful expansion into commercial and teaching roles all over Indonesia. In contrast to the somewhat marginal place of Christians in Asia, the three million Toba Batak Christians are aggressive and unapologetic about their status as Indonesians.

Sumatra and Indonesia

Economically there were at least three Sumatras in the early part of this century. Each of the three major cities was the center of a separate rail and road system - Medan in the north, strongly European and Chinese in character, with its closest external links to British Malaya rather than to other Dutch centers; Padang in the centre, the oldest but sleepiest of the major towns; and oil-rich Palembang, whence road and rail systems led southward to the ferry to Java. The trans-Sumatra highway was first discussed in 1916, but was not finally completed until 1938. In the same year the colonial government erected the first pan-Sumatran administration, with a governor in Medan supervising ten residencies.

In 1917 some Sumatrans formed the Young Sumatran League centered in the high schools of Batavia, and in 1921-2 sponsored Sumatra unity conferences in Sibolga, Bukittinggi and Padang. Most of the support came from Muslim Minangkabaus. Christian Batak students became numerous enough in the 1920s to want their own organization, and by 1926 it was apparent that the only acceptable ideals above the ethno-linguistic level would be national Indonesian ones. In fact Sumatra contributed far more than its share towards the development of Indonesian nationalism, with figures such as Mohammad Hatta (later Vice-president), Soetan Sjahrir (first Prime Minister) and Amir Sjarifuddin (second Prime Minister) playing role in developing the ideas of national unity.

Even more important was the Sumatran role in developing a national literature. For most Sumatrans Malay had always been the principal written language, and its adoption as the language of nationalism involved no such problem as for the Javanese. The development of the modern Indonesian novel was almost entirely a Minangkabau affair, with Marah Rusli, Takdir Alisjabana, Nur Iskandar, Abdul Muis and the Muslim leader Hamka dominating the 1920s and 1930s. Given this strong contribution to Indonesian nationalism in many fields, and its lack of any inherent unity at an island-wide level, it is not suprising that Sumatra rejected all attempts to separate it from Java in the turbulent 1940s. The Japanese in 1945 belatedly fostered the idea of an independent Sumatra centered

Left: Finely crafted hilt of an Acehnese dagger. Right: A thoughtful Toba Batak.

in Bukittinggi, while the Dutch in 1948-9 tried to foster a Sumatran umbrella for the federal states they had set up in various parts of the island. But Sumatrans themselves had already decided in the 1920s that they could only bring their diverse ethnic groups together at the Indonesia level.

Revolution, Rebellion, Integration

When independence was declared in Jakarta on 17 August 1945, Sumatra was governed by ten separate Japanese administrations which had allowed very little Indonesian contact among them. The revolution against first the Japanese, then the British who occupied the three major cities in October 1945, and finally the Dutch, had to be fought separately in each residency, with little beyond radio broadcasts from Java to provide inspiration. Sumatra had to undergo some of the most violent aspects of the revolution before it could fit easily within a nationalist framework. In Aceh the *uleebalang* who had ruled under the Dutch and Japanese were violently overthrown in December 1945 by a Muslim-led coalition. Three months later the Malay sultans and Simelungun *raja* who had risen to often flamboyant prosperity, were similarly overthrown in what was dubbed a "Social Revolution" by the Marxists among its supporters. These movements were not controlled by the Republican administration, and they led to a breakdown in authority, especially in east Sumatra where nationalist gangs became a law unto themselves.

Even though these excesses caused a reaction among some groups, who sought Dutch protection in 1947-9, Sumatrans were probably more wholehearted in their rejection of Dutch authority than any other major part of the colony. During the period of six months (1948-9) when the Dutch occupied all the cities and towns of Java, Aceh was the only province which the Dutch thought best to leave alone, and Banda Aceh became the capital of what remained of the republic. Despite Dutch attempts to surround republican Java with a ring of minorities fearful of Javanese dominance, they were forced to accept the reality of republican sentiments in Sumatra.

Nevertheless, the vast island was far from integrated politically or economically when the revolution ended with the transfer of full sovereignty to Indonesia in 1950. Each former residency had its own battle-hardened military force not eager to return to civilian life, and each felt it had earned the right to play a part in the republic on its own terms. The lucrative smuggling trade to Singapore, which had seemed patriotic during both the Japanese occupation and the revolution, was not easy to give up to a central government in Jakarta which had little to offer in return.

The first crisis came in Aceh, which objected to incorporation with Christian Bataks into a province of North Sumatra, to the failure to declare Indonesia a Muslim state, and to the poor rewards for its leaders within the new state. In 1953 the Islamic leadership of Aceh revolted against Jakarta, and declared Aceh part of Dar ul-Islam. Troops sent from Java reoccupied the Acehnese towns, but the rebels controlled the hinterland until 1959, when they surrendered in return for autonomous status for Aceh. Before then Toba Batak and Minangkabau military leaders had allied with national politicians dissatisfied with the centralism, corruption and pro-Communist policies of the central government, to form the Revolutionary Government of the Republic of Indonesia (PRRI) in February 1958. The central government reacted with great vigor, bombing Padang and Bukittinggi and sending a large force from Java. The fighting was over within six months; but it left Minangkabau, like Aceh in the same period, feeling like an occupied province in which locals were no longer trusted with high military or civilian office.

Under President Suharto Sumatran discontent has eased. The anti-Communist and free-market policies of the New Order are those Sumatran leaders in the PRRI had advocated, and the central government has had the resources to provide a generous return to the Sumatran provinces for their loyalty. The road system was finally restored in the 1970s to pre-war levels and better. Large multi-ethnic provinces were broken up until all except North Sumatra (pre-war East Sumatra plus Tapanuli) were back to the old Dutch residencies. The military presence became less obvious. One still hears grumbles about the *pusat* (center), but these are little different from those heard in Java and elsewhere.

Economic Development

Sumatra has often been called the island of Indonesia's future, with unbounded potential for development of its rich agricultural and mineral resources. It is certainly true that since the unification of Indonesia at the beginning of this century, it has been Sumatra that has grown fastest in population, exports, and wealth. Both by immigration (three million of Sumatra's present population were not born there) and natural increase, Sumatra has grown by over 3 per cent a year for most of this century, while the rest of the country has been closer to 2 per cent. Medan is the fastest growing of Indonesia's cities, from 5,800 in 1893 to nearly 3 million today.

Abundant arable land as well as a strong entrepreneurial tradition drew Sumatrans enthusiastically into the rubber boom in the 1920s, and into cloves, pepper, coffee, tobacco, oil palm and other crops since. In addition Sumatra has been Indonesia's biggest provider of oil, with the wells at Langkat and Palembang

Harvesting rubber (latex) from a tree in Sumatra.

being followed by newer ones at Pekanbaru and recently a vast natural gas field at Lhokseumawe.

Whereas Java provided most of Indonesia's exports in the nineteenth century, Sumatra has done so in the twentieth. In the 1930s Sumatran ports handled roughly half the value of Indonesia's exports, but this grew to nearly 70 per cent in the 1950s and 1960s, even without counting the large amount of smuggling. The growth of Java-based manufacturing and the greater centralization of the economy has recently reduced this dominance, but Sumatra still provides about 53 per cent of Indonesia's ever-expanding exports. Many of those who made their start handling these exports went on to become the biggest *pribumi* (native, i.e. non-Chinese) entrepreneurs of Indonesia in the 1950s and 1960s. However, the centralization of the economy and the importance of political connections have tended to reduce the role of Sumatrans in the economy in the last 20 years.

This wealth has given Sumatrans a relatively comfortable standard of living, even though the infrastructure of communications, electricity grids and piped water remains less developed than that of Java.

From the 1920s to the 1960s Sumatrans may have had on average double the income of the Javanese, though this gap too has narrowed with the new industry-based development in Java, so that the poorer southern provinces – Lampung and Bengkulu – are no longer above the national average. But still Sumatrans attend school longer, own more cars, bicycles and TV sets (about 12 per cent of Sumatran households in 1980), and spend more on food and clothing than Indonesians on average. The confident spirit of individual enterprise that has marked Sumatrans through the centuries will continue to serve them and their country well.

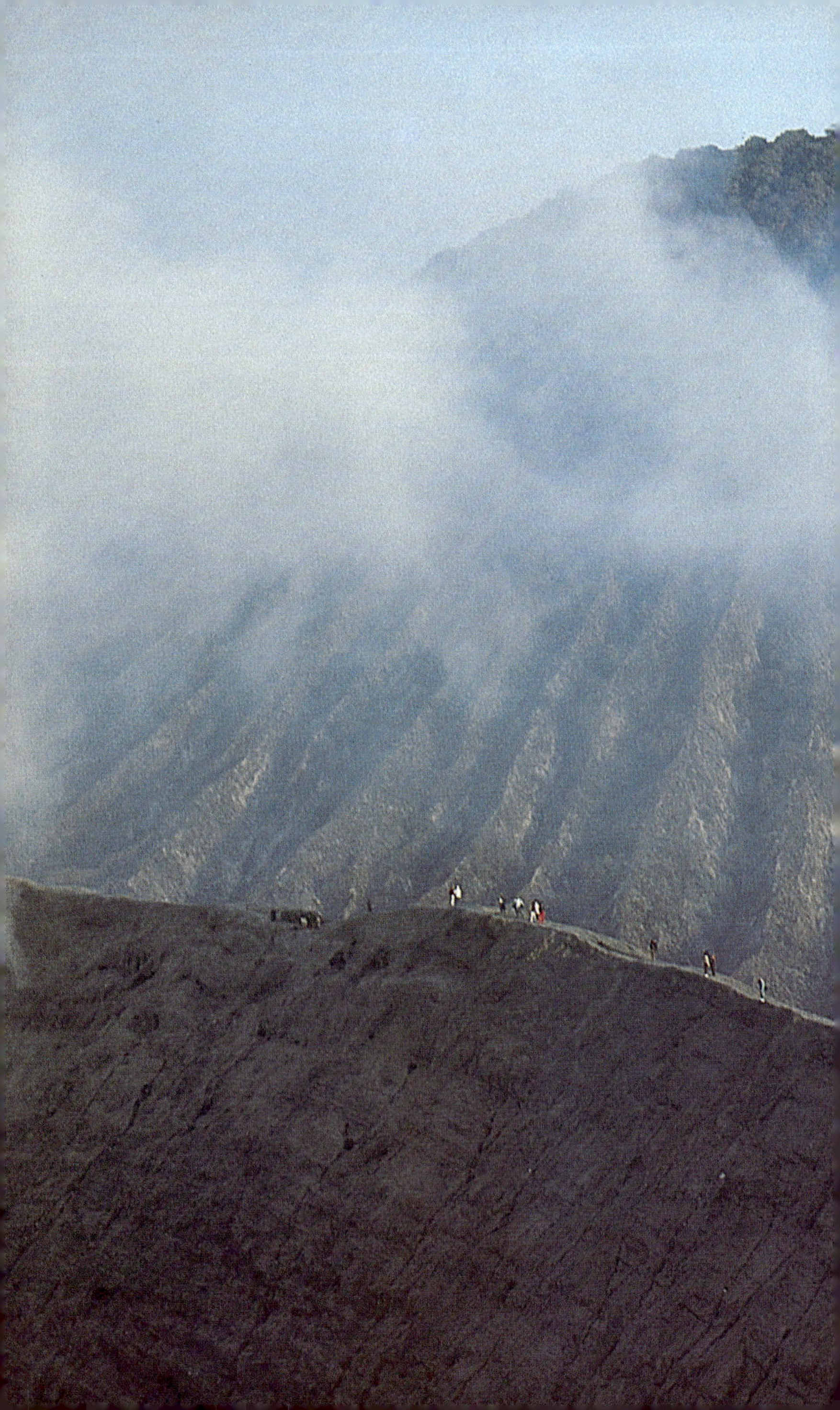

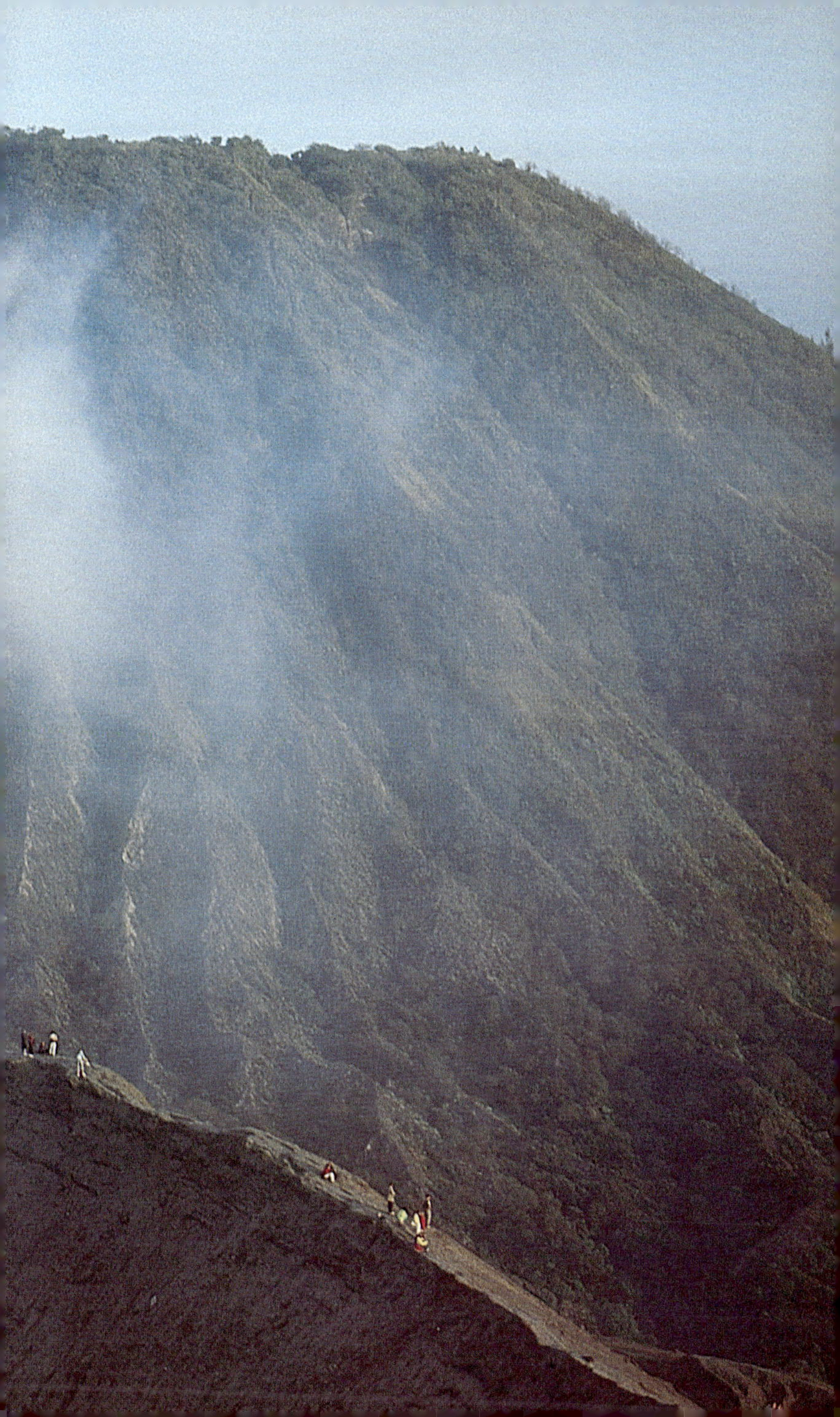

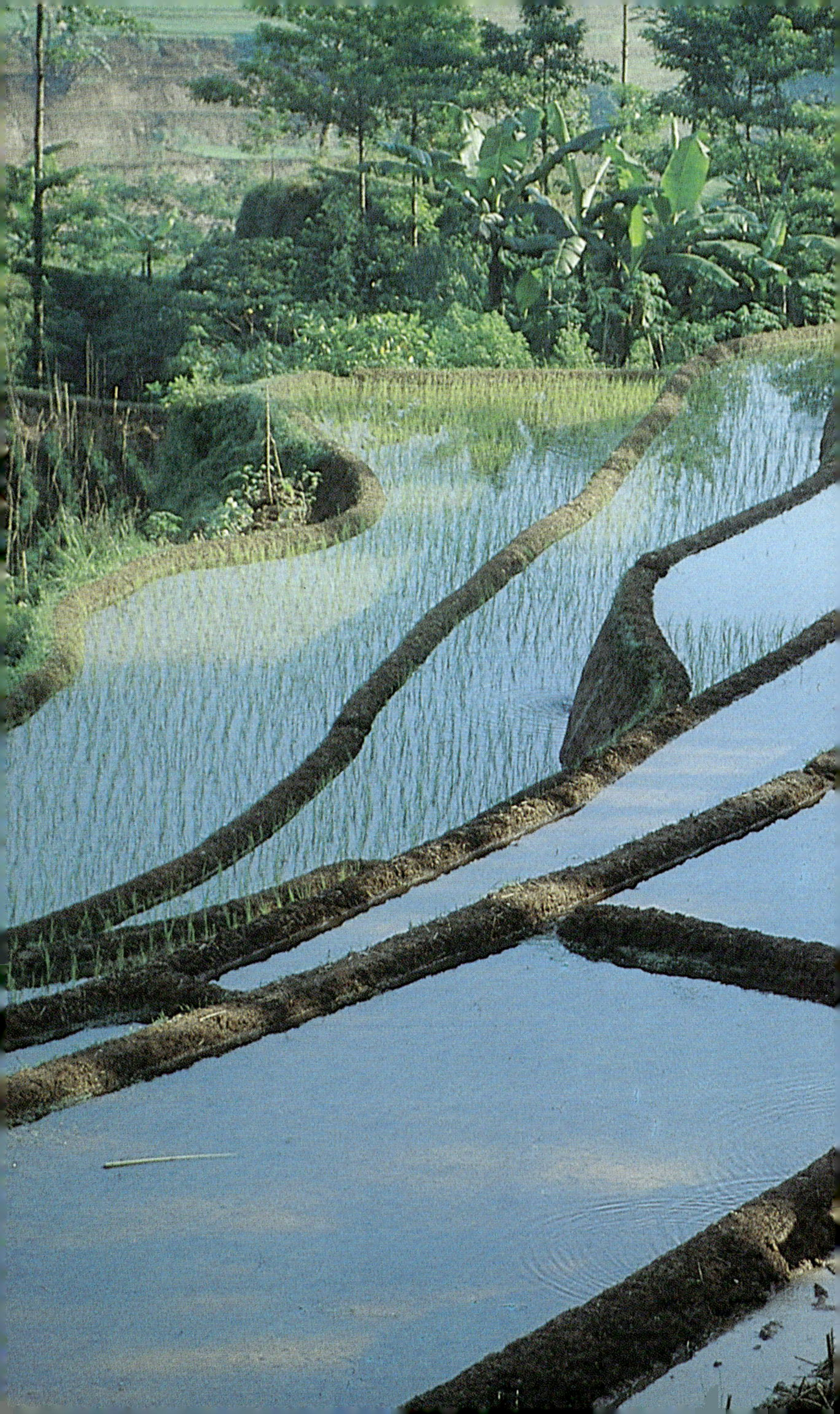

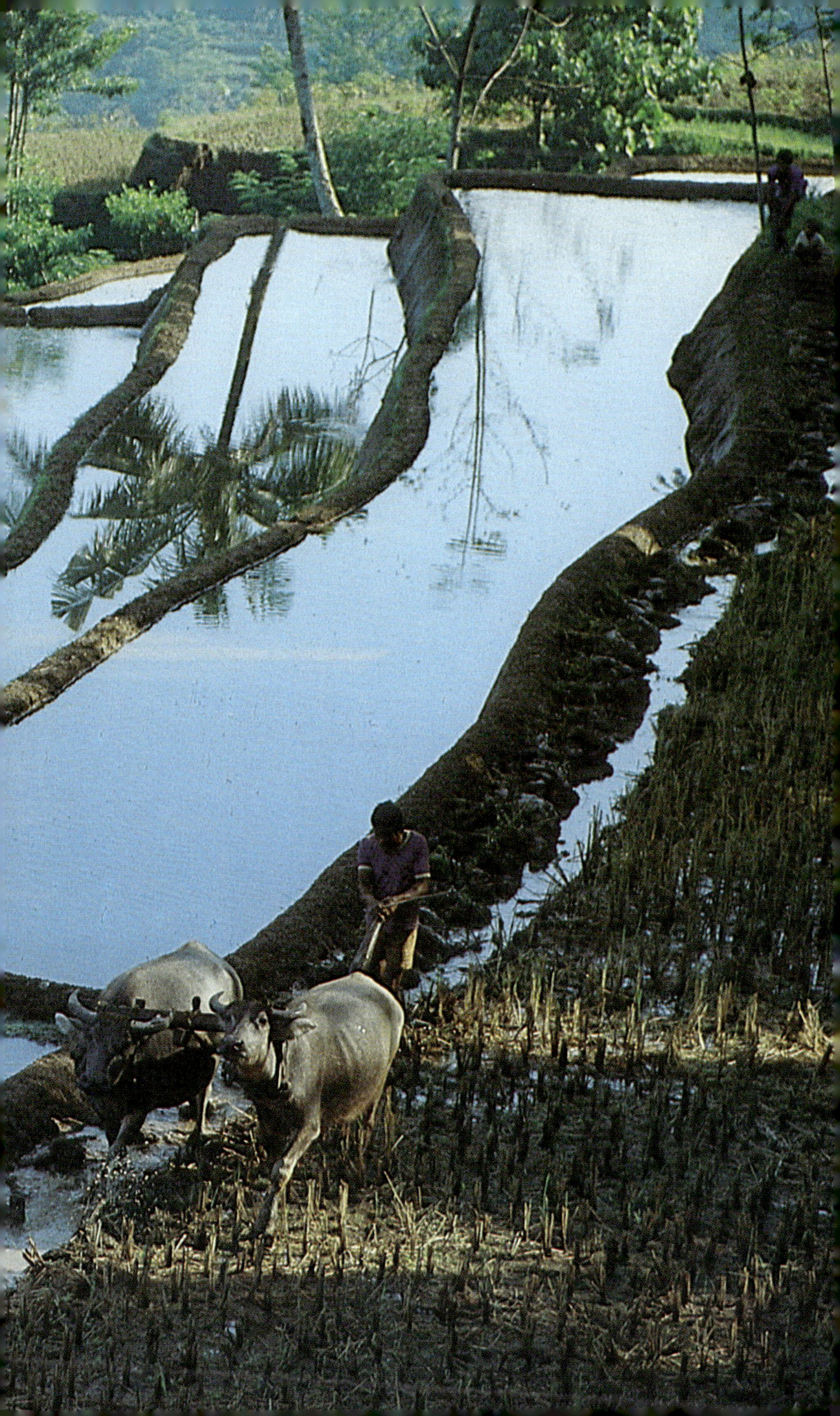

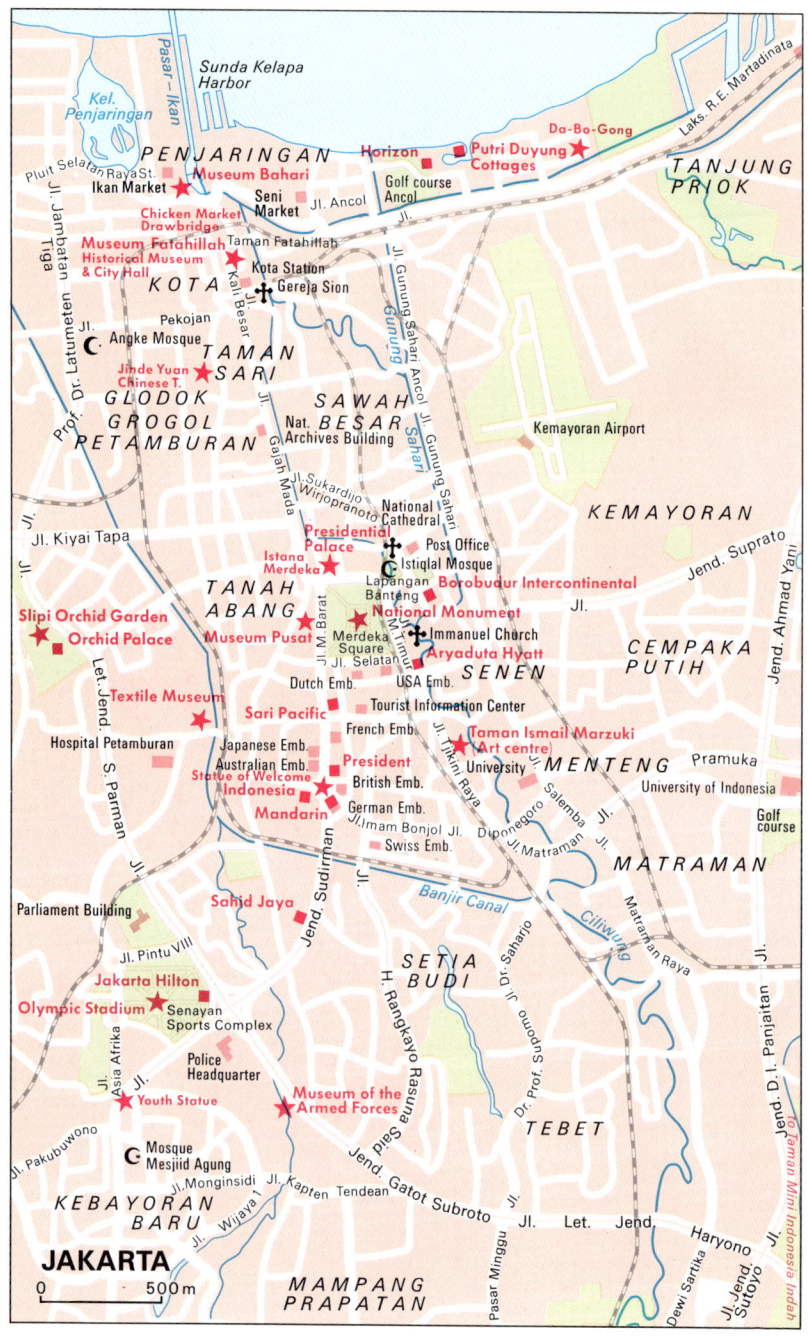

JAKARTA

SPRAWLING METROPOLIS

JAKARTA

JAKARTA

Sweltering on its humid coastal plain, this vast, sweaty, profuse, multifarious, vibrant place concentrates all Indonesia's diversity. At the city center, Jakarta seems to celebrate that diversity in the almost absurd juxtaposition of the white dome of Southeast Asia's largest mosque, **Istiqlal** (1978), with the neo-Gothic spires of the **National Cathedral** (1901) and the Grecian columns of the Protestant **Emmanuel Church** (1839) - while the secular spire of the **National Monument** towers over all three. One Jakarta neighborhood may contain every major ethnic group of Indonesia, some Chinese and a European or two. This is the place to acquire a preview or an overview of the vast range of Indonesian regional arts and crafts. **Taman Ismail Marzuki** is the nation's center for the performing arts; **Pasar Seni** at **Ancol** exhibits and sells visual art and handicrafts from all parts of the archipelago. Jakarta, Indonesia's much-maligned capital, also boasts the country's most interesting street life, its best selection of eating places, its finest museums, and historical monuments.

Preceding pages: On the rim of Bromo volcano. A farmer working on his rice terraces.

Jakarta is stereotyped as a city of chaos and contradiction: slums in the shadow of skyscrapers, rickety *becak* jockeying for position with shining BMWs on traffic-snarled streets, barefoot cripples begging outside the closed doors of air-conditioned shopping complexes. Many have seen it as a monument to the yawning gulf between the aspirations of Indonesia's elite and the everyday life of its masses, at once the country's greatest showpiece and its greatest shame. But for the careful observer Jakarta embodies Indonesia's unique syntheses as well as its painful antitheses. One block behind the roaring transport arteries lie almost miraculously quiet *kampung* neighborhoods where some of the calm and charm of rural Indonesia lives on, adapted to the new urban setting.

Jakarta is perhaps the one truly *Indonesian* city, the major melting-pot – give or take the odd coagulation of ethnic enmity – of the nation's diverse races and cultures. It is the crucible in which the cosmopolitan Indonesian culture of the future is being forged, not only by officialdom and the media, but also by an arcane youth subculture. Jakarta sets the standards of fashion and behavior for all Indonesia's urban youth, standards which are by no means pure imitations of the West. Few cities have changed more in

Sailing vessels at anchor in Sunda Kelapa Harbor, Jakarta.

recent times than Jakarta. The dizziest changes really began with the Pacific war, when the invading Japanese inaugurated the city's present name. For more than three centuries the world had known it as Batavia, the capital of Netherlands India.

The Dutch city had been a commercial and military foundation on the site of a Muslim port, Jakarta or Jayakarta, on a natural harbor at the mouth of the Ciliwung river. Earlier still, the port had been an entrepot for the Sundanese Hindu kingdom of Pajajaran, but in 1527 it was captured by Muslims from Banten and Demak. Little more remains from pre-Dutch days than a single inscribed stone pillar in the National Museum, commemorating a Hindu-Portuguese treaty of 1522. But the modern **Sunda Kelapa Harbor**, with its stately sailing vessels, and the pre-industrial marine technology on sale in the nearby **Pasar Ikan** market, still recall some of the atmosphere of the old Asian trading world into which the Dutch intruded all those centuries ago.

Jayakarta was destroyed in 1619 by the Dutch East India Company (VOC) under its ruthless fourth Governor-General, Jan Pieterszoon Coen. The compact little fortified town built in its place corresponded with the present-day district of **Kota**, and though the walls themselves were mostly demolished in 1810, something of this first Batavia is still to be seen. West of the harbor, VOC warehouses from 1652 now house the **Bahari Museum**, with Indonesian maritime exhibits; further south is a large but dilapidated **Company wharf**, once used for ship repair. Ruins of VOC installations can also be seen offshore, on the inner islands of the **Pulau Seribu** (Thousand Islands) archipelago, now a weekend beach retreat for wealthy Jakartans. The area of most complete preservation from Company days, however, is Batavia Town Square, now called **Taman Fatahillah**. The square is commanded by the 1710 **City Hall** (*Stadhuis*), which was restored in 1973/74 and now houses the **Historical Museum of Jakarta**. This solid building, said to have been inspired by its counterpart in Amsterdam, sports horrific dungeons as well as opulent chambers; public tortures and executions were carried out on the square in front. The museum collection includes fine furniture and VOC regalia. Also in Taman Fatahillah are art and *wayang* museums and a Portuguese cannon from Malacca called **Si Jagur**, said to make barren women fertile if they sit astride it. The canal and houses along Jl Kali Besar, and the restored **Chicken Market drawbridge** at its north end, illustrate a doomed attempt to recreate a Dutch environment in this tropical place.

Jan Pieterszoon Coen's fort withstood attacks by huge Javanese armies in 1628 and 1629, but Coen himself, ominously, died of cholera during the second siege. For the next two centuries, Batavia's most feared enemy was not arms but disease. Apart from cholera, the city's stagnant canals bred another deadly threat, malaria. Batavia's pestilences soon earned it the grim epithet of "the Dutchmen's grave". By the 1680s some seaward areas of the lower town were already practically uninhabitable. In the following century many Dutch residents abandoned Kota for healthier areas further south which were gradually becoming cleared of bandits and wild beasts. Thus began a southwards drift of the city's center of gravity which has continued ever since. One beautiful eighteenth century country house is now the **National Archives Building**, halfway along Jl. Gajah Mada on the west side. The **Istana Negara** (State Palace), north of the National Monument, is another. By the early nineteenth century, much government and social activity had shifted to the present-day symbolic center around **Merdeka Square** (formerly the *Koningsplein*) and **Lapangan Banteng** (*Waterlooplein*), where a new city presently rose – literally from the rubble of the old, which was quarried for scarce building material. Impressive public buildings appeared: an empire-style palace, now the **Department of Finance**, begun by Daendels in 1809 but not completed for almost two decades; a theatre, now the **Gedung Kesenian** (1821); the neoclassical **Supreme Court** (1848); and a lavish residence for the commander of the colonial army in Jl. Taman Pejambon, which later became the venue of the *Volksraad* or Indies parliament and is now famous as **Gedung Pancasila**, the building in which Sukarno first mooted the principles of the Indonesian constitution. On Merdeka Square there is the **National Museum**, opened in 1868 by the Batavia Society of Arts and Sciences, the oldest scientific institution in Southeast Asia (founded 1778). Its collections of Hindu-Javanese antiquities, ethnographic objects, Chinese pottery and plundered treasure are world-renowned. The **Istana Merdeka** or presidential palace, on the north side of the square, was completed in 1879; 15 Dutch governors-general ruled here before three Japanese army commanders and then two Indonesian presidents climbed into their warm, worn seat.

A Queen City

With better planning and medicine, Batavia gradually shed its reputation as a place of death and was transformed into the *Koningin van het Oosten*, Queen City of the East. At the end of Dutch rule, though already under increasing pressure from motor traffic and immigration, it was still an orderly, pleasant city of wide streets, shady parks and dignified if rather stolid architecture. And it was still only a moderate size: southern suburbs like **Kebayoran Baru** were laid out only after the war.

Batavia was Dutch, but most of its inhabitants were not. In the first place, its

A Batavia church, built in 1736 and destroyed in 1808.

prosperity always depended substantially upon the enterprise of its Chinese community, who braved persecution to build their homes, businesses and temples here. The district of **Glodok**, immediately south of Kota, was allocated to this pariah community after a notorious massacre of Chinese in 1740, and is still Jakarta's Chinatown. In its narrow, crooked streets on Jl. Petak Sembilan is Jakarta's oldest Chinese temple, the **Jin-de Yuan** or **Dharma Jaya**, a Buddhist foundation of 1650. An older name for this temple, Kwan-Im, became the Indonesian word for all Chinese temples, *klenteng*. It boasts fine roof ornamentation and various sacramental antiques. Another interesting *klenteng* is the **Da-Bo-Gong** on Jl. Pantai Sanur, near the gaudy "dreamland" recreation park of **Ancol**.

A less familiar minority is recalled by the **Portuguese Church**, now known as **Gereja Sion,** on Jl. Pangeran Jayakarta, just south of Kota Railway Station. The "Black Portuguese" were Eurasian flotsam from the breakup of the Portuguese Asian empire. They were brought to Batavia from Malacca and India by the Dutch, who built this attractive, restrained little (Protestant!) church for them between 1683 and 1695. The baroque pulpit and much else are original. One VOC governor-general, Zwaardecroon, was buried here in accordance with his wish to "sleep among the common folk".

And then there were the Indonesians, the "natives" who came to form the bulk of the population. Distrustful at first of the local people, the VOC imported manpower from elsewhere in the archipelago to serve it as craftsmen, slaves and soldiers: Balinese and Macassarese both became familiar languages on the streets of Batavia. The *kampung* between Jl. Bandengan Selatan and Jl. Pekojan, just west of Kota, retains something of the old-world cosmopolitan atmosphere of VOC

Batavia. Nearby, in Gang Mesjid 1, off Jl. Pangeran Tubagus Angke, the small **Mesjid Alanwar** or Angke Mosque, dating from 1761, incorporates Hindu-Balinese architectural elements. From such milieux emerged the *orang Betawi*, the "Batavian", prototype of the modern Jakartan, whose dialect and customs came to set the tone of everyday life in the city. Even the Dutch adopted *Betawi* ways, donning the *sarong* for home wear and abandoning their stuffy imitations of Dutch town-houses for open bungalows with Javanese roofs and galleries. Much late colonial residential architecture is to be seen in the suburbs of **Menteng** and **Kemayoran**. Today, low dwellings with red clay roof tiles, not high-rise blocks or suburban compounds, still define Jakarta's architectural character.

After independence the real transformation began. Old monuments were toppled: grander and uglier ones took their place. In-migration and incompetence frustrated the dreams of architects and ideologues; careless destruction and careless construction rendered Batavia almost unrecognizable within two decades.

Many of Jakarta's most famous landmarks date from this period: the **Senayan Sports Complex**, built with Russian money in 1962; the first of its luxury hotels, the **Hotel Indonesia** on Jl. Thamrin; and a remarkable collection of crude, powerful statues in the "Heroes of Socialism" tradition. Many of the latter have attracted deflating nicknames: "Hot Hands Harry", "pizza man" and "mad waiter" for the **Youth Statue** at the south end of Jl. Sudirman, who grimaces as he holds aloft what appears to be a flaming dish; "Hansel and Gretel" for the wholesome couple portrayed by the **Statue of Welcome** on Jl. Thamrin, built for the 1962 Asian Games. Of the striking **Irian Jaya Liberation Memorial** ("the chainbreaker") on Lapangan Banteng, it used to be quipped in Sukarno's time that the giant's cry was "empty!" - in reference to the Department of Finance behind him.

Sukarno's ultimate monumental legacy was the **National Monument** or **Monas**, otherwise known as "Sukarno's last erection". Part Hindu *lingga* (phallic symbol), part marble hymn to progress, it rises 137 metres above the centre of Merdeka Square. Still Jakarta's greatest landmark, Monas offers superb panoramic views and an interesting museum depicting the current official version of Indonesian history in 48 dioramas.

Sukarno also bequeathed Jakarta a population doubling every decade, a phone system which required businesses to employ special staff just to dial numbers over and over again, and a reputation as Southeast Asia's dirtiest, least organized, most dangerous capital. After the regime change, Jakarta's new governor Ali Sadikin set out to change the city's image. He repaired roads and bridges and built schools and hospitals, but also took cruel and much-criticized measures to eliminate the "eyesore" of street peddlers and *becak* from the central areas. A bloody police campaign against urban crime in 1983 repeated the theme of ruthless cleansing. Nor has the new era seen an end to extravagant prestige projects. Mrs. Suharto's **Taman Mini Indonesia Indah** ("Beautiful Indonesia in Miniature"), a mammoth theme park in the south of the city designed to provide a sanitized overview of all the country's regional cultures, epitomizes the "showcase" mentality.

To the westener unused to the texture of life there, Jakarta still gives the impression of being perpetually on the verge of terminal breakdown. Spreading like some concrete epidemic, Jakarta remains undefeated by its growth. In 1945 there were 900,000 Jakartans; but today there are eight million. Yet Jakarta's infrastructure and appearance, hard though it may seem for the newcomer to believe, continue to improve.

JAKARTA
Accommodation
INEXPENSIVE: Concentrated around Jl Jaksa/Jl Kebon Sirih, South of Merdeka Square. **Bali International**, Jl Wahid Hasyim 116, Tel: 345058. **Bloemsteen**, Jl Kebon Sirih Timur 1/173. **Borneo Youth Hostel**, Jl Kebon Sirih Barat Dalam 35. **Wisma Delima**, Jl Jaksa 5. **Djody Hostel**, Jl Jaksa 27. **Wisma Ise**, Jl Wahid Hasyim 168, Tel: 333463. **Karya Hotel**, Jl Jaksa 36. **Nick's Hostel**, Jl Jaksa 16. **Hostel Noordwijk**, Jl Jaksa 14, Tel: 330392. **Wisma Petra**, Jl Wahid Hasyim, Tel: 325149. **Pondok Soedibjo**, Jl Kebon Sirih 23. **Wim's Homestay**, Jl Kebon Sirih Barat Dalam 1, Tel: 327723.
MODERATE: **Marcopolo**, Jl Teuku Cik Ditiro 19, Tel: 375409. **Menteng I**, Jl Gondangdia Lama 28, Tel: 352508. **Kartika Chandra**, Jl Gatot Subroto, Tel: 510808. **Menteng II**, Jl Cikini Raya 105, Tel: 326312. **Sabang Metropolitan**, Jl Haji Agus Salim 11, Tel: 354031. **Transaera**, Jl Merdeka Timur 16, Tel: 351373.
LUXURY: **Hyatt Aryaduta**, Jl Prapatan 44-46, Tel: 357631. **Borobudur Intercont.**, Jl Lapangan Banteng Selatan, Tel: 370108. **Jakarta Hilton**, Jl Jen Gatot Subroto, Tel: 587981/ 583051. **Horison**, Jl Pantai Indah, Taman Impian Jaya Ancol, Tel: 680008. **Indonesia**, Jl MH Thamrin, Tel: 320008. **Jakarta Mandarin**, Jl MH Thamrin, Tel: 321307. **President**, Jl MH Thamrin 59, Tel: 320508. **Sahid Jaya**, Jl Jen Sudirman 86, Tel: 584151. **Sari Pacific**, Jl MH Thamrin, Tel: 323707.

Food
STREET FOOD: warung abound everywhere; Singapore-style sanitized versions at **Sarinah** stores at Jl Thamrin & Kebayoran Baru.
INDONESIAN: **Ayam Goreng Mbok Berek** (Javanese fried chicken), Jl Panglima Polim Raya 93, Tel: 770652. **Bu Tjitro** (Javanese), Jl Senen Raya 25A, Tel: 371197. **Jun Nuan** (seafood), Jl Batuceper 69, Glodok. **Pondok Jawa Timur** (Javanese), Jl Prapanca Raya, Kebayoran Baru. **Sari Bundo** (Padang), Jl Ir H Juanda 27, Tel: 358343. **Senayan Satay House**, Jl Kebon Sirih 31A, Tel: 326238. **Sinar Medan** (Acehnese), Jl HA Salim. **Tinoor Asli** (Manado), Jl Gondangdia Lama 33A, Tel: 336430.
CHINESE: **Bakmi Gajah Mada**, Jl Gajah Mada 92. **Cahaya Kota**, Jl Wahid Hasyim 9, Tel: 3533015. **Istana Naga**, Jl Jen Gatot Subroto (Kav 17, Case Bldg), Tel: 511809.
COLONIAL: **Arts & Curios Restaurant**, Jl Kebon Binatang III/8A, Cikini. **Club Noordwijk**, Jl Ir H Juanda 5A, Tel: 353909. **Oasis**, Jl Raden Saleh 47, Kebayoran, Tel: 347819.
WESTERN: **George & Dragon**, Jl Telukbetung 32, Tel: 345625. **Sari Pacific Coffee Shop**, Sari Pacific Hotel.

Shopping
TEXTILES & CLOTHES: **Batik Keris**, Sarinah Jaya department store, Blok M. **Danar Hadi**, Jl Raden Saleh 1A, Tel: 342390/343712. **Iwan Tirta**, Jl Panarukan 25, Tel: 349122. Many smaller shops in Tanah Abang, Pasar Baru & Kebayoran Baru.
HANDICRAFTS & CURIOS: **Jakarta fleamarket**, Jl Surabaya, Menteng. **Handicraft Center**, Sarinah Jaya dept store, Kebayoran Baru. **Indonesian Bazaar**, Jakarta Hilton. **Pasar Seni**, Ancol. Concentrations of smaller shops at: Jl Palatehan I, Kebayoran Baru; Jl Kebon Sirih Timur, Menteng; Jl Majapahit, Kota; Jl Gajah Mada, Kota.

Museums / Galleries / Zoos
Museum Bahari (maritime), Jl Pasar Ikan 1, Kota, Tel: 6693406/6692476. Tuesday-Thursday 8.00-16.00, Friday & Sunday 8.00-15.00, Saturday 8.00-12.30, Monday closed. **National Museum**, Jl Merdeka Barat 12, Tel: 360551. Sun & Tue-Thu 9.30-15.00, Fri 9.30-11.30, Sat 9.30-13.30, Mon closed. **Ragunan Zoo**, Jl Raya Ragunan (16 km S of town), Tel: 782975. Open daily 7.00-18.00. **Museum Satria Mandala** (military), Jl Gatot Subroto 14, Tel: 582759. Tue-Sun 9.00-16.30, Mon closed. **Jakarta History Museum**, Jl Taman Fatahillah 1, Kota, Tel: 677424. Tues-Fri 9.00-16.00, Sat 9.00-13.00, Sun 9.00-16.00, Mon closed. **Museum of Fine Art & Ceramics**, Jl Fatahilah 2, Kota, Tel: 676091. Tu-Thu 9.00-14.00, Fri 9.00- 11.00, Sat 9.00-13.00, Sun 9.00-14.00, Mon closed. **Museum Sumpah Pemuda** (history of nationalism), Jl Kramat Raya 106, Menteng, Tel: 356142. Mon-Fri 8.00-15.00, Saturday 8.00-14.00, Sun closed. **Museum Taman Laut Ancol** (oceanarium), Jl Lodan Timur, Ancol, Tel: 680519. Monday-Saturday 9.00-18.00, Sun 9.00-20.00. **Taman Mini Indonesia Indah** ('Beautiful Indonesia in Miniature', theme park incl cultural & zoological museums), Jl TMII, Pondok Gede, Tel: 8400525. Daily 9.00-17.00. **Textile Museum**, Jl Karel Satsuit Tubun 4, Tanah Abang, Tel: 365367. Tue-Thu 9.00-14.00, Fri 9.00-11.30, Sat 9.00-13.00, Mon closed. **Wayang Museum**, Jl Pintu Besar Selatan 27, Kota, Tel: 679560. Sun & Tue-Thu 9.00-14.00, Fri 9.00-11.00, Sat 9.00-13.00, Monday closed.

Cultural performances
Jakarta's and Indonesia's premier cultural venue is **Taman Ismail Marzuki (TIM)**, Jl Cikini Raya 73, Tel: 322606. Constantly changing pro-

GUIDEPOST JAKARTA

gramme of displays & performances, daily 8.00-20.00. **Pasar Seni**, Ancol, also has nightly cultural entertainment. **Taman Mini Indonesia Indah** (see Museums) has live dance, music & drama on Sun. **Bharata Theatre**, Jl Kali Lio 15 (near Pasar Senen) stages *wayang orang* Tue, Wed, Fri & Sat at 20.00-23.00.
University of Indonesia's **School of Folk Art**, Jl Bunga 5, Jatinegara, rehearses 11.00 daily except Sunday. *Gamelan* performances every Sunday 10.00 in **Wayang Museum** and alternate Sun at same time in **National Museum** (see Museums).

Tourist Information
Jakarta Tourist Information Centre, Jakarta Theatre Bldg, corner Jl MH Thamrin/Jl Wahid Hasyim, Tel: 354094/364093. Monday-Thursday 8.00-15.00, Friday 8.00-11.30, Saturday 8.00-14.00. **Directorate General of Tourism**, Jl Kramat Raya 81, Tel: 359001. Sunday-Thursday 8.00-15.00, Fri 8.00-11.30, Sat 8.00-14.00.

Money change
Many big banks along Jl MH Thamrin.

Post
Central Post Office, Jl Pos, Pasar Baru. Monday-Saturday 8.00-16.00.

Telephone
Kantor Telekomunikasi (24-hour long-distance service), Jakarta Theatre Bldg, corner Jl MH Thamrin/Jl Wahid Hasyim.

Hospitals
Rumah Sakit Fatmawati, Jl Fatmawati, Tel: 760121-4; or **Pertamina Hospital**, Jl Kyai Maja 29, Tel: 707214.

Immigration
Directorate General of Immigration, Jl Teuku Umar 1, Menteng, Tel: 349811/349812. Mon-Thu 8.00-1400, Fri 8.00-12.00, Sat 8.00-14.00.

Diplomatic missions
Australia: Jl MH Thamrin 15, Tel: 323109. **Belgium:** Jl Cicurug 4, Tel: 348719. **Canada:** 5th floor, Wisma Metropolitan I, Jl Jen Sudirman Kav 29, Tel: 510709. **Denmark:** Jl Abdul Muis 34, Tel: 346615. **France:** Jl MH Thamrin 20, Tel: 332807. **Germany:** Jl Thamrin 1, Tel: 323908. **Italy:** Jl Diponegoro 45, Tel: 340964. **Japan:** Jl MH Thamrin 24, Tel: 324303. **Netherlands:** Jl HR Rasuna Said Kav S-3, Tel: 511515. **New Zealand:** Jl Diponegoro 41, Tel: 330552. **Singapore:** Jl Proklamasi 23, Tel: 348761. **Sweden:** Jl Taman Cut Mutiah 12, Tel: 333061. **United Kingdom:** Jl MH Thamrin 75, Tel: 330904. **USA:** Jl Merdeka Selatan 5, Tel: 360360.

Transport
AIR: Soekarno-Hatta (Cengkareng) International Airport, 23 km W of town, handles all foreign & domestic flights. Taxis & Damri buses (to Kemayoran, Rawamangun, Blok M & Gambir) provide city link.
INTERNATIONAL AIRLINES: **Cathay Pacific** (Tel: 326807), **Thai International** (Tel: 320607) & **Quantas** (Tel: 327707) all in BDN Bldg, Jl Thamrin. **Philippine Airlines** (Tel: 370108) & **Swissair** (Tel: 378006) both in Borobudur Intercontinental Hotel, Jl Banteng Selatan. Elsewhere: **British Airways**, 1st floor, Mandarin Hotel, Jl Thamrin, Tel: 333207/ 333092/333198. **Japan Airlines**, Wisma Nusantara Bldg, Jl Thamrin, Tel: 333909. **KLM**, Hotel Indonesia, Jl Thamrin, Tel: 320708. **Lufthansa**, Panin Centre Bldg, Jl Jen Sudirman 1, Tel: 710247. **Singapore Airlines**, Sahid Jaya Hotel, Jl Jen Sudirman 86, Tel: 584021/584041. **UTA**, Jaya Bldg, Jl Thamrin 12, Tel: 323507.
DOMESTIC AIRLINE OFFICES: **Garuda**, Jl Ir H Juanda 15, Tel: 370709; Nusantara Bldg, Jl Thamrin, Tel: 330464; Hotel Borobudur, Tel: 370108 ext 2241/2242. **Merpati**, Jl Angkasa 2, Kemayoran, Tel: 413608/417404. **Bouraq**, Jl Angkasa 1, Kemayoran, Tel: 6295150/6595179. **Mandala**, Jl Veteran 1/34, Tel: 368107.
SEA: Passenger vessels berth at **Tanjung Priok Harbour**, 10 km NE of town. Inquire at **Pelni** office, Jl Pintu Air I, Tanjung Priok, Tel: 358398.
RAIL: Kota Station, Jl Stasiun Kota 1, for *Bima II* & *Mutiara* night expresses to Surabaya (via Yogya & Semarang), & morning train to Merak & Sumatra. **Gambir Station**, Jl Merdeka Timur; for other trains to Central & East Java & (with bus connection) Bali, and for Bogor & Bandung.
Tanah Abang Station for evening train to Sumatra. Some travel agencies, eg **Carnation,** Jl Menteng Raya 24, Tel: 344027, arrange tickets in advance.
ROAD: Pulo Gadung Terminal, corner Jl Bekasi Timur Raya/Jl Perintis Kemerdekaan, for buses to Central Java & points East; **Cililitan Terminal**, Jl Let Gen. Sutoyo, for Bogor & Bandung; **Kalideres Terminal**, Grogol, for the West & Sumatra. All three long-distance bus terminals served by local buses from Gambir railway station.
INTERNAL: Taxis are metered (*Bluebird* are most reliable), *bajaj* not. Buses frequent and cheap; *patas* fastest and most comfortable.

PULAU SERIBU
Onrust (Kapal) & **Bidadari** islands have regular ferry services from Tanjung Priok; **Putri** & **Melinjo** resorts can be reached by charter speedboat from Ancol marina or by air. Contact **Putri Pulau Seribu Paradise**, Jakarta Theatre Bldg, Jl Thamrin 9, Tel: 359333-4.

WEST JAVA

WEST JAVA

BANTEN
THE SUNDALANDS
BANDUNG
CIREBON

Jakarta happens to be located in Java, but it is hardly of Java. The contrast between the metropolitan capital and the surrounding province is dramatic. For although West Java contains some big cities of its own, its soul is rural. The least densely populated province of the island, it offers unrivaled scenery, extensive nature reserves, and refreshing mountain weather, all within a few hours of Jakarta's confusion. Its prosperity, its friendly people and its excellent transport facilities make it one of the most genuinely relaxing parts of rural Indonesia in which to travel. Nor is West Java devoid of cultural and historical interest.

West Java first became known to Europe as Sunda – a land, a kingdom, a language and a people all distinct from Java. The sixteenth century Portuguese were so impressed by this country that they misapplied its name not only to the whole island of Java, but to the whole archipelago; to this day, Sumatra, Java, Borneo and Celebes are still known collectively as the "Greater Sunda Islands". The first known kingdom on Java, the Hindu state of Tarumanegara, flourished on the north coastal plain of West Java in the fifth century. A millenium later, the first Portuguese ships to weigh anchor here were welcomed by another great Hindu kingdom, Pajajaran, a contemporary and rival of the great East Javanese Majapahit. Since 1433, the capital had been at an inland location, Pakuan, today's **Bogor**, where Dutch governors-general would later reside. But in 1522, when Pajajaran concluded an alliance with Portuguese Goa, it was still master of the north coast too, including the lucrative ports of Banten and Sunda Kelapa (now Jakarta). The Portuguese were to have helped protect the Hindu power against the violent westward expansion of Islam along the coast. But when they next returned in 1527, both ports had been captured by Muslims and made vassals of the young sultanate of Demak, 400 km to the east. Landlocked, Pajajaran declined, and 50 years later its capital was conquered by Banten.

While Javanese-speakers flocked to the booming coastlands, and Banten became a great trading and military power, Sunda proper retreated to the mountains and high plateaux in the south and became a rustic folk culture without cities or courts. In this condition, and so close to Batavia, what now became known as the "Sundalands" were easy prey for the Company: by 1684 the entire Sundanese-speaking area was under direct Dutch

Left: The National Monument in Jakarta.

WEST JAVA

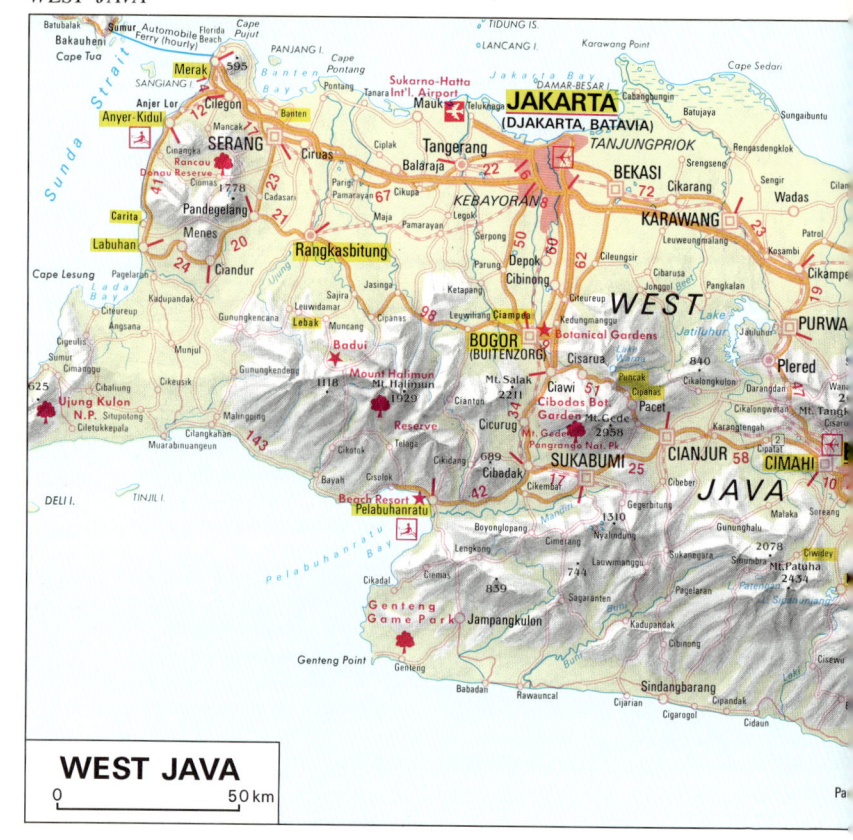

control, while the coastal sultanates of Banten and Cirebon retained nominal independence into the nineteenth century. In due course, the Sundanese too were Islamized, and indeed became known as purer and stricter Muslims than their Central Javanese neighbours. But in language, custom, and art, and in their own minds, the Sundanese never assimilated with the outgrowth of ethnic Java which had cut them off from the Java Sea.

So today there are two West Javas: the Javanized, maritime north coast and the Sundanese interior. This human division coincides closely with the most obvious physical one. The north is flat and featureless, a hot, wet, 50 km-wide littoral plain, advancing a little further seawards each year, laden with the rice which feeds Jakarta's masses. Sunda proper is a towering, stately mass of welded volcanoes – the **Priangan**, or Parahyangan, "Abode of the Gods", clothed in tea plantations and virgin forest, shrouded in cloud, falling steeply into the sea on the wave-lashed, portless south coast.

The broken island of **Krakatau**, out in the Sunda Strait, is an outlier; many of Priangan's other volcanoes are still active. At Cianjur, Bandung, Garut and Tasikmalaya, the mountains part to cradle high depressions, meticulously terraced to grow fragrant rice. To the east, the Priangan fades imperceptibly into the more intermittent volcanic terrain of Central Java.

BANTEN AND THE FAR WEST

90 km west of Jakarta via Serang is the fishing village of **Banten**, known to history as Bantam. Looking at this quiet little place today, it is hard to believe that for a century this was the greatest trading port of Java, the city which Batavia itself was founded to challenge. Wrested from Hindu control by Gunungjati of Demak in the 1520s, Banten became an independent Muslim sultanate which grew rich on the commerce of the Sunda Strait and the pepper of Lampung on the far side. Banten attracted English, French and Danish "factories" before a civil war gave the VOC the opportunity to intervene and end its glory forever in 1682.

The village is dominated by the tiered *meru* roof of the sixteenth-century **Masjid Agung**, one of Java's oldest mosques and a good example of transitional Hindu-Islamic architecture. The peculiar pagoda-like minaret is said to be the work of a Chinese Muslim, and the adjacent shuttered building that of a Dutch one! Early Java Islam was an eclectic institution. South of the *alun-alun* (central square) are the remains of two large palaces, the **Pakuwonan** and the **Istana Kaibon**, and a little further on is the tomb of the third king, Maulana Yusuf, who ruled in the 1570s. Northwest of these remnants of Banten's greatness is a monument to its fall – the ruins of **Fort Speelwijk**, constructed in 1682 to keep the city safely under the Dutch heel. Built overlooking the sea, the fort is now 200 m inland; coastal silting has played its part in the decline of Banten as a port. Since 1985, archaeological finds from Banten have been displayed in the **Banten Site Museum** on Jl. Mesjid Banten Lama.

For most visitors, the most important attractions of Java's far west are natural. The national park at **Ujung Kulon** ("West End") is one of Indonesia's prime nature reserves and a fine example of successful state action to preserve wildlife. This unsullied wilderness shelters hornbill, *banteng* (wild cattle) and crocodile as well as the only breeding population of Javan rhinoceros to survive the long transformation of Java from jungle to market garden. **Krakatau**, 40 km out in the Sunda Strait, is the remains of a great volcano which blew itself to pieces in 1883 in one of the greatest explosions ever recorded. Its scarred, primordial landscapes are reached by sea from **Labuhan**, which is also the usual jumping-off point for Ujung Kulon. Along the coast north of Labuhan are West Java's finest and safest beaches, with accommodation at **Carita**, **Anyer Kidul** and **Florida Beach** (near **Merak**, the terminal for the ferry to Sumatra).

THE SUNDALANDS

A manioc vendor at work at Bogor market.

Travelling from Jakarta, Sunda proper begins at the rain-drenched town of **Bogor**, 50 km south of the capital where the first big volcano, **Salak**, begins to rise. The area has a long history of civilization. Fifteen hundred years ago it was part of Tarumanegara, Java's first Hindu kingdom. Fifteen kilometers west of the town near **Ciampea**, the footprints of a fifth-century king, together with a miraculously sharp inscription, adorn the great riverside boulder of **Batutulis Ciampea**. Three kilometers southeast of the town, another inscribed stone or **Batutulis** is the only surviving reminder that in the fifteenth century Pajajaran had its very capital here. But Bogor's kings had vanished into legend before Gustaaf Willem Baron van Imhoff founded a country estate here in 1745. Bogor began its rise to renown as Buitenzorg ("Carefree"), retreat and later official residence of the governor-general of Netherlands India. The present **Istana Bogor** (Bogor Palace), elegant and white in its undulating green lawns, dates from 1856, and has seen many a lavish gathering of both Batavia's and Jakarta's elite. Its pre-war furnishings were looted by the Japanese; the present contents are owed to the acquisitive zeal of the late President Sukarno and the generosity of his many benefactors. They include paintings and sculptures, erotic and otherwise, by many of Indonesia's foremost artists. Sukarno was in *de facto* house arrest here from 1967 until his death in 1970.

The real pride of Bogor is the **Kebun Raya**, or Bogor Botanical Garden, which covers a beautiful 87 hectares next to the palace compound. It was founded in 1817 by the Prussian-born Dutch government naturalist Caspar Reinwardt, with the help of two Englishmen from Kew Gardens. This institution was in the forefront of the Victorian colonial enterprise of documenting, classifying, taming and

Angling in fish ponds near Bandung.

transforming tropical nature. And harnessing it for profit: the *cultuurstelsel* crops were tested and improved here, the oil palm introduced from Africa (1848) and *Hevea* rubber from Brazil (1883). Plantation magnates showered the gardens with funds to keep their money trees pest-free. Today, Bogor is still one of the world's foremost botanical institutions, with 17,000 living specimens from all over Indonesia and far beyond. On the same site are the **Museum Herbarium Bogoriensis** and **Bogor Zoological Museum**, besides extensive library and laboratory facilities. The gardens with their ponds and quiet groves are also favorite venues for picnickers and lovers. The busy, muddy town of Bogor itself has simply sprouted up around the Kebun Raya, but it is the home of one of the few remaining *gamelan* gongsmiths on Java.

Beyond Bogor is the **Tatar Sunda**, the rugged plateau of the Sundanese heartland and the home of the Sundanese arts. The elements are those of Java, but the balance is different. The Sundanese have their own *gamelan*, but they are better known for the more rustic tones of the *kecapi* (a type of lute), *angklung* (a device of bamboo tubes suspended in a frame and shaken with an almost metallic hollow sound), and *suling* (a soft-toned flute), often accompanying a dreamy female voice. The *wayang golek*, a prosaic but charming three-dimensional wooden version of the *wayang kulit* shadow play, is also known further east, but it is closest to the Sundanese heart. In performance, the romance of the *Ramayana* is preferred here over the philosophy of the *Mahabharata*. The *jaipongan* is a popular Sundanese dance event in which males pay for dancing opposite a professional woman performer, very suggestively and yet without touching her.

This area was formerly famous for its coffee, which became "Java coffee" to Europe and America. As early as the 1720s, the VOC was forcing the Sundanese peasantry to pay tax in coffee beans; this archaic imposition was not completely abolished until 1917. In the twentieth century, the place of coffee has largely been taken by tea. At **Puncak** ("Peak"), the highest part of the dizzy road from Bogor to the plateau, the hillsides are fragrant with tea. Women pickers still sweat to harvest this valuable crop, sometimes with their children on their backs. Incredibly, another important crop in this 1900m mountain pass is fish: big carp (*ikan mas*) are kept in countless fishponds, and smaller fish in the shallow water of empty ricefields during the off-season. At **Cipanas** there is a famous volcanic spa where the mountains disgorge sulpurous water at 43° Centigrade. Governors-general have sworn by its restorative powers and their country house still stands here. Not far away is the **Cibodas Botanical Garden**, a high-altitude extension of the gardens at Bogor, and beyond that the forested peaks of two volcanoes comprise the magnificent **Gede-Pangrango National Park**.

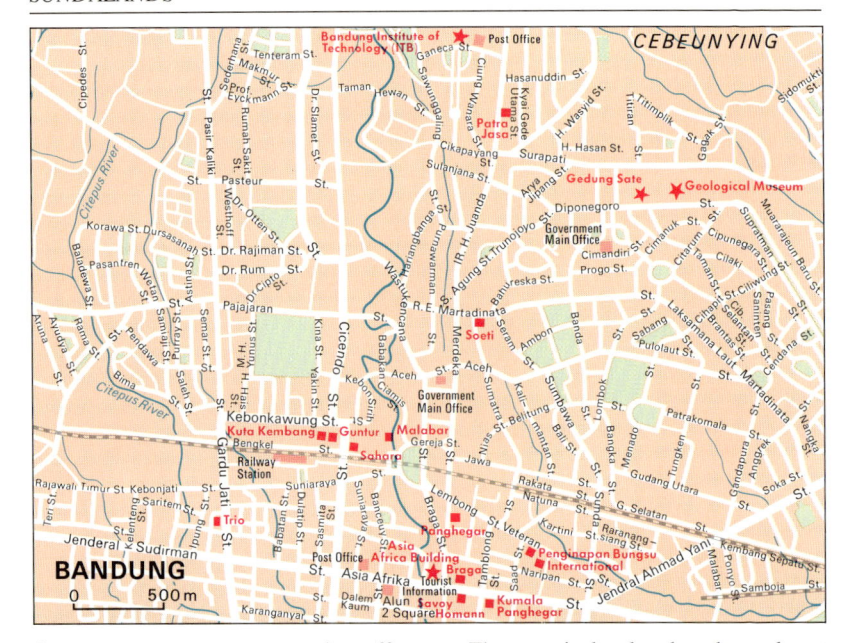

The most isolated and unchanged part of the Sundalands is the westernmost massif, straddling the *kabupaten* of Banten and Priangan Barat. At its center is the vast, rarely visited, almost literally trackless **Mount Halimun Reserve**. On the western slopes is a cluster of settlements inhabited by the intriguing **Badui** people, a remnant of old Sunda which resisted Islamization by the drastic expedient of isolating itself almost completely from the outside world both by distance and a series of strict taboos against travel and contact with strangers. The 40 families – never more – of white-robed "Inner Badui" acquired a cultish aura of secrecy and magic which kept outsiders in awe, while the more numerous black-clad "Outer Badui" acted as their ambassadors to the profane world – truly an astonishing piece of social history. The Badui area is usually reached from Rangkasbitung in the north, via the little town of **Lebak** where Multatuli was stationed and sacked and where his great novel *Max Havelaar* was consequently set. Part of the journey to the Badui must be made on foot. But no one may stay in the inner "forbidden area", for although the cult of the Badui is under heavy pressure from education, population growth and tourism, its days are not yet over. A far cry from the Badui is the Halimun massif's eastern window on "civilization", the seaside resort of **Pelabuhan Ratu**. When Sukarno stayed here, fresh bread rolls were flown in by helicopter from Bandung. At the **Samudra Beach Hotel** which the late president built, one room is always kept vacant for the malevolent Queen of the South Sea, a goddess who lures swimmers to their deaths in the crashing waves of this stormy coast.

BANDUNG

In **Bandung**, the Dutch gave Sunda the capital it had not had since the fall of Pajajaran. The original fiefdom of Bandung was established in 1641 by decree of Sultan Agung of Mataram, but its center was further south; the present city grew up around a Dutch administrative center established on the Great Post Road in 1811. In 1864 it became the capital of the Priangan plateau. Soon conveniently linked to Batavia by railway, it was favored by the colonials for its cool climate and fine location on the mountain-girdled bed of an ancient lake, and became a center for all kinds of Dutch activities not directly tied to the big ports. In 1916 the command of the colonial army was transferred here from Batavia, and Indonesia's officers are still trained here. In 1920 the **Bandung Institute of Technology** was opened, still one of Indonesia's most prestigious universities. With its comfortable bungalows and floral boulevards, Bandung was Java's most European city - even, some said, the "Paris of the East". In 1942, it was to have been the mountain stronghold which would defy Japan's onslaught; but its defenses crumbled even as the last planes took off for Australia. Today, reclaimed by the Sundanese but contested by more than the usual mix of immigrants from other regions, it is a busy, shabby city of almost two million, thriving on the light industries which came here in the 1970s. Bandung is the site of one of the New Order's most spectacular and controversial industrial projects, **IPTN Aircraft** plant. But while the old atmosphere has succumbed to the smog and the newer soubriquet of "City of Flowers" is poorly deserved, Bandung retains its historic and architectural interest, its intellectual dynamism, and the institutions which make it the seat of Sundanese culture.

Bandung Institute of Technology (ITB) is in the north of the town on Jl. Ganeca, an out-of-town campus location when it was built in 1920. Architect Maclaine Pont used the traditional houses of the Mandailing Batak in North Sumatra as the model for his beautiful and functional design. Sukarno received his engineer's degree here in 1926, not before helping to found the study club which would grow into the Indonesian Nationalist Party (PNI). To this day ITB students have a reputation for outspokenness; unapproved political publications have led to trials of student leaders. Not purely a technical university, ITB has an art gallery which is open to the public. Other 1920s buildings include the venerable **Gedung Sate** (1920) on Jl. Diponegoro and the **Geological Museum**, opened by the Dutch in 1929, over the road. Nearby is Bandung's tallest and most striking post-war building, the new local government headquarters, like some futuristic water-tower.

The streamline curves of the 1930s vision of modernity grace many buildings in the central area and the old elite suburb of Dago, but the most spectacular and well-maintained art deco relic is the opulent **Savoy Homann Hotel** on the main thoroughfare, Jl. Asia-Africa, once a section of the Great Post Road. Perhaps

Bandung's outstandig historic building, though, is the **Gedung Merdeka** on the same street - not for its crude inter-war civic architecture, but because it was the venue for a grand diplomatic event, the first and only Asia Africa Conference, in 1955. Here Sukarno played host to Nehru, Nasser, and Ho Chi Minh and laid the foundations of today's Non-Alligned Movement amid the euphoria of that seemingly distant time of falling empires. "Bandung spirit builds the world anew" blazed a giant slogan from the building's eaves then, while the armed Darul Islam rebels watched from the hills and the country lurched towards bankruptcy. Also known as the Asia-Africa Building, Gedung Merdeka houses an interesting museum of photos and other memorabilia of the conference.

Immediately west of Bandung is the pre-war army town of **Cimahi**; nearby, the Citarum river, Sunda's biggest, passes over spectacular falls. Fifty kilometers downriver, the Citarum flows into the huge **Jatiluhur Reservoir**, where a

Fruit and vegetables for sale in a typical Cirebon warung.

French-built dam and hydroelectric station feed Jakarta's and West Java's ever-growing demand for water and power.

North of Bandung, Dutch-style flower gardens, vegetable plots and even dairy farms grace the slopes of some of Java's highest volcanoes in homely defiance of the wild tropical backdrop. A very Asian use has been found here for fancy European livestock: the locals have long discovered that ram-fighting is more exciting than cockfighting. Here also are the famous spa resorts of **Ciater**, with almost Roman-looking hot baths, and **Maribaya**. **Lembang**'s Grand Hotel opened its doors in 1926. The best-known summit of this massif is the readily accessible **Tangkuban Prahu** with its triple craters of blasted boulders and boiling mud.

Even more dramatic landscapes lie on the opposite, southern side of Bandung, though at a greater distance. Above

Ciwidey, 30 km southwest of the city, is a fine cold mountain lake like a Scottish loch. Ciwidey itself is a living center of the craft of blacksmithing (agricultural tools are made as well as decorative knives), which otherwise is becoming hard to find even in tribal Sumatra. **Mt. Papandayan**, 60 km southeast of Bandung via the tea town of **Pengalengan**, is a bigger, angrier Tangkuban Prahu.

There are two routes from Bandung to the east: the old Great Post Road, which returns to the north coast, and a quieter southern route which ultimately winds its way to Yogyakarta. The first town on the southern road is **Garut**, a favorite mountain resort in colonial times, now a quintessentially Sundanese country town featuring some of the last stilt-houses in Java. Sunda retained the old pre-Hindu, Malay-like design long after the houses of Java proper came down to earth, but "Javanization", snobbery and the price of timber are putting an end to it now. North of Garut at **Lake Cangkuang**, near Leles, is West Java's only significant Hindu temple, imaginatively restored in the 1970s. Alongside, perversely (or perhaps appropriately, in syncretic Indonesia) is the grave of one Arif Muhammad, traditionally the pioneer of Islam in the area. The Garut region is even more volcanically active than points west. In 1982, it suffered badly from a series of major eruptions of **Mt. Galunggung**, east of Garut town, which covered the countryside in a searing black blizzard of ash. In **Kawah Talagabodas**, the crater of Galunggung's less deadly twin, a spectacular green sulphurous lake is to be seen. After Garut the next major stop is **Tasikmalaya**, famous for its woven craft products in rattan, pandanus and bamboo. Tasikmalaya also has a *batik* industry: the traditional designs are similar to those of Central Java.

Tasikmalaya's **Citanduy river** roughly marks the linguistic border between Sunda and Java; 40 km further on is the administrative boundary where Central Java officially begins. Just before the latter is the turn-off to one of Java's most accessible nature reserves, **Pangandaran**, like Ujong Kulon a narrow-necked peninsula. Pangandaran is also a popular cheap beach resort.

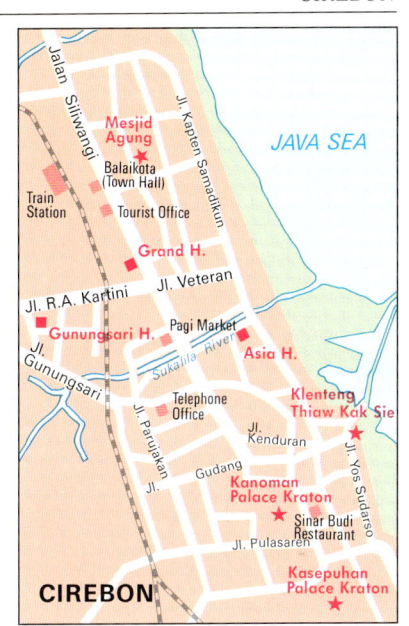

CIREBON

Two hundred kilometers along the coast east of Jakarta, beyond the ricebowl town of Karawang, or 100 km from Bandung along the Great Post Road that Daendels built, is the historic city of **Cirebon**. Cirebon was a Muslim city-state, another child of Demak's westward crusade in the early sixteenth century. Six kilometers north of the city is the holy **Tomb of Gunungyati**, the great Aceh-born warrior who also conquered Banten and probably Sunda Kelapa (Jakarta) too, before he came to rule Cirebon for Demak. He is revered as one of the *wali songo*, the nine saints who turned Java to the true faith, and his grave is still a place of pilgrimage. Like Banten, Cirebon was a Javanese colony in a Sundanese area. It played an important part in the Islamization of Sunda, but in doing so became partly Sundanese itself. Its deviant Javanese dialect is full of Sundanese words; its music and dance are substantially Sundanese too. Unlike Banten, Cirebon fell prey to the expansion of Mataram under Sultan Agung, and ever since it has remained closely associated with Central Java, whose courts and arts it has emulated. Today it is the *pesisir kliwon*, the western rim of Java proper.

During Cirebon's vassalage to Mataram, one of its rulers, Girilaya, weakened the sultanate in time-honored Javanese fashion by dividing it between his sons. To this day there are two separate palaces or *kraton*: the **Kraton Kesepuhan**, for the sultans of the house of Sepuh, in the southeast of the city, and the **Kraton Kanoman**, for the Anom sultans, more centrally located next to the market of the same name. The Kesepuhan houses a small but worthwhile museum of royal

This old woman is producing batik in a Cirebon factory.

memorabilia. The oldest part of the Kesepuhan dates from 1529; its *sitingghil* (pavilion) features a Hindu-style split gate, while elsewhere the use of Delft tiles for decoration is further evidence of the sultanate's eclecticism. In matters of religion, though, the Sepuh sultans were less flexible, as the impressive and equally old **Mesjid Agung** next door demonstrates. This grand mosque is built alongside the *alun-alun* (town square) in Javanese fashion, but skewed uncompromisingly towards Mecca; the Central Javanese would have left the building square and simply prayed diagonally once inside. The Kraton Kanoman, of later origin, is run-down but atmospheric. Many other old buildings line Cirebon's tortuous streets; this is one of Java's better preserved towns.

Battered by the wars of its more powerful neighbors, Cirebon was taken under the all-too-muscular wing of the

Wayang golek puppets in action during a performance in Cirebon.

Company in 1681. It staggered beneath the weight of Dutch exactions - Cirebon *corvee* laborers even helped building Batavia's roads – but retained its importance as a trade port, largely thanks to its strong Chinese community. There is a fine old Chinese temple, the **Klenteng Thiaw Kak Sie**, near the harbor. More unusually, the Chinese have made a unique contribution to Cirebon's artistic life. A Chinese architect designed the **Taman Sunyaragi**, a grotesque fantasy in brick and plaster 4 km out of town on the southwestern bypass. This extraordinary honeycombed folly was built in 1852 as a pleasure palace-cum-hermitage for Cirebon's royalty, then intent on following those of Yogya and Solo in their flight from ignominious political reality into a tacky cultural dream-world. A happier artistic synthesis has resulted from Chinese participation in the local textile business. Cirebon's renowned *batik* motifs are Chinese-inspired: swirling dark clouds (*megamendung*), rock designs, flying birds, even Chinese lions and dragons. The main *batik* centers are in the nearby semi-rural villages of **Trusmi**, **Kalitengah**, **Kaliwuri** and especially **Weru**. **Indramayu**, a fishing village 50 km to the north, has its own *batik* tradition.

In this century, Cirebon has figured in the Indonesian imagination as nothing more grand than "Kota Udang", the "Prawn City", after its best-known industry; the pre-war **Balaikota** (town hall) features the crustacean as an unlikely decorative motif. Recently, the town has experienced an artistic renaissance as a center of the *wayang topeng* genre of masked dance-drama. At **Linggajati**, 22 km southwest of the city, Java's old masters acknowledged that the times had changed by concluding their first diplomatic agreement with the Republic of Indonesia, in November 1946. Their successors maintain the resort in true Dutch style.

GUIDEPOST WEST JAVA

BANTEN
Most visitors stay in **SERANG** (eg **Hotel Serang**, Jl A Yani 5, Tel: 81641), **CILEGON** or **MERAK**. *MUSEUM:* **Banten Site Museum**, Jl Mesjid Banten Lama. Mon-Thu 7.30-13.30, Fri-Sun 7.30-11.30.

WEST COAST
FLORIDA BEACH (Merak): **Merak Beach**, Tel: 15 or Jakarta 367838. **CILEGON: Krakatau Steel Guest Hs.**, Kota Baja. **CARITA: Carita Krakatau Beach** (book through Hotel Wisata, Jl MH Thamrin, Jakarta, Tel: 320252). **Selat Sunda Wisata Cott.** (book through Jl Panglima Polim Raya 21, Kebayoran Baru, Jakarta, Tel: 714683). **ANYER: Anyer Beach Motel**, Jl Raya Karang Bolong, Tel: Jakarta 367594. **LABUHAN: Losmen Dian Dukatu**.
Ujung Kulon National Park: Accessible overland (motorcycle-taxi) from Sumur, or direct from Labuhan by charter boat. Permit required from conservation office (PHPA) in Bogor (Jl Ir H Juanda 9) or Labuhan. Guest bungalows on **Handeleum Island** & **Peucang Island** also available through PHPA.

BOGOR
INEXPENSIVE: **Elsana Transit Hotel**, Jl Sawojajar 36, Tel: 22552. **Wisma Karunia**, Jl Sempur 35-37. **Penginapan Pasundan**, Jl Veteran 19, Tel: 28249. *MODERATE:* **Salak**, Jl Ir H Juanda 8, Tel: 22091. **Wisma Permata**, Jl Raya Pajajaran 35, Tel: 23402.

Food
Asinan Bogor, Jl Kapt Muslihat. **Pondok Nineung**, Jl Dr Semeru 6, Tel: 21785.

Shopping
GONGMAKER: **Pak Sukarna's**, Jl Pancasan 17. *HANDICRAFTS:* **Batik Keris**, Jl Merdeka 6. **Nusa Penida**, Jl Ir H Juanda. **Kenari Indah**, Jl Bondongan Blok 30. **PP Dobbe & Son**, Jl Kantor Batu 19. More in *pasar* & around gardens.

Museums & Gardens
Bogor Zoological Museum, Jl Ir H Juanda 2, Tel: 22177. Sat-Sun & Tue-Thu 8.00-16.00, Mon 9.00-16.00, Fri 8.00-11.00 & 13.00-16.00. **Bogor Botanical Gardens**, Jl Ir H Juanda II, Tel: 22220. Daily 8.00-16.00. **Museum Herbarium Bogoriensis**, Jl Ir H Juanda 22-24, Tel: 22035. Mon-Thu 7.00- 14.00, Fri 7.00-11.00, Sat 7.00-13.30, Sun closed.

Tourist Information / Post office
Jl Ir H Juanda 38A, Tel: 21350. **Post office:** Jl Ir H Juanda.

Hospital
Jl Raya Pejajaran, Tel: 24080.

PUNCAK AREA
INEXPENSIVE: **Kopo Hostel**, Jl Raya 502, Cisarua, Bogor, Tel: 4296. **Pondok Pemuda Cibodas**, Cibodas botanical gardens. *MODERATE:* **Chalet Bali International**, Jl Puncak, Cisarua, Bogor. **Cibulan**, Cibulan, Cisarua, Bogor. **Sanggabuana**, Jl Raya 4-6, Cipanas, Cianjur, Tel: 2227. **Sindanglaya**, Jl Raya 43, Pasekon, Cianjur, Tel: 2116. *LUXURY:* **Bukit Raya**, Jl Raya 219, Cipanas, Cianjur, Tel: 2505. **Puncak Pass**, Jl Raya, Sindanglaya, Cianjur, Tel: 2503/2504.

Food
Countless restaurants, especially Sundanese fish restaurants, along main road (Jl Raya Puncak).

PELABUHAN RATU
INEXPENSIVE: **Sindang Laut**, Jl Kidang Kencana, Tel: 38. *MODERATE:* **Bayu Amirta**, Tel: 31, or Bandung 50882. *LUXURY:* **Samudra Beach**, Sangkawayana, Pelabuhan Ratu, Sukabumi, Tel: 23. Reservation in Jakarta, Hotel Indonesia, Tel: 322008.

BANDUNG
INEXPENSIVE: **Dago**, Jl Ir H Juanda 21, Tel: 58696. **Malabar**, Jl Kebon Jukut 3. **Losmen Mawar**, Jl Pangaran 14, Tel: 51934. **Sahara**, Jl Oto Iskandar Dinata 3, Tel: 51684. **Penginapan Sakadarna**, Jl Kebon Jati 34, Tel: 40181. **Wisma Remaja** (student hostel), Jl Merdeka 64, Tel: 50155. *MODERATE:* **Brajawijaya**, Jl Pungkur 28, Tel: 50673. **Cisitu Guesthouse,** Jl Cisitu 45, Tel: 82420. **Guntur**, Jl Oto Iskandardinata 20. **Istana**, Jl Lembong 22/24, Tel: 57240. **Harapan**, Jl Kapatihan 14, Tel: 51212. **Melati II**, Jl Kebonjati 27, Tel: 56409. **Pacific**, Jl Pungkur 97, Tel: 56027. **Pangarang Sari**, Jl Pangaran 3, Tel: 51205. **Soeti Guesthouse**, Jl Sumatra 52, Tel: 51686. **Trio**, Jl Gardu Jati 55, Tel: 58056.
LUXURY: **Kumala Panghegar**, Jl Asia-Afrika 140, Tel: 52141. **Panghegar**, Jl Merdeka 2, Tel: 57584. **Patra Jasa**, Jl Ir H Juanda 132, Tel: 81644. **Savoy Homann**, Jl Asia-Afrika 112, Tel: 58091.

Food
STREET FOOD: Concentrations around *Alun-alun* & on Jl Oto Iskandardinata.
INDONESIAN: **Babakan Siliwangi** (Sundanese), Jl Siliwangi. **Bakmi Raos**, Jl Kejaksaan 19. **Dago Tea House**, Pajajaran University Campus, off Jl H Juanda. **Handayani** (Javanese), Jl Sukajadi. **Koja Sate House**, Jl Pasir Koja 1. **Naya** (snakes), Jl Pasteur. **Pakarjan**, Jl Pasir Kaliki. **Sate Ponorogo**, Jl Jen Gatot Subroto. **Ponyo** (Sundanese), Jl Malabar. **Pak M Uju** (Sundanese), Jl Dewi Sartika 7A.

GUIDEPOST WEST JAVA

CHINESE: **Queen**, Jl Dalam Kaum 53A. **The Rose Flower**, Jl Jen Ahmad Yani 32. **Tjoen Kie**, Jl Jen Sudirman 46. *WESTERN:* **Tizi's**, Jl Hegarmanak 14, near ITB campus. European-style bakeries & pavement cafes are Bandung's speciality; several on Jl Braga.

Shopping
Local specialities include puppetry, ceramics, leather goods. Craft shops cluster at Pasar Baru, Jl Braga, & Jl Asia-Afrika. **Sarinah** dept. store, Jl Braga 10, has an own handicrafts section. *PUPPETS:* **Cupu Manik**, Gang Haji Umar 2, off Jl Kebon Kawung. *SNAKESKIN:* **Banowati**, Jl Geger Kalong Hilir. *FLEAMARKET:* **Pasar Jatayu**, on Jl Arjuna, 1 km from railway station.

Museums / Galleries / Zoos
Ceramics & Textiles Research Inst., Jl A Yani 318. **Museum Geologi**, Jl Diponegoro 57, Tel: 73205. Mon-Thu 9.00-14.00, Fri 9.00-11.00, Sat 9.00-13.00. **Museum Konperensi Asia Afrika**, Jl Asia Afrika 65, Tel: 438031. Mon-Thu 8.00-13.00, Fri 8.00-11.00, Sat 8.00-12.00. **Museum Mandala Wangsit Siliwangi** (military), Jl Lembong 38, Tel: 50393. Open weekdays. **West Java State Museum**, Jl Oto Iskandarinata 638, Tel: 50976. Tue-Thu 8.00-14.00, Fri 8.00-11.00, Sat-Sun 8.00-12.00.
Taman Sari Zoo, Jl Kebun Binatang 7, Tel: 82770. Daily 7.00-17.00.

Cultural performances
Yayasan Pusat Kebudayaan (YPK), Jl Naripan 7, is the city's cultural centre: *wayang golek* Sat 21.00-4.00, other performances weekdays. **ASTI** (State Institute for Performing Arts), Jl Buah Batu 212, has occasional public music & *wayang*. Other arts venues: **Rumentang Siang Theatre**, Jl Baranang Siang 1 (usually Friday nights). **Pak Ujo's**, Jl Padasuka 118, Tel: 71714. **Pasundan Restaurant** (Hotel Panghegar), Jl Merdeka 2, has Wed night (20.00) cultural performances. **Sanggar Tari Purwa Setra**, Jl Otto Iskandar Dinata 541A, for nightly *jaipongan*.

Tourist Information
Bandung Tourist Office, *Alun-alun*, on Jl Asia-Afrika, Tel: 71724. Mon-Thu 8.00-20.00, Fri 8.00-11.00, Sat 8.00-14.00.
West Java Provincial Tourist Office, Gedung Merdeka, Jl Asia-Afrika (but enter from Jl Braga). Mon-Thu 8.00-14.00, Fri 8.00-11.00, Sat 8.00-12.00, Sun closed.

Post office
Jl Asia-Afrika, near Jl Oto Iskandarinata intersection.

Hospital
7th Day Adventist Hospital, Jl Cihampelas 135, Tel: 82091.

Transport
AIR: Direct links with all Java airports, Denpasar & Palembang. **Husein Sastranegara Airport** is 4 km NW of town, by taxi or by *bemo* from Kebun Kelapa bus station. *Airline offices:* **Garuda**, Jl Asia-Afrika 73, Tel: 51497; **Merpati**, Jl Veteran 46, Tel: 437893; **Bouraq**, H. Preanger, Jl Asia-Afrika 81, Tel: 431631.
RAIL: Single central station. Many services to Yogyakarta, Surabaya (via Yogyakarta), Bogor & Jakarta (but not directly to Cirebon).
ROAD: Kebun Kelapa Bus Station, Jl Dewi Sartika, for Bogor & Jakarta. **Cicaheum Bus Station**, 45 minutes out of town by *bemo* from Kebun Kelapa, for Yogya & the East.

PANGANDARAN
Two dozen *losmen* at narrow point of peninsula. More upmarket, **Wisma Pelangi**, Tel: Bandung 81531 to book. New developments westwards on Parigi Bay, eg at Cijulang.

CIREBON
INEXPENSIVE: on Jl Siliwangi: **Famili**, no.76, Tel: 2324; **Sidodadi**, no.84, Tel: 2305; **Islam**, no.116; **Priangan**, no.122, Tel: 2929; **Damai**, no.130, Tel: 3045; **Semarang**, no.132, Tel: 3231; **Slamet**, no. 183, Tel: 3296. Elsewere: **Asia**, Jl Kalibaru Selatan 33, Tel: 2183. **Fatimah**, Jl Gunungsari 21. **Gunungsari**, Jl Gunungsari 49. **Nusantara**, Jl Gunungsari 39-41, Tel: 3941. *MODERATE:* **Grand Hotel**, Jl Siliwangi 98, Tel: 2014. *LUXURY:* **Cirebon Plaza**, Jl Kartini 46, Tel: 2061. **Omega**, Jl Tuparev 20, Tel: 3072. **Patra Jasa Motel**, Jl Tuparev 11, Tel: 3792.

Food
Restaurant Canton, Jl Pagongan 8A, Tel: 2967. **Kencana** (Sundanese), Jl Karang Kencana. **Kopyor**, Jl Karanggetas 9, Tel: 4343. **Maxim's** (seafood), Jl Bahagia 45, Tel: 2679/3185. **Sinar Budi** (Padang), Jl Karanggetas 20, Tel: 3846.

Shopping
BATIK: **Taman Batik Asri**, Jl Pasar Pagi 9. **GKBI** (*batik* cooperative), Jl Pekarungan 33. Out of town (high quality): **H Mohammed Masina**, Trusmi, near Weru. Cirebon *topeng* masks: **Pak Kandeng**, Suranenggala village, on road to Gunungjati's grave.

Museums
Museum Kraton Kasepuhan, Jl Kasepuhan 37, Tel: 4001. Open daily 9.00-16.00.

Tourist Information / Post office
Jl Siliwangi 88. **Post office:** Jl Yos Sudarso.

Transport
Railway station, Jl Siliwangi; long-distance bus station, '**Stasiun Taxi Kota**', Jl Gunung Sari.

CENTRAL JAVA

CENTRAL JAVA

THE MOUNTAINS
BOROBUDUR
PRAMBANAN
YOGYAKARTA
SOLO
NORTH COAST

THE MOUNTAINS

The western part of interior Central Java is the land of the **Serayu**, the only big river in Java to empty southwards into the Indian Ocean. Despite its apparently central location, this fertile basin and the coastal plain, formerly known as Bagelen, to its south has historically been isolated both from the north coast *pesisir* and from the royal lands to the east. Consequently, these areas have retained archaic cultural features no longer to be found elsewhere, including traditional five-village federations and a unique oral imitation of *gamelan* music.

Near the headwaters of the Serayu is the **Dieng Plateau**, an important monumental center as well as one of Java's strangest and most magical places. Dieng is a treeless moor at 2000 m, ringed by pine-clad mountains; sometimes it bathes in limpid sunlight, but eerie mists and chill rains may descend at any time. The earth is equally moody, proffering jewelled crystals from kaleidoscope pools or belching poison gas from ugly fissures. In the dawn of Indic civilization in Central Java, Hindu kings chose this elemental theatre – the name means "Abode of

Left: A temple at the site of Prambanan.

the Gods"– as the setting for the earliest Indonesian monuments still standing today. Apart from the maverick **Candi Bima**, which features rows of staring heads (apparently a unique imitation of an architectural style from Orissa), the eight surviving temples have a restrained, even austere aspect. All of the temples are dedicated to Shiva; they date from the end of the seventh century to around 780. At the east end of the plateau is **Goa Semar**, a cave traditionally used as a place of meditation. In 1974, Goa Semar was the unlikely scene of an infamous private meeting between Suharto and the then Australian prime minister Gough Whitlam, shortly before Indonesia invaded East Timor.

Though **Dieng** has the earliest temples, it was at **Gedong Songo** that the "standard model" of the Javanese temple was established, upon which later architecture would elaborate: a cubic central mass containing a shrine chamber, set on a wider plinth and capped by a tall roof which recedes in steps to give the impression that it is taller still. The Gedong Songo temples lie 50 km east of Dieng as the crow flies, scattered over the summits of six high sites on the southern flank of **Mt. Ungaran.** They all date from between 730 and 780, and the main temple in each group is dedicated to Shiva. Be-

101

MOUNTAINS

cause of its exposed location, this is reckoned the most dramatic temple site in Java. Nearby is the hill station of **Bandungan**, mountain resort for wealthy citizens of the north-coast city of Semarang, which is only an hour away.

For all its spectacle, Mt. Ungaran is only a minor outlier of Java's volcanic spine. To its southeast is the swampy basin of **Lake Rawapening** and the town of **Ambarawa**, where train passengers bound for Yogyakarta used to transfer to a remarkable Swiss-type rack-and-pinion railway to negotiate a long steep incline. Until 1977, when the Semarang-Magelang-Yogyakarta line closed in the face of competition from uglier, less comfortable and more dangerous, but also quicker and cheaper, road transport, Ambarawa was still a living railway town. In 1978 its station became the national **Museum Kereta Api** (Railway Museum). Fifteen years ago, Java as a whole was still a paradise for train buffs, but rust and progress have banished steam to the tiny sugar lines and to this refuge, where some 25 pre-1930 Dutch and German locomotives are exhibited. Some, however, are still in running condition, including Ambarawa's 1902 cogwheel engine, which will haul visitors up the 18-km toothed rail to **Bedono** by arrangement.

In the fields 2 km south of Ambarawa is a big Dutch fortress, today known simply as **Benteng Ambarawa** (Ambarawa Fort). In the mid-nineteenth century this was intended as the lynchpin of Java's defense against invasion by a European enemy. No invasion came, and the fort was declared obsolete in 1892, but with its squat outlying blockhouses and staring gun ports it is still a formidable sight. Further south again is **Banyubiru**, a notorious concentration camp for Dutch civilians during the Japanese occupation and still a major jail.

The twin volcanoes of **Merbabu** (3142 m) and **Merapi** (2914 m), mid-way between the Java Sea and the Indian Ocean, dominate Central Java at this point. Both offer rewarding panoramas: Merbabu from **Kopeng**, and Merapi from **Kaliurang**, Yogyakarta's beautiful hill resort; Merapi can be climbed (with a guide) from **Selo**, in the saddle between the two mountains. Merbabu is an extinct volcano, that looks north towards Semarang. Merapi, by contrast, is vigorously and dangerously active, and presides over the living heart of the island, where the worldly glory of Java began and ended and where its cultural soul still lies.

BOROBUDUR

Inner Java begins with **Borobudur**, located south of the cool upland town of **Magelang** in the valley of the Progo river. Borobudur is one of the universal symbols of Indonesia. Its massed *stupa* grace travel books and textbooks, advertise hotels and clove cigarettes. This is the world's largest Buddhist monument, and arguably the most extraordinary and impressive antiquity in Indonesia.

The great symmetry of Borobudur has trapped experts into some embarrassing confusions. For more than a century, a lot of learned Western writers eulogized its unity of conception as a model of the whole Mahayana Buddhist cosmos. Then it was suddenly realized that Borobudur was not only constructed in at least four separate stages, but was actually started, and completed, by Hindus. The first two terraces were built at the confluence of two rivers – the Ganges and Jumna of the architect's imagination – in the mid-eighth century. In about 790 the new Buddhist Sailendra dynasty, reluctant to tolerate such a prominent manifestation of the rival religion, took over the huge work and continued it as a Buddhist monument. In the ninth century they had time to make more modifications (involving extensive demolition as well as addition) before the wheel of history came full circle and the Sailendra were eclipsed by the descendants of their old adversaries, the Sanjayas. Finally, these new Sanjayas made their own small "improvements" to the monument, though they refrained from any attempt to reconvert Borobudur to Hinduism! But only a century later, Borobudur fell into disuse when the center of power moved to East Java.

Borobudur is a true forest of symbols. Some of its messages have been deciphered, others remain obscure. The overall form alone projects a multiple symbolism: in plan, it is a *mandala*, a geometric figure promoting meditation; in profile, it is Meru, the Hindu cosmic mountain, or perhaps a single giant *stupa*, emblem of the Buddha's enlightenment. The monument is a terraced pyramid of hewn volcanic rock. The five lower terraces create four concentric galleries running all the way around the structure. Buddhist ritual demands that pilgrims circle a shrine clockwise before approaching its center; Borobudur's multiple galleries provide for a circumambulation of over 5 km. On their walls are 1500 pictorial relief panels, once vividly decorated with painted stucco, for the edification of the spiraling pilgrim. Those on the first gallery depict episodes from the many lives of the Indian messiah, who died for the last time twelve hundred years before the first stone of Borobudur was laid. Higher up are scenes, often obscure, from Buddhist texts. The upper three terraces have no walls, and support 72 miniature, perforated *stupas*, each half-concealing a meditating Buddha, his serene features glimpsed in patchwork light. Reaching through the stone cowl to touch one of these figures brings good fortune. This is the zone of growing abstraction, a prelude to the pure form of the central *stupa*, which represents enlightenment itself. Invisible inside the great stupa are two small, sealed chambers containing nothing – a void.

Apart from being a great religious monument, Borobudur is an important source of historical information. In their pious friezes, its makers unwittingly gave us priceless stone windows on their own lost time: here are the houses, the ships, the clothes, the musical instruments and dances not of Buddha's India, but of ninth-century Java. A thousand years later, it was Europe which first grasped Borobudur's importance. The ubiquitous Raffles discovered it in 1814, beneath a millenium of volcanic debris. In 1911 the Dutch completed the first restoration. By 1968, the earthen core was rotten and the whole structure in danger of collapse; a major UNESCO program was launched to save it, and the work was completed in 1983.

Two smaller Buddhist temples are associated with Borobudur. **Candi Mendut**, 3 km to the east, was once described by a great Dutch scholar as "the jewel among the antiquities of Central Java". Although its exterior has some fine detailed reliefs, Mendut's fame rests primarily upon the beautiful statuary in its shrine chamber. A 3-m sitting Buddha preaches the law, flanked by two smaller Bodhisattva figures, also seated. The one on his left is Lokesvara, the Bodhisattva who refused to become a Buddha as long as all men on earth were not saved. Offerings are still brought here on *Waicak*, the anniversary of the Buddha's enlightenment. **Candi Pawon** is a miniature Mendut located midway along the east-west axis between Mendut and Borobudur.

YOGYAKARTA AND REGION

South of Borobudur, the Progo flows out onto the broad coastlands of the **Daerah Istimewa Yogyakarta** (Yogyakarta Special Region) the only princely state-within-a-state which has survived the national revolution of 1945-49. The region's history begins at **Prambanan**, 17 km east of Yogyakarta town itself. Scattered about this village is the finest concentration of temples in Indonesia. The oldest are contemporary with Borobudur, and like Borobudur they are Buddhist monuments, built during the Sailendra era. **Candi Kalasan**, the first to

Detail from the marvellous Borobudur reliefs.

be encountered on the way out of Yogyakarta, was consecrated in 778; its Buddha statue is gone, but the external carving is still marvellously intricate, the more so considering it was originally only a base for even finer detail in plaster. Kalasan represents Indonesian Buddhism in a more sectarian form than Borobudur: it was dedicated to a cult goddess, Tara. **Candi Sewu**, the "Thousand Temples", is another early Buddhist establishment, featuring 240 small shrines arranged in a complex *mandala* pattern around a large central building; in its present ruined state it has the air of a lost city.

When the Sanjaya returned to power after 832 to establish the kingdom sometimes known as "First Mataram", they intermarried with the Buddhist Sailendra and even sponsored the construction of Bhuddist temples themselves. **Candi Plaosan** and **Candi Sari**, both translations into stone of a two-storey wooden temple design of the time, are the result. Nevertheless, the new dynasty was a Hindu dynasty, and the greatest of its architectural works, said to have been built to rival Borobudur, is the great Hindu temple complex now known as **Candi Prambanan**.

Splendor of Prambanan

Like Borobudur, Prambanan is often said to surpass even its Indian prototypes. The Opak river was actually diverted to make way for the three extensive precincts which once surrounded this temple. The outer walls and shrines are now a builder's yard of jumbled stone blocks, but the central edifices have been very largely restored to their original glory. There are three major sanctuaries, one for each member of the Hindu trinity: Candi Brahma, Candi Visnu and Candi Siwa. Since Javanese Hinduism tended to make Shiva the highest god and arrange the others around him, the 47-m spire of Candi Siwa in the center is taller and

A New Year offering at Candi Mendut.

more architecturally perfect than the twin temples to Brahma and Vishnu on either side. An inscription commemorating its consecration in 856 describes it as "a beautiful dwelling for the god". Inside is an enormous statue of Shiva in four-armed human form; since the normal iconography would represent the god simply as a giant penis, this figure may stand for the king who is believed to have commissioned the sanctuary, Rakai Pikatan.

In other chambers around Shiva are the pot-bellied sage Agastya, the god's elephant-headed son Ganesha, and his wife Durga. In local legend, Durga is Loro Jonggrang, a "Slender Maiden" turned to stone by a rejected suitor. "Even Europeans", notes a Dutch textbook of 1919, "come to ask the statue of Durga for some favor or other, or for protection"; today, flowers and other offerings are still always to be seen at her feet. Her Javanese name is sometimes given to the whole temple complex. Opposite Candi Siva is a subsidiary shrine featuring a powerful statue of Shiva's mount, the divine bull Nandi. The inner panels of the balustrade around Candi Siwa illustrate the *Ramayana* epic in a monumental cartoon of stone reliefs; Candi Brahma carries the second installment.

Prambanan is of timeless beauty. The triple towers which rose eleven centuries ago remain weirdly futuristic, providing a stunning backdrop for the adjacent **Loro Jonggrang Theatre**, an open-air stage where the famous Ramayana Ballet dance performances are held over four consecutive moonlit nights each month in the dry season.

The Prambanan group also comprises several other less important Hindu temples, including the recently excavated **Candi Sambisari**, small but perfectly preserved by volcanic ash. But none are much later than Prambanan. In the first half of the tenth century, King Sindok transferred the center of power to East

Keeping an eye on the news at lunchtime.

Java, where it remained for the next 600 years. Then, in the sixteenth century, after the fall of the last and greatest East Javanese state, Majapahit, the island's center of historical gravity migrated back to the lands beneath Merapi as mysteriously as it had left. According to Javanese tradition, this process culminated in the re-foundation of Mataram, this time as an Islamic kingdom, by Kyai Gedhe Pamanahan. His son, Senopati, initiated the imperial expansion which was to make this second Mataram the last of Java's great indigenous states.

Senopati journeyed to the desolate south coast to meet with Ratu Loro Kidul, the Queen of the South Sea, who promised him the support of her spirit army. The beaches around **Parangtritis** are still the center of the cult of this siren goddess, who lures young men to their deaths by enticing them to swim in her dark ocean. On the birthday of the ruler of Yogyakarta, with whom Ratu Loro Kidul is still in communion, the sultan's hair and nail clippings are offered to her here.

The coastline has a windswept, restless beauty. The shifting dunes are ash-gray; against a leaden sea and a stormy sky, they are like a charcoal sketch. Because of powerful and treacherous currents, bathing is indeed dangerous, but a freshwater swimming pool constitutes part of the simple tourist facilities which have grown up here.

Senopati's court was at **Kota Gede**, now virtually a suburb of Yogya town, 5 km southeast of the center. His grave, and that of his son Krapyak, who succeeded him in 1601, can be seen here in a dark, flower-strewn chamber – accessible on Monday and Friday, subject to the hire of respectful Javanese clothing. The mausoleum was reconstructed after a fire at the beginning of this century, but its musty, incense-scented interior still reeks more strongly of the past than any sunlit temple. In the quiet grounds is a pool

YOGYAKARTA

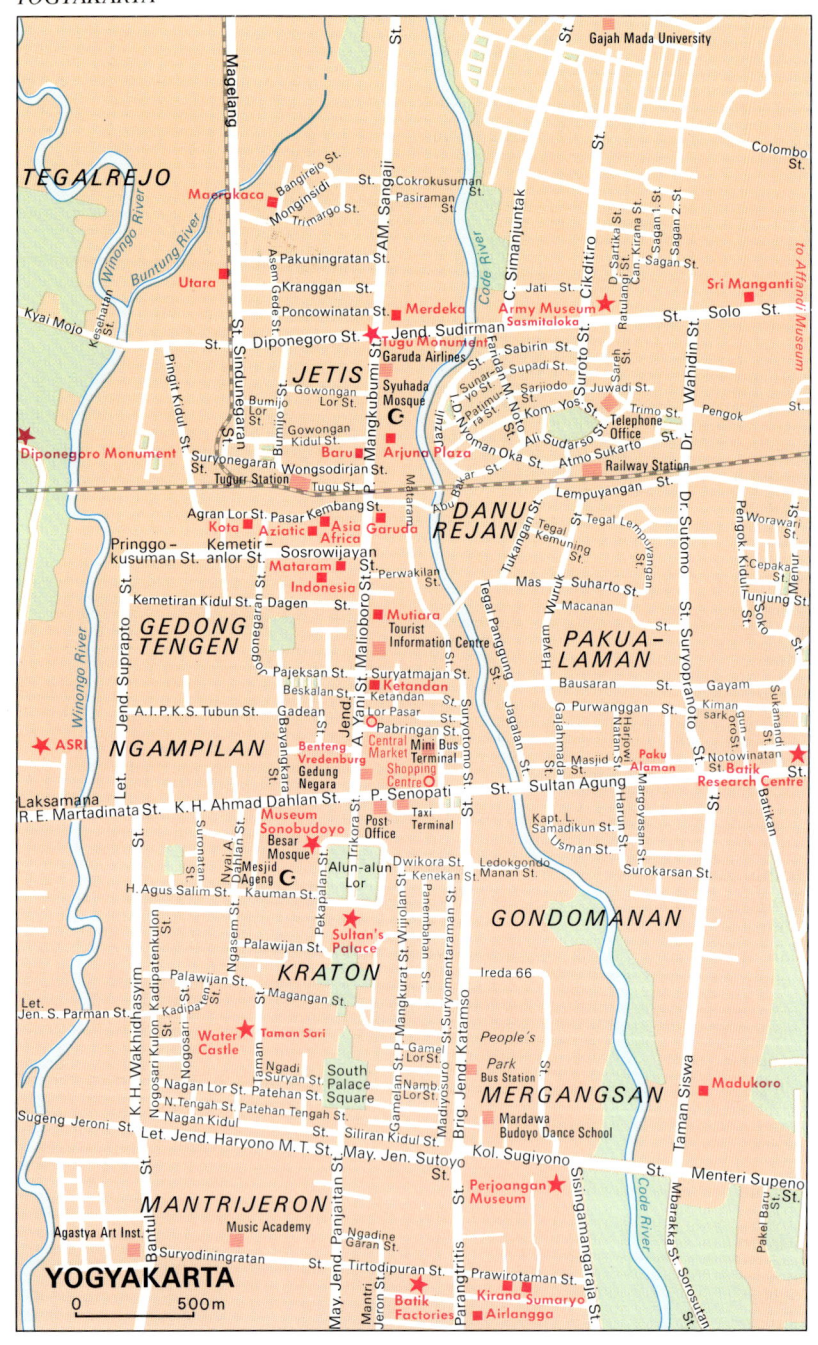

with a sacred albino turtle. Kota Gede is also known as a silverwork center.

Krapyak's son Agung is buried not with his father and grandfather at Kota Gede, but in a spectacular hilltop mausoleum at **Imogiri**, midway between Yogya and the sea. Agung was the greatest of Mataram's rulers, conquering Surabaya in 1625, besieging Dutch Batavia in 1628 and 1629, and finally taking the title of sultan in 1641. At his death in 1646 he was lord of all Central and East Java and the greatest conqueror in Indonesia since the time of Majapahit. The burial place which he created for himself reflects his glory. A great sun-dappled stairway of 345 steps leads to a fortress-like edifice containing not only Agung's own black tomb but also those of all his successors. After the sultanate split in 1755, both Yogyakarta and Surakarta rulers continued to be interred here, in separate wings of the building. The tombs are still objects of veneration, and may only be viewed on auspicious Mondays and Fridays.

Yogya Town

The town of **Yogyakarta** is a unique phenomenon in Indonesia. Apart from being the cultural capital and foremost tourist destination of Java, Yogya (pronounced "Jogja") is a city of more than half a million, a major administrative center, the site of more than 40 universities and academies, and a past capital of the Republic of Indonesia. Yet its sophistication comes deceptively cloaked in the simple garb of a giant village.

Though it stands amid a whole constellation of earlier royal sites, the modern town dates only from the mid-eighteenth century. The death of Sultan Agung heralded a century of chaos and decline for Mataram. Agung's son Amangkurat I was a tyrant who alienated most of his vassals, with the result that his successor Amangkurat II (reigned 1677-1703) could only claim his throne thanks to the Dutch, to whom the sultanate was now beholden. Three "Javanese Wars of Succession" followed before stability was restored in 1755 by the radical means of a permanent division of Mataram into two kingdoms. Paku Buwono III and his line were to rule Surakarta, while his uncle Pangeran Mangkubumi became the first ruler of Yogyakarta under the title of Hamengko Buwono, which is still borne by his descendants.

One of the first deeds of Hamengko Buwono I was to order the construction of the **Kraton Yogyakarta**, the palace which is Yogya's core. This *kraton* is a city within a city. Thousands of people live and work within its walls – *batik* makers, servants and guards as well as the musicians, jesters and *polowijo* or "weeds" (albinos and dwarfs) of the sultan's retinue, and the royal family itself. The central buildings, the first of which were completed in 1757, comprise a maze of *pendopo* – open or semi-open pavilions – which are separated by courtyards planted with shady trees. The outer walls, each a kilometer long and 3 m thick, caused the Dutch much consternation when they were added in 1785; but they did not prevent a thousand or so British Indian sepoys from taking the *kraton* against 11,000 defenders in 1812, with the sole casualty of a Scots officer stabbed to death by a princess whom he was carrying away as booty.

Not surprisingly, that debacle was the end of the independent military prestige of the court, which now accepted the superior power of the returning Dutch and devoted itself to self-beautification and the development of the Javanese arts. Although it seems timeless, today's *kraton* is essentially the *kraton* of this "theatrical" period, featuring opulent Indo-Dutch furniture, oil paintings by the nineteenth-century Javanese artist Raden Saleh, and several huge *gamelan* orchestras. Perhaps it is this very element of artifice

YOGYAKARTA

Gamelan orchestra at the kraton. Right: Ramayana dance performance.

which gives the palace its powerful otherwordly atmosphere. The ninth sultan who reigned 1939-88 nevertheless brought the court back down to earth just in time to secure its future, supporting the republic in 1945-49 and even giving over part of the palace to house the first independent Indonesian university, **Gajah Mada**, now a campus in the north of the city. Today, the *kraton* houses a museum and stages regular *gamelan* and classical dance performances.

Taman Sari ("Fragrant Garden"), also known as the Water Castle, is even purer fantasy. Located to the southwest of the main buildings, this labyrinthine ruin was the opulent pleasure palace of the first sultan. The adjacent bird market of **Ngasem** is built on the dry bed of an artificial lake across which Dutch visitors were once rowed in gilded boats to a manmade island. Only the smaller central bathing pools have been restored; the rest is in an evocative state of tropical decay.

Immediately in front of the *kraton* is the **Alun-alun Lor**, the main town square. It is here that tiger-buffalo fights were once staged for the entertainment and instruction of European dignitaries: the tiger represented Europe, the buffalo Java, and the steadfast strength of the buffalo seldom failed to overcome the ferocity of the tiger. On the west side of the square is a very Javanese **Mesjid Ageng** (Grand Mosque), built in the form of a *pendopo*. Three times a year, on the *garebeg* festivals, the sultan takes part in a spectacular procession from the palace to the mosque, accompanied by flower-bedecked heaps (*gungungan*) of rice, evidence of his charity. The greatest of these events is *Garebeg Maulud*, when the square seethes with performers and pedlars, and two ancient *gamelan* from the palace play majestic music for a solid week leading up to the procession.

Not far north of the *alun-alun* is the original Dutch fort, **Benteng Vredenburg**. In 1765, the first sultan agreed to build a castle for VOC troops in his city. But despite his industriousness in the field of pleasure gardens, and the fact that the 4-km walls around his own palace were apparently built in two weeks flat, the sultan did not manage to complete Vredenburg within his lifetime; Governor-General Daendels finally put a firm end to the procrastination in 1808. Opposite the fort is **Gedung Negara**, the handsome nineteenth-century home of the Dutch Resident. Further east on Jl. Sultan Agung is the **Paku Alaman**, the palace of Yogya's junior royal house, created by Raffles in 1813 as a counterweight to the court of Hamengko Buwono which he had just had occasion to storm. The Paku Alaman, which is not open to the public, is a less lavish version of the main *kraton*.

The British attack on Yogyakarta of 1812 ended the military power of the Javanese courts proper, but it was not quite the last stand of the aristocracy as a whole. In 1825, after years of court corruption and intrigue, increasing erosion of aristocratic privileges by the European government, and several ominous natural disasters, a Muslim visionary and scion of the royal family, called Prince Diponegoro, raised a rebellion against both the *kraton* and the Dutch which lasted five years and cost more than 200,000 lives.

Styled retrospectively as a freedom fighter, Diponegoro is one of the best-known figures in Indonesian history. He was brought up at **Tegalrejo**, 5 km northwest of the *kraton*, where his residence has been reconstructed as the **Monumen Diponegoro**, displaying some relics of the hero and realistic paintings of the war. In 1830 Diponegoro was finally tricked into capture 40 km northwest of Yogya at **Magelang**, which has another commemorative museum, **Museum Diponegoro**. More than a century of oppressive peace followed, the beloved *rust en orde* (peace and order) of Dutch colonialism, described by one nationalist of the 1930s as "the peace of death". When that peace was broken at last by Japan and the Indonesian revolution, Yogya was once again at the center of the whirlwind as capital of the infant republic from January 1946 until its seizure by Dutch troops in December 1948. The **Museum Sasmitaloka Jenderal Soedirman** celebrates the most important Indonesian military hero of this time, an Islamic schoolteacher who, wasted by tuberculosis, led the republic's armed forces from a litter which is still kept here.

Yogya's main street is **Jl. Malioboro**, famous for its stalls selling leatherwork and souvenirs by day and food by night. *Gudeg*, a mild jackfruit curry, is Yogya's speciality. Central Javanese food is the sweetest and least spicy in Indonesia, and makes much use of the soybean products *tahu* and *tempe*.

Insulated by Dutch policy from the changes sweeping other parts of Java in the late colonial period, Yogya was free both to maintain cultural traditions which faded elsewhere and to innovate energetically indigenous Javanese themes. The Dutch helped with the preservation, as the fine **Sonobudoyo** cultural museum, opened in 1935, testifies; the innovation was all Yogya's own. Both tradition and innovation have contributed to the town's present aesthetic wealth. In the field of *batik*, the main trend was conservative. Around **Taman Sari** and in the **Jalan Tirtodipuran** neighborhood, workshops produce traditional patterns, including those formerly reserved for royalty.

Wayang kulit, the ancient shadow-play, is a whole way of life in Yogya. There are numerous craftsmen producing the intricate leather puppets and two schools for *dalang* or puppeteers. Several institutions offer regular public performances of this magical spectacle, sometimes of traditional all-night duration. As a repertoire, the Indian epics of *Ramayana* and *Mahabharata* are generally preferred over more recent Javanese and Middle Eastern stories. Yogya's dance, by contrast, tends to be highly untraditional. Although some sacred and court dances are preserved, the masked dance-dramas known from the eleventh century and still popular in West and East Java are seldom performed in Yogya. They have been replaced by the unmasked *wayang wong*, an eighteenth century innovation, and the *sendratari*, a Western-influenced dance spectacle without dialogue, of which the best known example is the "Ramayana Ballet" staged at the **Loro Jonggrang Theatre** at Prambanan. *Ketoprak* is a form of contemporary folk drama which became popular in the 1920s.

Since 1922, when the arts-orientated Taman Siswa school system was founded here, Yogya has also been a dynamic center of the visual arts. Pioneers like Affandi, whose gallery **Museum Affandi** is open to the public, used European oils and perspective to defy the old Islamic taboos against human representation and create Indonesia's first wave of self-consciously individualistic art.

SOLO AND SURROUNDINGS

The twin courts of Yogyakarta were only two of four princely states to survive the incremental Dutch conquest of Java. The others were at **Surakarta**, more commonly known as **Solo**, at the eastern foot of Merapi. Not as quick to move with the times as those of Yogya, the Solo courts were unable to reconcile themselves to the republic and in June 1946 their prerogatives outside the palace walls were abolished forever. Today, their old territories are simply part of the province of Central Java.

Eight kilometers before Solo on the road from Yogya is the village of **Kartasura**, where a single crumbling brick wall is the only reminder that the capital of Mataram was here for 66 years. The Javanese courts were extraordinarily footloose: war, misfortune or the whim of a new king could lead to the wholesale transportation of the capital (sometimes literally, for important *pendopo* could be dismantled and carried) to a new, safer or more auspicious site, leaving behind a mostly wooden ruin quickly reclaimed by tropical nature.

Kartasura was founded in 1680 when the previous capital at Plered (near Kota Gede, Yogyakarta) was occupied by a pretender; in 1743, after three years of disastrous war against the Dutch and their allies, Pakubuwana II decided to abandon the obviously unlucky site and in 1746 he moved to the **Kraton Hadiningrat** at Solo, the fifth and last capital of Mataram. Though badly damaged by a fire in 1985, the palace is still worth seeing. It contains a museum of regal pomp, a cannon from Portuguese Malacca (the "wife" of the one in Jakarta's Taman Fatilah), and a peculiar pagoda in which the "emperors" (as the Dutch called them) trysted with the Queen of the South Seas. There is also an important library of Javanese manuscripts. The last of the great Javanese court poets, Raden

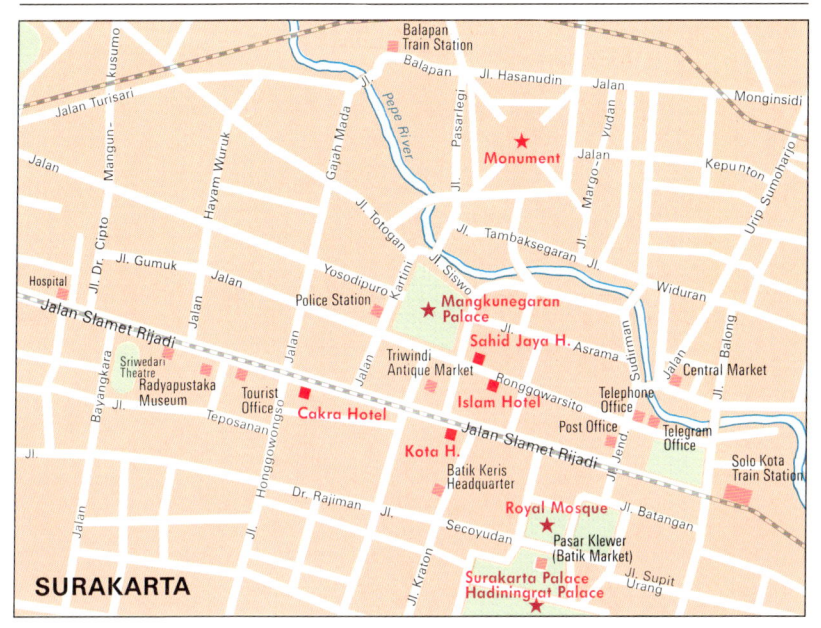

Ngabei Ronggawarsita, worked here until his death in 1873.

The Solo *kraton* remained the capital of all Mataram for less than a decade. The king's brothers were still in revolt, and his son not only saw Mataram divided between Yogya and himself but also had to suffer the foundation of a new junior court, the **Mangkunegaran**, under his very nose in Solo. Since the fire in Kraton Hadiningrat, this palace has rather upstaged the main *kraton* as a tourist attraction, sporting an imposing central *pendopo* of Javanese teak with an Italian marble floor, a famous *gamelan*, and a museum of *topeng* masks and *wayang* puppets. It was twice restored by a Dutch architect, Thomas Karsten, before the war, and remains the best maintained of Java's *kraton*. President Suharto's wife is related to the house of Mangkunegara. The Mangkunegaran Palace is north of the Kraton Surakarta, across the railway line. Further down the same line is an independent cultural museum, **Museum Radyapustaka**, founded in 1890. Indonesia's first railway line, begun in 1867, linked Solo to Semarang. In still earlier days the Solo river, Java's longest, carried boat traffic from Solo to the Strait of Madura, almost 300 km away.

In those times, Solo's wealth derived from the fertility of its lands and the labor of its subjects. Today, light industry is increasingly important. Solo's *batik* industry is organized on a bigger scale than that of Yogya. Some of the biggest *batik* companies in Indonesia, including **Batik Keris**, have their headquarters here. But traditional Solo *batik*, famous for its natural soft brown dyes against a mellow yellowish background, is still available. **Pasar Klewer** is the main *batik* market.

Solo has no great temple complex in its vicinity to match Yogya's Prambanan. But 36 km to its east on the slopes of Mount Lawu is one of the island's most intriguing and unusual antiquities, **Candi Sukuh**. Though lying within present-day Central Java, this temple belongs historically to East Java and to Majapahit. Built around 1430 during the declining years

113

of the empire, Sukuh is the end of the process of architectural and religious assimilation which began at Dieng: still a Hindu temple of sorts, but with the Indian elements all but overwhelmed by Javanese innovations. The central monument is a stepped pyramid, almost like a Mexican ruin. Some see this as a resurgence of a form of terrace used for ancestor worship long before Indian influences arrived in Java. Sukuh seems to be associated with a cult of the *wayang* hero Bima, but is also full of sexual imagery suggesting a fertility cult. A realistic set of male and female genitalia in stone, fragrant with recent flower offerings, adorns the floor of one of the entrances. Despite the airy views from the 910-m site and the erotic humor of the reliefs, Sukuh is an unsettling, almost demonic place in its setting of dark pines. The bestial imagery – giant turtles, elephant men, staring pigs – is as weird as a Bosch painting.

Sukuh is not quite the latest pre-Muslim temple to have survived. **Candi Ceto**, built 50 years later, is also on Mt. Lawu, 7 km further north and 600 m higher. Little remains of the original structure, but *pendopo* and Balinese split gates have recently been built on the old terraces. Near **Karangpandan** on the road to Sukuh and Ceto is the spot which the current president has chosen as his final resting place. Suharto was born and raised in the Yogya area, but **Makam Suharto** looks out over the broader *sawah* of the Solo valley. Suharto's elaborate mausoleum *pendopo* was completed in 1977, but will not be open to the public until he lies there in state.

Beyond Karangpandan, a road winds up through misty forests to the mountain resorts of **Tawangmangu**, which has a unique horticultural garden, and **Sarangan**, the usual starting-point for an ascent of Mt. Lawu. Sarangan is beyond the provincial boundary, and commands views over the old railway town of **Madiun** and the first great ricebowl of East Java.

Sangiran, 15 km north of Solo, is an important archaeological site first excavated in the 1930s. The 250,000-year-old skulls found here are at the center of an intriguing debate as to wether they represent a link between *Homo erectus* and *Homo sapiens*. The **Sangiran Site Museum** displays replicas of crania and fossils of the fauna of their time.

THE NORTH COAST

Tegal and **Pekalongan** are the first towns on the Central Javanese coast east of Cirebon. Tegal is a rising light industrial center known mainly for its ubiquitous emigrants, who sell street food in their *war-teg* (*warung* Tegal) from Jakarta to Surabaya. Pekalongan, however, is *Kota Batik,* "Batik City", where the wives of generals and diplomats order their *batik*. Before the war, Eliza van Zuylen, a Eurasian working in Pekalongan, set technical standards for *batik* manufacture which have never been equalled, with her Dutch-inspired floral patterns. During the war, Japanese models inspired the town's famous "Hokukai Batik". Today, Javanese, Arab, Chinese and European entrepreneurs design and produce *batik* here, and while there is reputedly such a thing as "traditional Pekalongan *batik*" the real "tradition" is one of innovation. The very best workshops, taking up to eight months to complete a single piece, are in surrounding villages like **Kedungwangi**.

The port of **Semarang**, not the old royal town of Solo, is the provincial capital and biggest city of Central Java. From 1678, when it was the first part of Mataram to be ceded to the Company, until 1948, when it was the base for an airborne assault on Yogya, Semarang was a Dutch beach-head on the Javanese heartland, and a conduit through which its wealth was extracted. Dutch warehouses and offices are still much in evidence downtown. An eighteenth century church, **Gereja Blenduk**, with a green copper dome and an imposing classical portico, is still in use, although the baroque organ is no longer in working order. Much of its congregation is Chinese: Chinese traders were here long before the Dutch made Semarang their own, and have outlasted them as masters of Semarang's commerce. The **Sam Poo Kong Temple** in the southwest of the city is dedicated to a sanctified Chinese Muslim said to have visited this coast in the fifteenth century – Chinese and Indonesians worship together here. **Klenteng Gang Lombok** is a more conventional Chinese temple, dating from 1772. Although the old Chinatown is still distinguishable around the *klenteng*, the richer Chinese businessmen have abandoned the blackout-ridden old town center to join their Indonesian patrons in the elite suburb of **Candi Baru**, on the hills overlooking the city.

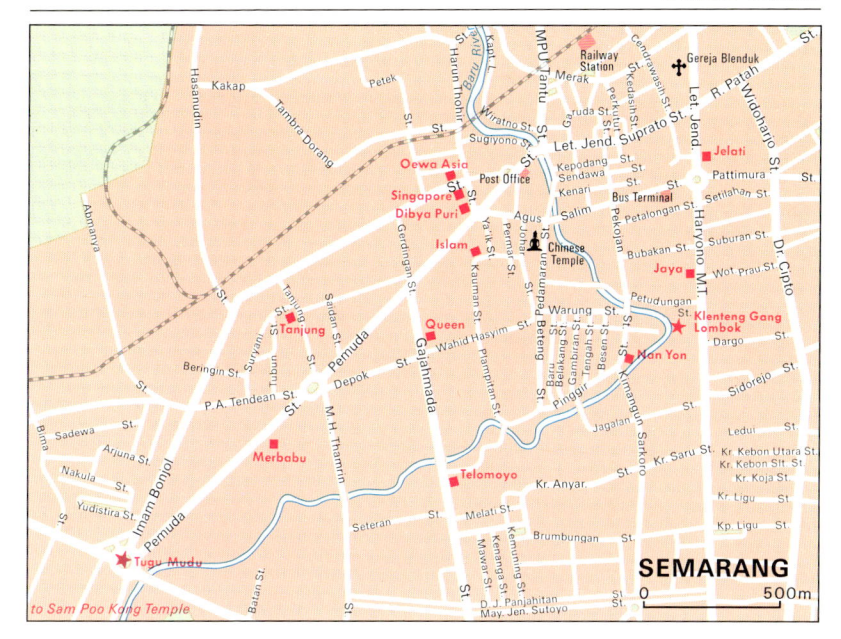

Because of the massive social changes it engendered, Semarang has had a turbulent twentieth century history. Henk Sneevliet, the Dutchman who introduced Marxism to the Indies in 1913, was active here in the Railway and Tram Workers' Union; he and his Javanese comrade Semaun made Semarang the capital of early Indonesian radicalism. Thirty years later, 2000 nationalist rebels died here in one of the most bizarre and tragic battles of the Indonesian revolution, when Japanese troops recaptured the city on British orders in October 1945, after initially allowing the Indonesians to take over. The **Tugu Muda** monument in the center of the city honors the Indonesian sacrifice. The black irony was maintained when six days later the Japanese were relieved by "British" troops who were in fact Indians, themselves not-so-willing colonial subjects.

Mosques

Every year, Java's north coast advances imperceptibly seaward. Semarang owes its growth partly to the fact that it has not suffered as badly from the creep-

All in a day's work.

ing mud as old rivals further east. When the Europeans first arrived, the greatest trading ports of Java were not Banten, Jakarta, Cirebon and Semarang, but obscure places, now almost forgotten by the world, on the curve of coast between Semarang and Surabaya.

Demak, whose fleets once conquered most of the coastal kingdoms of Java – and founded the rest – is now stranded 12 km from the sea. Apparently founded by a Chinese Muslim, Demak was Java's first Islamic state and first exponent of *jihad*. In the late 1520s it snuffed out the last fading embers of Majapahit's glory and became the first Islamic link in the chain of Moslem dynasties through which Solo and Yogya trace their legitimacy back to the ancient Hindu empire.

Folklore has it that four of the engraved pillars of Demak's **Mesjid Agung** mosque were brought from the Majapahit court. Certainly they are very old, although the remainder of the building was completely rebuilt in 1845 and again in 1987, when Suharto himself presided over the reopening. This is Java's most holy mosque; traditionally, seven pilgrimages here on the annual feast of *Garebeg Besar* were supposed to be worth one complete *haj* to Mecca.

More interesting still is the mosque at **Kudus**, which is of pure pre-Muslim design. Not only are the split gates reminiscent of a Balinese temple, but the redbrick minaret in front is so similar to a Hindu *kulkul* or gong tower that it may actually have been one. "Kudus" is a corruption of *al-Quds*, Jerusalem; this is the only place in Java to have acquired an Arabic name.

The mosque, which bears the date 1549, is known as *al-Manar* or *al-Aqsa* after the one in Jerusalem. It was founded by Sunan Kudus, who is said to have been the head of the mosque at Demak before he moved here. Sunan Kudus is one of the *wali songo*, the "nine saints" who take popular credit for the Islamization of Java. His carved, curtained grave behind the mosque has been a revered shrine for four centuries. The old port area of northeastern Java is also the homeland of the *wali*: another, Sunan Kalijaga, is buried at **Kadilangu**, 2 km south of Demak.

The domestic architecture of Kudus is more Middle Eastern than its mosque, with high, whitewashed, windowless streetside walls. Many of the female population work in the town's clove cigarette factories. The rich, sweet scent of *kretek* smoke was known for the first time only in the 1890s, and only started to make converts on a large scale in the 1920s, yet now it seems a timeless and essential part of Indonesia. Kudus was the first center of the *kretek* industry. Its cottage producers lost out after the war to new factories elsewhere, but the big Chinese-owned Djarum plant has regained much of the ever-growing market from Gudang Garam in Kediri.

Jepara comes closer to remaining a port than Demak or Kudus, but still misses the sea by a couple of kilometers. In the sixteenth century, ships from China, Burma, India, Persia and Arabia moored in its vanished harbor, and its own navy besieged Portuguese Malacca three times. Today it is a quiet, rather isolated place best known for its woodcarving in teak and mahogany.

The most famous child of this part of north-central Java is Raden Ajeng Kartini, Indonesia's foremost national heroine, whose birthday is celebrated as "Kartini Day" every 21 April. Born in 1879 in **Mayong** near Kudus, where there is a commemorative monument, Kartini was a daughter of the regent of Jepara, who allowed her to attend European school at a time when most Javanese aristocrats found female education unacceptable. Her wholehearted enthusiasm for Ethical Policy ideals dumbfounded even the Dutch themselves. In moving letters later published as *Door Duisternis tot Licht* (Through Darkness to Light), she expressed in lucid Dutch her desire to help bring education and emancipation to Javanese women. Kartini died tragically at 25, a few days after the birth of her first child. Her life and works are celebrated in Jepara by the **Museum Kartini di Jepara**, and in **Rembang**, where she spent her single year of married life, by the **Museum Kartini di Rembang**. She is buried by the old mosque in **Mantingan**, 19 km south of Rembang on the road to Blora.

A few kilometers east of Rembang is the little-known *batik* center of **Lasem**, where 50 small factories produce hand-drawn designs, often floral in theme, for sale in Surabaya. The industry is in the hands of the Chinese, who have been here for seven generations. Lasem resembles a nineteenth-century southern Chinese town.

Though separated from the historic coastland only by a low range of chalk hills, the **Lusi river valley** has always been one of Java's backwaters. This is almost the last place where you can see the rare *wayang* form called *krucil* or *klitik*, which uses flat, toy-like wooden puppets. At the beginning of this century, the villages around **Blora** were the scene of an extraordinary type of anticolonial resistance movement. An illiterate peasant called Surantika Samin founded a nativist religion stressing family and village loyalty, rejection of the money economy, and passive resistance to any form of external authority. Fed by resentment against forestry regulations in this teak-growing area, the movement spread: taxes remained unpaid, schools unattended. The messiah himself was exiled in 1907, but seven years later his followers were still keeping Dutch troops busy, and Saminism survived into the 1960s in this region. The **Museum Grobogan** near Purwodadi contains some historical, ethnographic and handicraft exhibits from the Lusi area.

DIENG AND GEDONG SONGO
Accommodation at:
DIENG PLATEAU
Several small *losmen* and a restaurant on the plateau, but many prefer to stay 1 hr downhill in Wonosobo.

WONOSOBO
INEXPENSIVE: **Petra**, Jl Jen Yani 81. **Losmen Surya**, corner Jl A Yani/Jl Penjara. **Losmen Widuri**, Jl Tanggung 20. *MEDIUM:* **Bima**, Jl Achmad Yani 5. **Nirwana**, Jl Tanggung 18.

Restaurants
Dieng Restaurant, Jl Kawedanan 23. **Asia Restaurant**, Jl Kawedanan 35, Tel: 165.

GEDONG SONGO
Usually visited from Semarang, but nearby **Bandungan** has several hotels.
Other antiquities of Central Java are seldom more than day excursions from Yogyakarta.

AMBARAWA AND MAGELANG
Museums
Railway Museum, Jl Stasiun, Ambarawa. Daily 8.00-17.00. **Museum Palagan Ambarawa** (military), Jl Mgr Sugiopranoto, Ambarawa. Daily 7.00-18.00. **Museum Diponegoro** (Prince Diponegoro Memorial Museum), Jl Diponegoro 1, Magelang, Tel: 2308. Sun-Wed 8.00-14.00, Fri 8.00-11.00, Saturday 8.00-13.00. **Museum Soedirman** (Gen Sudirman Memorial Museum), Jl Ade Irma Suryani C7, Magelang. Monday-Saturday 8.00-12.00, Sunday closed.

YOGYAKARTA
Accommodation
INEXPENSIVE: Mostly in travellers' ghetto S of railway station. On Gang I: **Beta Losmen, Home Sweet Home, Hotel Jogya, Losmen Bu Purwo**. On Gang II: **Bagus Hotel, Ghandi Losmen**. On Jl Pasar Kembang: **Ratna Hotel**, no.17A, Tel: 2675. **Asia-Afrika Hotel**, no. 25, Tel: 4489. **Hotel Kota** is at end of Jl Pasar Kembang on Jl Gandekan Lor. Away from station: **Hotel Aziatic**, Jl Sosrowijayan 6. **Indonesia Hotel**, Jl Sosrowijayan 9. **Intan Hotel**, Jl Sosrokusuman 1/16. **Hotel Puri**, Jl Sosrokusuman. **Prambanan Guesthouse**, Jl Sosrokusuman 18/20, Tel: 3303.
MODERATE: On Jl Prawirotaman – **Airlangga Guesthouse**, no.4, Tel: 3344. **Sriwijaya Guesthouse**, no.7, Tel: 55153. **Wisma Indah Guesthouse**, no.12, Tel: 88021. **Duta Guesthouse**, no.20, Tel: 5219. **Metro Guesthouse**, no.7/71. **Rose Guesthouse**, no.22, Tel: 2715.
Elsewhere: **Arjuna Plaza**, Jl Mangkubumi 48, Tel: 86862. **Gajah Mada Guesthouse**, Jl Bulaksumur, Gajah Mada university campus, Tel: 88461/ 88688 ext 625. **Hotel Mendut**, Jl Pasar Kembang. **New Batik Palace**, Jl Mangkubumi 46, Tel: 2149. **Pura Jenggala Guest House**, Jl Cendrawasih 2, Tel: 2238. **Indraloka Homestay Service**, Jl Cik Ditiro 14, Tel: 0274/ 3614, arranges boarding with Indonesian families.
LUXURY: **Ambarrukmo Palace**, Jl Adisucipto, Tel: 88488/88984. **Garuda**, Jl Malioboro 72, Tel: 2113. **Mutiara Hotel**, Jl Malioboro 18, Tel: 3272/4530/4531. **Puri Artha**, Jl Cendrawasih 9, Tel: 5934/5. **Sahid Garden**, Jl Babarsari, Tel: 3697. **Sri Manganti**, Jl Urip Sumoharjo, Tel: 2881. **Sriwedari**, Jl Adisucipto, Tel: 88288.

Food
STREET FOOD: Along Jl Malioboro, late-night *gudeg*, *sate* & *sop kaki kambing* (goat-foot soup) stalls. *INDONESIAN:* **Suharti Mbok Berek** (fried chicken), Jl Solo (beyond Ambarrukmo Palace Hotel). **Juminten** (Javanese), Jl Asem Gede 22, Kranggan 69. **Bu Citro** (Javanese), Jl Adisucipto, near airport entrance. **Warung Makan Sederhana**, Jl Mangkubumi 61B. **Sinar Budi** (Padang), Jl Mangkubumi 41.
CHINESE: **Moro Senang**, Jl Solo 55 (beyond airport). **Sintawang**, Jl Magelang 9. **Tiong San**, Jl Gandekan 29, a block W of Malioboro.
TOURIST FOOD: Kuta-style Indo-western eateries in *losmen* area S of station. Favored are **Bu Sis** & **Superman**, Gang I, **Anna's**, Gang II. Better and pricier approximations to western food at **Legian Garden Restaurant**, Jl Perwakilan 9 (junction Jl Malioboro/Jl Suryatman) & **Hanoman's Forest**, Jl Prawirotaman.

Shopping
Pasar Beringharjo (municipal market) off Jl Yani/Malioboro. **Yogyakarta Crafts Centre**, (big govt cooperative), opposite Ambarrukmo Palace Hotel.
LEATHER GOODS: Many shops are on Jl Malioboro, eg **Toko Setia**, nos.79 & 165.
Wayang kulit puppets: **Ledjar**, Jl Mataram DN I/370 (E of Malioboro). **Moejosoehardjo**, Jl S Parman Sari 37B (W of Winongo river), Tel: 2873. **Swasthigita**, Jl Ngadinegaran MD 7/50 (off Jl Panjaitan, S of *kraton*), Tel: 4346.
SILVER (Kota Gede): **Tom's Silver**, Jl Kota Gede 3-1 A, Tel: 3070/2818. **MD Silver**, Jl Keboan, Kota Gede, Tel: 2063.
ANTIQUES & CURIOS: Many shops on Jl Malioboro, incl **Toko Asia**, and in Taman Sari area. For higher prices and more reliable antiquity: **Jul Shop**, Jl Mangkubumi 29, Tel: 2157. **Ardianto**, Jl Pejaksan 21.
BATIK: Hundreds of outlets. Fixed prices at **Terang Bulang**, Jl Ahmad Yani 76. Two dozen factories around Jl Tirtodipuran, S of *kraton*, sell

cap (printed) *batik*. Taman Sari/bird market area is center for cheap *batik* painting; for more expensive originals, see 'Galleries'.

Museums & Zoos

Biology Museum of Gajah Mada University, Jl Sultan Agung 22, Tel: 4011. Mon-Thu 8.00-13.00, Fri 8.00-11.00, Sat & Sun 8.00-12.00. **Museum Dirgantara Mandala** (air force), Adisutjipto Air Force Base, Tel: 3647-9. Mon-Thur 8.00-13.00, Sat & Sun 8.00-12.00, Friday closed. **Yogyakarta Kraton Museum**, Tel: 2036. Friday 8.30-11.30, other days 8.30-12.30. **Gembira Loka Zoo**, Jl Gembira Loka. Daily 7.00-18.00. **Museum Perjuangan** (nationalistic history), Jl Sugiyopranoto 24. Mon-Thu 8.00- 14.00, Friday 8.00-11.00, Sat 8.00-15.00. **Museum Pusat TNI Angkatan Darat** (military), Jl Jen Soedirman 47, Tel: 86417-8. Mon-Thu 8.00-13.00, Sat-Sun 8.00-12.00, Friday closed. **Museum Sasana Wiratama** (Prince Diponegoro Commemorative Museum), Tegalrejo, Tel: 3068. Daily 7.30-18.00. **Museum Sasmitaloka Panglima Besar Jen Sudirman** (General Sudirman memorial museum), Jl Bintaran Wetan 3, Tel: 2663. Mon-Thu 8.00-13.00, Fri 8.00-11.00, Sat 8.00-12.00, Sun closed. **Museum Sonobudoyo**, Jl Trikora 3, Tel: 2775. Tue-Thu 7.30-13.30, Fri 7.30-11.00, Sat Sun 7.30-13.00, Mon closed.

Art galleries

Museum Affandi, Jl Solo 167, Tel: 88526. Daily 9.00-15.00. **Amri Yahya Gallery**, Jl Gampingan 67 (close to ASRI). **ASRI** (Indonesian Academy of Fine Arts), Jl Gampingan (W of city center beyond Winongo River). **Bagong Kussudiardjo**, Jl Singasaren 9, off Jl Wates.

Cultural performances

GAMELAN: **Kraton Yogyakarta**, rehearsals Mon & Wed am. **Pakualaman Palace**, every 5th Sunday 10.00. **Ambarrukmo Palace Hotel**, 10.30-12.30 & 15.30-17.30 daily in lobby.
WAYANG KULIT: **Agastya Art Institute**, Jl Gedong Kiwo MDIII/237 (off Jl Bantul in SW of town), every day except Saturday, 15.00-17.00. **Sasono Hinggil** (pavilion to S of *kraton*), 2nd Sunday of each month, 21.00-dawn. **Ambar Budaya**, Yogyakarta Craft Center, Mon/Wed/Fri 21.30-22.30.
DANCE: **Pendopo Dalem Pujokusuman**, Jl Brig Jen Katamso 45, Mon/Wed/Fri 20.00-22.00. The kraton dancers rehearse every Sunday 10.30-12.00. Several dance schools open rehearsals to visitors: **Krido Bekso Wirama**, Jl Wahid Hasyim; **ASTI** (State Dance Academy), Jl Colombo (N of city); **Bagong Kussudiardjo**, Jl Singasaren 9, off Jl Wates. **Ramayana Ballet** staged at full-moon nights at Prambanan May-Oct; check tourist office for details.
DRAMA: **Taman Hiburan Rakyat**, Jl Brig. Jen Katamso, every night.

Tourist information

Il Malioboro 16, Tel: 2182 ext 30. Mon-Sat 8.00-21.00.

Money change

Bank Niaga & Bank Bumi Daya on Jl Sudirman, & **Bank Negara 46**, next to post office. **Hotel Garuda** changes money on Sunday & after hours.

Post office

Corner Jl Senopati/Jl Jen A Yani. Monday-Thursday & Saturday 8.00-13.00, Friday 8.00-11.00.

Hospital

Rumah Sakit Bethesda, Jl Jen Sudirman 70, Tel: 2281.

Transport

AIR: Adisucipto Airport, Jl Solo, E of town. *Airline offices:* **Garuda**, Jl Mangkubumi 56, Tel: 4400; **Merpati**, Jl Sudirman 9-11, Tel: 4272; **Bouraq**, Jl Sudirman 37, Tel: 86664.
RAIL: One central station. 9 trains a day to Jakarta, 3 to Bandung, 6 to Surabaya.
ROAD: For buses to surrounding towns, **Terminal Umbulharjo**, 5 km SE of centre near Kota Gede, though some buses for Borobudur leave from **Terminal Pingit**, Jl Magelang. Long-distance buses leave from bus co offices on Jl Mangkubumi & Jl Diponegoro, or from Jl Sostrowijayan, where also ticket agencies are.
INTERNAL: Taxis hired on Jl Senopati by post office, or at bigger hotels. **Horsecarts** *(andong)* available at station, post office or public market. **Becak** everywhere, esp Jl Malioboro. **Minibus** terminal off Jl Senopati, behind shopping center. **Bicycles** can be hired from **Hotel Aziatic** or two *losmen* on Gang I.

SOLO
Accommodation

INEXPENSIVE: Between the two palaces – **Central**, Jl HA Dahlan, Tel: 2842. **Keprabon**, Jl HA Dahlan 14, Tel: 2811. **Kota**, Jl Slamet Riyadi 113, Tel: 2841. **Mawar Melati**, Jl Imam Bonjol 44, Tel: 6434. **Pak Mawardi's Homestay** ('The Westerners'), Jl Kemlayan Kidul 18, Tel: 3106. **Losmen Timor**, Jl Kepraban Wetan I/5. **Wigati**, Keprabon Wetan IV/4. Near railway station: **Hotel Gajah Mada**, Jl Gajah Mada 54. **Kondang Asri**, Jl RM Said 86. **Wismantara**, Jl RM Said 53. *MODERATE:* **Indah Jaya**, Jl Srambatan 13, Tel: 5444/7445 (near station). **Putri Ayu**, Jl Slamet Riyadi 293, Tel: 6145 (2.5 km out of town on road to Yogya). **Ramayana Guest House**, Jl Dr Wahidin 15, Tel: 2841 (near Putri

Ayu). **Hotel Trio,** Jl Urip Sumarharjo 33, Tel: 2847.
LUXURY: **Cakra Hotel,** Jl Slamet Riyadi 171, Tel: 5847/7000. **Kusuma Sahid Prince Hotel,** Jl Asrama 22, Tel: 6356-8/6901-2/7022. **Mangkunegaran Palace Hotel,** Jl Mangkunegaran, Tel: 5683/2226. **Sahid Sala,** Jl Gajah Mada 104, Tel: 3889/5889.

Food
STREET FOOD: Best on **Jl Teuku Umar,** off Jl Slamet Riyadi.
INDONESIAN: **Andalas,** Jl Ronggowarsito (near Mangkunegaran Palace Hotel). **Bakso Taman Sari,** Jl Gatot Subroto 42C (between Secoyuden & Slamet Riyadi). **Sari** (Javanese), Jl Slamet Riyadi 351 (3 km from town center). **Segar Ayem** (Javanese), Jl Secoyudan (opp Pasar Klewer). **Timlo Solo** (Javanese), Jl Urip Sumoharjo 106. Lots of small eating places around station and on Jl Achmad Dahlan.
CHINESE: **Centrum,** Jl Kratonan 151. **Orient,** Jl Slamet Riyadi 337A (near Sari). **Populair,** Jl Achmad Dahlan 70. **Ramayana Restaurant,** corner Jl Imam Bonjol/Jl Ronggowarsito (off Jl Slamet Riyadi).

Shopping
Pasar Gede (general market), end Jl Urip Sumoharjo. **Jl Secoyudan** is main shopping street. Fleamarket is **Pasar Triwindu,** Jl Diponegoro, in front of Kraton Mangkunegaran.
ANTIQUES & CURIOS: **Eka Hartono,** Jl Dawung Tengah 11/38. **Parto Art,** Jl Slamet Riyadi 103. Several more on and just off Jl Slamet Riyadi & Jl Urip Sumarharjo. Repro furniture from **Mirah Delima,** Jl Kemasan RT 11.
WAYANG PUPPETS: **Usaha Pelajar,** Jl Nayu Kidul (N of bus station).
DANCERS' REQUISITES: **Toko Bedoyo Serimpi,** Temenggungan 116 (corner Hayam Wuruk/Ronggowarsito).
BATIK: **Batik Danar Hadi,** Jl Slamet Riyadi. **Batik Keris,** Jl Yos Sudarso 37. **Batik Semar,** Jl RM Said 132. Textiles market is **Pasar Klewer,** by main *kraton*.

Museums & Zoos
Museum Kraton Surakarta, Tel: 2889, open 9.00-14.00, Friday closed. **Museum Istana Mangkunegaran,** open 9.00- 12.00, Sunday closed. **Museum Radyapustaka,** Jl Brig Jen Slamet Rijadi 235, Tel: 2306. Tuesday-Thursday 8.00-14.00, Friday 8.00-11.00, Saturday 8.00-12.00, Monday closed. **Sriwedari Zoo,** Jl Ir Sutami 109, Tel: 6379. Daily 7.00-17.00.

Cultural performances
GAMELAN MUSIC: **ASKI,** Pagelaran Alun Utara - rehearsals most mornings 9.00-14.00.

COURT DANCING: **Mangkunegaran Kraton,** Wednesday 10.00- 12.00.
WAYANG ORANG & KETOPRAK: **Taman Sriwedari,** Jl Slamet Riyadi, nightly 20.00-23.00; **Taman Hiburan Bale Kambang,** nightly from 20.00, matinee Sunday 10.00.
WAYANG KULIT: **Radio Republik Indonesia** (near r/way station), 3rd Sat of each month.

Tourist information:
Municipal Tourist Office, Jl Slamet Riyadi 235, Tel: 6508.

Money change:
Bank Bumi Daya & **Bank Niaga,** Jl Slamet Riyadi (nos. 8 & 18), & **Bank Negara Indonesia 1946,** Jl Jen Sudirman 19.

Post office:
Jl Sudirman, open Monday-Thursday & Saturday 8.00-13.00, Friday 8.00-11.00.

Telephone office:
Jl May. Kusmanto, Tel: 108.

Transport
AIR: Only Garuda fly to Solo - office in forecourt of Kusuma Said Hotel, Jl Sugiopranoto, open Monday-Friday 7.00-16.00, Saturday 7.00-13.00, Sunday & holidays 9.00-12.00. **Adi Sumarmo Airport** is 9 km W of town. Direct flights to Singapore began recently.
TRAIN: 5 trains each day to Yogya, one to Semarang, 6 to Surabaya, all from **Solo Balapan** station.
ROAD: For inter-city buses, **Terminal Cilingin,** 3 km N of centre on Jl Tagore. Some night bus companies operate from Jl Urip Sumoharjo, and some minibuses to Yogya from Jl Yos Sudarso.
INTERNAL: Minibus station opposite Pasar Klewer near Kasusuhunan palace. Taxis wait nearby at Jl Kratonan. Bicycle hire from **Pak Mawardi's** (see accommodation).

PEKALONGAN
Accommodation
INEXPENSIVE: **Losmen Asia,** Jl Wahid Hasyim 49, Tel: 41125. **Gajah Mada,** Jl Gajah Mada 11A, Tel: 41185. **Hotel Murni,** Jl Mansyur 4. **Sari Dewi,** Jl Hayam Wuruk 1.
MODERATE: **Hayam Wuruk,** Jl Hayam Wuruk 152- 158. **Hotel Istana,** Jl Gajah Mada 23-25, Tel: 61581.
FIRST CLASS: **Nirwana Hotel,** Jl Dr Wahidin 11, Tel: 41691/41446.

Food
Pekalongan Remaja, Jl Dr Cipto 20, Tel: 21019 (Chinese). **Serba Ada,** Jl Hayam Wuruk 125.

Batik
Ahmad Yahya, Jl Pesindon 221, Tel: 41413. **GKBI** (national batik cooperative), Jl HA Salim

39, Tel: 183811. **Tobal Batik**, Jl Teratai 7A. Many other shops on Jl KH Mansyur & Jl Hayam Wuruk. Out of town: **Oey Soe Tjoen**, Jl Raya 104, Kedungwuni.

Transport
Minibus station: Behind Pertamina petrol station, Jl Hayam Wuruk. **Intercity bus station** is 2 km out of town.

SEMARANG
Accommodation
INEXPENSIVE: **Losmen Bahagia**, Jl Pemuda 16-18. **Losmen Djelita**, Jl MT Haryono 32-36, Tel: 23891. **Hotel Jaya**, Jl MT Haryono 87, Tel: 23604. Many small, cheap *losmen* along Jl Imam Bonjol.
MODERATE: **Oewa Asia**, Jl Imam Bonjol 1, Tel: 22547. **Queen Hotel**, Jl Gajah mada 44-52, Tel: 27063. **Sky Garden Motel**, Jl Setiabudi, Grogol, Tel: 312733-6. **Telomoyo**, Jl Gajah Mada 138, Tel: 20926/25436/27037.
LUXURY: **Metro Grand Park**, Jl H Agus Salim 2- 4, Tel: 273717. **Patra Jasa Hotel**, Jl Si Singamanaraja, Tel: 314441-7. **Siranda Hotel**, Jl Diponegoro 1, Tel: 313271-5.

Food
INDONESIAN/SEAFOOD: **Sate Ponorogo**, Jl Gajah Mada 107, Tel: 20637. **Soen**, Jl A Yani 164, Tel: 316174; **Kompleks Warna Sari** (food centre), Jl Gajah Mada. *CHINESE:* **Gajah Mada**, Jl Gajah Mada 43, Tel: 23753. **Pringgading**, Jl Pringgading 54, Tel: 288973. More on Gang Lombok, in Chinatown next to *klenteng*.
COLONIAL: **Toko Oen**, Jl Pemuda 52, Tel: 21683.

Shopping
Pasar Johar, off Jl Pemuda, is main market. **Bird market**, Jl Kartini, near stadium.
BATIK: **Cenderawasih**, Jl Pemuda 46, Tel: 25986. **Batik Danar Hadi**, Jl Gajah Mada 186, Tel: 25999. **Batik Keris**, Complex Pertokoan, Gajahmada Plaza.
ANTIQUES & CURIOS: **Pandjang**, Jl Widoharjo 31A, E of bus station; also several shops on Jl Pemuda.

Museums
Central Java State Museum, Jl Abdul Rahman (1 km from airport). **Museum Jamu Nyonya Meneer** (museum of herbal remedies), Jl Raya Kaligawe km 4, Tel: 285732. Monday-Friday 10.00-15.30.

Cultural performances
WAYANG ORANG & KETOPRAK: Nightly at **Ngesti Pandowo**, Jl Pemuda 116, **Sri Wanito**, Jl Dr Dipto, & **Wahyu Budoyo**, Kopleks Tegal Wareng, Jl Sriwijaya.

DANCE: Performances at **Taman Hiburan Rakyat**, Jl Sriwijaya.
WAYANG KULIT at **Wisma Pancasila** (Jl Simpang Lima, South end of Jl Gajah Mada), 2nd Saturday of each month, 21.00- dawn.

Tourist Information
Municipality Tourist Office, Wisma Pancasila bldg, Jl Simpang Lima (central square, South end of Jl Gajah Mada), Tel: 288690. Mon-Thu 8.00-14.00, Fri 8.00-11.00, Sat 8.00-13.30. **Central Java Prov. Tourist Office**, Jl Pemuda 171. Mon-Thu 8.00-13.00, Fri 8.00-11.00, Sat 8.00-12.00.

Post office
Pasar Johar, top of Jl Pemuda.

Hospital
St. Elizabeth, Jl Kawi 1, Candi, Tel: 315.

Transport
AIR: Ahmad Yani Airport, 8 km W of Semarang. Airline offices: **Garuda**, Jl Gajah Mada 11, Tel: 20178; **Merpati**, Jl Gajah Mada 23, Tel: 23027.
RAIL: One main station, **Tawang**, on main Jakarta-Cirebon-Surabaya line.
ROAD: Inter-city bus terminal is **Terminal Bis Terboyo**, 6 km from center, reached by *mikrolet* from Terminal Sendowo (see below).
INTERNAL: Main internal bus/mikrolet station is **Terminal Sendowo** on Jl Suari, south of Gereja Blenduk. No metered taxis; hire taxis at **Pasar Johar** or behind Metro Grand Park hotel.

KUDUS
Accommodation
INEXPENSIVE: **Losmen Amin**, Jl Manur 448. **Losmen Dewi Tungal**, Jl Kenari 2. **Losmen Slamat**, Jl Jen Sudirman 63. *MODERATE:* **Notosari**, Jl Kepodang 17, Tel: 21245. **Hotel Duta Wisata**, Jl Sunan Muriabarongan 194, Tel: 694.

Food
Garuda Restaurant, Jl Jen Sudirman 1; good street food at *Simpang Tujuh* in front of *kabupaten* office.

JEPARA, REMBANG, PURWODADI
Museums
Museum Kartini di Jepara (Raden Ajeng Kartini Memorial Museum), Jl Kartini 1, Jepara, Tel: 118. Mon-Thu 7.00-14.00, Fri 7.00-11.00, Sat 7.00-13.00, Sun closed. **Museum Kartini di Rembang** (Raden Ajeng Kartini Memorial Museum), Jl Gatot Soebroto 8, Rembang. Mon-Thu 9.00-14.00, Fri 9.00-12.00, Sat 9.00-13.00, public holidays 9.00-17.00.
Museum Pemerintah Daerah Grobogan (Grobogan local museum), Grobogan, Purwodadi. Mon-Thu 8.00-13.00, Fri 9.00-11.00, Sat 8.00-12.00, Sun closed.

EAST JAVA

EAST JAVA

NORTH COAST
SURABAYA
MADURA
MALANG
MAJAPAHIT
PENATARAN
BROMO AND BEYOND

East Java is vernacular Java, country Java, deep Java. It was here that Javanese art finally mastered its Indian models, that ancestor-worship and mysticism triumphed over theology, that a peasant bandit came to found a great dynasty. East Java saw the most powerful of all Java's kings, but there have been no kingdoms here now for almost three centuries: no courtly arts, but also no empty pomp, no grovelling deference, and no eclipse of folk traditions. Devoid of living kraton, far from the capital and relatively poor in tourist facilities, East Java attracts fewer visitors than the other two Javanese provinces. But in many ways it offers a fairer and more diverse view of the island's life and people.

THE NORTH COAST

To the north of the volcanic spine is a wide plain where the twin rivers of Solo and Brantas wind through teak forests, sugar fields and rice paddies to their sprawling deltas on the Strait of Madura. A final modest ridge of dry limestone, the "North Chalk Hills" (of which Madura island is an extension) separates the Solo river valley from the Java Sea. In terms of

Left: Panoramic view of the Merapi volcano.

culture and history as well as physical geography, the seaward part of this area is a continuation of the Central Javanese *pesisir*. **Tuban**, 100 km along the palm-shaded beach from Rembang, is another ancient port, once Majapahit's main harbor. It boasts the grave of a minor *wali*, Sunan Bonang. Inland is **Bojonegoro**, where the **Sendangduwur Mosque** features a beautiful sixteenth-century *gapura* or ornamental doorway. The intricately carved reliefs above the lintel show flowers and coral flanked by a striking pair of garuda wings.

On the broken northeast corner of Java, the ancient port of **Gresik** rivals Demak in the brilliance of its past. According to Chinese records Gresik was founded in the fourteenth century by traders from Canton. Blessed with a fine sheltered anchorage, it became a major international trading center, and was the first port of Java to be visited by Europeans - Portuguese traders en route for the Moluccas. The Portuguese writer Tome Pires, who lived in Malacca between 1512 and 1517, described Gresik as "the jewel of Java in trading ports". Again like Demak, Gresik was a major early center for the dissemination of Islam, not only in Java, but throughout eastern Indonesia. **Makam Maulana Malik Ibrahim** in Desa Candipuro is the revered tomb of the very

SURABAYA

EAST JAVA

0   20km

first of the *wali*, Malik Ibrahim, and his family. The tombstone was probably imported from Gujarat in India; according to its inscription, the saint died in 1419. Two kilometers south of the center of Gresik, on a hill called **Giri**, is the even more famous grave of **Sunan Giri**. Unlike the other *wali*, Sunan Giri founded a line of spiritual lords to continue his authority after his death. These were feared both by the Dutch, who called them "the popes of Java", and by the rulers of Mataram, who respected their learning and spiritual power. In 1680 the line was finally exterminated by its combined enemies, but Giri has remained a place of pilgrimage to the present day. In life, the *wali* could work miracles; in death, they are still *kramat*, capable of bestowing divine favors on the devotees.

Still, Gresik is probably losing its sacred aura. The kind of Islam which moves today's youth has more to do with morals and loudspeakers than with saints and graves. Sawmills are the new face of Gresik, where Kalimantan's razed forests are reduced to plywood and pulp. The old Gresik lingers only in the narrow streets of the "Arab quarter", and around the holy tombs themselves.

SURABAYA

It was not silt which caused Gresik's eclipse: plenty of exotic sailing craft still bob on the polluted waters of Gresik har-

and noise, but it is an interesting and gripping place. This is a living cultural center, both in the formal sense of plays and performances, and in the sense of the fusion and regeneration of folk cultures.

Surabaya is cosmopolitan, but without the jarring pseudo-Western glitter of Jakarta. Give or take an air-conditioned shopping complex or two, Surabaya's atmosphere is more purely Indonesian, with a special east Indonesian flavor. For as Surabaya grew as an export point for Javanese products, it also became the hub of the maritime trading network for the eastern archipelago as a whole. Much of its population is from nearby Madura, but there are also large numbers of Banjar from Kalimantan, Bugis and Minahasans from Sulawesi, and Ambonese from the Moluccas.

Surabaya's colonial boom was in a sense a renaissance, for the port has a long history. In 1620, it was a fortified trading city over 30 km in circumference, a state in its own right with lordship over Gresik and Sidayu. But five years later Mataram took it by siege, thus ending Surabaya's luster for more than two centuries. According to tradition, the conquered king's son was ordered to take up the life of an ascetic at the holy grave of Surabaya's founder – yet another *wali*, Sunan Ngampel, who was a pupil of Malik Ibrahim of Gresik. His grave is still to be seen in **Kampong Ngampel**, the origin of the city, now lost in the old commercial district between the forks of the Kali Mas on which Surabaya is built.

A little further south, where Jl. Rajawali crosses the west branch of the river, is the famous **Red Bridge**, once the beating heart of Dutch Surabaya. In 1920, rush hour here was "an indescribable press of four- and two-wheeled carriages, carts loaded with merchandise, travelling sailors, native and Chinese merchants, coolies...". Today's roaring motorized battle leaves one at an even greater loss for words, but the neighbor-

bor. The culprit was the mighty colonial port of **Surabaya**, just 25 km along the coast to the southeast. Ceded to the Dutch by Mataram in 1743, Surabaya was still smaller than Gresik in 1800. But it had been selected as the chief Dutch entrepot and administrative center for East Java, and the massive growth of the colonial economy in the nineteenth century made Surabaya the busiest port and the biggest city in the Dutch Indies, outstripping even Batavia and ranking almost alongside Singapore in international importance. Today, Surabaya has been overtaken again by Jakarta in size, but at 3.7 million it is still number two in the country and still growing fast. Surabaya's sweet name belies a reality of heat, dirt,

SURABAYA

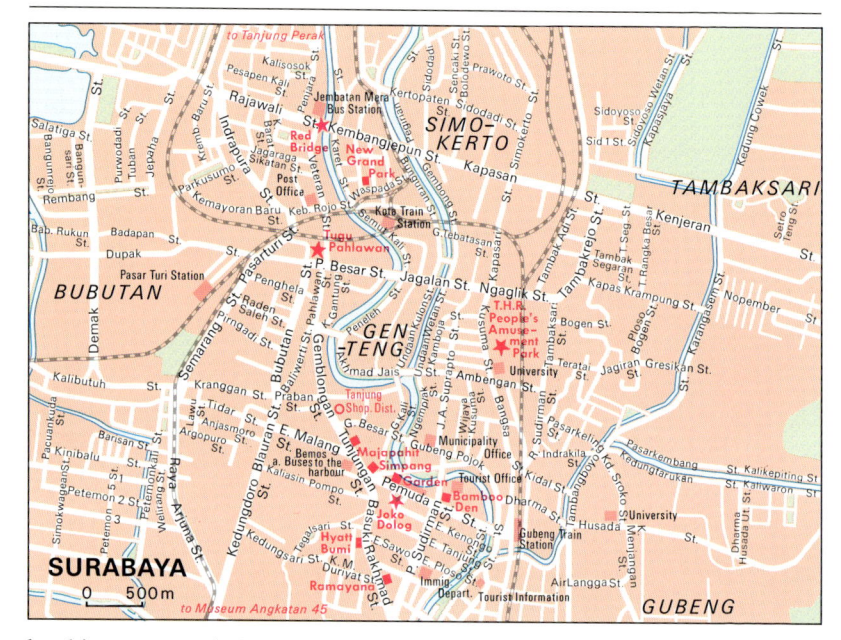

hood is now evocatively dowdy with its run-down Dutch warehouses and pre-war offices.

When the Red Bridge neighborhood was in its prime, it was also the geographic center of the city, halfway between the docks in the north and the gracious suburban administrative precinct served by **Gubeng Station** in the south. The dock complex at **Tanjung Perak** is still much as it was, except for the new air-conditioned passenger terminal. Coolies still unload sacks of copra, pepper and cloves from boats from such places as Tarakan, Tolitoli and Ternate. Scrubbing, hammering sailors struggle to keep ageing warships seaworthy: as in Dutch times, this is Indonesia's main naval base. But in the south, urban growth has swamped the old civic boulevard, **Jl. Pemuda**, which is now a commercial thoroughfare lined with banks and hotels. Nevertheless **Grahadi**, the residence of the Dutch governor, still stands here on immaculate lawns, an island of tranquillity preserved by the presence of today's Governor of East Java. On a plinth opposite the residence stands the corpulent figure of **Joko Dolog**, a thirteenth century statue from the Malang area which has long been Surabaya's trademark.

Around the corner on Jl. Tunjungan is a building which recalls both the heyday and the end of colonialism in Indonesia. The **Hotel Majapahit**, opened in 1910 as the Hotel Oranje, was Surabaya's finest. Countless planters, ship-owners and cruise passengers were served *rijsttafel* in its palatial dining room and sipped Bols on its polished terraces. The unsightly air-conditioning units bolted to the more expensive rooms are a concession to modernity, but otherwise this pavilion-style hotel retains its old-world grace. In 1942 the invading Japanese renamed it Hotel Yamato, and after their defeat an attempt to make it Oranje again precipitated an incident which helped spark off the biggest and bloodiest battle – indeed, some say the only real battle – of the national revolution. The blurred monochrome photographs of this event have not lost their power to move: they show Indonesian youths scaling the building's squat tower to tear off the blue strip from the Dutch tricolor on the flagpole, leaving the *merah putih*, the red and white flag of the republic.

There were as yet only a few actual Dutchmen in the city; order was officially in the hands of 6000 British Indian troops. When these seemed about to be massacred by more than 100,000 Indonesian fighters bent on various combinations of revolution and *jihad*, the British flew in Sukarno and Hatta to arrange a ceasefire. But there was more fighting, and on 10 November 1945, a day now commemorated as Heroes' Day (*Hari Pahlawan*), the British began a bloody punitive sweep through Surabaya, supported by a naval and air bombardment. Many of the defenders fought in the ancient state of selfless frenzy which has entered the English language as "amok", and the fighting lasted three weeks. Though the Republicans lost thousands of men, the Battle of Surabaya was a turning point in the revolution, convincing the outside world that the republican leaders were not simply a group of isolated collaborators who would soon be denounced by their own people. Those who fought and died on the Indonesian side are commemorated by the **Tugu Pahlawan** or Heroes' Monument, and the whole city is often honored with the epithet "Kota Pahlawan", City of Heroes. An army museum containing relics of the revolution, the **Museum Angkatan 45**, is located in the far south of town.

East Java is the original home of much of the island's classical cultural heritage. The first great works of old Javanese literature were composed here, including the *Arjunawiwaha*, the *Bharatayuddha* and the *Ramayana*, all classic Old Javanese versions of ancient Sanskrit myths. Episodes from East Java's history supply the raw material for the *Panji* and *Damar Wulan* romances, which provide

Javanese girl performing a Ramayana dance in Surabaya.

lighter alternatives to the Indian epics of *wayang* repertoire. Panji is a perfect knight whose pursuit of his true love, the equally flawless Dewi Anggreni, gives him ample scope to demonstrate his courage and honor. Damar Wulan, a more demotic hero, is a stable boy who manages to marry a princess of Majapahit.

The East Javanese have their own genres as well as their own scripts. The Panji cycle is often played by the *wayang gedog* - essentially a form of *wayang kulit*, but with a slightly different style of puppet and accompaniment from a seven-tone *pelog gamelan* rather than the customary five-tone *slendro* type. Sunan Giri himself is said to have introduced this *wayang* form. *Ludruk* is a special Surabayan form of drama in which the settings are contemporary urban households and the human actors speak the local *arek* dialect. Coarse, realistic and satirical, *ludruk* epitomizes the strong populist vein in East Javanese art and society. The whole range of the region's performing art can be sampled in Surabaya, although for dance, the most prestigious venue of all is the **Candra Wilwatikta Open Air Theatre** near Pandaan, 45 km south of the city. Traditional arts form a living part of folk culture in Surabaya in a way they are beginning not to in Jakarta. The decrepit red light districts of **Jarak** and **Bangunrejo**, for instance, are still the haunt of *ronggeng*, dancing-girls-cum-prostitutes who dance by the roadside just as they did when Raffles deplored them almost 180 years ago.

Surabaya is also a good place to watch *reog*, one of Java's oldest and strangest entertainments. *Reog* is the local name for the ancient trance dance which occurs in different forms and under different names from Banten to Bali. In West and Central Java, the main performer rides a flat hobby horse of woven bamboo and is literally whipped into his trance state while weird clowns look on, a surreal scene which sets the imagination roving. In East Java and Bali, grotesque monster masks are used. The *Reog Ponorogo* (after Ponorogo, a small town south of Madiun) performed in Surabaya combines both types in a spectacle of orchestrated madness.

MADURA

The barren island of **Madura** lies off Surabaya like a stray piece of maritime eastern Indonesia somehow towed to the Javanese coast. Madura has a pronounced dry season, and when the rain does fall it is quickly swallowed up by the limestone hills. One result is that the inhabitants eat more maize and cassava than rice, and breed cattle instead of water buffalo. Another is that the Madurese have always been far more dependent upon the sea, and far more wholeheartedly orientated towards the other lands beyond it, than have the Sundanese, Javanese or Balinese. Madura is an island of picturesque fishing villages, blinding white salt pans, and multi-colored *prahu* drawn up on golden beaches. The north coast is the best place in Indonesia to spot traditional *prahu*, and the last place on earth where some designs are still built.

Oppressed by Javanese dynasties and dissatisfied with the dry poverty of their own island, the Madurese seem to have spent much of their history trying vainly to master Java. Sultan Agung of Mataram conquered Madura in 1624, forcing its petty states to unite under the line later known as Cakraningrat. But as Mataram grew weak, the tables were turned. Again and again, Madurese armies were the crucial factor in the wars for the Javanese throne. But they were never numerous enough to be more than that: a factor. Twice – in 1677 and 1742 – they actually took the court of Mataram, only to lose it again. Today, emigration seems to be succeeding where arms failed. Of the 12 million Madurese, Madura itself supports barely 3 million: the rest live on the mainland, and in parts of the north coast east of Surabaya they make up virtually the whole of the population.

The Madurese are the epitome of Indonesian martial valor, but unfortunately for their place in the modern schoolbooks their only consistent antipathy has been towards Java, against which they have more often fought alongside Dutchmen than opposite them. The regents of Madura were granted extravagant titles and privileges by the Dutch in return for services rendered. The Cakraningrats became official custodians of the remote *Oosthoek* of the East Java mainland, and even bore the title of sultan for a time. Several Cakraningrats are buried in the **Air Mata** cemetery near **Arasbaya**. This contains Muslim graves richly decorated in pre-Muslim style, including one backed by a huge carved stone screen in the form of the *gunungan* which signals

A racing bull and his owner on Madura.

the end of a *wayang kulit* performance. In the east of the island, a separate dynasty ruled for the Dutch at **Sumenep**, where their eighteenth century palace, **Kraton Sumenep**, still stands. Part of it has been converted into a small museum of royal regalia. The royal tombs of Sumenep are at the **Asta Tinggi Cemetery**, 1 km outside the town. One of the princes of Sumenep was a personal friend of Stamford Raffles, and supplied much of the information which Raffles used to put together his classic *History of Java*, still selling after more than 170 years. The **Mesjid Jamik** mosque is roughly contemporary with the palace and features the graceful Hindu roof which was superseded on later Javanese mosques by the squat Arab *qubbah*. Also remarkable are the classical colonnades gracing many colonial buildings in this quiet country town.

For many, Madura seems to bear out the supposition that harsh lands produce harsh people. But others say that the Madurese of today are simply like the Javanese of old, before their courts became effete and their people deferential to the Dutch: proud, brave, vengeful, quick to anger, and fascinated by long knives. These characteristics are perhaps reflected in the Madurese approach to religion. Madura was not one of the first areas to be Islamized, but it took on the new faith with the zeal of many a late convert. In the twentieth century it has been one of the bastions of Islamic politics. Madura is undoubtedly *kasar* ("coarse"), the cultural antipode of the Javanese *kraton*. But the angular, ascetic faces and loud, aspirated speech of Madurese men nevertheless inspire wary respect on the mainland. Their unpredictable temperament is also said to render approaches to Madurese women a matter for extreme caution. This is widely regretted because Madura's beautiful daughters are the sole guardians of the secret of *goyang Madura*, an apparently indescribable lovemaking technique.

A more accessible attraction is the unique sport of bull-racing, Madura's prime tourist attraction. Pairs of massive pedigree bulls cover 130 metres in 10 seconds flat while their "jockeys" hang grimly on to light wooden sleds lashed between each pair. Honor, life and limb, and a great deal of money are at stake. The cash prizes were introduced 80 years ago by the Dutch local government in order to encourage the breeding of better stock; since then, both the bulls and the prizes have continued to get bigger. Qualifying races are held throughout the island before the October final in **Pamakesan**, the administrative capital. This tournament is a major social and cultural event, complete with *gamelan*, dancing, and armed brawls.

Madurese *batik* has a distinct style featuring highly stylized bird, fish and leaf motifs in an almost autumnal reddish-brown colour derived from tree bark. It smells different from *batik* produced elsewhere. In Madura, *batik* is exclusively a cottage industry, and all the wax is applied by hand. The main center of production is **Tanjungbumi** on the north coast. Despite its proximity to the teeming city of Surabaya, the north and interior of Madura is in every way one of the most traditional parts of western Indonesia. Outward symptoms include the *destar* headdress still worn habitually by older men, the *sarong kebaya* of the women, and the preponderance of ox- and horsecarts on the roads.

SURABAYA TO MALANG

South of Surabaya, 40 km of flat, teeming, glistening, rice-laden delta country separate the city from the mountains. Half-way across, in **Sidoarjo**, estuarine fish are farmed in brackish pools and *krupuk* (expanded rice crackers) are manufactured. A dozen workshops also make finely traced red- and white-*batik*. Surabaya's most popular resort is **Tretes**, 22 km beyond Sidoarjo on Mt. Arjuna, the volcano which, on a clear day, seems to loom over the streets of the city itself. The summit is part of the little-known **Arjuno-Lalijiwo Reserve**, with many tough and spectacular walks. Tretes is comfortable and scenic but not one of the retreats of the real elite. It features a large number of Madurese prostitutes.

In topographic make-up, East Java is more straightforward than the rest of the island. The mountains of Central Java still have something of the tangled, interlocked confusion of the Sunda highlands. But in the east, this storm of rock gives way to an even, powerful swell. Over the 400 km between Solo and the eastern tip of Java, majestic cone alternates with fertile basin in a single stately row of volcanoes, none less than 2000 m high. All have multiple peaks, but each is clearly a single massif. Each basin cradles one major town – from west to east: Solo, Madiun, Kediri, Malang, Lumajang, Jember, and finally Banyuwangi on the Bali Strait. The great oscillations of alti-

"...by the sweat of your brow" – man-made terraces. Left: Untamed nature on Java.

tude, combined with a climate much more seasonal than that of the rest of the island, make this backbone of East Java a land of predictable but nonetheless jarring extremes: heat and cold, rain and aridity, barrenness and lushness.

The historic core of East Java is not as tightly concentrated as Central Java's Magelang-Yogya-Solo arc. The old kingdoms spread and shifted over a wide area, and their remnants are scattered in a broken circle around the **Arjuna- Butak-Kelud** mountain group, which straddles the island between Surabaya and the south coast. Although there are signs of Hindu civilization in East Java from the eighth century, the area only entered the mainstream of history with the mysterious shift of power from Central Java in the early tenth century. The first kings of the East Javanese era are hazy figures and the site of their capital has never been found, but their earliest substantial monuments are in the foothills of **Mt. Arjuna**, not far from Tretes.

One of these foothills, **Gunung Penanggungan**, is of special interest, for it was regarded as a miniature of Mt. Meru, the Hindu world-mountain. Not content with creating artificial Merus in their architecture, the Hindu Javanese also sought holy mountains in their natural environment. The shape of Penanggungan, with four spurs around a central peak, rendered it especially suitable, and it still provides a dramatic and appropriate backdrop for dance performances at the **Candra Wilwatikta** open-air theater near **Pandaan**. On the slopes of Penanggungan are upwards of 80 shrines, most of them very small and weathered. The earliest, but also the most attractive and complete, are, of all things, royal bathing places. **Candi Jalatunda** and **Candi Belahan** were the tenth-century prototypes for many such elaborate *mandi* elsewhere in East Java and in Bali. Both consist of mossy tanks of eroded stone set back into sculpted hillsides –

Candi Jawi, one of the Singosari temples.

dark, magical places. At Belahan, the blessed water spouts from the nipples of the goddesses Laksmi and Sri, the wives of Vishnu. It is not known exactly what ceremonies were performed here, but a fourteenth-century text hints at erotic rites. Whatever their connotations, these bathing places were important enough to receive the ashes of kings. An urn containing ashes and gold was found during the excavation of Jalatunda. Belahan was converted in 1049 into a funerary monument for one of Java's most famous rulers, Airlangga, whose statue as Vishnu once stood between the fountain goddesses but is now in the Mojokerto Archaeological Museum.

Airlangga was a half-Balinese hermit-king who reunited East Java in 1019 after a divisive war and ruled it until his death in 1049. Before he died, however, he divided the country again by splitting his lands between his two sons. The new border line was known as the *pinggir rekso* or "guarded frontier". Running north and south from the summit of **Mt. Kelud**, it coincides with the real linguistic division between Central and East Java. The western kingdom was Kediri, centered on the town of the same name. Also known as Daha, this was at first the dominant of the two. Kediri did much for Javanese literature, but left precious few monuments. The eastern kingdom created by Airlangga was called Janggala. By the beginning of the thirteenth century it was a mere vassal of Kediri, but in 1222 a usurper called Ken Arok, who had murdered the regent of Janggala seized power in the east and founded a new dynasty which overthrew Kediri. This was **Singosari**, a name still borne by a village north of Malang. It lasted only 70 years, but it has left the richest part of East Java's monumental legacy.

Singosari Temples

One of the most complete Singosari temples, **Candi Jawi**, is not far from

Jalatunda. This is neither a Buddhist nor a Hindu shrine, but a combination of both. The foundation is Hindu, but a Buddhist stupa crowns the monument.

In the Singosari period, syncretism superseded coexistence in the relationship between the two faiths. Religious thought became less rigorous, more mystical, more emotional, more Javanese. Hinduism was now fully identified with worship of the god Shiva. And Shiva was Buddha, and the human kings were incarnations of both.

The builder of Candi Jawi, King Kertanegara (1268-92), had it house a statue of himself as a "Siwabuddha" – Shiva on one side and Buddha on the other. Almost without exception, the East Javanese temples are monuments to kings as well as deities.

As religion drifted from its Indian moorings, so did architecture, with stunning results. A far cry from the squat Indian reproductions at Dieng, Jawi is a further develpment of the free, soaring style beginning to emerge at Prambanan. Its waisted silhouette has the tropical weirdness characteristic of the East Javanese temples, projections of the unfettered Javanese imagination.

Other Singosari temples are found south of Candi Jawi in the high country around Singosari village itself. **Candi Kidal**, near Tumpang, was even more slender and spire-like than Jawi, and has paid in earthquake damage for the presumptuous skill of its architect. Kidal is currently being restored to its full 12.5 meters height.

Candi Jago, in Tumpang village, has a different form, with a high three-level base and a smaller off-set shrine building. It is most remarkable for its reliefs, executed in a two-dimensional style quite unlike the rounded realism of the Borobudur carvings, and probably influenced by the *wayang kulit* shadow puppets - more evidence of the progressive "Javanization" of Java's art. Some of the figures shown, like the grotesque *panakawan* clowns, are still popular *wayang* characters. Heads and feet are turned sideways, as in an Egyptian mural. Other panels depict the wooden architecture of the thirteenth century, so like that of modern Bali. **Candi Singosari** is almost the only visible remnant of the old capital. The last and most elaborate of the dynasty's temples, it was never quite finished. The sculptors worked from the top down, for the final detailed ornamentation is complete only on the upper parts. Disaster overcame Singosari in 1292 or 1293 when it was overthrown by a king called Jayakatwang from Kediri. A hundred meters from the temple are a pair of huge, vile *raksasa* (giant) statues which may once have stood ineffectual guard at Singosari's gate.

Malang, which has been described as the most attractive town in Java, is the natural base for exploring the Singosari temples and the mountains around them. Like the Sundalands, Malang's high valley is perfect for coffee, and the town grew up in the nineteenth century on the wealth which the government coffee system squeezed from the soil and its children. When compulsory cultivation ended, both locals and Europeans preferred to plant the tobacco and fruit for which the place is now known, while the attractiveness of the cool climate for the Dutch also kept its fortunes from flagging. Malang is hilly and varied, without the dreary, straight, shuttered main street of many towns of its size. Along with the Dutch architecture, it also seems to retain a ghost of Dutch civic discipline and concern for neatness.

Still, Malang is a Javanese town – much more purely so now than kaleidoscopic Surabaya – and something of a cultural center in its own right. *Topeng Malang*, for instance, is a special local form of the masked dance genre, enacting stories from the Panji cycle. Once one of Java's most widespread dramatic types, *wayang topeng* has retained its popularity in only two disparate geographic settings, Cirebon and Malang. In Malang it is a real folk tradition, used to celebrate marriages and circumcisions. At the **Sasono Budoyo Catholic Church** in Malang, *gamelan* music and even Javanese dance are used in services. Protestant churches in Indonesia, from the Dutch Reformed to the American Baptists, have tended to be agents of cultural assimilation; with the Catholics, the assimilation is the other way around. This tactic has certainly paid off in Java, where Catholicism has done well out of the drift to Christianity caused by the combination of government insistence upon adherence to an official religion, and widespread Javanese antipathy to rigorous Islam. Not that religious antipathies are much in evidence in Malang, where the central mosque and the Protestant church stand side by side on the main square.

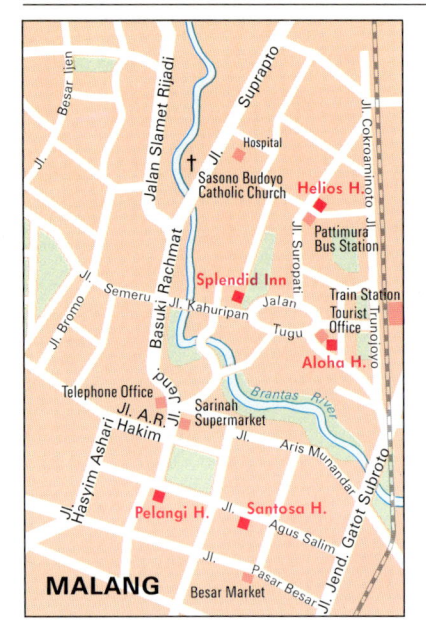

Other faded colonial idylls lie in the vicinity of Malang. **Lawang**, 18 km to the north along the main road, was even more popular than Malang as a place of retirement for Dutch civil servants and rich Chinese businessmen. Lawang's town square is probably the most attractive and tranquil in Indonesia, with grass, fountains, a restrained stone monument, and a dignified white town hall at one side. **Kebun Raya Rurwodadi**, a little further beyond Lawang, is an outstation of the national botanical gardens at Bogor. The beautifully located swimming pool and restaurant at **Selecta**, 23 km northwest of Malang via Batu, was once the very symbol of the good life which ordinary Dutchmen could aspire to in the colonies while stiff respectability and economic recession ruled at home.

Near Selecta is the source of the great **Brantas river**, Java's second river after the Solo. The Brantas rises barely 40 km from the sea, but reaches it by an extraordinary route which gives it a length of 252 km: first southeast to Malang, then down through a sharp defile to a west-east section parallel with the south coast, then back north and east via Kediri and Mojokerto to form the great delta south of Surabaya. This delta was the stage for the greatest act in Hindu Javanese history after the fall of Singosari.

MAJAPAHIT

A few months before his end the last Singosari king, Kertanegara, had the temerity to offend Kubhlai Khan, conqueror of China. Kubhlai sent an ambassador to demand Java's acknowledgement of the suzerainty of the Middle Kingdom; Kertanegara returned him with a mutilated face. By the time the inevitable punitive expedition arrived in Java, Singosari had already been sacked and the king killed by his own rebels from Kediri. But, ironically, the Chinese army was to ensure that a new and greater Javanese dynasty arose from the ashes. A son-in-law of Kertanegara, Wijaya, was devious enough to persuade the Chinese

Javanese women selling their wares in the village of Trowulan.

to help him defeat the rebel Jayakatwang. He then turned upon them and drove them back to their boats to become undisputed lord of East Java. In 1294, Wijaya founded a new capital on the delta of the Brantas, and called it **Majapahit**. The lower Brantas valley was exceptionally fertile, still rich in rice and sugar and one of the most densely populated places on earth. At the same time, access to the sea meant access to the trading wealth now represented by Surabaya. Majapahit became a great walled city of palaces, temples and canals. What remains of it is scattered over 15 square kilometers around the village of **Trowulan**.

Like other Javanese capitals, Majapahit was mostly wooden. But because even its more permanent monuments were built of red brick in place of stone, it has stood the test of time particularly badly. Much imagination is needed to picture it as it was when the court poet Prapanca described it in 1365, beautiful and unearthly as a Balinese temple but immeasurably grander and finer. The dry sump of **Segaran** was a 6-hectare pool of limpid water. In the surrounding fields were gilded pavilions where King Hayam Wuruk and his *patih* (prime minister) Gajah Mada received guests and watched tournaments and sacrifices. The gateway of **Bajang Ratu** led to the courtyard of a vanished temple, where flowering trees produced the petals which were strewn in the king's path wherever he went. **Candi Brahu** was the greatest of the city's temples, overlooking the field of Bubat where envoys from West Java once camped, bringing a Sundanese princess to be Hayam Wuruk's bride. **Candi Tikus** was a royal bathing-place.

Museum Purbakala Trowulan contains hundreds of archeological finds, including terracotta heads which look so Greek that some have speculated on European influence. One stormy masculine face has been identified, justifiably or not, as that of Gajah Mada himself, and its image graces Indonesian textbooks and even government buildings. Because Majapahit seems to have had dependencies throughout the archipelago, it is important to modern Indonesians as a historical precedent for their state. Some of the city's monuments have been more reconstructed than restored, and the army has built a huge new **Pendopo Agung** on an original foundation.

The Muslim graves at **Tralaya**, 2 km south of the site museum, have revolutionized traditional views of the history of Java. They date from 1376 onwards, and, bar one found in Trowulan itself, they are the oldest Muslim burials in Java. It used to be accepted that Islam spread from the bottom up, winning converts among traders and commoners oppressed by Hindu caste and kingship. But the Tralaya graves seem to be those of the Majapahit nobility, perhaps even members of the royal family, suggesting "top-down" Islamization. One of them still has the form of a Hindu *lingga*.

A regent of nearby **Mojokerto**, Kromodjojo Adinegoro, was responsible for the upsurge of interest in the Majapahit ruins at the beginning of this century. He founded an archaeological museum which was transferred to the government in 1912 and is still open today as the **Museum Purbakala Mojokerto**.

In what sense Majapahit "ruled" the outer islands in the fourteenth century is open to question, but it certainly ruled East Java and its kings and priests made processions around the religious sites in all parts of the land. Apart from continuing to honor Singosari shrines, they also built outlying temples of their own. **Candi Tegowangi** and **Candi Surowono** near **Pare** are both Majapahit sites. Pare is a typical East Javanese small town – so typical that it was chosen by Clifford Geertz to be immortalised under the pseudonym "Mojokuto" in his classic work *The Religion of Java*. **Museum Purbakala Tirtoyoso** in **Kediri** also has Majapahit exhibits. Kediri was the last refuge of Hindu-Javanese power during the period of Islamization. Racked by disorder after the death of Hayam Wuruk in 1389, Majapahit staggered on until hemmed in by Islamic sultanates. When the Portuguese arrived in 1512, the "pagan" state had retreated to Kediri – whether it still called itself Majapahit is not known. Fifteen years later it was conquered by Demak, ending the Hindu-Javanese era. Today Kediri is home of the clove cigarette empire, Gudang Garam.

PENATARAN

Further up the Brantas beyond Kediri, the region around **Tulungagung** and **Blitar** is rich in antiquities. The less important ones date from the Singosari period and before. **Candi Sawentar**, in the village of the same name near Blitar, is a temple like Jawi and Kidal. **Goa Selamangleng** near Sanggrahan, southeast of Tulungagung, is a hermit's cave carved with scenes of the temptation of Arjuna. But the real attraction is a Majapahit sacred site, **Penataran**. Located above Blitar on the slopes of Mt. Kelud, Penataran is East Java's largest and finest surviving temple complex.

Whereas the great monuments of Central Java seem to aim at power through mass, the emphasis at Panataran is on space. There are three wide courtyards, linked by ornamental gates and rising progressively in the direction of the mountain. Appended to the rear of the complex is a bathing place in the tradition of Jalatunda and Belahan, and another has been fully restored in nearby **Penataran village**. The main sanctuary was at the top and back, but only the foundation remains. In better condition are **Candi Naga** on the second level, with guardian serpents draped along its eaves, and the restored **Dated Temple** on the first, a perfect miniature version of Candi Jawi or Kidal. So called because an inscription

Silversmith at work with his traditional tools.

records its construction in 1369, the Dated Temple is now the emblem of the Brawijaya army division.

The stone reliefs decorating almost every surface at Penataran, including the sides of humble foundation structures, represent the highest development of that medium in East Java. As at Candi Jago, the illustrations are highly stylized. Their themes are bewilderingly various, including such curiosities as the Bubuksha-Gagang Aking story as well as the more classical Indian epics. Gagang Aking ("Dry Stalk") is a Hindu ascetic who starves his way to wisdom; his younger brother Bubukshah ("Glutton") is a Buddhist who reaches enlightenment in comfort. Less narrative iconography features animals, especially mythical ones: weird, unearthly, power-laden creatures. East Javanese art is infused with an awareness of the supernatural world behind observable phenomena.

At **Sentul**, not far outside Blitar on the way to Penataran, is Indonesia's greatest twentieth century shrine, **Makam Proklamator**. This is the tomb of Sukarno, the man whom history threw up to ride the tide of revolution and lead an apparently impossible new nation through its first, most dangerous years. Hardly known for self-effacement in his life, Sukarno nevertheless had the humility to ask to lie as a commoner in death, alongside his mother in the small town where he spent much of his youth. Or perhaps he knew he was already beyond both humility and pride? No inscription marked the simple grave, which for eight years was distinguished only by a sun-faded parasol, ancient symbol of power. Sukarno's resting place made a provocative contrast with the lavish mausoleum which his successor, Suharto, completed for himself in 1977 at the age of 56. In 1978, the events of 1965 were judged far enough past to allow Sukarno's rehabilitation as a national hero. An elaborate monument was built over the grave, and

Semeru volcano. Right: Orchards in blossom.

today it is a big and lucrative tourist destination, complete with restaurants and souvenir stands.

BROMO AND BEYOND

East Java as far as Malang has always been somewhere near the mainstream of Javanese history. Even after the coming of Islam and the return of power to Central Java, the old eastern core remained part of Mataram's *mancanegeri*, or outer domains, an important source of tribute as well as rebellion. But east of Malang was a land so remote from the world of most Javanese that they classed it with the outer islands, calling it the *tanah sebarang wetan*, the "land on the far side in the east". The Dutch later called it the *Oosthoek*, the "eastern salient". Java's eastern peninsula consists mostly of rugged mountains. There are no big cities, no ancient monuments, just wild tropical landscapes - Java in the raw.

No landscape is rawer than that of the famous **Mt. Bromo**. At 2,392 m, Bromo itself is actually the smallest of three peaks rising from the center of a vast extinct crater, the **Tengger** caldera. Over the last two centuries, Bromo's mouth has alternated between crater lake and gaping vent; today, unlike its two neighbors, it is active. The volcano-within-volcano configuration is like Mt. Batur in Bali, but while Batur has a blue lake at its foot, Bromo has a sea of sand. Not for nothing is Bromo East Java's most popular tourist destination. The view into the volcano's maw is as humbling as anything in nature, and the landscapes of the Sand Sea are like the end of the world, or the beginning. The scale of the outer caldera is such that visitors feel like ants in the ruins of a cathedral. Bromo is usually ascended before dawn, on horseback or on foot, from the village of **Ngadisari**. An alternative route begins at the old Dutch health resort of **Tosari**.

Bromo is the holy mountain of the remarkable Tenggerese, a 60,000-strong ethnic group native to the surrounding **Tengger Highlands**. Once a year they gather for a ceremony of appeasement on the razor-sharp rim of the mountain, hurling fruit, vegetables and flowers into the steam below. At one time it was a human sacrifice which was cast into the fire. The Tenggerese are not Muslims, but the last surviving fragment of the culture of Majapahit. Hayam Wuruk himself exempted the Tengger villages from tax and ordered them to worship Bromo (Brahma); six centuries later, they are still fulfilling their obligation. The Tenggerese retain a pre-Muslim calendar, and their priests or *dukun* possess beakers engraved with zodiac signs and fourteenth-century dates. Rice will not grow well in the cool, high air, and the main crops of the Tenggerese are maize, onions, carrots and cauliflower. Until recently they built wooden longhouses unlike any other dwellings in Java; now they live in tin-roofed shacks.

Vast as it is, Tengger is only part of the massif separating Malang from the next valley to the east. The southern part is formed by the perfect cone of **Mt. Semeru**, at 3676 m the highest mountain in Java. Also called Mahameru, this is the island's definitive Meru or world-mountain. The rest of Java's mountains are supposed to have been pieces which crumbled from Semeru when the gods fumbled its transplantation from the Himalayas. The anomaly of a second Meru at Mt. Penanggungan near Pandaan (see above) is explained by the circumstance that the top of Semeru was also lost in flight and fell to form the smaller mountain. Semeru is more or less continuously active and has caused considerable devastation at times; ash from the eruption of 1911 fell even on Bali.

The north coast of the *Oosthoek* is an unexciting stretch of ricefields and mangrove forests, interrupted only by the sands of **Pasir Putih**, a beach resort near **Situbondo**. The coastal population is made up almost entirely of Madurese, who have come here through history as soldiers, traders, plantation laborers and farming settlers. The Madurese in **Bondowoso** have developed a new sport for their favorite animal: bull fighting. This is bloodier for the bulls than the racing practiced on the home island, but not so dangerous to human life: bull fights bull, not matador.

The Madurese were able to make much of this part of Java their own because of the repeated wars which swept and depopulated the area during the seventeenth and eighteenth centuries. **Blambangan**, a name which now refers only to a small peninsula in the far southeast, was once a powerful Hindu kingdom extending westwards as far as Mt. Bromo. But caught between expansive empires to the west and their stubborn Balinese enemies to the east, Blambangan could not maintain a stable independence. It became a no man's land where bandits and refugees built precarious kingdoms between

Woman cutting bananas in East Java.

the power blocks. Sultan Agung conquered Blambangan in 1639, but, unable to hold it permanently against the Balinese, he decided to transport as much as possible of its population to Central Java as slaves. In 1697 the reformed kingdom was conquered again by the ex-slave Surapati, arch-enemy of the VOC. Amid the chaos, Blambangan retained the Hindu religion, and in fact has the distinction of being the last major region of Java to do so. Uniquely, it was the Dutch who ensured its ultimate Islamization, sponsoring two Muslim princes as rulers of Blambangan in order to reduce Balinese influence there; but nevertheless they had to fight a war in 1771-2 to have their way.

Today, almost the only remnant of Blambangan is the Balinized dialect spoken by the 400,000 *Osing* people who live around **Banyuwangi** on the Bali Strait. Until 1881, Banyuwangi was the base from which the Dutch handled all relations with Bali and Lombok, then still independent. In 1920, it was still a substantial port, exporting bananas and copra to Australia. Coconut trees still line the coast, and the incongruous place name of **Glenmore**, on the road from Banyuwangi to Jember, is a reminder of the international plantation investors which the lowlands here once drew. The ferry to Bali now leaves from **Ketapang**, 8 km north of Banyuwangi, but the older port remains a common stopover for inter-island travelers.

Behind Banyuwangi the land sweeps upwards towards the **Ijen Plateau**, the dead crater of Java's easternmost volcanic massif. Like Tengger, Ijen now contains several sub-craters, of which **Kawah Ijen**, by virtue of its periodic activity and spectacular appearance, is the best known. The sheer walls of this crater enclose an eerie lake of opaque, milky green water from which a bitter river springs. Several thousand people live on the Ijen Plateau. Some hunt across the

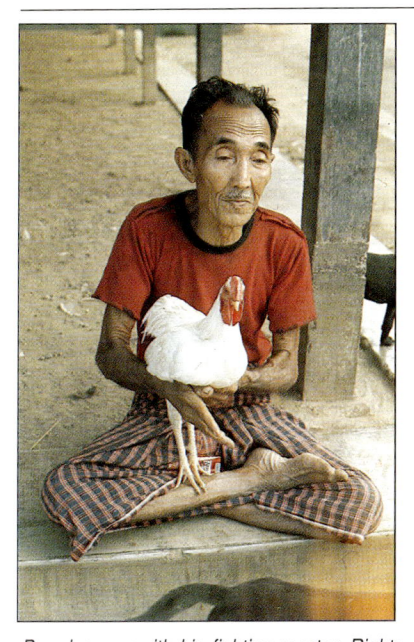

Proud owner with his fighting rooster. Right: Traditional dance on Madura.

peaks for volcanic sulphur, which they collect with hand tools like the medieval miners of Europe; oil refineries and fertilizer plants will buy the acid just the same. Others plant and pick coffee, exactly as it was done a century ago in the mountains of West Java.

In some ways, the eastern tip of Java is remarkably like the western tip. Sparsely populated and wild, both have served as refuges for threatened wildlife as the advancing ploughs and chainsaws have driven the wilderness back to the extremities of the island. The environments are, however, very different. **Baluran National Park**, on the northeast tip of the *Oosthoek*, gets no more rain each year than parts of England, and much less evenly distributed. In the dry season (April to October), much of it is like an African savannah, with crackling dry grass and herds of *banteng* and deer gathering warily around the waterholes. Baluran reserve also encompasses other environments including vast mangrove swamp and upland forest.

Banyuwangi Selatan Reserve is a newer park on Blambangan peninsula, the cartographic mirror-image of West Java's Ujung Kulon. Its protected fauna includes the *ajak*, a wild dog once universal in Java but ruthlessly hunted by farmers. **Plengkung**, at the point of Grajangan Bay on the west side of the peninsula, is said to offer the best surfing waves in Indonesia.

Meru Betiri Reserve, on a remote section of the south coast which can be unreachable in the wet season, was set up in 1972 to protect the last few tigers on Java. This is one of the most unspoiled places on the island. Only the coffee and rubber plantation at **Sukomade**, itself a remnant of pre-war Java, intrudes upon a wilderness where turtles breed on the beaches and hornbills in the trees. But despite World Wildlife Fund, the reserve has failed in its primary goal: the Javanese tiger is gone forever.

SURABAYA
Accommodation
INEXPENSIVE: Gubeng Station area – **Bamboe Denn**, Jl Pemuda 18, Tel: 40333. **Wisma Ganesha**, Jl Sumatra 34; **Gubeng**, Jl Sumatra 18. **Santosa**, Jl Embong Kenongo 40, Tel: 43306. Elsewhere: **Olympic**, Jl Urip Sumarharjo 65. **Stasiun**, Jl Stasiun Kota 1; **Pavilyun**, Jl Genteng Besar 98. *MODERATE:* Gubeng Station area – **Bina Dirga Angkasa**, Jl Embong Kenongo 52, Tel: 42687. **Remaja**, Jl Embong Kenongo 12, Tel: 41359. **Royal**, Jl Panglima Sudirman 68, Tel: 43547-8. **Wisma Mawarani**, Jl Embong Kenongo 73, Tel: 44839. Elsewhere: **Kalimantan**, Jl Pegirian 202A. *LUXURY:* **Elmi**, Jl Panglima Sudirman 42-44, Tel: 475150-8. **Garden**, Jl Pemuda 21, Tel: 470000. **Garden Palace**, Jl Jos Sudarso 11, Tel: 479251. **Hyatt Bumi Surabaya**, Jl Basuki Rachmat 124-128, Tel: 470875. **Majapahit**, Jl Tunjangan 65, Tel: 43351. **Mirama**, Jl Raya Darmo 68, Tel: 69501.

Shopping
Jl Tunjungan/Jl Basuki Rachmat is main shopping street. *ANTIQUES & HANDICRAFTS:* concentrated on Jl Tunjungan (incl 3rd floor of **Pasar Tunjungan Surya**), around Bumi Hyatt hotel. Also on Jl Raya Darmo (**Bangun**, no. 5, **Rokhim**, no. 27, **Whisnu**, no. 68-74).

Museums & Zoos
Museum Angkatan 45 (military), Jl May Jen Sungkono. **Loka Jala Srana Naval Museum**, Kompleks AAL Morokrembangan, Tel: 291092 ext 440. Mon-Wed 8.00-13.00, Fri 8.00-10.00, Sat 8.00-12.00, Sun closed. **Museum 'Mpu Tantular'** (East Java Provincial Museum), Jl Taman Mayangkara 6, Tel: 67037. Tue-Thu 8.00-13.00, Fri 8.00-10.00, Sat 8.00-12.00, Sun 9.00-14.00, Mon closed. **East Java Art Museum**, Jl Pemuda 3, Tel: 45608. Mon-Thu 9.00-12.00, Fri 9.00-10.00, Sat 9.00-11.00, Sun closed. **Surabaya Zoo**, Jl Setail 1, Surabaya. Daily 7.00-18.00.

Cultural performances
Taman Hiburan Rakyat (THR, People's Amusement Park), Jl Kusuma Bangsa, - various drama nightly from 20.00. **Taman Budaya**, Jl Genteng Kali 85, for higher-brow culture & music starting 20.00; morning rehearsals often open to public too. **Candra Wilwatikta Open Air Theatre**, Pandaan, stages *sendratari* dance on 1st & 3rd Sat of each month Jun-Nov.

Tourist Information / Post office
East Java prov. tourist office, Jl Pemuda 118, Tel: 472503. Mon-Thu 7.00-1400, Fri 7.30-11.00, Sat 7.30-12.30. **Post office:** Jl Kebon Rojo (near Tugu Pahlawan), Mon-Fri 8.00-16.00, Sat 8.00-12.30. Branch office Jl Pemuda.

Transport
AIR: Important domestic air transport hub, flights to most Indon. cities. **Juanda Airport** is 15 km S of town; taxis are sole link. Airline offices: **Garuda**, Jl Tunjungan 29, Tel: 44082; **Merpati**, Jl Urip Sumoharjo 68, Tel: 406481; **Mandala**, Jl Raya Darmo 109, Tel: 66861; **Bouraq**, Jl P Sudirman 70-72, Tel: 46428.

SEA: Many departures daily from **Tanjung Perak** & adjacent **Kalimas** harbour. **Pelni** office: Jl Pahlawan 20, Tel: 21041, open Mon-Fri 8.00-12.00/13.00-16.00, Sat 8.00-13.00. Ferry for Madura leaves from Ujung Baru in Tanjung Perak, or catch bus direct from Joyoboyo terminal (see below).

RAIL: 3 stations. **Pasar Turi** handles services to Jakarta via Semarang. **Kota** (alias **Semut**) & **Gubeng** are terminals for inland route W (via Solo, Yogya & Bandung) and for Malang & Banyuwangi. Some trains arriving at Gubeng continue to Kota. Surabaya is unavoidable transfer point for rail passengers for Bali; Bali fares include ferry & road transfer Banyuwangi-Denpasar.

ROAD: 3 main bus stations. **Jembatan Merah** for N coast towns from Gresik to Semarang. **Joyoboyo**, S edge of city, for rest of E Java (incl Madura) & Solo. **Bratang** station, 3 km E of Joyoboyo, handles really long-distance buses (Jakarta, Bali etc). Some bus cos have offices on lanes off Jl Basuki Rachmat.

INTERNAL: **Taxi Cab Surya**, Jl Kranggan 100, Tel: 471340, has metered taxis. Very dense and regular *bemo* network. Main terminals: **Jembatan Merah** (beside intercity buses) & **Wonokromo**, near Joyoboyo bus station. Larger *bis kota* also do some routes inside town.

MADURA
SUMENEP: *INEXPENSIVE:* **Losmen Damai**, Jl Jen Sudirman 39, or **Losmen Matahari**, Jl Jen Sudirman 42. **Wijaya I**, Jl Trunojoyo 45-47, is pricier. Street food on *alun-alun* in evening.
RESTAURANTS: **17 Augustus**, Jl Diponegoro. **Nasi Burung**, Jl Trunojoyo; for Chinese food, **Mawar**, Jl Diponegoro 47A. *SHOPPING:* **Mustika Kempang**, Jl Trunojoyo 78, for *batik*. **A Ba'bud**, Jl A Yani, for crafts & antiques. *MUSEUMS:* **Museum Daerah Bangkalan**, Jl Letnan Abdullah 1, Bangkalan. Mon-Thu 8.00-12.00, Fri 8.00-10.00, Sat 8.00-11.00. **Museum Pemerintah Daerah Tingkat II Sumenep**, Jl Dr Sutomo, Sumenep. Mon-Thu 7.00-14.00, Fri 7.00-11.00, Sat 7.00-13.30.

MALANG
INEXPENSIVE: **Bamboo Denn**, Jl Semeru 35, Tel: 24859. **Helios**, Jl Pattimura. **Losmen Menara**, Jl Pajajaran 5, Tel: 22871. **Santosa**, Jl

GUIDEPOST EAST JAVA

KH Agus Salim 24, Tel: 23889.
MODERATE: **Aloha**, Jl Gajah Mada 7, Tel: 26. **Pelangi**, Jl Merdeka Selatan 3, Tel: 27456. **Splendid Inn**, Jl Majapahit 4, Tel: 23860. **YMCA**, Jl Basuki Rachmat 68-76, Tel: 23605.

Shopping
BATIK: **Wisma Batik** (Danar Hadi), Jl Basuki Rachmat. *ANTIQUES & CURIOS:* Several stores on Jl Basuki Rachmat; also try **Pasar Besar** market, Jl Pasar Besar. *OTHER:* **Pasar Burung** (bird market), Jl Tjembaran.

Tourist Information / Post / Medical
Tourist Office, Jl Tugu (beside town hall). Mon-Thu 7.00-14.00, Fri-Sat 7.00-11.00. **Post office:** Jl Agus Salim, S side of town square. **Teleph. office:** Jl Basuki Rachmat. **Medical**: Big practice at Jl Kawi 13; **Hospital** on Jl Suprapto.

Transport
AIR: Only **Merpati** flies to Malang. Merpati office, Jl Jagung Suprapto 50, Tel: 27962; own taxi service to airport. Flights to most Java cities & some Bali/Nusatenggara airports.
RAIL: Trains to Surabaya or once a day direct to Solo, Yogya & Jakarta via Blitar & Kediri.
ROAD: **Sawahan** minibus station for Surabaya, Batu, Blitar (for Penataran temple) & most destinations. **Pattimura** in NE of town handles long-distance buses, though some may leave from **Gadang** & **Dinoyo** terminals out of town.
INTERNAL: **Pattimura Station**, Jl Pattimura, is *bemo* hub.

MAJAPAHIT
TROWULAN: No *losmen* in Trowulan; visitors wanting to be closer than Surabaya stay in **Jombang** (eg **Losmen Melati**, Jl Pang Sudirman 63). **MOJOKERTO:** Cheap accommodation at **Losmen Merdeka**, Jl Pramuji 73. **Penginapan Mutiara**, Jl Setia Mulio, & **Losmen Nagamas**, Jl Pahlawan 23. **Sriwijaya** (Jl Desa Pacot, Tel: 12/9) is more expensive.
ARCHAEOLOGICAL MUSEUMS: **Museum Purbakala Mojokerto**, Jl Ahmad Yani 14. Tue-Sat 7.00-13.00, Mon closed. **Museum Purbakala Trowulan**, Jl Mojokerto 349, Mojokerto, Tel: 544. Tue-Sun 7.00-16.00, Mon closed. **Museum Purbakala Tirtoyoso**, Jl Jen A Yani, Kediri. Mon-Wed 8.00-13.00, Fri 8.00-1100, Thu/Sat/Sun closed. **Museum Balai Penyelamatan Arkeologi**, Jl Syodanco Soeprijadi 40, Blitar, Tel: 81365. Sun-Thu 7.00-13.00, Fri 7.00-11.00, Sat 7.00-12.00.

MOUNT BROMO
Via **Ngadisari:** Leave North coast road at **Probolinggo**, catching minibus to **Sukapura** or if possible **Ngadisari**; both have simple accommodation. From Ngadisari, 3 km walk to **Cemoro Lawang** on caldera lip, 2 more hrs on foot or 1 hrs by hired pony to Bromo summit. Only accommodation above Ngadi sari is medium-priced **Bromo Permai Hotel** at Cemoro Lawang – book in Probolinggo, Jl Raya Panglima Sudirman 237-242, Tel: 21510/21983.
Via **Tosari:** Bus inland from **Pasuruan**, then overnight at **Tosari**. From Tosari, 2 hrs to rim and another 2 to Bromo. Guide advisable.

MOUNT SEMERU
Usual approach is from Malang by minibus via **Tumpang** & **Gubuklakah** to **Ngadas**, then on foot via Rano Pani (where guides available) & Rano Kumbolo. Very strenuous, requires full camping equipment, food & water.

BANYUWANGI
INEXPENSIVE: **Baru**, Jl Pattimura 82-84, Tel: 21369. **Bhakti**, Jl Jen Sudirman 117, Tel: 21129. **Wisma Blambangan**, Jl Dr Wahidin 3, Tel: 21598. *MODERATE:* **Banyuwangi**, Jl Dr Wahidin 10, Tel: 41178. At **KETAPANG: Manyar**, Jl Situbondo.

Museums
Museum Daerah Blambangan Banyuwangi, Jl Sri Tanjung 1, Banyuwangi. Mon-Thu 7.00-13.00, Fri 7.00-10.30, Sat 7.00-12.30.

Tourist information
Jl Diponegoro 2, Tel: 41761.

Transport
SEA: Ferries leave for Bali from 2 terminals at Ketapang, 8 km N of town, at least 12 times daily.
RAIL: Banyuwangi station is easternmost terminus of Java's rail system: trains run to and from Yogya & Surabaya.
ROAD: 3 bus stations. For Blambangan & the S, **Terminal Brawijaya** in the S. For Ijen Plateau, **Terminal Banjarsari** in the W. For Surabaya & the N, **Terminal Blambangan** on Ketapang Rd.

EASTERN NATURE RESERVES
Conservation Office (PHPA) at Jl A Yani 108 in Banyuwangi, Tel: 41119, issues entry permits, although permits for Baluran also available in **Wonorejo** near reserve turn-off. **BALURAN:** park entrance is at Batangan, 37 km N of Banyuwangi. HQ at Bekol, 12 km inside park. Bamma Guesthouse here must be booked in advance at PHPA. **BLAMBANGAN** *(Banyuwangi Selatan):* No roads South of Grajangan, 52 km from Banyuwangi by road. Surfing camp & park interior must be reached on foot or by boat from Grajangan or direct from Bali. **MERU BETIRI:** Access along dirt roads from Genteng (via Pasanggaran) or from Glenmore. Accommodation at Wisma Sukomade in Sukomade estate or at the PHPA Resthouse at Rajegwesi.

BALI

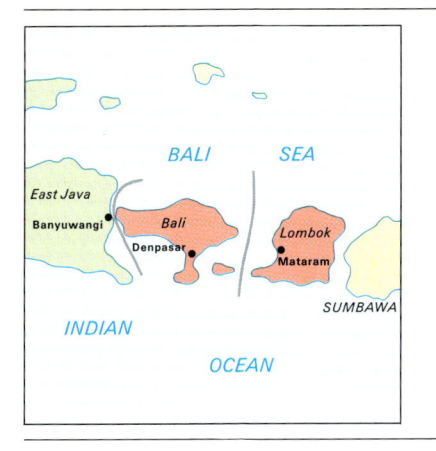

BALI / LOMBOK

DENPASAR
SANUR AND KUTA
BALINESE HEARTLAND
UBUD
THE MOUNTAINS
NORTH COAST
KARANGASEM
LOMBOK

DENPASAR

Denpasar is Bali's "big city", the valve through which the power and culture of Jakarta enters this most self-contained and self-assured of dominions. Here are the lurid cinemas, the deafening, sugary made-in-Indonesia pop music, the ubiquitous government signboards, the antnest *bemo* terminals of urban Java. But glimpses of an older Balinese Denpasar still gleam through. And even in Bali, culture and art at the highest level need the patronage of the state, so like other provincial capitals, Denpasar is not without its contemporary highbrow interest.

The local name for Denpasar is **Badung**. Before its colonial conquest, Badung was one of the richest and most powerful of the Balinese kingdoms. Its fertile territories stretched northwards as far as Lake Bratan in the central mountains. The very old but restored temple of **Pura Maospahit** is one of the few surviving remnants of the town's pre-Dutch history. The name refers to the Javanese dynasty of Majapahit, from which all Balinese royalty claim descent. Although the first Dutchmen set foot on Bali as early as 1597, the island offered few in-

Left: For the eyes and palate: women carrying Balinese delights.

ternational trade products, and hence never fell within the deadly sights of the Company. In the 19th century, diplomatic relations were established and north and east Bali forced to become Dutch vassals, but most of the southern kingdoms remained independent. By the beginning of the 20th century, however, the colonial government stepped up its imperialist claims, and Badung was the first to learn how radically the military balance had changed. The issue of a plundered wreck provided a pretext for war, and in 1906 the **Main Square** of Denpasar became the site of one of the most tragic and poignant events in Indonesian history. Realizing that they had no chance of victory, the Balinese elected to make an honorable end to the dynasty on earth and rebuild it together in heaven. Armed only with spears and *kris*, they marched towards the Dutch lines. The king, his family, and hundreds of his subjects were mown down by repeater rifles.

After this sad beginning, the Dutch governed Bali with restraint. Roads were built, slavery and widow-burning banned; but planters and businessmen, and for a long time missionaries too, were deliberately excluded from the island as threats to its cultural identity – and its political stability. Denpasar was rehabilitated as an administrative center. The

DENPASAR

Puri Pemecutan palace, destroyed in 1906, was rebuilt in authentic style in 1907; it is now used as a hotel. The **Bali Museum**, on the square, was set up by a museum society in 1931 to present the archaeological and artistic wealth of an island then only just emerging from centuries of isolation and oblivion. Today it exhibits contemporary tools and handicrafts as well as dance costumes and ancient artefacts and sculptures. The architecture of the museum buildings includes imitations of temple and palace styles from all regions of the island.

In 1945, Denpasar succeeded Singaraja as the governmental capital of the whole island. Though most of the Balinese rajas accepted the authority of the revolutionary republic, Bali was quickly back in Dutch hands and in 1946 Denpasar hosted the conference at which the federal "State of East Indonesia" was called into being. Reunited with the republic after independence, Denpasar was not spared a typical trapping of this period, Sukarnoism: a triple life-size piece of social realism in bronze still commands the main square. But the state has also sponsored the development of indigenous Balinese arts, a lucrative national resource as well as a unique cultural phenomenon. **Kokar**, the state academy for instrumental and performing arts, established in 1960, trains musicians and dancers. Rehearsals are open to the public. The newer **Abian Kapas Arts Centre** is an extravagant example of "traditional modern" Balinese architecture.

The **Pura Jagatnata** state temple next door to the museum is another interesting modern building. Unusually, this temple is dedicated to Sang Hyang Widi, worshipped here as the Balinese supreme being, the highest god. Sang Hyang Widi is undoubtedly a genuine original feature of Bali's complex, multi-faceted religion, appearing on old manuscripts as a strange, small white figure with a three-pronged penis and flames shooting from his joints. But in pre-war Bali he only played a small role in popular ceremony and temple ritual. The holiest shrines, if dedicated to a specific deity at all, were for Shiva of the Hindu trinity, or Surya, the sun god. Popular religion was robustly polytheistic. The change in emphasis has to do with external pressures upon Bali since independence. In modern Indonesia, polytheism is neither intellectually nor politically respectable. As a state-sponsored religion, Balinese Hinduism has to toe the *Pancasila* line and worship an explicit highest god.

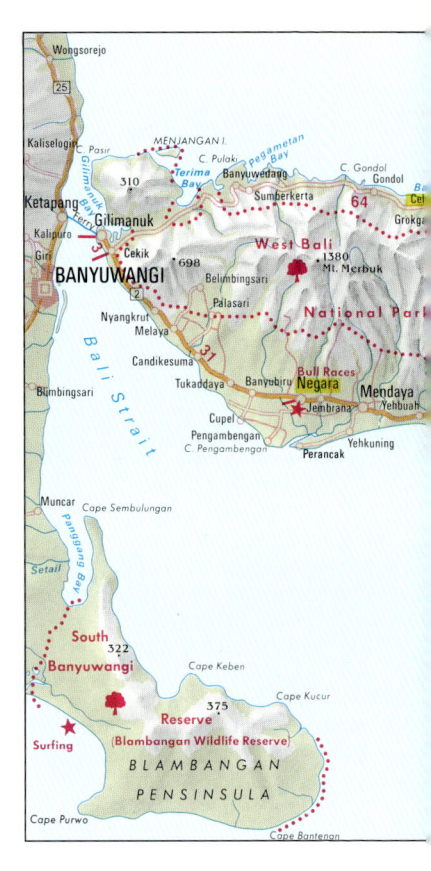

Modern Bali tourism began in Denpasar. Before the war, the Bali Hotel, known today as the **Natour Bali Hotel**, used to cater to Dutch vacationers and well-heeled world-travelers. At that time, however, the town still lay out of reach of the transport arteries of the Indies. The south of Bali had no port suitable for large vessels; visitors disembarked from their steamers at Singaraja on the north coast, and traveled to Denpasar overland. All this changed with the jet age and the opening of the **Ngurah Rai International Airport** just 12 km south of the city center. The world came to Denpasar - but soon learned to pass it over. At first, everyone stayed in the town and traveled to the sea or the mountains during the day. But as Denpasar grew busier, noisier and less like the paradise people expected of Bali, an exodus began to new resorts that sprang up on the beaches themselves.

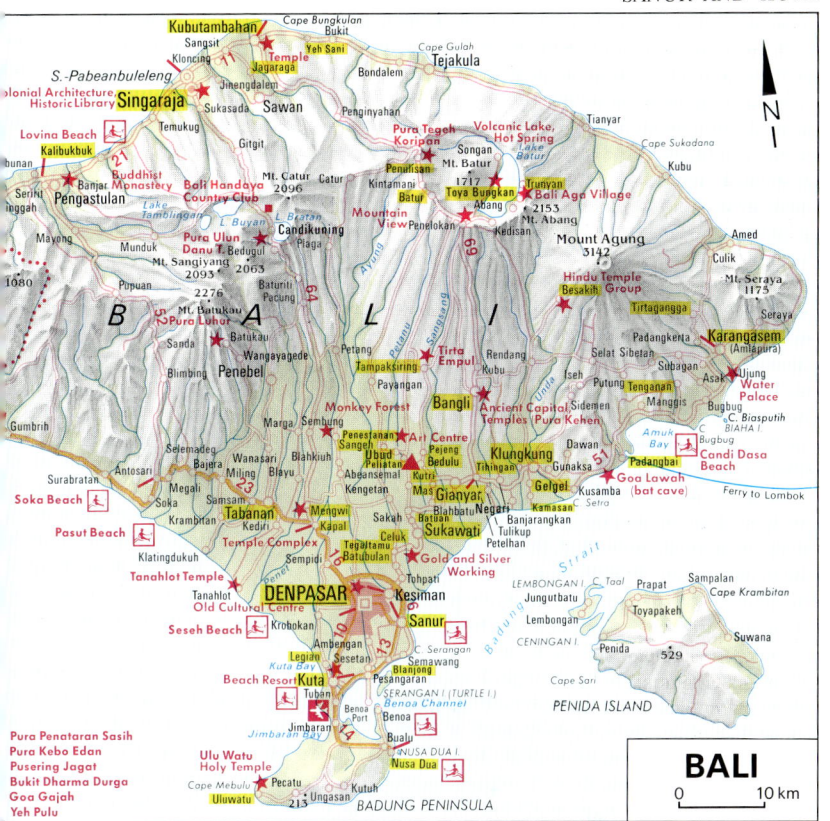

SANUR AND KUTA BEACH

The lotus-eaters have settled on almost all of the sandy coasts south of Denpasar, on both sides of the sinuous southern tip of Bali. This is where the overwhelming majority of Bali's visitors are "deplaned", accommodated, sunned, massaged, intoxicated, lightly edified by suitably abridged cultural performances, and put back on board when their time or their money run out.

Even in dreamland, money is real, and the neighborhoods are divided by class. Broadly speaking, the east coast is for the well-to-do, the west is for the budget crowd. **Sanur Beach**, the closest to Denpasar, is in the first category. Here stand

SANUR AND KUTA

the **Bali Hyatt** and its ilk. In the 1930s, quiet Sanur was the home of some of the European intellectuals who anticipated and inspired the West's love affair with Bali. The beachside house of one of them, the Belgian painter Le Mayeur, has been converted into the **Museum Le Mayeur**, with displays of his works. Today it is squeezed in between two big hotels, one of which, the **Bali Beach Hotel**, is the island's only skyscraper. After its completion in the 1960s, the gruesome prospect of a Balinese Miami Beach growing out of the sand prompted the authorities to enact a far-sighted law prohibiting new buildings "above the height of a palm tree".

Sanur is a very old port. At **Blanjong**, a short distance inland, an inscribed pillar records the victories of a tenth century king over unidentified enemies. Discovered in 1932, the inscription is written in Sanskrit and Old Balinese and dated 914. Contrary to common belief, Indian civilisation had already established itself on Bali long before the reign of Majapahit. On nearby **Serangan Island**, on the other hand, **Pura Sakenan** has Bali's closest approximation to a Javanese *candi*. Elsewhere on this island lives a colony of Bugis sailors from South Celebes.

More Sanur than Sanur is the **Nusa Dua** luxury beach resort on the **Bukit peninsula**, which hangs like a bulbous pendulum from the southern tip of Bali. Created with the help of the World Bank in 1970, Nusa Dua is a beautiful, isolated reserve for the rich. Most of the rest of the peninsula is a barren limestone plateau edged by spectacular cliffs falling sheer to the sea. Perched on the westernmost headland is one of Bali's most important sea temples, the beautiful **Ulu Watu**. Nirartha, a Brahmin saint who sought refuge in Bali after the fall of Majapahit in Java, is said to have achieved *moksa* – miraculous union with the godhead – in this temple.

Kuta, the bargain basement beach, has given its name to a whole rag-tag culture of surfboards and *batik* shorts, ramshackle *losmen* and rickety motorbikes, *nasi goreng* and yoghurt, rice wine and marijuana.

Kuta faces west and offers stunning ocean sunsets nightly, as does its slightly more up-market northern extension, **Legian**. Since its discovery by surfers in the early 1970s, Kuta has become the liveliest and most popular tourist destination in Indonesia. Blissfully devoid of historical interest, it lives in an eternal present of sea, sweat and music. Everything is for sale on its toyland streets, from the classiest fashion in southeast Asia to the tackiest souvenirs. Even the bodies of Balinese boys are for sale, and find plenty of takers among Australia's fine daughters.

At the south end of Kuta beach, the main runway of Ngurah Rai juts out into the sea, and 747s full of holidaymakers pass gracefully over the heads of beachcombers. Those bemused by Kuta may find this an apt place to ponder its absurdities.

Bali's southern playground is changing very fast, and it is not easy to know what will become of it. Though there will always be cheap *losmen* in Kuta, the raw, young, ragged, wide-eyed, world-smitten, outcast travellers' scene of old is rapidly passing away. In its place are hard-headed, young, one-season gypsies getting their tropical rites of passage for their money before going on to be secretaries or stockbrokers in London or Munich.

Though air-conditioned French restaurants are in Sanur to stay, the real rich no longer set the tone; in fact, they have adopted much of the lightweight, rice-eating, technicolor lifestyle of the backpackers. Though sometimes dismissed as Australia's Costa del Sol, tourist Bali remains a multifarious, shocking, inventive, endlessly cosmopolitan place.

Right: Balinese religion still lives on.

THE BALINESE HEARTLAND

The heartland of Balinese culture is only a few kilometers from Kuta beach, in the compact foothills of the mountains above Denpasar. The outside world loves Bali's warm seas, but for the Balinese themselves salt water carries connotations of departure and death; they have never been a seafaring people. Theirs is a terrestrial, agrarian civilisation, nurtured and tended along with the emerald rice on the terraced slopes which rise, first gently, then dramatically, towards the north. A rim of volcanic mountains forms a snug little amphitheater, a forcing house for the cultivation of a singular, exotic culture. The volcanic soil is fertile, and countless streams provide constant water for irrigation. Some 80% of Bali's population live in this semicircular bowl, and six of the nine states of old Bali had their capitals here, each claiming a long, narrow strip of land between the mountains and the sea.

A highly developed system of agricultural management based on the *subak*, a sort of traditional irrigation cooperative, allows the Balinese to devote much of their time to the sacramental art and ceremony which seem to dominate their lives and their society. There are ceremonies for everything: to mark events in the life-cycle and the agricultural cycle; to propitiate gods and spirits good, bad and indifferent; to expel evil from a person, a village or the whole island; to commemorate the foundation of a house, a palace or a temple. There are celebrations for which the celebrants themselves disagree on the reason. In the past, there was yet another stratum of ceremonial, now largely vanished, for maintaining the theatrical pomp of the royal courts. The development of Bali's massive artistic wealth was tied up with its need for ritual music, dance, decoration and architecture all of them reaching their highest development in the southern piedmont area.

High above the sea – the temple of Ulu Watu.

The most striking and ubiquitously tangible manifestations of Balinese culture are the temples. They are the means by which the Balinese leave their cultural imprint upon the landscape as does no other people in Indonesia. Even in the most historic parts of Java, graceful buildings are few and far between, but the hills of south-central Bali are encrusted with 15,000 temples. Each village must have at least three for different ritual purposes, and there are many more corresponding to other social communities both smaller and larger than the village, including some which are of significance to everyone on the island. Nothing contributes more to Bali's unearthly beauty than this forest of tiered *meru* towers, carved gateways, roofed shrines and guardian statues. Like Penataran in East Java, the temples of Bali are not stone masses but spacious walled compounds enclosing various wooden and brick structures. The "split gate" (*candi bentar*) which usually serves as an entrance has become a symbol of the island and of Indonesia as a whole: a giant reproduction of one greets entering Jakarta on the road from Cengkareng airport.

Lovely though they are, not many of the temples are very old. Some deliberately sham antiquity: a new one at **Tegaltamu**, just beyond **Batubulan** on the main road out of Denpasar, features eleventh-century reliefs copied by their sculptor from an archaeology textbook. However, a concentration of genuine antiquities can be found in the district of **Pejeng**, between the **Petanu** and **Pakerisan** rivers. This seems to have been the center of Hindu civilisation in Bali before the coming of Majapahit. Until recently, the Balinese regarded this period as a dark and barbarous age; traditionally, the true history of Bali begins with the East Javanese administration and clergy installed by Gajah Mada after the invasion of 1343. The last independent king is remembered as a pig-headed monster.

Nevertheless, **Pura Penataran Sasih**, the central temple of the old Pejeng kingdom, is still venerated. Penataran Sasih is famous for the sacred drum known as the **Pejeng Moon** kept in an elevated pavilion at the rear of the temple. This is a man-sized all-metal kettledrum of a type first developed by the Dong-son culture of northern Vietnam in the first millenium before Christ. It may have been cast in Bali, in which case it is the largest and finest surviving artefact of the early Indonesian metal age.

The drum is moulded in one piece and expertly decorated with staring faces and geometric designs. Possibly 1000 years older than the temple itself, the Pejeng Moon derives its name from a Balinese account of its origin, which portrays it as a fallen celestial body, unrelated to human history. When the first Dutchman climbed up to examine and measure it in 1906, the locals professed amazement that he came back down alive.

Near Penataran Sasih, the small compound of **Pura Kebo Edan** contains a 3.6 m statue known as the **Pejeng Giant**. The remarkable protuberances on the dancing giant's penis have often been interpreted as indications of his miraculous powers. But there is a more realistic explanation: the use of one or more "penis pins", inserted through the organ at right angles and secured with knobs on both sides, was widespread in pre-Hindu Indonesia and current until very recently in Borneo. Such pins increased female sexual pleasure and their insertion provided a formidable initiation rite for the male.

The name of **Pusering Jagat** ("Navel of the World"), another temple nearby, recalls the former importance of the Pejeng area for the whole of Bali. This temple houses the so-called **Pejeng Vessel**, an intricately engraved stone container for holy water bearing a chronogram indicating the date 1329. Water is central to Balinese religious practice; indeed, the whole religion is sometimes called *ag-ama tirtha*, "holy water religion". The water formerly held in the Pejeng Vessel represented *amerta*, the elixir of immortality which the Hindu gods produced by churning the primeval ocean. **Bukit Dharma Durga**, south-east of Pejeng near the village of **Kutri**, is the site of another fine historical relic, a statue of the six-armed Hindu goddess Durga standing on the slain demon bull. Unusually fluid and lifelike, this is probably a posthumous image of the tenth century Balinese queen who was the mother of Airlangga, the first great ruler of East Java.

The best-known of all the Pejeng antiquities is **Goa Gajah** or "Elephant Cave", near Bedulu. A whole rock face has been chiselled into a baroque frieze of fantastic plants and animals; the cave itself forms the gaping mouth of a mad-eyed demon, which was mistaken for the eponymous elephant when the site was rediscovered in 1923. This strange monument was probably a hermitage for eleventh century priests. Few would describe Goa Gajah as beautiful, but it is certainly striking and contains some splendid workmanship. A Balinese, it is said, likes threatening temple decorations; the ugly faces repel any dangerous powers and make him feel safe. The elaborate bathing place below the cave was excavated as recently as 1954. The resemblance to Belahan in East Java suggested by the nymph-shaped spouts is not accidental, but a result of early dynastic links. **Yeh Pulu**, one kilometer from Goa Gajah between the Petanu and Jurang rivers, is an enigmatic giant rock relief, 2 m high and 25 m long. It has no parallels in Indonesia but is thought to date from after the Majapahit conquest. The **Museum Purbakala Gedung Arca** north of Bedulu offers a synopsis of the rich archaeology of the Pejeng area.

The most striking of Bali's pre-Majapahit monuments, however, stands a few kilometers further where the valley of Pakerisan becomes a steep ravine cut-

Entrance to the cave temple of Goa Gajah.

ting into the rising flank of the Mt. Batur massif. At **Gunung Kawi** in **Tampaksiring**, nine full-scale *candi* façades, each set in a deep niche for protection, have been hewn out of two solid rock walls facing each other across the river. Nearby is an elaborate cloister, also of solid rock, for the monks who once tended them. Painstaking Dutch scholarship has revealed that the five main monuments probably commemorate King Anak Wungsu (1049-1077) and the wives who burned themselves on the royal pyre to be with him in the next life (the last such suttee on Bali took place in 1903). The carving is more conventional than at Goa Gajah, but the scale of the undertaking far more impressive. River water diverted through a channel at the base of the monuments was supposed to bring a god-king's blessing of fertility to the ricefields downstream. Just beyond Tampaksiring is the famous watering place of **Tirta Empul**, with atmospherically mossy but rather recent bathing pools and temple. The water is holy without having to be consecrated and has magical and curative properties. On a hill overlooking the site is an "occasional palace" built in 1954 by Sukarno, who was always associated closely with his mother's native Bali.

Foreign Inspiration

The urbanizing village of **Ubud**, on the west bank of the Petanu, is the usual center for the exploration of antiquities and of a legion of other attractions in south-central Bali. Ubud is the geographic and cultural hub of rural Bali, and the island's artistic capital. Yet it was never a royal capital, and the fact that it is now to Bali what Yogyakarta is to Java has to do with the 20th century infusion of European ideas and styles which has made Balinese art what it is today. At the beginning of this century, the art of Bali was exclusively traditional in the truest sense of the word. It was an aspect of daily life and ritual, a way to beautify the environment and a means of honoring the gods. There was some slow innovation, but no emphasis on individual creativity; artists neither signed their work nor experimented with new media and forms. It is often remarked that the Balinese language has no word for "art" as a category of activity in its own right. For better or for worse, the introduction of "art for art's sake" fell to a tiny band of European paradise-hunters who found their way to Ubud in the halcyon days between the Dutch conquest and the Japanese.

Foremost among this lucky few was the remarkable Walter Spies, a romantic who had been a painter in the Ukraine and a musician in Batavia before ending his wanderings in Bali. The Euro-Balinese house which Spies built in **Campuan**, west of the center of Ubud, is now for (pricey) rent as part of the **Tjampuan Hotel**. His major contribution was in the field of painting. Bali had escaped the Islamic ban on human and animal representation, but knew little of perspective and possessed limited painting media. Spies' instruction and his own flamboyant style inspired a generation of young Balinese artists, who combined it with their own imagination and experience to produce lush, teeming tableaux of Balinese life, landscape and mythology.

Ubud's **Museum Puri Lukisan** displays many early works of the Pita Maha art society, which Spies founded together with a Dutch artist, Rudolf Bonnet, and a local aristocrat, Gede Agung Sukawati. Sukawati went on to become a respected Indonesian statesman, whose funeral in 1979 was hailed as "the last great Balinese cremation". The greatest of the Pita Maha school was probably I Gusti Nyoman Lempad, whose drawings of cremation towers and *Ramayana* scenes can be seen in the **Neka Gallery**. In **Penestanan**, west of Campuan, a colony of young artists continues the Pita Maha tradition. There are scores of other studios and small galleries in and around Ubud, and despite the stultifying influence of the tourist market, many continue to produce innovative work. But today Ubud suffers from success. There are bars and even a supermarket; the local inhabitants, who won recognition in the early 1980s for their pioneer attempts to manage tourism by teaching visitors informed respect for the place and its culture, are being swamped again.

The invigorating European influence of the pre-war period was not limited to visual art. The dramatic, hypnotic *kecak* or "Monkey Dance" to which every tourist is now treated was choreographed in 1928 by Spies and a German film-maker. Nevertheless, the elements were Balinese; only the indigenous genius of Bali made the fusion possible. That this genius lives on in the heart and lives of the people is amply demonstrated by the villages en route from Denpasar to Ubud, each of which seems to specialize in some particular craft or performance.

Batubulan, the birthplace of the *kecak* and now the site of Denpasar's music and dance academy, is also a center of stonecarving, where teenage craftsmen liberate gods and demons from blocks of locally quarried soapstone. Eminently unsuitable as souvenirs, they have been little affected by tourism. Batubulan statues grace and guard temples all over Bali.

Celuk, a little further up the road, produces delicate gold and silver jewelry. As in most parts of Indonesia, metalsmiths in Bali are traditionally a closed and privileged group; even Brahmins must address them in high Balinese. In Celuk, however, almost every family cashes in on the trade. Nevertheless, traditional methods, using manual bellows and a metal spike knocked into a tree trunk for an anvil, have survived. **Sukawati** is an important custodian of the Balinese *wayang kulit* tradition, of all the island's arts perhaps the one least influenced by the west. Bali almost certainly derived its shadow-play from East Java, but has developed its own style with small, robust puppets, less delicate and insect-like than those of Yogya.

Mas is a woodcarving center. In the past, wood carvings were always elaborately finished in brilliant colors, but the Western love of things "natural" got the better of the Balinese passion for decoration, and most are now left unpainted. Themes vary from traditional Vishnu and Sita figures to sleek realistic animals and psychoticly twisted heads.

Batuan and **Peliatan** both have famous dance groups, performing to the crashing, shimmering cascades of the Balinese *gamelan*, so different from the deep, drifting current of its Javanese counterpart. Dancers are the stars of Bali, from the pre-pubescent girls who alone may perform the delicate, vibrant *legong* to the sinewy athletes who execute the warlike *baris*. But for every dancer and musician who performs for big foreign crowds, there are still more who reserve their skills for themselves, their families, their villages and their gods. Balinese culture is poised between life and art. Money and much else draws it towards pure art, but nobody can predict what will become of it if the ritual which anchors it in living experience becomes extinct.

Klungkung, in the eastern wing of Bali's green amphitheater, is a good place to glimpse what the royal art of Bali looked like before the western infusion. This area was for a long time the seat of civilization in Bali. The first Majapahit viceroys ruled from a site near the old capital of Pejeng, but after the fall of Majapahit in Java, Bali was reunited under the *Dewa Agung* or god-king of **Gelgel**, just south of Klungkung on the seaward side. The state temple of **Pura Dasar** still stands there. The Gelgel dynasty sponsored a renaissance of Hindu culture in Bali just when it was being obliterated in Java, and built the so-called *Sad Kahyangan* or Holy Temples, of which everybody agrees there are six in all but disagrees upon which they are. Eventually Gelgel declined and lost its grip upon its vassals. As in Java, such misfortune called for a change of palace, and around the beginning of the eighteenth century the dynasty moved 3000 meters to the present capital of Klungkung, where it retained a residual spiritual authority over the other states until the Dutch conquest.

The **Kerta Gosa** in the center of modern Klungkung is a hall of justice, retained under the Dutch as the seat of the highest indigenous court on the island. Built in the mid-eighteenth century, it is an open-sided *pendopo* pavilion of the type long favored for official buildings in Java. The inside of the roof is entirely covered by intricate concentric friezes depicting divine punishment and reward, perhaps intended to induce honesty in the witnesses. The current paintings were done in the 1940s, but the style is traditional and the figures are executed in the flat, almost cartoon-like *wayang* style typical of Balinese art before the advent

Wooden ceiling in Klungkung. Left: Monkey dance during a barong performance.

of Spies. The ceiling of the **Bale Kambang** or "Floating Pavilion" of the nearby Klungkung palace is similarly decorated. This style of painting is sometimes also known by the name of a village near Gelgel, **Kamasan**, where it is still practiced on cloth as an art form in its own right. Kamasan also has silversmiths and goldsmiths. Another notable craft center in the Klungkung area is **Tihingan**, where *gamelan* gongs are forged.

The nine minor states into which Bali split with the disintegration of the Gelgel empire were, besides Gelgel's successor Klungkung: Badung, Bangli, Buleleng, Gianyar, Jembrana, Karangasem, Mengwi and Tabanan. **Bangli** is 26 km by road north-west of Klungkung, on the threshold of the mountains proper; a vantage point nearby offers panoramic views out over the whole lush cradle of southern Bali. Bangli's state temple, **Pura Kehen**, is one of the most beautiful on the island, almost always included among the six holy *Sad Kahyangan*. Kehen is built on three rising terraces, and the central courtyard contains an 11-tier *meru* tower. An inscription of 1204 proves that there has been a temple on this site since before Majapahit. **Gianyar,** also in the east of the amphitheater between Klungkung and Pejeng, was the most vigoros and expansive of the kingdoms in the late nineteenth century, but its request for Dutch help in 1899 was the beginning of the end for them all. The **Puri Dalem** palace at Gianyar is one of the few still inhabited by a royal family.

The capital of the kingdom of Badung stood – as already noted – on the site of present-day Denpasar. Two more of the nine, Mengwi and Tabanan, were also in the core piedmont area, but west of Denpasar and Ubud. **Mengwi**, now a modest village 20 km north-west of Denpasar, was snuffed out by internal war and divided among its neighbours in 1891, before the Dutch arrived. The state temple, **Pura Taman Ayun**, is unusual

Sunset over Tanah Lot temple. Right: Statue in the Monkey Forest.

for its large size and lily-lined moat. This temple was founded in 1634, although most of the present structure dates only from 1937. In the nearby village of **Kapal** is an older temple, **Pura Sada**, with a split gate from the time of Majapahit and a reconstructed *prasada* or *candi*-like sanctuary, rare in Bali.

The second royal site in this region, **Tabanan**, lies further to the west, amid some of the most fertile of all Bali's bounteous rice lands. The cultural center here is called **Gedung Mario** in memory of Bali's greatest 20th century dancer and choreographer, I Nyoman Mario, a native of Tabanan. Other attractions of the western half of the piedmont include the **Tanah Lot Temple** on the Tabanan coast, a clifftop sea temple like Ulu Watu, and the **Monkey Forest** near Sangeh, where tame monkeys swarm through a grove of nutmeg trees. Nutmeg is one of the two crops – the other was cloves – which first drove Europeans to Indonesia, and, for that matter, Columbus to America. But it is native only to the Moluccas, the Spice Islands proper, 1500 km further east; the Monkey Forest is the only nutmeg stand on Bali, and who planted it remains a mystery.

THE MOUNTAINS

Mountains are central to Balinese culture. Before the advent of Hinduism, the ancestors already lived there; that the Indian gods should have similar tastes surprised no-one. The direction in which the mountains lie, *kaja*, is naturally favorable, just as the seaward direction, *kelod*, is a source of evil influences. But while there is no mountain without a deity, the uplands are not so hospitable to human life, and only a tiny fraction of Bali's people live there. When all travel still occurred on foot, the mountains were seen as a distant and sacred realm, visited only when religious festivals demanded it. They still feel a world away from the warm, rich airs of the lowlands. The mountains of the far west are almost completely uninhabited, and have been designated as a vast nature reserve, the **West Bali National Park**. Until he sighted his last big game hunter in the 1930s, the Balinese tiger had his last refuge in this truly wild place. The old state of Jembrana, around present-day **Negara**, clung to the narrow southern coast of the wilderness as a marginal, out of the way country. Substantially Muslim today, Negara is more an outpost of East Java than an appendage of Bali; in fact, it is best known for its Madurese-style bull races. Balinese say that the west, the domain of the setting sun, is an inauspicious direction. Negara, being both in the west and by the sea, could hardly face worse prospects.

Mt. Batukau is the westernmost of the semicircle of very high mountains which rims the southern amphitheater. Like its antithesis, the sea, a great peak demands to be honored by a temple: hence the remote **Pura Luhur**, set among mossy forests on Batukau's southern flank. Access to this temple is via Tabanan. Further east, one of the two main roads across the island skirts the serene mountaintop lake of **Bratan**, suspended in the dead crater of a volcano of the same name. The flimsy thatched pavilions of the lowland Balinese house would be of little use in this alpine country; in their place are sturdy cottages of wood and tile. The lakeside temple of **Ulun Danu** is one of the most atmospheric in Bali. A little further up the road is an anomalous piece of worldly luxury, the **Bali Handaya Country Club** with its international class 18-hole golf course.

The most striking landscape feature of mountain Bali is the 12 km-wide caldera which contains the center of the volcano and lake of **Batur**. Bali's highest temple, **Pura Tegeh Koripan** (also known as Pura Sukawana) is located on the wind-swept western rim near **Penulisan** and grants superb views on a clear day. Inscriptions found here date back to the eleventh century and it is thought that this was the mountain sanctuary of the Pejeng kings, the *kaja* counterpart of the temple of Penataran Sasih.

The village of **Batur**, also on the lip of the caldera, was located in the crater itself until 1926, when it was destroyed by a major eruption of Mt. Batur. The shrine of the lake-goddess in the **Pura Ulun Danu** temple was carried to the rim as the only part of the original temple to have survived the lava flows. Small wonder that the Balinese, at the mercy of their mountains, are one of the most superstitious people on earth. Tempting fate for the sake of tourist dollars, some are still bold enough to make their homes by the foot of the beast in **Toya Bungkan**, where hot volcanic springs supply pools at the lakeside for steaming starlit baths. The eccentric Sumatran author Takdir Alisjabana has established a center here for the development of Balinese art and dance.

On the far side of Lake Batur is the isolated village of **Trunyan**, one of the few inhabited by the people classified as "Bali Aga". These are distinguished from other Balinese mainly by their willingness to concede that they are of indigenous rather than Javanese descent. They do, however, retain a number of unique customs including that of leaving their dead to rot above ground in bamboo cages, a grisly tourist attraction. Not surprisingly, Trunyan, and the Batur area in general, is one part of Bali where visitors are tolerated rather than welcome.

Seat of the Gods

Not content with the candidates in East Java, the Hindu dynasties of Bali sought to bring Mt. Meru, the cosmic mountain, closer to home. **Mt. Agung**, at once the highest (3142 m) and the most easterly (hence the most auspiciously located) of Bali's major peaks, was the natural choice. As the abode of the departed ancestors of pre-Hindu times, Agung served as an Olympus of sorts. The foundations of the great temple at **Besakih**, 950 m high on the southwest flank of Agung, were probably laid as a prehistoric terraced sanctuary for ancestor worship. By the eleventh century Besakih was in use by Hindu kings; in the fifteenth the Dewa Agung of Gelgel, descendant of Majapahit viceroys, made it his ancestral temple. Gelgel's successor, Klungkung, is still responsible for the upkeep of key parts of the monument, but every regency and many other groups of various sorts now have their own shrines. For Besakih is the mother temple of Bali, the one truly pan-Balinese religious site. Through the centuries of division after the decline of Gelgel, Besakih represented the spiritual unity of Bali.

The size and beauty of the Besakih complex, containing around 30 temples in all, reflect its unique status. The style is austere, relatively free from the excessive ornamentation of many other Balinese monuments. Its jagged split gate and black *meru* flowers silhouetted against the misty slopes of Mt. Agung are a haunting and unforgettable sight. The central shrine in particular expresses the humility beneath the often cheeky exuberance of Balinese religious art. It consists simply of three empty thrones, one each for Brahma, Vishnu and Shiva. Sculptors may parody lesser deities and demons, but do not presume to idolize the *Trisakti* themselves.

Once every century, Besakih is the focal point of the *Eka Dasa Rudra* ceremony, designed to stablilize and purify the whole cosmos just as lesser rites ensure harmony in the family and village. *Eka Dasa Rudra* involves millions of man-hours of labor in the preparation of offerings and the execution of rituals. In March 1963, the great ceremony was actually in progress when Mt. Agung erupted, killing more than 2000 people and devastating the surrounding countryside. Lava streams reached the sea in some places, yet Besakih itself was unscathed. The catastrophe was clearly a bad omen of cosmic proportions, and has often been linked to the communal violence of two years later, in which up to 100,000 communists are thought to have been killed in Bali. The carnage was seen partly as a purge of the evil influences which had displeased the gods. That Bali was one of the worst slaughterhouses of 1965 gives the lie to the idyllic image of a harmonic, happy, resilient society projected by 60 years of travel literature and a good deal of serious research.

THE NORTH COAST

The northern coast of Bali has been set apart from the rest of the island both by geography and by history. Before the construction of the present road network in the 1920s and 30s, the east-west mountain spine was a formidable barrier to

Mt. Agung – the seat of the gods.

overland communication, and the Balinese were reluctant seafarers. Drier and less fertile than the south, the north is naturally poorer in food resources, although it has compensated over the years by exporting slaves, coffee, cattle and copra. North Bali had a respectable Hindu kingdom of its own, **Buleleng**, but it was overcome by the Dutch almost half a century before the fall of the south. A self-confident and aggressive power in the early 19th century, Buleleng invoked the wrath of the Dutch in 1846 by snubbing their ambassadors and plundering one of their ships. After two attempts a punitive expedition finally took control of the kingdom in 1869. The Buleleng commander took poison, and the Dutch set about building the town of **Singaraja** on the site of the old capital. Buleleng women were ordered to cover their customarily naked breasts "to protect the morals of the Dutch soldiers"; that respectably brassièred Balinese now frown upon topless tourists is a wonderful historical irony.

As the main Dutch beachhead, Singaraja achieved significance as a port and administrative center. In 1882 it was placed under direct rule and elevated to residency capital for Bali and Lombok; in the first years of independence it controlled all of Nusa Tenggara from Bali to Timor. Today, even sea traffic has for the most part deserted Singaraja for the new port of **Celukanbawang**, and the old capital is a rather pretty small town with tree-lined streets and *dokar* horsecarts.

Hotel Singaraja used to be the Governor's mansion. The **Gedong Kertya** historical library, founded in 1928, is a repository for the precious *lontar* palm leaf manuscripts and copper plate inscriptions which record Bali's indigenous history, mythology and medicine.

The temples of North Bali show some surprising differences from those of the south. *Meru* towers, for instance, are much less common, and a soft pink sand-

Ritual food offering to appease the gods.

stone is used in place of the usual grey rock and brick. But most striking are the carvings: perhaps due to some spiritually corrosive effect of the long Dutch presence, those adorning northern temples are often absurdly secular and playful. The temple at **Jagaraga**, where the army of Buleleng was defeated in 1849, sports big-nosed Dutchmen in a pre-war motor car and a steamship under attack by a sea monster. **Pura Maduwe Karang** in **Kubutambahan** has domestic scenes, lovers, and a man on a bicycle. Domestic architecture in North Bali features corrugated iron roofs in place of the rustic thatch of the south, confirming the general impression that in scenery, there is no competition. But the north coast does have superb and relatively unspoiled black sand beaches around **Kalibubuk** and at **Yeh Sanih**.

KARANGASEM

Karangasem, in a tight little coastal depression at the foot of Mt. Agung, was the easternmost of Bali's pre-colonial kingdoms. After the calamitous eruption of Mt. Agung in 1963, superstition caused the capital to be renamed **Amlapura**, signifying a break with the unhappy past. Like Buleleng, Karangasem was poor in local resources and hence apt to foreign adventure. In the late 18th and early 19th centuries, it played a major role in the extraordinary Balinese enterprise of conquest and colonisation of the neighboring island of Lombok – a miniature Asian colonialism in the shadow of the bigger European one. In 1849, after siding with Buleleng in a losing war against the Dutch, Karangasem was awarded by the Governor-General to its own former vassal Mataram, in Lombok.

Restored to independence by the Dutch themselves in 1894, Karangasem became the kind of malleable native state of which Batavia could be proud. Its kings devoted themselves to architectural escapism in the style of their Javanese counterparts. Their traditional home is the **Puri Agung Karangasem**, a modest red brick compound, but their descendants live in the flamboyant but dilapidated **Puri Kanginan**, an eclectic amalgam of European, Chinese and Balinese styles. The last Raja also built two outlying follies: a pleasure palace on the coast (1921) and a neo-traditional bathing complex inland at **Tirta Gangga** (1946). Despite damage sustained from the eruption of 1963 and from political vandalism during the same period, the latter is still a pleasant place to swim under the gaze of bizarre statues from the end of a romantic era.

Overseas expansion distracted Karangasem's attention from its own immediate hinterland. Just 7 km from the capital, at **Tenganan**, a community has survived which, like the far less accessible one at Trunyan, considers itself linked to Bali's pre-Majapahit civilisation. At Tenganan the cultural idiosyncracies are strikingly visible. The entire village is walled, and the houses arranged symmetrically along two wide stone lanes. Tenganan is the only place in Indonesia, and one of only three in the world, where the fabulously difficult technique of "double *ikat*" weaving is practiced. This involves dyeing both warp and weft threads before they are combined on the loom; tiny errors could ruin the pattern, yet the *kain geringsing* produced often features intricate designs. The art of preparing and writing *lontar* leaf books, in Bali's own Indic script, also survives here.

Karangasem now has its own slice of tourist action: **Candi Dasa**, on the main road from Karangasem to Klungkung, which has only recently come of age as a beach resort. Less expensive than Sanur and less frantic than Kuta, Candi Dasa is allegedly where the cognoscenti go and certainly where the yuppies go.

The innocuous little port of **Padangbai**, on a flawless pearl-shaped bay west of Candi Dasa, connects Bali to the neighbor which it once dominated, **Lombok**. South of the ferry's course, the arid island of **Nusa Penida**, once a penitentiary for exiles from Klungkung, is a premonition of the change of environment awaiting passengers on the far side.

LOMBOK

Long regarded – not least by the Balinese themselves – as an ugly stepsister to her glamorous neighbour, Lombok is currently emerging from obscurity and becoming an eastern extension of the Bali tourist playground. In a sense this is true to the history of the island, which for the last three centuries has been dominated by Bali. But Lombok is also the western threshold of the harsh and variegated natural and cultural world of Nusa Tenggara, utterly different from rich, homogeneous, introspective Bali.

The Lombok Strait is no trifling shelf like that which divides Bali from Java, but a huge cleft scoured by powerful currents, the route of nuclear submarines passing undetected between the Indian Ocean and the Pacific. A formidable barrier for animal migration, it marks the zoogeographical Wallace Line which conventionally divides the Asian fauna of the western archipelago from the Australasian sphere of the east. The parrots and parakeets of Lombok, absent from Bali, portend the transition. Lombok also serves as a transition between the seasonal but reliable climates of East Java and Bali, and the dangerous semi-aridity of the rest of the lesser Sundas, where the capricious rainshadow of the Australian continent may linger into the monsoon season to bring drought. Lombok blooms like Bali only at high altitude and in areas of intensive irrigation; its population density is only half that of its neighbor, and some parts suffered a famine in 1966.

Mt. Rinjani dominates the entire Lombok landscape. The Balinese say that

Agung and Rinjani are husband and wife, but the latter is larger, more central and at the same time more isolated. At 3726 m, Rinjani is the second highest mountain in Indonesia outside the snowcaps of Irian Jaya. A road to the crater has been planned, but for the moment the climb takes three days there and back, is suitable only for the fit and well-equipped, and should not be attempted in the wet season when the paths become waterfalls. Only serious mountaineers aim for the peak itself; most climbers are content with the emerald, pine-ringed crater lake of **Segura Anak** which fills the caldera.

Rinjani and its lake are sacred to the indigenous people of Lombok, the *Sasak*. These speak a language closely related to that of Bali, and like the Balinese they are farmers rather than seafarers. But for all intents and purposes, the similarities end there. Never deeply penetrated by the Indian and Javanese influences which transformed Bali, the Sasak have retained the thatched stilt-houses, the *ladang* agriculture and a good deal of the animist religion of virgin Indonesia. Back-strap hand-looms are in common use: **Sukarare** is the main rural weaving center, but almost every village has its family weavers. Sasak basketware is also widely prized. The Sasak which have remained truest to their *adat* (tradition) are those who class themselves as *Waktu Telu*, a term of obscure origin indicating incomplete compliance with the duties of Islam. Though self-professed and authentically circumcised Muslims, the *Waktu Telu* do not find it necessary to pray the prescribed five times per day, nor to observe the fasting month. Some openly venerate ancestor shrines as well as the spirit of Lake Segura Anak. The homeland of the *Waktu Telu* lies on the isolated northern side of Mt. Rinjani around **Bayan** and **Senaro**.

The majority of Sasak, however, are more orthodox Muslims inhabiting the mosque-studded lowland corridor which cuts across the island south of Rinjani. These are the *Waktu Lima* Sasak, even more antithetical to the Balinese in spirit. The number of *Waktu Lima* seems to be growing at the expense of the *Waktu Telu* as state pressure and smoldering resentment against Lombok's resident Hindu Balinese combine to make Islamic orthodoxy more attractive.

As in other parts of the archipelago, it is not clear exactly how Islam came to Lombok. Local tradition suggests a connection with the legendary Muslim evangelist Sunan Giri, who is buried near Surabaya in East Java. Equally likely is that the Macassarese of South Celebes, who dominated the Lesser Sundas in the seventeenth century, played a major role. In either case, Islam was well enough anchored to survive two centuries of Hindu Balinese rule. From the end of the seventeenth century onwards, the Balinese state of Karangasem founded colonies in Lombok which subdued the Sasak and made their *datu* or lords into Balinese vassals. The most intensively colonized area was in the west of the island, around the foremost Balinese colonial state, **Mataram**, namesake of two historic Javanese dynasties. With the application of intensive Balinese irrigation techniques, Mataram became a major rice producer and exporter; it is still the greenest part of Lombok and the home of the majority of the Lombok Balinese, who make up about 20% of the island's total population.

The town of Mataram itself is now the seat of the provincial government of Nusa Tenggara Barat (Lombok and Sumbawa) and home to an absurd number of civil servants and soldiers. The bureaucratic nature of Indonesian society is most evident in such places, fairly populous but lacking major commerce and industry. Every other building seems to sport a government signboard, and every other person is a government employee. Mataram's old port was **Ampenan**, once a major center of commerce but now a broken-down jetty bypassed even by the Bali-Lombok ferry, which docks further south at **Lembar**. **Cakranegara**, where the Mataram princes built their courts, has become a commercial extension of Mataram, with a large Chinese community. **Pura Meru** in Cakaranegara is Lombok's largest Balinese temple. Presumed to date from the early eighteenth century, it contains more than 30 shrines and was intended to symbolize the unity of the Balinese plantations in Lombok under Mataram's leadership – a function reminiscent of Besakih in Bali itself. The **Puri Mayura** royal garden is a last remnant of the *kraton* of Cakranegara. Its centerpiece is a *bale kambang* (floating pavilion), set on an island in an ornamental lake. Nearby is a more recent palace building housing a collection of photographs and memorabilia from Dutch times. The rest of the old palace, including the high defensive walls which surrounded it, were razed in the fateful Lombok War of 1894.

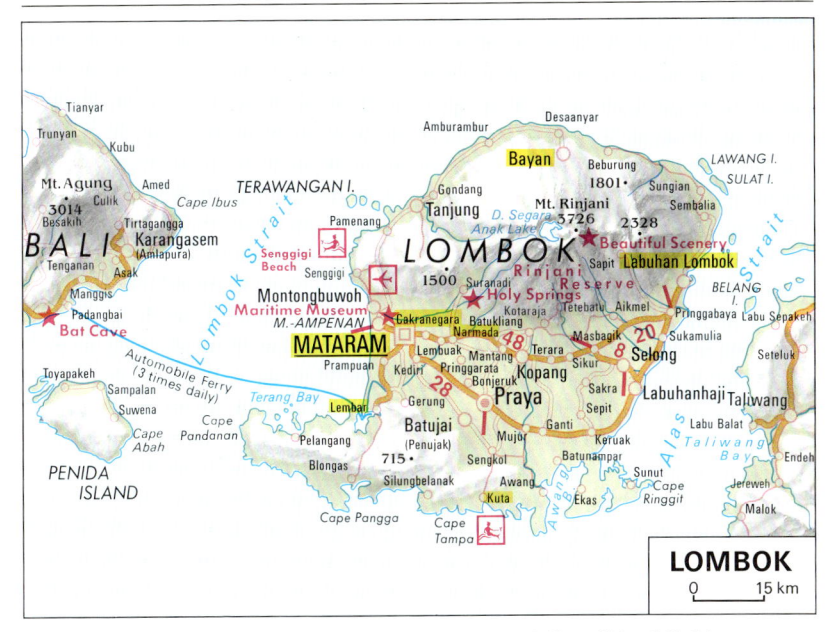

From 1849 until its fall, Mataram was a substantial power, ruling not only the whole of Lombok, but eastern Bali (Karangasem) too. But the Mataram Balinese were better soldiers and engineers than administrators, and their clumsy oppression provoked a series of Sasak uprisings. In 1894, a Sasak appeal for help provided the Dutch with an excuse to clip Mataram's wings. Troops landed at Ampenan, and the old king was forced to accept an ultimatum, whereupon the Dutch marched confidently to Cakranegara. But the crown prince ambushed them as they camped within the *kraton* walls. Using modern rifles obtained from European traders, the Balinese wounded 272 and killed 113, including the second in command, P.P.H. van Ham. He was buried at **Karang Jankong** between Cakranegara and Ampenan, where he died trying to lead the survivors back to the coast. The Indies press cried treachery, and the otherwise sluggish Dutch national sentiment boiled over. Within three months, reinforcements had retaken Cakranegara

Stick fighting – a popular sport and tourist attraction on Lombok.

after a pulverizing artillery barrage. The Mataram dynasty was abolished, and the whole island came under direct colonial government.

With the conquering army came a Dutch scholar, Dr. J. L. A. Brandes, anxious to save from destruction any literary treasures surviving in this most distant and vigorous offshoot of old Hindu Indonesia. In the village temple of **Pagutan** he found the one and only manuscript of the fourteenth century panegyric *Negarakrtagama*, the major source of information about Majapahit and arguably the most important single document of Indonesian history. It is impossible to know what other priceless material vanished; when Brandes arrived, many *lontar* books had already been burned to boil tea on Dutch campfires. For decades the *Negarakrtagama* was kept in the Netherlands, but on the occasion of the Dutch royal visit to Indonesia in 1970 it was presented to the National Museum in Jakarta.

In the irrigated country around the capital, the immigrant Balinese nobility recreated their native world of temples and bathing places. On **Mt. Pengsong**, 5 km south of the town, a series of white shrines stands on a rocky outcrop. In the small town of **Narmada**, some 10 km east of Cakranegara, a modest hill has been transformed into a complex of tiered gardens, pools and pavilions. The design is said to be a symbolic replica of Mt. Rinjani and its crater lake; ceremonies held on the mountain itself are also held here simultaneously. **Suranadi** above Narmada is a place of pilgrimage on account of its holy springs, that match those at Tampaksiring in Bali. The **Lingsar** temple complex combines Hindu and *Waktu Telu* shrines, and features a pond containing, of all things, holy albino eels which emerge from dark conduits when fed with pieces of hard-boiled egg.

The art and ceremonial culture of Balinese Lombok duplicate those of the mother island. The Sasak arts, for their part, combine styles from many different sources, including the Hindu overlord. *Cupak Gerantang* is a dance popular all over the island telling the story of the East Javanese culture hero, Panji; in the east of the island the dancers wear masks like Balinese *topeng*. *Rudat* and *Oncer*, vigorous male dances, seem more indigenous in inspiration. *Gamelan* music is played everywhere.

The beaches of Lombok share the excellence of its mountains. **Senggigi Beach**, with a new and expensive luxury hotel, is the one which is being pushed by the local government, but there are miles of empty sand in the **Meninting** area north of Ampenan and at **Kuta** (no relation) in the south. The offshore islands of **Gili Air**, **Gili Meno** and **Gili Trawangan** in the north-west are famous for their coral reefs. **Labuhan Lombok**, on the east coast, is the way to Sumbawa.

DENPASAR
INEXPENSIVE: **Adi Yasa**, Jl Nakula 23, Tel: 22679. **Darma Wisata**, Jl Imam Bonjol. **Wisma Taruna Inn**, Jl Gadung 31, Tel: 26913.
MODERATE: **Denpasar**, Jl Diponegoro 103, Tel: 26336. **Elim**, Puri Oka, Jl Kaliasem 3, Tel: 22165. **Pemecutan Palace**, Jl Thamrin 2, Tel: 23491. *LUXURY:* **Natour Bali**, Jl Veteran 2, Tel: 25681-5.

Food
STREET FOOD: night markets at **Kereneng Terminal** & **Kumbasari Shopping Centre**.
INDONESIAN: **Restaurant Betty**, Jl Kartini, off Jl Gajah Mada. **Gajah Mada Restaurant**, Jl Gajah Mada. **Rumah Makan Wardani, Tapakgangsul**. *CHINESE:* **Puri Selera**, Jl Gajah Mada 16. **Atoom Baru**, Jl Gajah Mada 106, Tel: 22794.

Shopping
Sanggraha Kriya Astra (state handicrafts centre), Tophati, on road to Batubulan. **Abiankapas** arts centre has some items for sale. Many smaller craft shops along Jl Gajah Mada. Weaving factory at **Pertenunan Carma**, Jl Letda Suci 2, south of Bali Museum.

Museums
Bali State Museum, Jl Letnan Kolonel Wisnu, Tue-Thu 8.00-13.30, Fri 8.00-11.00, Sat/Sun 8.00-12.30. **Art Museum**, Jl Bayusuta. Daily 8.00-16.30.

Cultural performances
Abiankapas arts centre has *kecak* nightly 18.00-19.00. **Kokar** academy rehearsals may be open to public; timetables vary. In **Batubulan**, *barong* dance every morning 9.00-10.00. **Ayoda Pura**, Tanjung Bungkak, on Sanur road, has *kecak* dances nightly 18.00-19.00. **Hotel Puri Pemecutan** stages regular *wayang kulit*.

Tourist Information / Post
Badung Tourist Office, Jl Surapati. Mon-Thu 7.00-14.00, Fri 7.00-11.00, Sat 7.00-12.00. **Dinas Pariwisata**, near GPO in administration complex south of town, is state tourist authority for whole island. **Post: Denpasar Post Office**, administration complex; Kuta & Sanur branches generally more convenient. **DHL Courier Service** is at Jl Tanjung Bungkak 92.

Transport
AIR: Ngurah Rai International Airport, 12 km S of town. *Bemo* for airport leave from **Stasiun Tegal**. Most people bound for Kuta or Sanur go straight there from airport. Denpasar airline offices: **Garuda**, Jl Melati 61, Tel: 22028; **Merpati**, Jl Melati 59, Tel: 2159; **Bouraq**, Jl Kamboja 45D, Tel: 23564.
SEA: port & Pelni agent at **Benoa**, 10 km to S.
RAIL: No railways on Bali, but rail office at Jl Diponegoro 172 sells tickets for Java plus Denpasar-Banyuwangi road/ferry connection.
ROAD: Suci Terminal or **Ubung Bus Station** for buses to Java; many bus offices around these terminals, but also agents in Kuta & Sanur. Suci also serves N & W Bali. **Tegal Terminal**, on Jl Iman Bonjol, for Kuta & the far south.
Kereneng Bus Station for C & E Bali.
INTERNAL: *Bemo* operate between the 4 bus stations. *Dokar* (horsecarts) available.

SANUR
INEXPENSIVE: **Hotel Rani**, **Hotel Sanur Indah**, **Hotel Taman Sari**, all on Jl Segara.
MODERATE: **Diwangkara Beach Hotel**, Jl Pantai Sanur, Tel: 8577/8412. **Laghawa Beach Inn**, Jl Tanjung Sari. **Mars Hotel**, Jl Raya Sanur. **Hotel Ramayana**, Jl Tanjung Sari, Tel: 664359. **Taman Agung**, Jl Tanjungsari, Tel: 8549. **Tourist Beach Inn**, Jl Segara. **Werdha Pura**, Jl Tanjungsari.
LUXURY: **Alit's Beach Bungalows**, Tel: 8567. **Bali Beach Intercont., Tel: 8511-7**. **Bali Hyatt**, Tel: 8271. **Wisma Baruna**, Jl Sindhu, Tel: 8546. **Bali Sanur Bungalows**, Jl Tanjungsari, 8423. **Sanur Beach**, Tel: 8011. **Segara Village**, Tel: 8407. **Sindhu Beach**, Jl Sindhu, Tel: 8351. **Tanjungsari**, Jl Tanjungsari, Tel: 8441. **La Taverna Bungalows**, Jl Tanjungsari, Tel: 8497.

Food
Warung food near the 3 cheap guesthouses. Hotels all have own restaurants: **Tanjung Sari Hotel Restaurant** & **Kuri Putih** in Bali Sanur Irama Bungalows are authentically Balinese. Independent restaurants mostly European, eg **Trattoria da Marco** off Jl Sanur. Exception: **Si Pino's**, Jl Sanur (opp Bali Beach entrance). Best Chinese restaurant: **Telaga Naga**, opp Bali Hyatt. Nearby **Kulkul** good for seafood.

Museums
Museum Le Mayeur, Sanur Beach. Thu-Fri & Sun 7.00-14.00, Sat 7.00-12.30, Mon closed.

Tourist Information / Post
in big hotels. **Post:** Kantor Pos Sanur, Jl Segara.

NUSA DUA
LUXURY: **Hotel Bualu**, Tel: 71310. **Hotel Nusa Dua**, Tel: 71210. **Bali Holiday Village** (Club Med). **Bali Sol Hotel**. All hotels self-contained - restaurants, cultural events etc. on premises.

KUTA AND LEGIAN
INEXPENSIVE: Upwards of 300 *losmen* & home-stays. A selection: **Arena Cottages**, off Poppies Lane. **Ayu Bungalows**, off Poppies Lane. **Janji Inn**, Gang Uluwatu, Legian.

GUIDEPOST BALI / LOMBOK

Kempu Taman Ayu, Poppies Gang. **Lasi Erwati's**, Poppies Gang. **Legian Mas Inn**, Legian. **Mirabo**, Legian. **Puspa Beach Inn**, Jl Bakungsari, Tel: 51988. **Senin Beach Inn**, Legian.
MODERATE: **Kuta Cott.**, Jl Bakung Sari, Tel: 24100. **Kuta Suci**, off Poppies Lane II. **Poppies Cott.**, Poppies Gang, Kuta, **Tel: 23059**. **Yasa Samudra**, Jl Pantai Kuta, Tel: 25305.
LUXURY: **Bali Mandira Cott.**, Jl Padma, Legian, Tel: 25785. **Bali Oberoi**, Kayu Aya (far N end) Tel: 25581. **Kartika Plaza Beach**, Kuta, Tel: 22454. **Kuta Beach Palace**, Legian, Tel: 25858. **Legian Beach**, Jl Melasti, Legian, Tel: 26811. **Natour Kuta Beach**, Kuta, Tel: 25791. **Pertamina Cottages**, far South, Tel: 23061.

Food
Restaurants & *warung* multiplying as fast as hotels & *losmen*. Most serve whole east-west spectrum, from Balinese *babi guling* (spicy spit-roast pork) & exotic Chinese seafood to hamburgers & "muesli & honey yoghurt".
Some recommendations: **Made's Warung**, between Jl Pantai Kuta & Poppies Gang. **Poppies Restaruant**, off Poppies Lane. **TJ's** (Mexican!), Poppies Gang. **Blue Ocean Hotel**, Legian. **Bali Indah**, Jl Buni Sari. **Lenny's**, Jl Legian. **Mini Restaurant**, Jl Legian. **Indah Sari**, Jl Legian.

Shopping
Kuta & Legian are major fashion centers in southeast Asia. Boutique concentrations: **Pasar Seni**, Jl Bakung Sari; beach end of Jl Melasti, Legian.

Entertainment
Banjar Pengaretan, Banjar Tegal & **Indra Prasta** in Kuta, & **Banjar Legian Kelod** & **Banjar Seminyak** in Legian, give Balinese dance performances. But real native entertainment is pubs, discos & nightclubs, segregated by continent: **Brunei Club**, **Gado Gado** & **Kayu Api** for Europeans, **Koala Blu**, **Rivoli** & **Casablanca** for Australians.

Tourist Information / Post
Government office on Jl Bakung Sari.
Post: **Kuta Postal Agent**, Jl Legian, sells stamps, stationery etc, also poste restante. Main **Kantor Pos** off Jl Ngurah Rai.

Medical
Government clinic on Jl Pantai Kuta.

Transport
Main *bemo* stand: Jl Legian/Jl Pantai Kuta intersection, but *bemo* also travel down Jl Legian. *Bemo* go to Tegal station, Denpasar, also S to Ngurah Rai airport. Many hotels & *losmen* hire out bicycles, motorcycles & jeeps.
Garuda airlines office: Kuta Beach Hotel, Jl Pantai Kuta, Tel: 24764.

UBUD AND SURROUNDINGS
INEXPENSIVE: **Arjuna Inn**, Campuan. **Munut Bungalows**, Campuan. **Oka Homestay**, Pengosekan. **Jati Homestay**, Pengosekan. **Negara Home-stay**, Peliatan. **Mandala Homestay**, Peliatan. **Mudita Inn**, Peliatan. **Puri Agung**, Peliatan. **Agung Pension**, Ubud. **Artini**, Ubud. **Frog Pond Inn**, Ubud. **I Made Sadia** homestay, Ubud. **Jaya Losmen**, Ubud. **Karyawan**, Ubud. **Hotel Menara**, Ubud. **Monkey Forest Hideaway**, Ubud. **Nani House**, Ubud. **Pondok Indah**, Ubud. **Tjanderi's**, Ubud.
MODERATE: **Kampung Aman**, Ubud. **Oka Kartini's**, Padangtegal. **Oka Wati's Bungalows**, Ubud. **Puri Saraswati**, Ubud. **Hotel Puri Saren**, Ubud. **Sika Garden Cottage**, Campuan. **Ubud Inn**, Pengosekan.
LUXURY: **Hotel Tjampuhan**, Campuan.

Food
Hotels & many *losmen* have own eating places, often open to non-residents. In addition: **Cafe Lotus**, Puri Saraswati, Ubud. **Cafe Wayan**, Ubud. **Griya Restaurant**, Ubud. **Murni's Warung**, Campuan. **Nomad Restaurant**, Ubud.

Shopping
Main street lined with kiosks selling carvings, basketry, antiques, *batik*, paintings. But most obtainable more cheaply direct from makers in Ubud & surrounding villages. Concentrations of artists' workshops in **Penestenan** & **Padangtegal**.

Museums / Galleries
Museum Purbakala Gedung Arca, (archaeology), Blahbatu, Tel: 26101. Tue-Sat 7.30-13.30, Sun & Mon closed. **Galleries**: **Museum Lempad**, home of late I Gusti Nyoman Lempad, Ubud. **Puri Lukisan Ratna Wartha**, Ubud, open daily 8.00-14.00. **Neka Gallery**, Padangtegal. **Museum Neka**, Campuan. **Agung Rai Gallery**, Peliatan.

Cultural performances
Check *Bali Post* for details of events.
DANCE: **Banjar Padangtegal**, Padangtegal - *Kecak* dance, Sun & Wed 18.00-19.00. **Pura Dalem Puri**, Peliatan - *Legong* dance, Sat 18.30-19.30. *WAYANG KULIT:* **Oka Kartini**, Peliatan, Wed 19.30- 20.30.

Tourist Information / Post
Both opposite Cafe Lotus on main street.
Post: in Padangtegal near Neka gallery.

Transport
Bemo leave cinema for Denpasar and elsewhere. Bicycle/motorcycle hire can be fixed through most *losmen*. **Surya International**, opp Puri Lukisan Museum, Tel: 51673/51786, reconfirms international flight tickets.

GUIDEPOST BALI / LOMBOK

BATUR CRATER
PENELOKAN: not highly recommended as place to stay. **KINTAMANI: Losmen Kencana, Miranda & Losmen Supermen** are budget-priced, **Puri Astina** more salubrious.
TOYAH BUNGKAH (Tirtha): *Inexpensive:* **Amerta, Mountain View ,Wayan Matra.** *Moderate:* **Toyahbungkah Art Centre.**

Transport
Bemo run between Kintamani, Penelokan, Kedisan & Toyabungkah. Boats ply between Kedisan, Toyabungkah & Trunyan.

SINGARAJA
Most people prefer Lovina Beach, 10 km further W. But plenty of accommodation in town:
INEXPENSIVE: **Losmen Ratna**, Jl Imam Bonjol 102. Rest all on Jl Jen A Yani, eg **Sentral** (no.48), **Garuda** (no.76), **Gelasari** (no.87, Tel: 21495).
MODERATE: **Sedana Yoga**, Jl Gajah Mada.

Museums / Post
Museum Gedong Kirtya (manuscripts museum), Jl Veteran 20, Tel: 41645. Mon-Thu 6.30-14.00, Fri 6.30-11.00, Sat 6.30-12.00.
Post office: East end of Jl Jen A Yani.

Transport
Minibus terminals: at W end of town for Denpasar & the W, at E end for Kintamani & Amlapura. Bus cos near Yani/ Diponegoro junction run direct to Java from Singaraja.

LOVINA BEACH
Reached by *bemo* from Singaraja's westerly bus station. Few facilities other than *losmen* & small restaurants. Tourist zone stretches a rarefied 10 km, encompassing **Anturan, Kalibukbuk, Lovina & Temukus.** One medium-range place: **Samudra Beach Cott.** Lovina. Rest is all budget: **Agung Homestay**, Anturan, **Baruna Beach Cott.**, Anturan. **Lila Cita Beach Inn**, Anturan. **Banyualit**, Kalibukbuk. **Ayodya**, Kalibukbuk.

AMLAPURA AND SURROUNDINGS
Amlapura itself has **Lahar Mas Inn** at west end of town & **Sidya Karya** on Jl Hasannudin, but most visitors prefer **Homestay Lila** in Abian Soan, 5 km west of town, or 5 budget *losmen* at scenic **Tirtagganga** to the North.

CANDIDASA
More than 40 *losmen*, the only buildings on this stretch of road & beach, all in budget price range.

Food
Some up-market eateries incl **Hawaii Restaurant, Sumber Rasa** (Chinese) & **Candra Warung**, but real *warung* are better value.

MATARAM & SURROUNDINGS
INEXPENSIVE: **Pabean**, Jl Yos Sudarso 146, Ampenan, Tel: 21758. **Pusaka**, Jl Hasanuddin 23, Tel: 23119. **Rinjani**, Jl Panca Warga 18, Mataram. **Wisma Triguna**, Jl Koperasi, Ampenan (near airport), Tel: 21705.
MODERATE: **Granada Hotel**, Jl Bung Karno, Mataram, Tel: 22275. **Wisma Melati**, Jl Langko 80, Ampenan, Tel: 23780. **Wisma Paradiso**, Jl Angsoka 3, Mataram, Tel: 22074.
BEACH HOTELS: **MENINTING:** (moderate) **Sasaka Beach. SENGGIGI:** (budget) **Pondok , Mascot Cott., Senggigi Beach** (first class).
INLAND: **Hotel Suranadi**, Suranadi (first class).

Food
INDONESIAN: **Arafat**, Jl Pabean, Ampenan. **Garden House Restaurant**, Mataram Shopping Centre, Jl Pejanggik, Mataram. **Jasmin**, Jl Kebudayaan 3, Cakranegara. **Madya**, Jl Hasanuddin, Cakranegara. **Minang**, Jl Hasanuddin, Cakranegara. **Mulia**, Jl Pabean, Ampenan. **Taliwang**, Jl Pejanggik, Mataram. *CHINESE:* **Asia**, Jl Selaparang, Cakranegara. **Pabean**, Jl Yos Sudarso, Ampenan. **Tjirebon**, Jl Yos Sudarso, Ampenan.

Shopping
Textiles: **Slamet Riyadi**, Jl Ukir Kawi, Cakranegara. *Antiques:* **Wayan Wika**, Jl Bangau 12, Cakranegara. **Sudirman's**, Jl Pabean 16A.

Museums
Nusa Tenggara Barat State Museum, Jl Panji Tilat Negara, Mataram, Tel: 22159. Tue-Thu & Sun 8.00-14.00, Fri 8.00-11.00, Sat 8.00-13.00.

Tourist Information / Post
Jl Langko 70, Ampenan, Tel: 21866/21730. Mon-Thu 7.00-14.00, Fri 7.00-11.00, Sat 7.00-13.00. **Post office:** Jl Ismail Marzuki, Mataram. Branch at Jl Langko, Ampenan.

Transport
AIR: Selaparang Airport, a short distance N of Mataram; taxis connect. Airline offices: **Garuda** (Tel 23762), **Merpati** (Tel 22226) & **Bouraq** (Tel 22670) all on Jl Langko/Jl Pejanggik.
SEA: 2 ferries each way per day (morning & afternoon) between Padangbai (Bali) & Lembar (a few km S of Mataram by *bemo*). To Sumbawa, 2 morning ferries per day from Labuhan Lombok on E coast.
INTERNAL: *Bemo* station - **Sweta**, a crossroads 2 km east of Cakranegara on main road.

Climbing Mt. Rinjani
Two approaches: from the N via **Senaru** (normal route), or from the E via **Sapit & Sembalun** (more difficult). Both arduous, require tents & supplies, take 3-4 days up & down. Guides recommended – can be found by hotels incl **Wisma Triguna**, Jl Koperasi, Ampenan.

167

ACEH

ACEH

BANDA ACEH

The Special District of Aceh is a world apart from the rest of Indonesia. More than 1500 km Mecca-wards from Jakarta, it sees itself as the proud and pure Islamic antithesis to the decadent tolerance and syncretism of Java. Aceh was the only province in which the Islamic opposition defeated the government party Golkar in the 1987 elections. For the Muslims of Sumatra, Acch is an object of wary admiration; for the Christians, an object of fear and an ever-present reminder of their stake in the New Order government which keeps Islamic forces in check.

For the foreign visitor, however Aceh is a much more interesting and attractive place than is generally realized. The Acehnese, it is true, do not take kindly to an affront, and as in other staunchly Islamic societies that includes offences against community and religious morality such as drunkenness, public petting or scanty dress. But provided such simple rules are not broken, they are a civilized and hospitable people, uniquely and refreshingly self-confident in their independence of thought and rejection of some of the shibboleths of modern Indonesia. The towns are quiet and clean by Indonesian standards, and not without historical and architectural interest. The interior is as beautiful as any, with pine forests alternating with open blang of dry grassland; ethnic groups distinct from the Acehnese proper inhabit the mountains. In the south is a vast national park and a world-famous white-water rafting river.

Despite their fierce ethnic pride, the Acehnese are very far from being a pure race. The racial heterogeneity of other Indonesian peoples is often exaggerated, with fanciful stories of "Veddoid", "Mongol" and "Polynesian" admixtures. But the Acehenese are truly of very mixed descent. Many could pass for Indians or Arabs; at **Lamno** on the west coast, there is even a community with European features – the legacy, they say, of a Portuguese shipwreck. Closer to home, slaves from Nias and the Bataklands have enriched the ethnic stew. Historically, this mixture was synthesized in a number of great polyglot trading ports on the shores of the Andaman Sea.

BANDA ACEH

The most important of these ports was **Banda Aceh**, the present-day provincial capital, at the very tip of the island of Sumatra. It was from here that Ali Mughayat Syah, the first sultan of Aceh, sallied out in the 1520s to conquer the

Left: Bringing home bananas in Aceh.

surrounding pepper- and gold-producing areas. By the middle of the 16th century Aceh was one of the three great powers of the Straits, locked in an endless series of triangular wars with the Sultanate of Johor and the Portuguese colony of Malacca, both over the water on the Malay peninsula. It also became the most distant vassal of the Ottoman empire in Turkey. Aceh experienced its "golden age" under the rule of the great Sultan Iskandar Muda (1607-36), briefly becoming the greatest power in the western archipelago. Iskandar Muda combined Machiavellian ruthlessness in politics with benevolent patronage of the arts; under him, Aceh was a center of Malay literature and Islamic scholarship.

Very little remains of the opulent seventeenth century capital. The *kraton* complex was located by a bend in the Krueng Daroy river, south of the modern city center. The **Pintu Khop** gateway connected the vanished palace with the **Taman Sari** pleasure garden. As *Pintu Aceh*, this gate has become a standard motif of Acehnese gold and silver jewelry. It was also copied in 1880 by the architect of the **Pendopo Gubernor**, the Dutch governor's residence, which stands a little downstream from Taman Sari and is still used by the present Indonesian governor.

In the Taman Sari garden stands an original building of extraordinary and mysterious design: the **Gunungan**. This unlovely construction resembles a large number of giant tombstones arranged in ascending order of size around a tall central column. The name means "mountain-like". Popular tradition has it that the Gunungan was built by Iskandar Muda to please one of his wives, herself a child of the mountains. Barely more credible is the scholastic assertion that this is yet another of those ubiquitous cosmic mountain models, like a Javanese *candi* or the heaped rice at a *slametan* feast; the Gunungan was built by Muslims in the seventeenth century, and there are almost no Hindu antiquities in Aceh. However, the northern tip of Sumatra is known to have been involved in international commerce since the ninth century, and can hardly have escaped Indian influence.

Not far from Taman Sari is the **Aceh State Museum**. The centerpiece of this complex is a replica of an Acehnese *adat* house, constructed, strangely enough, in Semarang, for a colonial exhibition of 1914. The traditional house of Aceh is a spacious, elegant version of the Malay stilt house, divided between men's and women's sections and distinguished by intricate fretwork ventilation panels in the gable which faces Mecca. Houses of this kind are still in use in some areas outside the capital, particularly on the west coast. The museum's displays include jewelry, ceremonial costumes and weapons such as the famous *rencong* fighting knife.

In the grounds of the museum lie the graves of the Acehnese rulers. Pride of place goes to that of **Iskandar Muda**, which is regularly repainted. Iskandar Muda was a monster who castrated an unsuccessful military commander and even murdered his own son; but he undoubtedly built a powerful state and gave the Europeans serious problems too, and has therefore earned the title of National Hero.

After his death in 1636, Aceh began to decline as the elite squabbled and royal authority was reduced to the capital. Its fortunes did not revive until the beginning of the 19th century, when the Napoleonic wars and the collapse of the VOC practically eliminated Dutch power in Sumatra. By 1820, Aceh was producing over half of the world's supply of pepper, and from 1838 onwards a vigorous and capable new leader, Tuanku Ibrahim, began a campaign of conquest which led invatably to a collision with the resurging Dutch. At first the British forced the Dutch to respect Aceh's independence, and for a while it looked as though Aceh would be another Siam, an obsolescent Asian state preserved by western diplomacy. But in 1871 a high-handed imperial deal was struck which lead to the longest and most bitter of all colonial wars: the Dutch gave England the Gold Coast in Africa in return for a "free hand" in Aceh.

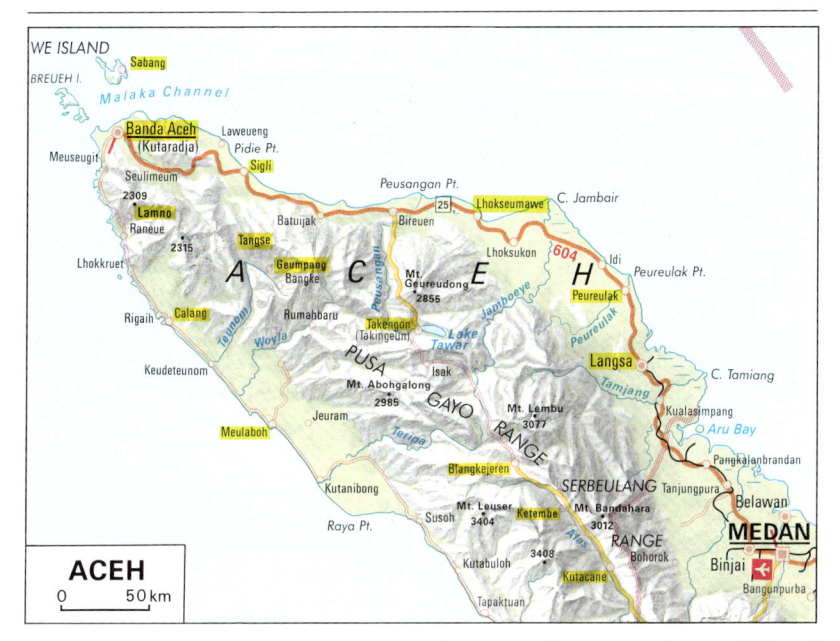

Some 2000 of the Netherlands Indies troops who died trying to exercise that "free hand" are buried in the **Dutch Cemetery** west of Taman Sari. For over 30 years, Aceh was Holland's Sahara, the Indies army its Foreign Legion. As a Dutch ditty of the time ran:

Wij zijn het leven moe,
Wij gaan naar Aceh toe.
(We're tired of life,
 We're going to Aceh.)

Most of the names chiselled here, however, are not Dutch, but Javanese, Ambonese, Minahassan - loyal, underprivileged brown servants of a distant European crown. This cemetery is still maintained with Dutch money; in 1949 its preservation was made a condition of the Dutch-Indonesian peace settlement. Perhaps the most telling monument is the fine memorial stele erected to the dead by the East Sumatra Tobacco Planters' Association. Few of the Acehnese who died resisting imperialism have the dignity of a marked grave. Even after the conclusion of the military campaigns, desperate Acehnese would occasionally stab an infidel on the street to secure their passage to paradise.

Another ironic reminder of the Aceh war is Banda Aceh's **Baiturrahman Mosque**. It was built by the Dutch in 1878, after they had secured the capital, as a peace offering to the recalcitrant guerillas in the hills. As such it was ineffective: in 1899, Dutchmen were still dying and the mosque was still empty. But after the last conclusive military actions of 1904, the Acehnese reconciled themselves to the expensive gift from the infidel. In 1935 two additional cupolas were added to the original singleton. A further extension after independence made it a total of five. Built in an almost fussy Imperial Indian style, and sporting a clock like a Victorian railway station, Baiturrahman has neither the austere grandeur of modern Islamic architecture nor the antique elegance of the *meru*-roofed mosques of old Java. But it is undeniably an imposing and superbly maintained building, and remains the unlikely pride of Aceh.

A no less unusual embodiment of Acehnese pride is the grounded Dakota aircraft suspended on a pedestal in a square across the road from the cemetery. This airliner, known as the **RI 001 Monument**, was donated to the beleaguered republic by the people of Aceh during the revolution. Having rounded up and imprisoned all the resident Dutchmen in 1942 in anticipation of the Japanese arrival, Aceh was prudently left alone by the Dutch military in 1945-9 and spent the revolution conspicuously being more republican than the republic itself. Disillusion and rebellion followed when Jakarta tried to exert some of its long-

The Grand Mosque in Banda Aceh by night.

hailed authority there. A fragile peace was restored only by recognition of Aceh's autonomy in matters of religion, education, and in some areas of law. Today, with limited Islamic law in force, films and books censored by the provincial authorities, and radical Islam strongly represented among students, there is little sign of an absolute break with the past.

Islands and Coasts

Banda Aceh is not quite Indonesia's northernmost outpost. That distinction falls to **We**, 12 km across the water from the harbour. The main settlement of this scenic and hilly island is **Sabang**, known to every Indonesian schoolchild from the slogan *dari Sabang ke Merauke*, "from Sabang to Merauke". (**Merauke** is more than 5000 km away on the Irianese border with Papua New Guinea.) During

Heading for the next island by prahu.

the campaign for West Irian, this expression served as a battlecry; today it is a smug reminder of Indonesia's physical greatness. In the days of steamships, Sabang was an important coaling station, with electric loading facilities and a 3000-ton floating dock. But diesel and competition from the port of Belawan near Medan reduced it to a backwater, and the harbor, nestled in green hills, now has an almost Caribbean natural beauty. There is, however, a large military presence. Sabang has served as a fortress against Japan and Malaysia; now its guns are trained on the Nicobar islands immediately to the north, lair of India's huge navy, potential battlefield of two emerging Asian superpowers.

One of the paradoxes of Aceh is that its Islamic zealotry is grafted to an *adat* society which, even by Indonesian standards, is relatively benevolent towards women. A newly-married couple lives in the wife's house, not the husband's. A married woman is the owner of her house, and often of rice land too. Inheritance is through both male and female lines. In the 17th century, four successive queens occupied the throne of Aceh, but the province's most famous daughter is Cut Niak Dhien, a heroine of the Aceh War. The **Cut Nyak Dhien Museum** in Banda Aceh is devoted to her. This remarkable woman took over command of a group of resistance fighters after her husband Teuku Umar was killed in a Dutch ambush in 1899. After considerable success as a guerilla leader, she was eventually caught and died in exile at Sumedang in West Java.

The place of Teuku Umar's death, on a lonely beach near **Meulaboh** on the west coast, is marked by a monument. Facing the empty Indian ocean rather than the teeming commerce of the Malacca Strait, the west of Aceh has always afforded a last refuge for rebels. The road down this coast is rough, but has been described as one of the prettiest in the world; it skirts

Ladang farmer at work in the Aceh highlands.

rugged rocky beaches where mountain streams pour with vain vigor into the pounding sea. The bay at **Calang** used to be known as the *Heksenketel* or the Witches' Cauldron, for the violence of its surf during the west monsoon.

On the tamer east coast, the story is very different. The coastal plains between Banda Aceh and Medan are both the cradle of Aceh's distant past and the epicenter of its planned industrial future. Long before the area was united under Ali Mughayat Syah, the first Islamic kingdoms in all of Indonesia were established at now obscure estuaries on Aceh's eastern seaboard. When the Venetian world-traveler Marco Polo, the first European known to have set foot in Indonesia, visited this coast on the way home from China in 1292, the people of "Ferlec" – present-day **Peureulak**, near **Langsa** – had already been converted to Islam by "Saracen" traders. The earliest surviving physical evidence of Islam in Indonesia, the **Malik as-Salih tombstone**, can be seen in a village about 18 km east of Lhokseumawe. The Arabic calligraphy on this modest monument, which was apparently imported from Cambay in India, is still clear almost seven centuries later. It is dated 1297 and commemorates a ruler of Samudra, a kingdom that gave its name to the whole island of Sumatra. Closer to Banda Aceh, the town of **Sigli** was once Pedir, the port from which Indonesian pilgrims set sail for the Islamic Holy Land; Aceh was nicknamed *Serambi Mekah*, the "front porch of Mecca".

Before Aceh was even fully subjugated, the Dutch, with bayonets fixed, built a railway along this hostile shore, both for strategic reasons and to open up the country to commercial agriculture. The line has been disused for two decades, but the ghostly shells of old stations are still to be found in Sigli and elsewhere, and rubber and oil palm still grow along the rusting track.

White-water adventure on the Alas River.

In terms of economic importance, however, all else has been eclipsed by Aceh's new miracle moneyspinner, liquefied natural gas (LNG). In 1971, one of the biggest natural gas fields in the world was discovered near the unknown and unspellable little town of **Lhokseumawe**. Export earnings from LNG have made an important contribution to Indonesia's economic growth under the New Order, although the fact that the revenues are strictly under central control is always fuel on the fire of Acehnese regionalism. An army of foreign engineers and Indonesian laborers has transformed Lhokseumawe into a grotesque technological boom-town. A giant liquefaction plant forms the core of the most important industrial development zone in the country, which includes two fertiliser factories. By night, when carbide lights and gas flares illuminate the sky over the paddies, the complex offers a surreal spectacle. Rainbow oil on the water proclaims the advent of industrial pollution, one of the latest evils imported from Europe to arrive in the green tropics.

The Mountains

The contrast between Lhokseumawe and the staunchly traditional highlands immediately behind it could hardly be more dramatic. Even at the peak of their power, Aceh's coastal rulers never entirely mastered their mountain hinterlands. The Gayo and Alas peoples who lived there paid tribute to the sultans, but were not absorbed into the Acehnese culture. They did, however, convert to Islam. In the last stages of the Aceh war, they also gave refuge and support to the hard-pressed guerillas. For this they were punished in 1904 by the ruthless Dutch commander van Daalen, whose troops, frighteningly modern with their olive fatigues and jungle carbines, stormed and burned the fortified mountain villages in the famous *Gayotocht* campaign. Gayo settlements like **Tangse** and **Geumpang** are scattered throughout the northern interior, but the Gayo "capital" is **Takengon**, on the shore of a high blue mountain lake, **Lake Tawar**. No swidden-farming hillbillies, the Gayo produce some of the best irrigated rice in Sumatra, and also farm such commercial crops as coffee, tobacco, cloves and cinnamon. Gayo crafts include embroidery and a unique style of decorative clay pottery.

The road south from Takingon to **Blangkejeren** and the Alas lands was carved through the mountains during the Japanese occupation, using *romusha* forced labour. It is still unreliable in the wet season. In Blangkejeren are some of the surviving traditional houses of the area, long wooden buildings sheltering several families, each of which has its own apartment or *bilek* as in a Borneo longhouse. The Blangkejeren area produces high grade cannabis, formerly a popular alternative to sinful alcohol in Aceh. In recent years, however, the custom has come under pressure from *Operasi Narkotika*, and for a foreigner to partake is doubly dangerous.

The central feature of southern Aceh is the **Alas River**, which rises on the slopes of the great **Mt. Leuser** (3404 m) and tumbles for 100 km through a splendid gorge running parallel to both coasts. This is one of the wildest areas of Sumatra, and has been declared a national park, a refuge for the Sumatran rhinoceros, elephant, tiger and orang-utang among other rare wildlife. Orang-utangs confiscated from illegal captivity are returned to forest life at the park headquarters in **Ketembe**. The margins of the park are under pressure from agricultural settlers; **Kutacane**, the last substantial settlement on the Aceh side of the provincial border, is an outpost of farmers from the Bataklands.

Right: A batak staff portraying domestic hierarchy.

BANDA ACEH
INEXPENSIVE: **Losmen International**, Jl Achmad Yani 19, Tel: 21834. **Lading**, Jl Cut Meutia 9, Tel: 21359. **Losmen Lamprit**, Jl T Nyak Arif 7, Tel: 23995. **Wisma Sari**, Jl KHA Dahlan, Tel: 21528.
MODERATE: **Aceh**, Jl Mohd Jam 1, Tel: 21354. **Medan**, Jl A Yani 9, Tel: 22636. **Prapat**, Jl A Yani 11, Tel: 22159. **Rasa Sayang**, Jl Teuku Umar 439. **Seulawah**, Jl Neusu Timur, Tel: 21749. **Sultan**, Jl Polem, Tel: 22581. **Losmen Yusri**, Jl KHA Dahlan 74, Tel: 23543.
LUXURY: **Kuala Trip**, Jl. Mesjid Raya 24, Tel: 21879/21455.

Food
ACEHNESE: **Asia Baru**, Jl Cut Nyak Dhien. **Ujong Batee**, by beach on road to Krueng Raya, is a famous Acehnese seafood restaurant. Another is **Braden**, 9 km from town on road to Lhoknga. *INDONESIAN:* **Aroma Restaurant**, Jl Cut Nyak Dhien. **Dian**, Jl A Yani. **Minang Surya** (Padang), Jl Safiatuddin 10. *CHINESE:* **Tropicana**, Jl A Yani 56.

Museums
Aceh State Museum, Jl Sultan Alaidin Mahmudsyah, Tel: 21033/2335. Tue-Thu & Sun 8.00-14.00, Fri 8.00-12.00, Sat 8.00-13.00,

Tourist Information / Post
Jl Teuku Nyak Arief 35, Tel: 22841. **Post office**: Jl T Angkasa. **Telephone**: Jl Machmud Syah.

Transport
AIR: **Blang Bintang Airport**, 17 km from town. Flights to Sabang, Meulaboh & Tapaktuan, Medan & other big Sumatran cities. *Airline offices:* **Garuda**, Jl Merduati 6, Tel: 21305; **Merpati** and **SMAC** (for W coast routes), Jl Cut Niak Dhien, Tel: 21626.
SEA: Local boats leave from Uleelheue harbor, long-distance ships from **Krueng Raya**. **Pelni office**: Jl Uleelheue, Tel: 23976.
ROAD: **Terminal Teuku Umar** (in front of Rasa Sayang hotel) for long-distance buses; most bus offices on Jl Mohammed Jam. **Stasiun Kota**, in town center, for local services.

RURAL ACEH
TAKENGON: *(Budget)* **Batang Ruang**, Jl Batang Ruang 5, **Losmen Fajar**, Jl Mahkamah 92. *Moderate:* **Losmen Danau Laut Tawar**, Jl Lebekader, & **Renggali**, Jl Bintang.
MUSEUMS: **Museum Malikussaleh**, Jl May Jen T Hamzah Bendahara, Lhokseumawe. Mon, Wed, Thu 8.00-14.00, Sun 8.00-10.00. Tue & Fri closed. **Museum Sepakat Segenep**, Kutacane. Tue-Thu & Sun 8.00-11.00, Fri 8.00-11.00.

ACEH

NORTH SUMATRA

NORTH SUMATRA

MEDAN
BATAKLANDS
PADANG LAWAS
NIAS

This province is the most populous, most fertile, most diverse, most spectacular, most visited and best known part of the island of Sumatra. Its capital, Medan, is one of the great export ports of Southeast Asia; its crowning landmark, the vast blue halo of Lake Toba, is known the world over as a symbol of Indonesia's natural beauty.

Yet the rise of North Sumatra has been a relatively recent and rapid one. Less than a century and a half ago, when Java was already a market garden keeping sugar and coffee on the breakfast tables of Europe, interior North Sumatra was an unmapped wilderness inhabited by warring cannibals. More than 1500 years before, various tribes, who are collectively called Batak today, left their settlements at the foot of the Himalayas and moved to this rough mountain landscape. Medan was an insignificant village amid alluvial swamps, part of a minor sultanate disputed between the Acehnese and the Dutch.

The first European who set his who are eyes on Lake Toba did so in 1853; the first tobaccoin the whole of North Sumatra was planted near Medan in 1863. Not surprisingly, therefore, North Sumatra retains many clear reminders both of its unique indigenous cultural heritage and of its late colonial heyday.

MEDAN AND THE PLANTATIONS

Medan, Indonesia's third largest city, is a monument to capitalism: its power and creativity, but also its harshness and ugliness. Great wealth passes through here, and air-conditioned cars, shopping centers and clubs testify to the affluence of those who control the flow. But Medan is a place of cruel contrasts, almost untempered by the civic pride and facelifting operations lavished on the national capital or upon tourist towns; Medan has long ceased to be anybody's showcase. Broken pavements and zinc-roofed shacks line the dirty streets, and swarms of *becak* circulate aimlessly. But it has vigor and life, and an energy as intoxicating as its exhaust fumes. It is not too gigantic to overwhelm the visitor and boasts a number of architectural jewels from a time when it had not yet been engulfed by the shadier side of its success.

Medan rose on the tide of the economic *laissez-faire* which transformed the Dutch colonies in the late nineteenth century. The modern town's founding and spiritual father was the pioneer tobacco planter Jacob Nienhuys. The name of this commercial imperialist has survived better than those of his military counterparts – he is still honored by the **Nienhuys Fountain** outside the post office.

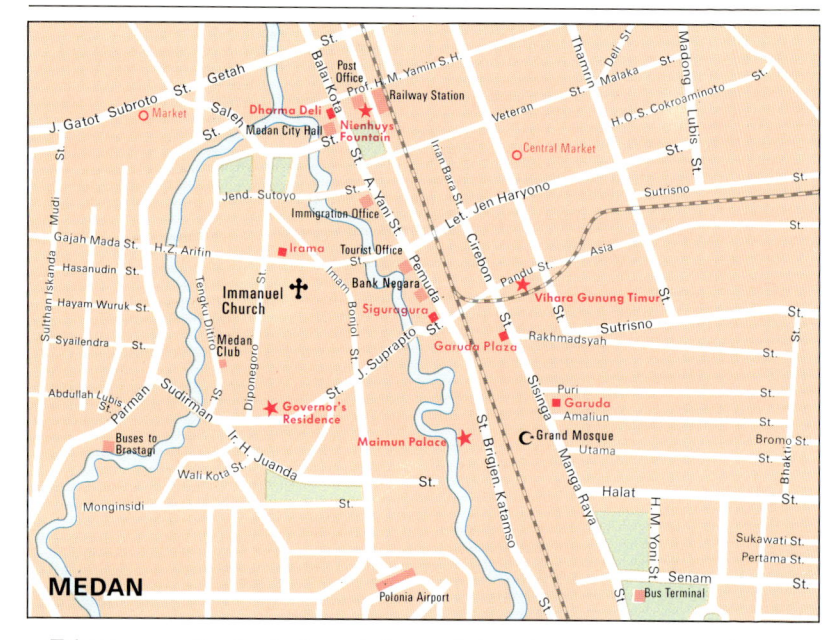

Tobacco was the beginning of the miracle, and Sumatran cigars are still a byword for those who understand such things. But other Midas crops followed: oil palm, tea, and above all rubber, riding not at the heels, but on the wheels of the young automobile industry. The land which grew all this wealth was known as the Deli *cultuurgebied* (Deli plantation zone), after the sultanate which had nominal sovereignty over it, and Medan was its metropolis.

The Sultan did more than comfortably out of his unholy alliance with Dutch capitalism: **Maimun Palace**, built for him by an Italian architect in 1888, is the most impressive royal residence anywhere in Indonesia. With its imposing arches and colonnades and stately grounds, the Maimun Palace remains the symbol of Medan. Care was also taken to pander to native religious sensibilities: the **Grand Mosque**, built in 1906, is the finest in Sumatra. Dutch props, however, could only prolong the downfall of the old social order; in 1945 and 1946 most of the aristocracy were overthrown by revolutionaries.

The assorted foreigners who made Medan – British and Americans as well as Dutch and Chinese – also put up some interesting buildings for their own use. Most of them are found along **Jl. A. Yani** and around **Merdeka Square**. The **Witte Societeit**, the exclusive European club, is now the Bank Negara. The old **Hotel de Boer**, once to Medan what Raffles Hotel was to Singapore, is the Hotel Dharma Deli. The lofty estate offices of **Harrison & Crossfield** are, appropriately enough, the headquarters of P.T. London Sumatra Indonesia; and the offices of Nienhuys' own company, the **Deli Maatschappij**, now belong to PTP Tobacco. The old **Governor's Residence,** on Jl. Jen. Sudirman, is still in use. The art-deco **Immanuel Church,** from 1921, still shakes to the power of Batak hymns.

During the occupation, the Japanese built a Shinto temple in Medan, one of only two in their short-lived Southeast Asian empire. When British troops reoc-

An ojek (motorcycle-taxi) driver taking a rest in Medan.

cupied the city in 1945, they stifled their instinct to burn it upon realizing that it would make a comfortable and stylish officers' mess. Today it is in use as the private **Medan Club**, on Jl. Kartini.

As in Indonesia's other centers of commerce, the Chinese community have been the principal heirs to Dutch business power. **Vihara Gunung Timur** on Jl. Hang Tuah is Sumatra's biggest Chinese temple; **Chinatown** is in the east of the city around Jl. Pandu. On Jl. A. Yani is the lavish pre-war mansion of one Chinese who did not live to see the succession, **Chong Ah Tie**. This unfortunate millionaire died of malnutrition in a Japanese prison camp; his mausoleum is in the **Pulau Brayan** cemetery. Sukarno forced the last foreign capitalists out of Medan when he nationalized their enterprises in 1957, but today the foreigners are back: Medan has foreign consulates, an international school, even a Japanese club and restaurants. Medan's port is **Belawan**, 28 km from the city center. In 1914, it was already handling more than 3000 ships per year; now it is a grim giant's playground of silos, warehouses and storage tanks, eternally under repair and extension.

What the European planters knew as Deli was the whole strip of land east of the central mountains from Aceh in the north to the Asahan river in the south. In this country, indentured Chinese and Javanese coolies, fed with opium to complete their dependency, were bought and sold like slaves by landlords whose decadent lifestyle gave the word Deli a taste of scandal as well as gold. The scientific side of the racket was handled by the earliest extension of the Buitenzorg botanical gardens, at **Sibolangit**, where it still runs today. Sibolangit has been joined by a more altruistic biological institution, the orangutan rehabilitation center at **Bohorok**, where a finger of the Leuser national reserve protrudes into North Sumatra from Aceh. The second

Enjoying their boat trip on Lake Toba.

town after Medan was **Pematang Siantar**, at the core of what is now the most productive plantation area of all, in the gently rising foothills of the spinal mountains. During the revolution, Pematang Siantar was briefly the Republican capital of Sumatra. **Pangkalan Brandan**, 80 km northwest of Medan, was the site of the first refinery to be built by the company which became Royal Dutch Shell, after a commercial oilfield was opened up in the neighborhood in the 1880s. This was the seed from which Indonesia's vast oil industry grew. Some antique equipment is preserved here, as significant a monument to Indonesia's modern history as any memento of the revolution.

Since 1957, most of the plantations of North Sumatra have been run as state enterprises, an unglamorous but reliable export machine ticking over in the growing shadows of oil and gas refineries. Today they are being streamlined and joined by new private plantations. The Deli strip is more than ever a plantation landscape, harshly geometric with its ordered ranks and squares of oil palms, rubber trees and tea bushes. Dusty access roads slice up the green blocks like long yellow wounds in the eroding earth. The latest chapter in North Sumatra's story of exploitation is being written high up on the Asahan river, where the three great concrete dams of the **Asahan Project** have drowned a spectacular gorge to supply hydroelectric power for the coastlands and for a huge Japanese aluminum smelter.

THE BATAKLANDS

As the *cultuurgebied* expanded, it encroached upon the territory of tribal peoples over whom the old sultanates had never established firm control. These original inhabitants of North Sumatra are known collectively as *Batak*, and their homeland is that section of Sumatra's mountain backbone between the Alas valley in Aceh and the Minangkabau

Old couple at a Toba Batak dance.

highlands of West Sumatra. At the widest point in the chain, the pine-covered peaks imprison extraordinary **Lake Toba**, at more than 1000 sq km the biggest lake in Southeast Asia. In turn, the lake encircles the sizeable island of **Samosir**. Batak country is one of the most productive and hospitable natural environments in Sumatra, and might have been expected to become a mighty state, as in Java. Instead, it remained a decentralized society of fortified villages without kings or sultans, ever torn by war but reintegrated by trade, kinship and religious ritual.

Heathens and cannibals, the Batak awakened the disgust of European visitors from Marco Polo to Stamford Raffles. Today, they take a tongue-in-cheek pride in their gory past, playing on their primitive image not only to attract tourists but also to intimidate other Indonesians. The Batak are among the most visible and dynamic ethnic groups in modern Indonesia. From their ranks have come writers, generals and two prime ministers. The stereotype Batak is an honest, blunt, volatile character; indeed, if a non-Batak Indonesian is compelled to speak less circuitously than the mores of his own ethnic group allow, he may apologize first for his "Batak-like" behavior.

In keeping with the fragmented nature of their old society, Bataks speak a number of different dialects and vary in custom and religion. Conventionally, the Bataks are divided into six categories: Karo, Pakpak, Simelungun, Toba, Angkola and Mandailing. Closest to Medan are the *Karo Batak*, who inhabit the valleys around the new administrative town of **Kabanjahe**. Despite their relative accessibility, the Karo are often described as the most traditional of all the Batak. Most Karo are nominally Christian, but missionaries have always had an uphill struggle here; ancestor worship is still practiced, and sorcery and witchcraft are taken seriously. Many "conversions" have been matters of political expediency. Kinship, and the clan system, which governs choice of marriage partners, dominate all social relations.

The Dutch built an agricultural college in **Brastagi**, 11 km north of Kabanjahe. In 1912, thousands of seed potatoes were experimentally distributed here among local Batak farmers; they and many other temperate crops caught on, and the area now supplies avocado, cabbage, carrots and flowers to Singapore as well as Medan. Brastagi was and is also a popular holiday resort – the **Bukit Kubu** is one of the most faithfully preserved colonial hotels in Indonesia. One attraction is the ascent of the imposing volcano **Sibayuk** which dominates the town. Another natural spectacle of the Karo area is the 120-m waterfall **Sipisopiso** near **Tongging**, overlooking Lake Toba. West of Tongging is the country of the **Pakpak** Batak, a small and obscure group noted as the guilty party in the last incident of cannibalism in North Sumatra, which took place in 1906.

Related to the Karo are the *Simalungun Batak,* occupying the northeast bank of the lake. At **Pematang Purba**, the house of a Simalungun chief has been preserved as a museum. The prime exhibit is the building itself, more than a century old and a beautiful example of Batak architecture. The all-wood construction is secured by notches and pegs, without a single nail; the roof covering is *ijuk,* thatch from the sugar palm. The gables and supporting piles are carved and painted in abstract patterns. A larger collection of Simalungun ethnographic exhibits is on display at the **Museum Simalungun** in **Pematang Siantar**, on the road down to the coast.

The most numerous and best known Batak tribe are the *Toba Batak,* from **Samosir island** and the lands on three sides of their eponymous lake. This is the group, with its megaliths, buffalo horns and hymn singing, which Indonesia and the world really know as Batak. In the late nineteenth and early twentieth centuries, the Toba Batak managed a happy leap from notorious but respected savagery to proud and still respected Christianity, without shedding all of their indigenous culture. They were converted by the German missionaries of the Rhineland Missionary Society, who placed a stronger emphasis than their Dutch colleagues upon the rapid creation of an independent church. Today the Toba Batak form the largest coherent Christian community in all Indonesia.

As the conventional first stop after Medan on the overland route through western Indonesia, Lake Toba has become quite a tourist trap in recent years. The original resort, and still the one favored by domestic visitors, is flashy **Prapat**, on the eastern shore at the ethnic boundary between the Simalungun and the Toba. But the international travelers prefer the earthier pleasures of Samosir island, parts of which, notably the **Tuktuk Peninsula** directly opposite Prapat,

Batak musicians. Left: Everyday life in a Batak village.

have consequently become an almost Kuta-like warren of *losmen*. Many of the locals have converted their picturesque traditional houses into lucrative tourist accommodations and have themselves retreated to nondescript bungalows to count their cash.

Tomok, the usual port of entry from Prapat, is a good place to see Toba Batak handicrafts and arts. Twenty years of tourism have almost exhausted the supply of actual Toba antiques, but dozens of families bring lengths of beautiful dark *ulos,* the handwoven cloth of the Batak, for sale to the visitors. Despite its present commercial role, this cloth is still important as an item of ritual exchange in Batak wedding ceremonies. The *Sigalegale* puppet dances weekly in Tomok – a tourist performance, admittedly, but the only one likely to be available. *Sigalegale* is a disturbingly lifelike wooden android, without any of the reassuring doll-like quality of the *wayang golek* puppet. Animated by an intricate mechanism of strings and pulleys, it dances to dispel the curse implicit in the death of a childless person, the spirit of whom is supposed to descend into the jointed mannequin. A sponge in the head enables the model to weep.

The great stone megaliths scattered around Tomok are another eerie remnant of old Batakdom. Like other peoples the length of the archipelago, the Toba Batak, normally content with perishable art and architecture, seem to have felt the urge to create more durable monuments for some especially hallowed purposes. Most characteristic of the Samosir megaliths are long stone sarcophagi with carved monster heads; though they look like coffins, these normally contained not a prostrate skeleton but the collected skulls of a whole family or clan, dug up and ceremonially re-interred after a year or so underground. Other such skull-tombs are in the shape of round stone urns. Not all are necessarily old – indeed, new ones are still made occasionally. A different style of megalith is to be found at **Ambarita**, where chairs and tables have been hewn out of single boulders – massive, squat and lichen-covered like some oversophisticated artistic joke. The villagers revel in their graphic explanation of the part played by this ponderous furniture in gruesome cannibalistic rituals.

Samosir is famous for its striking *adat* houses, distinguished by rakishly curved roofs which their inhabitants like to compare to the horns of a buffalo. The shape is an unconscious memory of a vanished design in which the main roof beam had to be curved because of the way in which it bore weight. Today it is pure styling, but none the less attractive, and none the easier to build, for that. Indeed, the art of building these houses is becoming distinctly rare, but there are still very many around, albeit mostly with shabby corrugated iron roofs in place of the original rustic *ijuk* thatch.

At **Simanindo** on the northern tip of the island, a particularly fine specimen has been restored to its original state. This was once the home of Raja Dapoton – not a real rajah with kingly powers, but the head of a *bius* or sacrifice-community, a quasi-religious federation of villages which celebrated its spiritual unity in an annual buffalo sacrifice. Buffalo were also slaughtered at the death of a *raja*, and the ten sets of horns attached to one of the main uprights indicates that ten generations of the same dynasty inhabited this house, which became a museum in 1968.

Simanindo as a whole is also a good example of a fortified *huta* or village. The stone and earth rampart with its narrow tunnel gate can still be seen. Formerly it was augmented by a formidable pallisade of sharpened bamboo stakes. The houses *(ruma)* were built in a single row on the lower side of the enclosure; opposite them were the smaller *sopo* or rice-barns, which also served as sleeping quarters for unmarried boys. Also in the courtyard stands a banyan tree, the condition and health of which were supposed to be intimately related with the welfare of the *huta* and its leading family.

The forsaken ruins of more spectacularly fortified *huta* are scattered on several elevations and clifftops in the interior of the island. The landscape here is a wide, dry highland of lava rock, pierced by narrow gorges with vertical, daunting walls embracing streams which turn to dangerous torrents after heavy rains. There are coffee and clove plantations between stretches of grassland and low forest. A popular two-day trek crosses the island from Tomok or Ambarita to **Panguruan** on the west coast. When it was built in 1909, this track was a first-class road, but today the eastern section is strictly for hikers. Panguruan was the Dutch administrative center for Samosir and the western shores of Lake Toba. Formerly it was connected to the mainland by a narrow peninsula, but in 1906 a canal was built which made Samosir a true island at last. A stone bridge spans the channel.

Three kilometers outside **Balige**, an attractive market town on the southern shore of the lake, is the grave of the most famous figure in Batak history: the tenth and last bearer of the title of *Singamanaraja*. Often described as god-kings or priest-kings, the Singamanaraja line exercised little actual day-to-day power but were held in religious awe by all Toba Batak. This ultimate member of the Singamanaraja was a serious obstacle both to the German mission and to the Dutch government. In 1883 he burned down two mission stations and a church, prompting military intervention in the Toba area; in 1907, the army finally tracked him down, captured and killed him. However, the ancestral home of the Singamanarajas located at **Bakara,** is currently being reconstructed.

Beyond **Tarutung** in the south is a

A saleswoman with textiles. Far right: On the way to a local festivity.

PADANG LAWAS

much more obscure country, the domain of the Muslim *Angkola* and *Mandailing Batak*. Not long before Christianity began to affirm its grip on the Toba area, the southern Bataklands were caught in the powerful shock waves of Islamic fervor generated by the Padri wars in Minangkabau West Sumatra. Today, though far from being the most devout of Sumatra's Muslims, these southerners are revolted by the dog-eating habits of their Toba neighbours, and often reluctant to call themselves Batak at all. Of the two groups, the Mandailing are the more southerly, occupying the narrow neck of mountains along the Trans-Sumatran Highway between **Padangsidempuan** and the border with West Sumatra. Traditional Mandailing houses are built on the same principle as those of the Toba, but are far bigger, and sometimes have multiple gables reminiscent of the Minangkabau style.

In the past, the Batak were often characterized as textbook "Proto-Malays" and placed firmly at the bottom of the conventional evolutionary ladder of Indonesian cultures. Yet they have clearly been influenced by Indian civilization. Batak even wrote using their own modification of an Indian alphabet: museums and souvenir shops in the Toba area display calendars and magical texts in this script, inscribed on bamboo and bark. As knowledge both of Batak anthropology and of Sumatran history has mounted, the Batak have come to seem more like a fragment of Indic Sumatra, hemmed in by Islam and defined by the absence of it, than a lost world of ancient tribes. As a source of the medicinal plant product camphor, the Bataklands participated very early in world trade. But the most tangible evidence of the past importance of North Sumatra is the startling collection of temple ruins at **Padang Lawas**, in a nowadays very out-of-the-way area south of **Gunungtua**, where tributaries of the **Barumun river** meet on the eastern flanks of the Barisan range.

Padang Lawas is among the outstanding mysteries of Indonesian archaeology. It constitutes the largest complex of antiquities in Sumatra, yet even the identity of the state which built it is unknown. There are no traces of urban settlement nearby, so it was probably an isolated religious sanctuary, like the Dieng plateau in Java. But for whom? Dated inscriptions here range from the eleventh to the fourteenth centuries, but none of them mentions a builder; one appears to be written in a Batak language. There are no rich bas-relief dioramas of everyday life, as in Java, to provide clues. Some have associated Padang Lawas with the lost empire of Sriwijaya, but so far this is only supposition.

The Padang Lawas antiquities were discovered by a German geologist in the mid-nineteenth century, but remained utterly obscure until another German, the eccentric freelance archaeologist and adventurer Friedrich Schnitger, excavated here in 1935. Schnitger's methods left much to be desired - his accounts, for instance, refer casually to emptying temples of their "rubbish". But he did succeed in saving some of the most important statues and inscriptions, which can now be seen in the national museum in Jakarta, and he recorded the state of the monuments before they deteriorated still further.

Of the twenty-odd temples, many are little more than tantalizing rubble today. This part of Sumatra offers no building stone; the main material used was brick, so that Padang Lawas has rotted as quickly as Majapahit. Some temples, however, retain their form and some of their decoration. The largest, known as **Biaro Bahal I**, has recently been restored. At 13 m tall, it consists of a hollow *candi* set upon a two-stage terrace and roofed by a hemispherical stupa.

Rather more is known about the iconography of these monuments than about their history. Almost all were Buddhist temples, but the Buddhism practiced here was of a peculiar and disquieting type. As with all great faiths, time and distance corrupted even this most elegant and intellectual of religions. In medieval Indonesia, it had become a royal cult existing alongside Hinduism and stressing various high-pressure mystical shortcuts to enlightenment. One of these shortcuts involved mastering the dark forces in the world by making direct contact with evil, and this was the technique celebrated at Padang Lawas. The dancing warriors and half-men on the temple walls are nothing less than demonic images. The ceremonies of the Bhairawa sect included mass human sacrifice; an old text compares the stench of the burning corpses to "the scent of ten thousand flowers". Priests, drunk on human blood, cackled, raved and danced into the night. Some authors have seen shades of this sophisticated barbarism in the Batak rites that others

Performing a war spirit dance on Nias. Left: Nias dancer.

considered for innocent savagery; if the former are correct, then even cannibalism among the Bataks was a memory of Indic "civilization".

NIAS ISLAND

A hundred and twenty kilometers off the west coast of North Sumatra is one of Indonesia's most spectacular freaks of cultural evolution, the island of **Nias**. Nias is the largest of a chain of islands running parallel to the long axis of Sumatra, a half-submerged echo of the mighty Barisan range. In Indonesia, islands do not mean isolation, and in colonial times, if not before, Nias was a significant participant in archipelagic trade. Yet the culture of Nias has somehow managed to pursue a maverick path of its own, elaborating on its Austronesian roots without significantly absorbing the waves of Indic, Islamic, and, until the last century, European influence which have swept over the rest of Sumatra. As a living experience, the old culture of Nias has now at last been substantially erased by more than a century of Protestant evangelism; there are more convincing "living museums" elsewhere in Indonesia, indeed even in Sumatra. But what gives Nias its special drawing power is the tangible, visible, spectacular and enduring style of its cultural products.

The Niassers are no throw-away, bamboo-and-rattan people: they prefer to leave their footprints in the sands of time, and the bigger the print, the better. Whole tree trunks, great blocks of stone, and eternal gold are their preferred media. Nias is Indonesia's most striking and most recent specimen of what used to be called a "megalithic culture": one in which the regular manufacture of huge stone monuments fulfils important social functions. An ingrained interest in size, solidity and permanence also gives a unique texture to Nias art and domestic architecture.

NIAS

While the elements from which the aesthetic is built up are recogniazble from elsewhere in the archipelago, the overall effect could be described as "un-Indonesian". A *behu*, for instance, is a stone obelisk, often topped by a bird statue, like something out of imperial Rome. A *nio-gaji* is like a giant stone mushroom, decorated, perplexingly, on the underside but not on the top. These and other megaliths were erected either at funeral celebrations or in connection with the great "feasts of merit" whereby chiefs destroyed and distributed their wealth to buy the right to increased rank and status. Less easy to come upon today are the carvings which, with an almost African blend of crudity and elegance, depict Nias warriors in strange flared sleeveless tunics and Norman helmets.

Most of what Nias has to offer by way of art and spectacle is concentrated in the southern part of the island, where around 30 traditional villages are still inhabited and many other groups of megaliths occur at abandoned settlement sites in the scrubby countryside. Southern Nias was fiercely resistant both to military and spiritual conquest. Dutch military expeditions burned villages here in 1847 and 1863, but not until 1908 was colonial power respected. The Rhineland Missionary Society had to withdraw its post here in 1886, and Christianity made little headway until after 1920. **Gomo**, an inaccessible place a roadless 15 km from the southeastern coast, is regarded as the cradle of the Nias race, but the most interesting village is **Bawomataluwo**, a short drive from the main southern port, **Teluk Dalam**.

The **Chief's House** in Bawomataluwo is the biggest in Nias and must rank as one of the finest pieces of architecture in Indonesia. The graceful curving roof sweeps up to a majestic height of 16 m at the ridge; the body is supported on a powerful lattice of wooden piles, each three-quarters of a meter thick. Even the unfortunate replacement of thatch by corrugated iron roofing does not destroy the effect. Inside, complex beamwork under the roof has eliminated the need for large numbers of uprights passing down through the living area, which is consequently as spacious as a castle. Shafts of light from open battens in the roof illuminate superior woodcarving on walls and beams.

The rest of Bawomataluwo is, correspondingly, the epitome of a south Nias traditional village. In front of the chief's house are two standing stones; one of them, an 8-tonne slab, was dragged 4 km uphill from its quarry to be erected here in 1914.

These megaliths stand at one end of a skilfully paved stone "runway", formerly used for dancing and ritual. One live performance from the old repertoire is still available, at a price, to tourists: it is the famous stone-jumping spectacle, in which athletic youths jump 2-m stone pyramids to prove their manhood. In the past, this feat was made even more formi-

On crystal-clear waters off Nias.

dable by bamboo blades and stakes attached to the obstacle. According to one story, the jumping-stone was originally intended as a simulation of the fortifications which a warrior would face when trying to enter an enemy village. Old Nias was a violent place, even by Indonesian standards. Its tribes lived in constant war with each other, mainly with the intent of procuring slaves for service, sale or ritual sacrifice. Foreigners bought, as well as kidnapped, many Nias slaves; one of the principal consumers in the eighteenth century was Dutch Batavia. Small wonder that an important village like Bawomataluwo is built in a matchless defensive location, on a steep prominence approached by a narrow switchback pathway of more than 400 steps. There are fine views over the surrounding countryside, which also contains many other interesting villages - **Hilisimaetano** is particularly recommended.

Despite its relatively recent "discovery" in the 1970s, Nias is no longer *outré* as a tourist destination. It seems particularly popular with Italians. Nevertheless, its eccentric location and limited facilities keep it off most standard itineraries. What development there is is very unevenly distributed. The local government has done its best to concentrate accommodation facilities in the administrative capital, **Gunungsitoli**, and tours and events in Bawomataluwo, which has become almost as worldly as Samosir. A specialist development is the ragged surfers' Mecca of **Lagundi Bay**, the blue water of which can be seen from Bawomataluwo. The waves which storm in here from the vast Indian Ocean are strictly for professionals. But throughout much of the Nias countryside - partly thanks to the appalling roads - a foreigner is a great and entertaining rarity. This is particularly so in the north of the island, which, though colonized and Christianized for longer than the south, has had less of the recent limelight.

MEDAN

INEXPENSIVE: **Irama**, in alley by junction Jl Sukamulia/Jl Listrik. **Melati**, Jl Amaluin 6, Tel: 516021, near ALS bus station (to Lake Toba). **Mona**, Jl Sukamulia. **Tapian Nabaru**, Jl Hang Tuah 6, Tel: 512155. **Siguragura**, Jl Let Gen Suprapto 2K, Tel: 323991. *MODERATE:* **Angkasa**, Jl Sutaom 1, Tel: 321244. **Garuda**, Jl Sisingamanaraja 27, Tel: 22760. **Dharma Deli**, Jl Balai Kota 2, Tel: 327011. **Dirgasurya**, Jl Imam Bonjol 6, Tel: 323433. **Pardede Intern.**, Jl Ir H Juanda 14, Tel: 323866. **Sumatra**, Jl Sisingamanaraja 21, Tel: 24973. *LUXURY:* **Danau Toba International**, Jl Imam Bonjol 7, Tel: 327000. **Garuda Plaza**, Jl Sisingamanaraja 18, Tel: 326255. **Polonia**, Jl Jen Sudirman 14, Tel: 325300. **Tiara Medan**, Jl Cut Mutiah, Tel: 516000.

Food

INDONESIAN: **De Boer**, Hotel Dharma Deli. **Bukit Kubu**, Jl Padang Bulan (7 km outside city centre). **Garuda**, Jl Pemuda 20C/D, Tel: 327692. **Vegetarian Indonesia**, Jl Gandhi 63A (beside Bioskop Benteng), Tel: 526812. *CHINESE:* **Bali Plaza**, Jl Kumango 1A, Tel: 515505/14852. **Hawa Mandarin**, Jl Mangkubumi 18. **Polonia**, Polonia Hotel, Jl Sudirman. *WESTERN:* **Lyn's**, Jl Jen A Yani. **Tip Top**, Jl A Yani 92A.

Shopping

ANTIQUES & CURIOS: The specialist street is Jl Jen A Yani. **Indonesia Art Shop**, no.1A. **Borobudur Art Shop**, no.32. **Toko Yulida**, no.33. **Toko Selatan**, no.44. **Toko Asli**, no.62. **Toko Bali**, no.68.
ART: **ABC Art Gallery**, Jl Jen A Yani 50. **Nu Chou** (Chinese brush painting), 74, Jl Thamrin (over Phoenix photo studio). **Simpassri** (local artists' display), Jl Jen Suprapto, off Jl Teratai.

Museums & Zoos

North Sumatra State Museum, Jl MH Joni, Tel: 25799. Tue-Thu 9.00-14.30, Fri 9.00-11.00, Sat 9.00-13.30, Sun 9.30-14.30, Mon closed. **Museum Juang 45** (revolutionary history), Jl Pemuda 17. Mon-Thu 8.30-13.00, Fri 8.30-12.00, Sat 8.30-13.00, Sun closed. **Museum Perjuangan 'Bukit Barisan'** (military), Jl H Zainul Arifin 8, Tel: 326972. Mon-Thu 8.00-13.00, Fri 8.00-11.00, Sat 8.00-12.00, Sun closed. **Medan Zoo**, Jl Brigjen Katamso, Desa Baru. Daily 8.00-16.00.

Cultural performances

Bina Budaya, Jl Perintis Kemerdekaan (opp Angkasa Hotel) - twice-weekly cultural events. **Taman Ria Amusement Park** - permanent cultural exhibits, also occasional performances. **Tapian Daya Cultural Centre** is on Jl Binjei.

Tourist Information

North Sumatra Tourist Office, Jl Palang Merah 66, Tel: 511101/512300. **Kantor Wilayah 1 Sumatera Utara/Aceh** (also covers Aceh province), Jl Alfalah 22, Tel: 322838.

Post

GPO, Jl Bukit Barisan, Tel: 23612/25945.

Hospitals

Rumah Sakit Umum Dr Pirngadi (General Hospital), Jl Prof HM Yamin 47, Tel: 23332.
Private hospitals: **St. Elizabeth**, Jl Imam Bonjol 38, Tel: 322455. **Herna**, Jl Mojopahit 118, Tel: 510766.

Consulates

Malaysia, Jl Diponegoro 11, Tel: 25315/323261.
Netherlands, Jl Abdul Lubis 7A, Tel: 526034.
Singapore, Jl Teuku Daud, Tel: 23356/327978.
United Kingdom, Jl Jen A Yani 2, Tel: 325735.
USA, Jl Imam Bonjol 13, Tel: 322200/322463.
Germany, Jl Let Jen S Parman 217, Tel: 322043/520908.

Transport

AIR: Medan is Indonesia's western air gateway, numerous flights to Penang and Singapore as well as major Indonesian cities. **Polonia Airport** is 2 km from city center; connection by *becak*, from outside gate, or taxi. The fit can even walk. *Airline offices:* **Garuda**, Jl Let Jen Suprapto 2, Tel: 25700/ 25702. **Merpati**, Jl Brig Jen Katamso 37, Tel: 516617. **MAS** (Malaysia), in Hotel Danau Toba International, Jl Imam Bonjol 17, Tel: 519333. **Singapore Airlines**, Jl Imam Bonjol 16. **SMAC** (Sabang Merauke Air Charter), Jl Imam Bonjol 59, and at airport.
SEA: Passenger boats connect Medan and Penang twice weekly; tickets from **Siguragura Travel Agency**, Jl Jen Suprapto 2K, or **Eka Sukma**, Jl Brig Jen Katamso 62A. *Bemo* for the port (Belawan) leave from Stasiun Sei Wampu, Jl Sei Wampu. **Pelni** operates services to Tanjung Pinang (Riau) & Jakarta. **Pelni office**: Jl Kol Sugiono 5, Tel: 25100/ 25190, or Jl Palang Merah, Belawan.
ROAD: Many long-distance bus cos, each with own terminal, eg: **ALS**, Jl Amaliun 2A, Tel: 22014. **ABS**, Jl Sutrisno 128, Tel: 322352. **ANS**, Jl Sising-amanaraja16, Tel: 25775/515775. Others on and around Jl Sisingamanaraja. Buses for Aceh leave from Stasiun **Sei Wampu**, Jl Sei Wampu, off Jl Parn W of city.
INTERNAL: Sambu terminal, near market, is main *bemo* station. But *becak* often more convenient. Taxis licensed but not metered.
Main taxi stands: Polonia Hotel, Danau Toba International Hotel.

BRASTAGI

INEXPENSIVE: **Bukit Tongging**, Jl Veteran 48G. **Wisma Dieng**, Jl Udara 27. **Ginsata** Hotel, Jl Veteran 79. **Wisma Sibayak**, near minibus station. Inexpensive bungalows just out of town: **Karo Hill**, **Papirpir**, **Laterisa**. *MODERATE:* **Brastagi Cottage**, Jl Gundaling. **Bukit Kubu**, Jl Sempurna 2. **Rose Garden**, outside of town. **Rudang Hotel**, Jl Sempurna, Tel: 43.

PRAPAT

INEXPENSIVE: **Pago Pago Inn**, Jl Haranggaol. **Soloh Jaya**, Jl Haranggol. On Jl Sisingamanaraja: **Singgalang**, **Samosir**, **PT Andilo Nancy**, **PT Dolok Silau**. *MODERATE:* **Astari**, Jl Samosir. **Budi Mulya**, Jl Samosir 17, Tel: 41216. **Mimpin Tua**, Jl Talun Sungkit 9. *LUXURY:* **Patrajasa Prapat**, Jl Prapat, Tel: 41796. **Natour Hotel Prapat**, Jl Marihat 1, Tel: 41012.

Cultural performances

Batak Cultural Centre, Jl Josef Sinaga 19, holds music and dance events Sat nights. **Prapat Hotel** also stages cultural performances. Weeklong Danau Toba festival held every June.

Shopping

Jl Sisingamanaraja for souvenirs. More exciting is **Saturday market** by Tigaraja ferry dock. **Labuhan Graha**, 25 km from Prapat, specialises in *ulos* cloth.

Tourist Information / Post

Pusat Informasi, Jl Samosir (at entrance to Prapat). **Post office**: Jl Sisingamanaraja.

Transport

PT Andilo Nancy & other agencies on Jl Sisingamanaraja sell long-distance bus tickets. Ferries for Samosir leave from Tigaraja dock near market.

SAMOSIR

INEXPENSIVE: Concentrated on Tuktuk peninsula, with more than 40 lakeside *losmen*, and at Tuktuk Pandan, a quieter enclave between Tuktuk & Ambarita. Elsewhere: **Rohandy's** & **Gordon II**, Ambarita. *MODERATE:* **Toba Beach**, Tomok. **Carolina**, Tuktuk. **Toledo Inn**, Tuktuk. **Pulau Tao Cott.**, on island off Simanindo. **Sopo Toba**, Ambarita.

Shopping

Tomok main street is permanent market for Toba Batak crafts and souvenirs.

Museums

Museum Huta Bolon, Simanindo, Samosir, open daily 9.00-17.00.

Cultural Performances

Inquire **Golden Tourist Information Service**, Tomok, & **Museum Huta Bolon**, Simanindo.

Transport

Regular ferries between Prapat & Tomok and between Tigaras & Simanindo. Road bridge approach via Tele on western side of lake.
Occasional buses run almost circumference of island (but loop unconnected in far South) and inland from the west as far as Roonggurni.

AROUND LAKE TOBA

Museum Pemda, Jl Pasanggrahan 1, Balige.
Museum Rumah Bolon Pematang Purba, Pematang Purba. Mon-Sat 7.30-16.30.

PEMATANG SIANTAR

Museum Simalungun, Jl Jen Sudirman 10, Tel: 21054. Mon-Sat 8.00-15.00, Sun closed.
Pematang Siantar Zoo, Jl Kapt MH Sitorus 10, Tel: 21511. Mon-Thu 8.00-15.00, Fri 8.00-11.30, Sat 8.00-14.00, Sun 8.00-18.00.

SIBOLGA

Bintang Terang, Pelabuhan Baru. **Indah Sari**, Jl A Yani 27-29. **Hotel Maturi**, opp Indah Sari. **Hotel Taman Nauli**, north of town.

NIAS

GUNUNGSITOLI: In town center, **Ketilang**, **Tenang**, **Wisata** & **Gunungsitoli**. 6 km out of town, higher-priced **Wisma Soliga**.
TELUKDALAM: Sabar Menanti, **Wisma Jamburae**, **Effendi**, all near waterfront.
LAGUNDI BAY: A dozen *losmen* with attached eating places in **Jamborai Village**.
OTHER: Most villages, incl Bawamataluo, can arrange overnight accommodation for courteous visitors, usually in headman's house.

Transport

AIR: Merpati & SMAC have scheduled flights Medan-Gunungsitoli (**Binaka Airport**, 19 km from town).
SEA: Jumping-off point for Nias is **Sibolga**, 107 km by road from Prapat. One boat per day leaves **Pelabuhan Lama** harbor for Telukdalam (S Nias), & one from **Pelabuhan Baru** for Gunungsitoli (N Nias).
LOCAL: Regular daily bus and less regular ferry run Gunungsitoli-Telukdalam, but roads elsewhere may only carry motorcycles or legs. Bicycles sometimes rented in south.

PADANG LAWAS

From **Padangsidempuan**, buses leave for **Gunungtua**, which has *oplet* services to **Portibi**, access point for ruins.
Portibi is also home of site caretaker, who can arrange guide.

MALAY SUMATRA

MALAY SUMATRA

ISLAND RIAU
MAINLAND RIAU
SOUTH SUMATRA PROVINCE
JAMBI

Colonialism and commerce may have made Medan in many ways the heart of Sumatra, but it is a very eccentric heart. The plantation zone is a freak of fertility at the northern extremity of a great band of malarial lowland jungle and acid mangrove swamp, which stretches for two-thirds of the length of Sumatra east of the Barisan range. The dominant element in this, perhaps the most quintessentially Sumatran landscape, is water.

Huge brown rivers wind ponderously across the wide, wet, olive-drab plain to discharge themselves over branching brackish deltas. At the coast, the mangrove-lined tidal channels interlock with each other until the divide between land and sea is unclear; the coastline seems to crumble gradually eastwards into a maze of islands.

The dominant people of this watery country are the *Malays,* historically the most influential and the best known of all Indonesia's ethnic groups. Not without reason did English writers, before the rise of modern national terminology, refer to the whole of island Southeast Asia as the "Malay Archipelago".

The Malay language was a *lingua franca* for traders from Aceh to the Philippines long before it became, in slightly different forms, the national language of both Indonesia and Malaysia. "Malay" was a synonym for the Muslim, maritime culture which united the trading ports of the island world, a flexible category which almost anyone could join by converting to the Islamic faith and speaking the Malay language. People calling themselves Malays were to be found every where in the archipelago, and even today members of interior tribes in Kalimantan still "masuk Melayu" ("enter Malayness") to become respectable in the cosmopolitan coastal towns. But the accepted homelands of the Malay people are eastern Sumatra and the Malay peninsula, on opposite sides of the Strait of Malacca.

Modern political geography has thus split the Malay world down the middle: in the space of a few decades, Sumatran Malays have learned to regard their cousins in Malaysia as foreigners, and Christians from Ambon as compatriots. But within Indonesia the Malays still perceive themselves as a distinct ethnic group. In Sumatra they dominate the three east-coast provinces of **Riau**, **Jambi** and **South Sumatra**, with a combined population of some eight million, about a quarter of that of Sumatra as a whole, for almost half of the land area.

Left: Riau women sell fruits and vegetables.

MALAY SUMATRA

ISLAND RIAU

Appropriately for a maritime people, the foremost seat of Malay culture in modern times has not been on the mainland but in the **Riau Archipelago**, which litters the Strait of Malacca at its narrow southern end, just off the tip of the Malay peninsula. This critical strategic location astride the most important shipping lane in the world has made Riau an historic focus of power and piracy, wealth and war. The cultural and historical interest of insular Riau combines with its accessibility and the desert-island beauty of its coasts and islets – almost uniqe in eastern Sumatra – to make this the most immediately attractive part of Malay Sumatra for the foreigner.

After the fateful fall of Malacca to the Portuguese in 1511, the descendants of the Malacca sultans established a new kingdom, Johor, further south. At various times the royal seat of Johor was not at present-day Johor, on the Malay peninsula opposite Singapore, but in Riau. As in Java, the repeated changes of capital were usually caused by succession quarrels and civil wars. In 1819, Raffles took advantage of one of these to snatch one of the Riau islands from under the noses of the Dutch; his prize was to become the city-state of Singapore, whose skyscrapers now gaze distainfully across the water. The British intervention saw the old state of Johor permanently divided into two kingdoms: Johor proper, on the British (now Malaysian) side of the strait, and **Riau-Lingga** on the Dutch (Indonesian) side.

Riau-Lingga was so called because it was itself an uneasy union of two separate courts: that of the native Malay sultan, and that of a Bugis viceroy. Old Indonesian political thought favored such two-headed states, but the ethnic division was unusual. The Bugis aristocrats were the descendants of interlopers from the east who, dispersing from their South Su-

ISLAND RIAU

lawesi homeland during the wars of the seventeenth and eighteenth centuries, had insinuated themselves into the governing elites of many Malay states. The Bugis court was established on the tiny island of **Penyenget**, across the harbor from **Tanjung Pinang** on the south side of the largest island of the Riau archipelago, **Bintan**. When the position of viceroy was abolished under Dutch pressure at the beginning of this century, Penyenget became the true capital of a united kingdom; but in 1911 it was abandoned when the refractory sultan was dismissed by the Dutch and replaced by a direct Dutch administration.

Penyenget is well worth a visit for its historic remains, which are now being progressively restored. The palace buildings themselves are ruined or vanished, but several royal tombs and an attractive old yellow mosque are in good condition. The mosque contains a unique library including some hand-scripted korans. Riau has an old reputation as a literary center for the Malay language, and when the Dutch decided in the 1890s to standardize the Malay language used in their Indies administration and school system, it was the Riau variant which they selected as the official model.

Long known as a den of smugglers, the fast-growing port of **Tanjung Pinang** bustles with the business, shady and otherwise, of three countries. The goldsmiths accept Singapore dollars, the televisions in coffee shops and restaurants are more likely to be blaring forth Kuala Lumpur advertising than Jakarta propaganda. There are some parks, supermarkets and concrete-box suburbs, but at its heart Tanjung Pinang is still a raw Malay trading town of wood and water. Houses are built on long piles over the sea, which is both front street and sewer. Local travel is by boat or along rickety wooden walkways suspended over slicks of waterborne garbage. Watercraft of all descriptions fuss bewilderingly to and fro while an amplified call to prayer floats across th harbour from a tin-roofed mosque. These are images repeated throughout the Malay parts of Sumatra. The **Riau Kandil Museum**, 2 km outside Tanjung Pinang, is an informative tribute to the way of life which they symbolize.

The commercial dynamism of Tanjung Pinang is mainly parasitic. Since the foundation of Singapore, Indonesian Riau has been forced to live in the economic shadow of its northern neighbors, picking up crumbs by providing odd services unavailable or prohibitively expensive over the water. There is, for instance, no direct surface link from Singapore to mainland Sumatra; sea passengers are forced to transfer in Tanjung Pinang. Just outside the town, the twin villages known anonymously as **Kampung 12** and **Kampung 16** provide for another type of visitors' demand – regulated prostitution, as cheap as only poverty can make it. Similar in conception, if not in scale, is the giant development project now underway to transform a large part of **Batam Island** into an industrial zone.

Beyond Batam and Bintan, Riau quickly becomes wilder. Most settlements are just tiny stilt-top fishing villages, sometimes perched out on fringing reefs, hundreds of meters from land and fresh water. Hundreds of islands are completely uninhabited. But at night, the straits between them are sprinkled with the man-made stars of pressure lanterns, used by fishermen to lure dazzled fish to *prahu* and stilt-houses on the dark water. The warm, shallow seas of island Riau are as clear as gin and contain a spectacular marine life; divers also come here for the wrecks which the wars and storms of the centuries have left among the coral.

Near **Tanjungbalai** on **Karimun** island, west of Batam, a Buddhist religious inscription has been cut in Indic characters into a flat rock. This utterly isolated antiquity is one of the earliest pieces of

Riau market trader selling her crops.

MAINLAND RIAU

evidence of Indian culture in Indonesia. The island of **Lingga**, due south of Bintan, was the seat of the Malay half of the Riau-Lingga state in the nineteenth century. The jungle-beleaguered remains of the royal palace and mosque, together with the graves of the Malay sultans, lie within walking distance of the little port of **Daik**. **Dabo**, on the adjacent island of **Singkep**, is the center of a small tin mining industry. In the days of the sultanate, Singkep paid its annual tribute in this metal. The province of Riau also includes the much more remote islands scattered thinly across the South China Sea as far east as Borneo and as far north as the nature reserve of **Pulau Laut**, on the same latitude as Brunei. Driving a wedge of Indonesian territorial water between the two halves of Malaysia, these otherwise insignificant outposts of the *merah putih* are jealously guarded for their strategic importance and suspected oil wealth.

Old Riau was a sea kingdom with dependencies on mainland Sumatra, but the modern province of Riau includes a huge slice of the mother island, known as **Riau Daratan** or Mainland Riau. The capital is no longer Tanjung Pinang but **Pekanbaru**, a new town about 160 km inland on the **Siak river**. Like every big river in eastern Sumatra, the Siak once supported a trading kingdom of its own – **Siak Sri Indrapura**, now an obscure little place half-way between Pekanbaru and the sea. The last palace of the defunct sultanate has been preserved there as the **Museum Asserajah El Hasyimiah**. Built between 1886 and 1889, this is an interesting piece of architecture from the beginning of the golden age of Dutch imperialism, a solid castle-like construction with Islamic styling, set in elegant gardens. The building was renovated and the museum established with financial aid from the new lord of the Siak, the (American) oil giant Caltex.

Caltex has also sponsored the meteoric growth of Pekanbaru itself. Until the discovery, on the eve of the Pacific war, of major oil deposits to its north, Pekanbaru was just a lively but small river-port at the highest navigable point on the Siak. Today it is a booming oil town with an international airport. Pekanbaru's roads, power, education and health services are all well above usual Indonesian standards thanks to the pastoral care of Caltex Pacific Indonesia. The wells themselves are scattered over a huge tract of forest, but the very earliest, which first flowed in March 1941, can be seen, complete with commemorative plaque, on the main road 3 km north of the **Minas** camp. The Siak river is navigable, but not for tankers, so the oil is pumped through a prodigious surface pipeline direct to the purpose-built port and refinery on the coast at **Dumai**, one of the biggest oil terminals in the world.

The forests of these oilfields are the home of one of lowland Sumatra's enigmatic tribal populations, known by local Malays as the *Sakai*. It is not really known whether they represent a pre-Malay "remnant" like the upland Bataks, or an isolated splinter of later migrations – fugitive slaves, perhaps. The Malays regard them with the customary mixture of contempt and fear, despising their lack of civilization but, half-animist themselves, fearing the spiritual power of the tribesmen. Oil drilling, as such, is relatively friendly to the environment, and has not destroyed the rain-forest habitat of the Sakai, nor its rich fauna, which includes tapir, rhino and even tiger. But the logging industry, which makes glad use of jungle roads constructed by the oilmen, poses a growing threat. The government is seeking to resettle the Sakai in permanent villages where they can be educated and controlled. Some have moved voluntarily to the Rumbai-Dumai road, where their thatched bamboo huts are in jarring contrast to the shining oil pipeline which has brought so much change to Sumatra.

Apart from the Siak, other important rivers of mainland Riau include the **Rokan** and the **Kampar**, renowned for the spectacular and dangerous tidal bores which surge along them from the sea at spring tides. River-dwelling Malays have made a sport of "surfing" the advancing wave in small canoes; on the Kampar, this forms the core of an annual festival.

High on the clear upper reaches of the Kampar, near the border with West Sumatra and at the foot of the Barisan range, is the only well-known antiquity of Riau province: a small but striking group of Buddhist temples known as **Muara Takus**. Of the several buildings visible, **Maligai Stupa** is the best preserved. The slender, waisted, uncluttered profile of this *stupa* reveals a gentler aesthetic at work than that which produced Padang Lawas.

Beneath its crumbling brick skin Maligai has a core of hard sandstone which has saved its graceful form from the ravages of time. The temples at Muara Takus probably date from the elfth and twelfth centuries. Like those at Padang Lawas, they have been associated with the shadowy empire of Srivijaya, which Chinese sources depict rising from nowhere in the late seventh century to dominate the whole of the western archipelago for 600 years. In 1937, a Dutch scholar suggested that Muara Takus was the site of the Srivijaya capital itself, thus giving Riau its own stake in a debate which has continued hotly ever since.

SOUTH SUMATRA PROVINCE

Much evidence suggests that Srivijaya was based not at a remote interior citadel but at a great trading port, and the conventional favorite has always been **Palembang**. The southernmost of the big Malay towns, modern Palembang is the capital of the important province of South

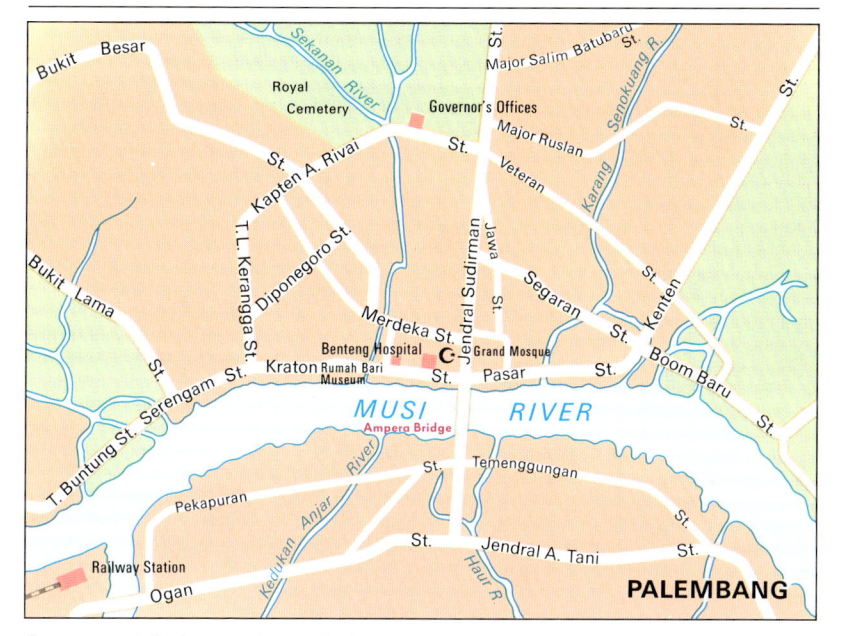

Sumatra and the largest city on the island after Medan. Palembang is not a coastal harbor but a river port, some 100 km from the mouth of the **Musi river**. But the Musi is Sumatra's largest river, draining an area of rain forest almost as big as Ireland; by the time it reaches Palembang it is already hundreds of meters wide and navigable for ships of 10,000 tonnes. Salt and fresh water are all the same to the amphibian culture of the Malays, who have reproduced the waterborne lifestyle of the Riau archipelago here in the heart of Sumatra. Piletop settlements line the banks of the Musi from Palembang to the sea, the piles increasing in length with the tidal range. At **Sungsang**, the floors stand a dizzy five meters above the river at low water, and visitors can walk for kilometers along high *nipah*-trunk boulevards. Formerly there were many dwellings which literally floated on rafts, although these are becoming rarer now. Many Palembang Malays prefer to build their homes over water even when roads and building land are available. A thousand years ago, the situation was probably not very different. One account of the Srivijayan capital mentions that while the king lived on dry land, his subjects made their homes on the water, where they were exempt from tax.

That the city was composed mainly of wooden pile-buildings helps to explain why so few relics of Srivijaya's greatness have survived. Of the moderate haul of inscriptions and Buddhist images collected here over the years, many have long since been removed to the National Museum in Jakarta. The remainder are on display in Palembang's **Rumah Bari Museum**. One of the finest is a serene Buddha carved in granite, a rock which does not occur near Palembang and must have been imported. Other exhibits include Chinese pottery excavated in the city. **Bukit Seguntang**, south of town, is supposed to have been the site of a religious sanctuary. Local legend has it that a descendant of Alexander the Great came down from heaven to this hill to become the first king of Srivijaya. Even allowing for tropical rates of decay, the absence of temple ruins is surprising given that when a Chinese pilgrim visited Srivijaya in 671, there were a thousand monks there studying Buddhist texts. So enough doubt remains for speculation on the location of Srivijaya to continue.

After the demise of Srivijaya in the fourteenth century, Palembang seems to have come under the rule of Javanese kings. Strong Javanese cultural influence is still evident. For instance, Palembang is one of only two places outside Java which have traditionally produced *batik* cloth. The traditional house of the Palembang elite, with its two-tier *limasan* roof, is also of Javanese inspiration; a fine example forms the centerpiece of the Rumah Bari museum.

Despite the Javanese influx, Palembang regained its independence, becoming one of the most powerful sultanates in Sumatra and a wily and resilient opponent of both Javanese and European expansion. The VOC defeated Palembang and established a fort there in 1659, but the sultanate retained considerable autonomy. The **Grand Mosque** in the center of town was founded in 1740, at a time of renewed wealth and expansion. At the **Royal Cemetery**, most of Palembang's sultans are buried. The best-known today is Mahmud Badruddin, whose slaughter of the resident Dutch garrison in 1811 led eventually to his exile in 1821 and to the end of real independence for Palembang. Under Dutch rule, Palembang increased in commercial importance and in 1900 it was the biggest city in Sumatra. The Chinese presence grew accordingly. On **Kemaro Island**, at the confluence of the Musi and two of its tributaries, there is a picturesque Chinese temple about a century old.

The standard symbol of modern Palembang is the monumental **Ampera Bridge**, the first and only road link between the two halves of the city across the brown depths of the Musi. When it was built 25 years ago, the central span of the Ampera bridge could be raised to the top of its high pillars to allow big ships to pass underneath; but ambitious mechanisms tend to have short working lives in Indonesia, and this one has been out of order for a long time.

The economic basis of Palembang's wealth has changed repeatedly over its long history. It is often said that Srivijaya, in contrast to the great Javanese kingdoms, possessed no agricultural hinterland, drawing its power instead from gold, luxury forest products, transit trade and military might. But today, skilful land management has made the drier parts of Palembang's hinterland a valuable garden of rice, rubber, coffee, cotton and fruit.

In the seventeenth century, pepper, native to the foothills of the Himalayas, was the main trade crop. But equally as important as the agricultural products have been the mineral ones. In the eighteenth century, Palembang had the good fortune to gain control of the newly discovered

Everyday life on muddy waters. Left: Chinese inhabitant of Tanjung Pinang.

sources of valuable tin on the islands of **Bangka** and **Belitung**, opposite the mouth of the Musi. Tin is still extracted on these islands, where many of the population are descendants of Chinese contract-coolies once shipped down from Canton to labor in the mines.

In the present century, oil has overshadowed all other exports. The first drilling concession in the Palembang area was issued in 1899, not long after the first finds in North Sumatra and long before the opening of the Riau fields. The South Sumatra Basin is now the biggest and most productive oilfield in Indonesia, exploited by the state oil giant, Pertamina, which has given Palembang its television station, sports stadium and clock tower. The Pertamina headquarters is at **Plaju**, just east of Palembang, where the cracking towers and gantries of a huge refinery and petrochemicals plant stand like a floodlit space platform in the jungle.

At the western margin of South Sumatra is a set of monuments from the opposite end of Indonesian history, the **Pasemah megaliths**. These mysterious carved stones lie scattered through the valley beyond **Lahat**, where a tributary of the Musi cuts into the Barisan range near the border with Bengkulu province. Some of the most striking megaliths, including the magnificent elephant sculpture known as *Batu Gajah*, have lately been removed to the museum in Palembang, but many remain, including an impressive concentration in **Tegurwangi** village, between **Pagaralam** and **Tanjungsakti**. Though they are conventionally described as "prehistoric", recent research indicates that some at least are from the seventh century or later, contemporary with Srivijaya. At any rate, these are no "stone age" monuments: many of the sculptures depict figures with metal swords and rings, and even bronze kettledrums of the Dong Son pattern known, to have come to Indonesia at the beginning of the Christian era. They must therefore represent a sustained megalithic tradition, comparable to Nias and Samosir. The monuments at Pasemah include avenues of upright stones, troughs with human heads at each end, giant rice-pounding blocks, stone terraces, hollow chests and statues as well as bas-relief carvings which utilize the natural curves of their parent boulders so skilfully that they resemble three-dimensional sculptures. Even the sparse local population, which claims descent from Javanese Majapahit, is at a loss to explain the purpose of most of the imagery, and nothing suggests that this remote valley will ever divulge the secrets of its past.

The desolate riverine wilderness north of the Musi is the home of the **Kubu** tribesmen, a marginal forest people comparable to the Sakai of mainland Riau. Malays make much of the story that although the Kubu live out their lives surrounded by rivers and swamps, their superstitious fear of water is so great that they never bathe. The ancestral hearth of the Kubu is supposed to lie on the River **Lalang**, in one of the emptiest parts of Sumatra.

JAMBI

Sandwiched between the giants of South Sumatra and Riau is the smaller province of **Jambi**. The central artery of Jambi, the **Batang Hari river**, rises in the mountains of West Sumatra and meanders for almost 800 km across the eastern plain, making it even longer than the mighty Musi, though not so broad or powerful. Like the Musi, the Batang Hari is an historic highway of Malay commerce. Indeed, the great ancient kingdom of the Batang Hari, Melayu, eventually gave its name to the whole Malay race.

This Melayu seems to have pre-existed even Srivijaya, sending tribute to imperial China as early as the fifth century. In the late seventh century, Melayu seems to have become a Srivijayan vassal, but it maintained an autonomous existence of sorts until 600 years later when it freed itself from Srivijayan influence with the help of Javanese allies, and ultimately inherited some of the fading luster of Srivijaya for itself. The capital is thought to have been at **Muara Jambi**, a short distance down the left bank of the Batang Hari from the present provincial capital, which bears the same name as the province. The ruins of seven temples can be made out on the riverside, but the standard of preservation is disappointing. Like Srivijaya, Melayu has left nothing photogenic for the sightseer. Nor does modern Jambi town have much to offer after Palembang, except some *batik* workshops and fine nineteenth-century Malay houses with carved gables and shutters.

From Jambi, the most interesting road runs west towards the mountains, following the current of Sumatran history after the demise of Srivijaya. In 1347, a prince called Adityavarman was sent from East Java to govern Sumatra, now known generally as Melayu, in the name of the kingdom of Majapahit. Born of a mixed marriage between a Melayu princess and a Javanese noble, Adityavarman had become a member of the same Bhairawa sect which built grim shrines at Padang Lawas; a huge statue found on the upper Batang Hari before the war and now on display in the National Museum in Jakarta, depicts him as a demonic snake-draped figure standing upon a corpse which in turn rests on a pedestal of human skulls. Adityavarman did not stay long in Jambi, but moved upriver to the Barisan mountains, taking with him both the historic luster of Srivijaya and Melayu and the dark aura of his sect. By the time the first European ships arrived in the Malacca Strait, Islamic sultanates were the masters of coastal and riverine Sumatra. But they continued to live in awe of a vague and mysterious king, who held court somewhere in the remote mountains of West Sumatra.

TANJUNG PINANG
INEXPENSIVE: **Johnny's Guest House**, on *gang* off Jl Bintan. **Hotel Surya**, Jl Bintan. **Hotel Tanjung Pinang**, Jl Pasar Ikan.
MODERATE: **Wisma Riau**, Jl Yusuf Kahar. **Sempurna Inn**, Jl Yusuf Kahar. **Penginapan Sempurna Jaya**, Jl Yusuf Kahar. **Hotel Sondang**, Jl Yusuf Kahar. At Trikora Beach: **Trikora Country Club Cottages**.

Museum / Post
Riau Kandil Museum, Jl Bakarbatu, 2 km outside town on road to Kijang. **Post office:** Corner Jl Merdeka/Jl Pos. Open Mon-Thu 9.00-16.00, Fri 9.00-11.00, Sat 9.00-13.00.

Transport
AIR: Kijang Airport, 20 km SE of Tanjung Pinang. Daily flights to Pekanbaru & Jakarta, less frequent to other Sumatran destinations. Connection to town by taxi. **Merpati** office: Jl Yusuf Kahar. **SEA:** frequent launches leave wharf for Batam island & Singapore. Boats leave at least 3 times weekly for Pekanbaru, via Siak Sri Indrapura. **Perintis** ships serve island Riau. **Pelni** ships to Jakarta & distant destinations board at separate harbor outside town. Pelni office in Tanjung Pinang: Jl Temiang 190. **INTERNAL:** Main taxi rank on Jl Gambir. Ojek (public motorcycle) is standard means of motor transport, but some minibuses too. Boats to Penyenget Island leave from main jetty.

BATAM ISLAND
Sekupang is arrival point for launches from Singapore's Finger Pier. **Nagoya** is Batam's developing new town, with restaurants & souvenir shops. **Hang Nadim Airport** has at least 3 Jakarta flights daily, and even a service to Bandung as well as most important Sumatran towns. Many luxury hotels under construction - **Batam View Hotel** & **Batam Fantasy Resort** already open.

PEKANBARU
INEXPENSIVE: One concentration of cheap *losmen* is Jl Nangka near bus station, eg **Hotel Linda**, no.133. Another is near harbor, eg **Nirmala**, Jl Pasar Bawah, Tel: 21314. Elsewhere: **Kelabang Sakti**, Jl Diponegoro 53.
MODERATE: **Anom**, Jl Gatot Subroto 3, Tel: 22636. **Badarussamsi**, Jl Sisingamangaraja 71, Tel: 22475. **Wisma Bunda**, Jl Prof Moh Yamin 104, Tel: 21728. **Indrapura**, Jl Dr Sutomo 86. **Sri Indrayani Hotel**, Jl N Bangka, Tel: 21870.

Tourist Information / Post / Hospital
Baparda, Jl Jen Sudirman 344. **Post office:** on Jl Jen Sudirman. **Hospital: Rumah Sakit Umum Pekanbaru**, Jl Diponegoro 2.

Transport
AIR: Simpang Tiga Airport, 10 km S of town, connection by taxi only. Daily direct flight to and from Singapore. *Airline offices:* **Garuda**, Jl Jen Sudirman 207, Tel: 21026/21575. **Merpati**, Jl HOS Cokroaminoto, Tel: 23558. **SMAC**, Jl Jen Sudirman 25, Tel: 23922. **Sempati**, Jl Sisingamangaraja 2. **WATER:** Boats leave down Siak river at least 3 times weekly for Siak Sri Indrapura & Tanjung Pinang. Tickets from Asia Restaurant near harbor entrance. **ROAD:** Long-distance bus terminal is at Jl Nangka in S of town; most bus co offices nearby.

MUARA TAKUS
Ruins are near **Pongkai** village, 26 km from main Pekanbaru-Bukittinggi highway. Appropriate side-road turns off at **Muaramahat**, where *bemo* available. Accommodation: **Losmen Arga Sonya**, Muaramahat.

PALEMBANG
INEXPENSIVE: **Aman**, Jl Lematang. **Asiana**, Jl Jen Sudirman 45E. **Jakarta**, Jl Sayangan 763, Tel: 21737. **Kenanga Inn**, Jl Bukit Kecil. **Segaran**, Jl Segaran 207. *MODERATE:* **Leparadis**, Jl Kapt A Rivai 257, Tel: 260707. **Swarna Dwipa**, Jl Tasik 2, Tel: 22322. *LUXURY:* **Sanjaya**, Jl Kapt A Rivai, Tel: 20272.

Museums
Rumah Bari Museum, Jl Rumah Bari. Sat-Thu 8.00-13.00, Fri closed.

Tourist Information / Hospital
Baparda, Jl Kapt Rivai (beside governor's office). Mon-Thu 7.30-14.00, Fri 7.30-11.30, Sat 7.30-13.00, Sun closed. **Hospital: Pertamina Hospital**, Pertamina complex, Plaju.

Transport
AIR: Talang Betutu Airport, 17 km N of the city. *Airline offices:* **Garuda**, Jl Kapt Rivai 20, Tel: 22933. **Merpati**, Jl Kapt Rivai, Tel: 21604.
WATER: Ferries leave from **Boom Baru** harbor for Bangka island and Bayungelincir (near Jambi). Smaller boats travel upriver as far as one day's journey.
RAIL: Railway station on Jl Ogan, 8 km from city center on South side of river. 3 services daily to Tanjungkarang and Java; 3rd class trains also run to Lubuklinggau, on road to Bengkulu & one of routes to the north.
ROAD: Terminal Bis Tujuluh for buses N to Jambi & Padang, W to Lahat and Bengkulu, & S to Lampung & Java.
INTERNAL: Stasiun Ampera, next to market by bridge, is main *bemo* terminal. Motorboats for charter West of bridge off Jl Kraton.

WEST SUMATRA

WEST SUMATRA

MINANGKABAU HIGHLANDS
BUKITTINGGI
PADANG
MENTAWAI ISLANDS

MINANGKABAU HIGHLANDS

If Sumatra has ever had a single heart, then it beats in the maze of green peaks and switchback ravines which make up the **Minangkabau highlands**, in the modern province of West Sumatra. Appropriately situated at the center of the island's mountain backbone, mid-way between Aceh and Lampung, this area has been both a sanctuary of tradition and an epicenter of change for all Sumatra. And the dynamic contradiction between these two roles has made West Sumatra a crucial contributor to the history and culture of modern Indonesia as a whole. The name of Minangkabau conjures up diverse and apparently ill-assorted images: on the one hand, a colorful antique culture of postcard architecture and quaint costumes and dances; on the other, a dynamic, educated, enterprising, outward-looking society of traders, teachers, soldiers and leaders.

The traditional cradle and cultural heartland of the Minangkabau people is the area known as **Tanah Datar**, around the small town of **Batusangkar** in the southern shadow of the 2,891-m volcano **Merapi**, the dominant peak of the high-

Left: Minangkabau woman wearing her impressive head plumage.

lands. According to legend, the earliest ancestors of the Minangkabau lived here in **Pariangan**, a village southwest of Batusangkar on the slopes of Merapi. Tanah Datar was the seat of the mysterious "Kings of Minangkabau", whose strange half-mystical authority radiated outwards from these hidden hills for four centuries. In terms of practical power, the *Raja Yang Dipertuan Sakti* of Tanah Datar seem hardly to have had much control even over their own homeland.

The Minangkabau themselves believed their kings to be descendants, alongside the emperors of China and Constantinople, of Alexander the Great. The truth is almost as impressive: the Minangkabau dynasty can be traced to the half-Javanese demon-worshipper Adityavarman, dispatched from the court of Majapahit in 1347 to govern Malayu (Sumatra) as a vassal ruler. For some unknown reason, the dynasty gradually retreated up the Batang Hari river to settle in Tanah Datar. The only tangible remnants of its first years in Minangkabau are the **Adityavarman stones**, rock tablets like gravestones inscribed in Sanskrit-based scripts. Examples can be seen by the side of the road near **Limakaum** and at several other sites in the Batusankar area. Some of the inscriptions are in an indigenous Indian-derived script

207

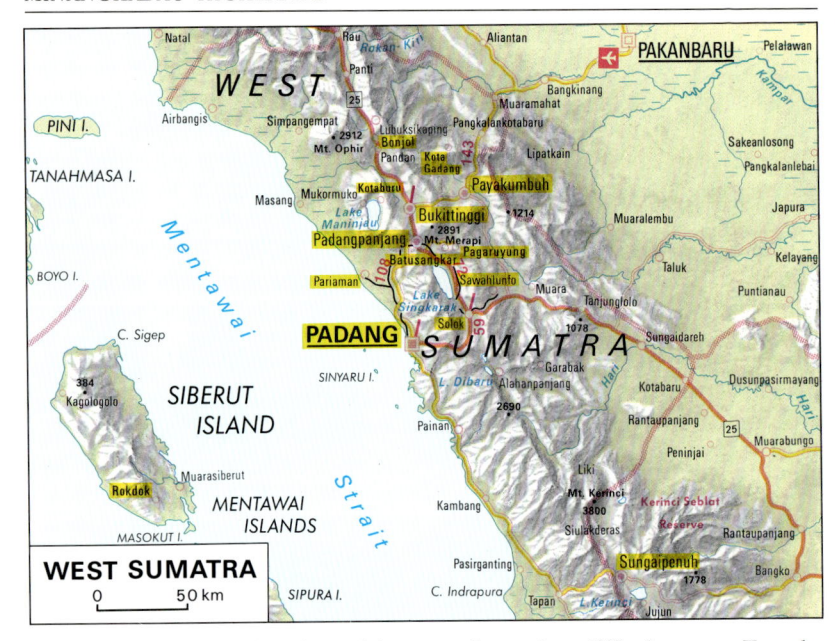

related to that of Java, others in an alphabet imported directly from India; most are undeciphered.

The first European to reach Tanah Datar and set eyes upon a Minangkabau king was Tomas Dias, a renegade Portuguese in the service of the Dutch East India Company. Dias marched over the mountains from eastern Sumatra in 1684. At the end of this astonishing journey, executed at a time when the interior of Sumatra was utterly unknown to Europeans, he was greeted by a 4000-strong escort bearing golden umbrellas and salvers. Passing through three gates into a palace guarded by 100 musketeers, he was then presented with a silver-inlaid musket, a halberd, a pure-bred horse and a set of pornographic pictures as royal gifts, together with the right to enslave and condemn to death in the name of the king.

Like most of their counterparts in Java, the ceremonial buildings of Minangkabau were built of timber, and have not survived. Again as in Java, royal centers tended to change location at slight provocation, and are difficult to trace. To make things still more complex, there was not one king but three: after the arrival of Islam in the sixteenth century, the old autocratic Indic kingdom was replaced by a peculiar triple monarchy in which a "King of Religion" (*Raja Ibadat*) and a "King of Custom" (*Raja Adat*), reigned alongside the "King of the World" (*Raja Alam*) himself. The last capital of the *Raja Alam* is known – it was at **Pagaruyung**, 5 km east of Batusangkar. Just outside this village, a replica of the old palace, **Istana Pagaruyung**, has been built by the government. The new building is far larger than it should be, but embodies the dramatic lines of traditional Minangkabau architecture, and is being fitted out as an informative museum of the Pagaruyung dynasty.

Minangkabau Architecture

The Minangkabau house is the most striking and distinctive in Indonesia, and many have called it the most beautiful.

Like the Batak, the Minangkabau have developed a long-redundant structural feature, the saddleback roof formed by a load-bearing ridge-beam, into an art form. Each roof section ends in a graceful horn which sweeps upwards to a narrow point, sometimes twice as high as the center of the ridge; with two telescoping extension roofs protruding from each end of the main central section, a big Minangkabau house cuts the skyline with a dramatic saw of curved spires. And many of them are truly big: designed to shelter an entire matrilineal clan, the largest reach 450 sq m in floor area. The wooden foundation piles continue upwards through the living area to support the roof, providing a framework of uprights between which partitions can be hung to create separate compartments for the individual families.

Externally, these houses are decorated with rectangular panels covered with floral motifs which hide the abutments of the beams supporting the floor. A short distance from each house are cubic rice barns, styled to match. A surprisingly large number of old *rumah gadang* still stand in Tanah Datar, notably in the villages of **Balimbing**, **Limakaum**, and **Pariangan** as well as Batusangkar and Pagaruyung; most, however, have surrendered their rustic palm-fibre thatch to the shining advance of corrugated iron. Further architectural interest in the Minangkabau uplands is provided by mosques, many of which display the multi-tiered *meru* roof pattern inherited from the Hindu period. One mosque near **Solok** in the far south of the area combines a three-layer *meru* with the more modern Middle Eastern *qubbah* dome to create a remarkable pagoda-like strucure.

Islam and Tradition

West Sumatra is generally reckoned to be a "serious" Muslim area, where sincere faith is an important part of life; the animist survivals here are weaker than in the Bataklands. But the dominant *adat* of West Sumatra, which involves matrilineal descent and inheritance, is also taken seriously, and here it is the patriarchal wisdom of Mohammed and his interpreters which is usually passed over. Some of the implications of Minangkabau *adat* are startling to Western sensibilities. A dead man's wealth, for instance, is inherited by his sister's children in preference to his own.

The present balance between Islam and Minangkabau tradition has not been achieved without friction. In the early nineteenth century, the greatest of all slips of the fault line between the two caused a tremor which both destroyed the ancient Minangkabau monarchy and initiated the conquest of West Sumatra by the Dutch. In 1803, far-off Mecca was conquered by a puritanical Muslim sect called the Wahhabites, whose bloody zeal inspired a handful of Minangkabau pilgrims, then present in the holy city, to plan a similar venture in their own country. Upon their homecoming, the "Padri", as they came to be known, launched a civil war aimed at purifying Minangkabau society of such evils as gambling, betel-chewing, and matrilineal inheritance. The reformers won steady ground against conservative chiefs, and around 1815 the Minangkabau royal line was all but exterminated. In 1821, surviving aristocrats signed the whole of the Minangkabau highlands over to the Dutch, whereupon the Padri quickly found themselves on the receiving end of someone else's crusade. The "Padri wars" were to engage colonial armies intermittently for 17 years. The first stronghold founded by the Dutch in the uplands was **Fort van der Capellen** in Batusangkar, long used as a school and now a police station. But the permanent center of colonial power was **Fort de Kock**, the foreign irritant around which the pearl of modern **Bukittinggi** has grown.

BUKITTINGGI

Like Bandung, Bukittinggi is a colonial foundation which, for want of an indigenous rival, has become a regional cultural capital. This, together with its fine climate and setting, makes Bukittingi the most attractive town in West Sumatra and the usual base for exploring the Minangkabau highlands. The town is 930 m above sea level on the edge of the **Ngarai Sianok** gorge, a sheer canyon incised into the white pumice of the surrounding plateau. The weather has been compared to that of Mediterranean Europe, and allows the cultivation of European flowers and vegetables. The name means "High Hill", a reference to the defensible rise which forms the core of the old settlement. When the fort was first built in 1825 it was christened *Sterrenschans*, the Fort of the Stars. Only later was it renamed Fort de Kock, after the army commander who presided over the defeat of Diponegoro's revolt on Java in 1830. Until the Second World War, Fort de Kock was the only name by which anyone except local natives knew what is now Bukittinggi. On the surviving ramparts of the fort, an emasculated Dutch cannon still surveys the countryside which it once terrorized.

The rebuilt palace of King Adityawarman at Batusangkar.

The very highest point in town is occupied not by the fort but by the **Taman Bundokanduang** park, comprising a zoo of the sickening old iron bars variety together with the **Rumah Adat Baandjuang Museum**. The centerpiece of the museum, which opened in 1935, is a very fine Minangkabau house built in 1844. Displays include local wedding and dance costumes, musical instruments and historic weaponry. The other museum in town is the **Army Museum**, next to the **Panorama Park**, which overlooks the Ngarai canyon. The most interesting exhibits here date from the regional rebellion of 1958, when Bukittinggi briefly became nothing less than the capital of a

"Revolutionary Government of the Indonesian Republic". The rebels aimed to free the outer islands from the economic centralism and political leftism of Java. Sukarno had Bukittinggi bombed and eventually captured by central government troops, causing lasting bitterness. But today the rebellion has been rehabilitated as an anti-Communist crusade, a sort of premonition of the birth of the New Order.

Modern Bukittinggi is a relatively clean, orderly place whose charm has not been drowned in poverty and petrol fumes. Sedate horsedrawn carts, rather than shameful *becak* or snarling *bajaj*, are the main small passenger conveyance. The town's best-known landmark is its **Jam Gadang**, or Big Clock. This is a European public clocktower fitted with a twee little decorative roof in horned Minangkabau style. So great is the renown of this unlikely timepiece that the whole town is occasionally known as "Kota Jam Gadang" after it. The clock stands at the central intersection, close to the lively main market. Bukittinggi owed its growth in the first place to its focal position in the network of roads which the Dutch drove through the uplands to facilitate their military pacification and economic exploitation. By 1915, Bukittinggi market was visited by some 40,000 people on fine Saturdays; it is still a dizzy experience, a uniqe opportunity to watch the Minangkabau in one of their favorite and most characteristic environments as well as a good place to buy their distinctive food and crafts.

The Minangkabau are opportunists, taking advantage of the chances open to them in any field, from petty trade to cash crops to Western schooling. Long before the Padri wars, the Minangkabau had developed coffee, a crop introduced to Indonesia by the Dutch, into a major source of wealth; once defeated on the battlefield, they wasted no time making a new sort of victory out of the educational opportunities provided by their enemies. Bukittinggi, blessed in colonial times with the only teacher training college in Sumatra, was at the heart of a Minangkabau intellectual bloom which produced a crop of writers and politicians out of all proportion to the population and the economic importance of the area.

Many of the distinguished Minangkabau figures came from tiny villages in the neighborhood of Bukittinggi. **Kota Gadang**, within walking distance on the opposite side of the Ngarai canyon, has produced no less than two Indonesian prime ministers. Yet it is indicative of the Minangkabau enigma that this illustrious little place also gives every impression of conservatism - priding itself, for instance, on its filigree silverwork and hand-embroidered cloth. Other villages in the area have their own craft specialities: brass dishes and betel boxes in **Desa Sunga**, silk weaving and woodcarving in **Pandai Sikat**, blacksmithing in **Sungaipuar**, basketwork in **Payakumbuh**.

The most characteristic Minangkabau craft product is *songket*, heavy cotton cloth highlighted with (now mostly ersatz) gold and silver threads. **Silungkang** village, in the far southeast of Tanah Datar, is one of the best-known sources of high quality *songket*. Traditional entertainments can also be seen in the villages. Minangkabau bullfights (bull versus bull), are staged in **Kotobaru** and **Kotolawas**, near Bukittinggi. Another big social event for male villagers is the wild pig hunt. Higher-brow entertainment is provided at the state-sponsored academy of Minangkabau performing arts in **Padangpanjang**. Traditional dance genres include the *Randai*, a vigorous all-male form incorporating movements derived from the martial arts, and the *Tari Lilin*, a dance for lithe women who must manage to keep hold of saucers bearing lighted candles. The Minangkabau folk orchestra is a combination of gongs, xylophones, drums and flutes.

Scenic Nature

Upland Minangkabau is also rich in natural spectacle. Stately **Mt. Merapi** makes a spectacular and popular climb, starting from Kotobaru. **Lake Maninjau** is a huge, ice-calm crater lake between Bukittinggi and the sea; further south, and likewise in the process of "development" into a tourist destination, is the equally large **Lake Singkarak**.

For those interested in wild flora and fauna, there are several nature reserves. **Batang Palupuh** is one of the few places where a living specimen of *Rafflesia arnoldi* can easily be found. In the **Anai Valley** near Padangpanjang and the dramatic **Harau Canyon** north of Payakumbuh, protected refuges have been created for the wild pigs, tapirs, leopards and tigers which are hunted with such passion elsewhere in Minangkabau. A much larger reserve, **Rimba Panti**, exists in the far north of the province.

The old heart of Minangkabau country comprised three fertile core territories or *luhak* – Tanah Datar, Agam (the Bukittinggi area) and Limapuluh Kota (the "fifty towns", around Payakumbuh). Together, these made up the *darat* – literally just "the land", meaning the ethnic homeland, the origin of the Minangkabau people and their culture. Roughly speaking, the *darat* covers the mountains and valleys between **Bonjol** in the north, where today's trans-Sumatran highway crosses the equator, to the attractive traditional village of *Cupak* in the south.

The antithesis of *darat* is *rantau*, a term which, in Minangkabau thought, covers not only the remainder of the province, but also the rest of Sumatra, Indonesia, and the world. The mountains are fertility, antiquity, security, purity, and home – the mother country, the high womb and cradle of the race. The sea is vast and capricious, the obscure and dangerous outer world. Yet the Minangkabau have not been an insular or xenophobic people: the *rantau* plays as important a part in their lives as the *darat*.

The cultural institution of *merantau* urges young men to leave home for a finite time to seek knowledge, wealth and maturity in the wider world. During *merantau*, the traveler is expected to support himself by means of enterprise and guile, considered the quintessential Minangkabau qualities. That the Minangkabau like to think of themselves as a savvy race is nicely illustrated by their own explanation of the origin of their ethnic name. A conflict between Sumatrans and Javanese, runs the story, was to be decided by a bullfight. Java's champion was a monster of an animal, but the wily Sumatrans brought on a half-starved calf. Mistaking the bull for its mother, the calf ran to suckle and ripped open the belly of the giant with a knife attached to its nose.

PADANG AND THE LOWLANDS

The Minangkabau people have certainly shown more enthusiasm and aptitude for the wiles of business than have most Indonesians. Nowhere is this more apparent than in the provincial capital of **Padang**, where even wholesale businesses are in the hands of *pribumi* traders rather than the familiar Chinese. Historically, European and indigenous commerce have combined to make Padang an important business center and the third largest city in Sumatra. In the seventeenth century, it was already a VOC outstation, hawking Indian cloth to the Minangkabau; in the eighteenth, the native merchants got the upper hand, and the foreigners were tolerated more or less at their pleasure. Between 1795 and 1819, the town was in British hands, whereafter the Dutch returned with renewed vigor and used Padang as a base for their campaigns against the Padri, developing it at the same time into a collection and export point for rice, coffee, tobacco and spices from Minangkabau, which the Dutch

Pawprint of the rare Sumatra tiger.

came to know as the "Padang Uplands". Since independence, the regional capital has been definitively reclaimed by the Minangkabau; traditionally part of the *rentau,* Padang is being absorbed into the darat, and now rivals Bukittinggi as a cultural as well as a political focus. Padang has a university and an arts center, and its **Adityawarman Museum** is the most important museum of Minangkabau anthropology, history and art.

Padang has also given its name to the remarkable style of cookery which has become the trademark of Minangkabau in the *rantau*. The Padang restaurant is as familiar throughout urban Indonesia as the fish and chip shop in Britain. But the best place to sample Padang food is, of course, Padang itself. At a decent *rumah makan Padang*, the waiter brings a selection of a dozen dishes, balanced precariously along the length of his arm. The ingredients range from beef and chicken to tripe, but what almost all recipes have in common is a quantity of chilli and other fiery spices which can be downright dangerous to the unprepared dinner.

Low, flat and exposed to drenching sea winds, Padang is an appallingly hot and wet place, especially during the west monsoon. It is not unusual for 17 cm of rain to fall on a single November night. Old Padang houses were fortified against the elements, resting on tall piles to surmount floodwaters and with wide overhanging roofs to combat the onslaught of sun and rain; the current pan-Indonesian concrete blockhouse style is far less practical as well as uglier. South of Padang, the coastline is rugged and scenic, with fine beaches at **Bungus** and **Pasir Putih**.

The special interest of **Pariaman**, a seaside town 36 km north of Padang, is the *Tabut* festival celebrated there at the beginning of the first month of the Muslim calendar. *Tabut* commemorates the martyrdom in battle of two of Mohammad's grandsons. Although it is associated with the Shiite sect, considered heretics by most Indonesian Muslims, this festival is held in many parts of the archipelago – but nowhere as dramatically as in Pariaman. In a communal ritual of almost Balinese color and extravagance, the Pariaman Minangkabau construct and destroy huge effigies of the Bouraq, a mythical flying animal supposed to have borne the souls of the heroes to heaven. Vibrantly painted, the images are danced through the streets only to be tossed into the sea, whereupon Minangkabau thrift suddenly resurges as spectators dive in to recover valuable pieces of decoration.

The railway connecting Padang to its mountain hinterland was completed in 1892, essentially to serve the big coalfield at **Sawahlunto**, which supplied fuel for the steam-driven sea and rail arteries of the Greater Netherlands. There is a branch line to Bukittinggi, but only freight trains operate on it now. Train buffs may just be lucky enough to cadge a ride on the footplate of one of the last commercial steam locomotives in Indonesia and the world.

West Sumatra is not one of the largest provinces of Sumatra, but at almost 50,000 sq km it is still bigger than any of those of Java. And with a population of only 3.8 million, heavily concentrated around Padang and the central *darat*, there are large tracts of wilderness. The greatest of these is in the south, some ten hours' drive from Padang. It forms the northern extremity of the huge new **Kerinci-Seblat Reserve**. This magnificent sanctuary is one of the Indonesian government's most dramatic conservation gestures. Covering 1.5 million hectares of high-altitude forest and marsh, it has segments in three separate provinces. **Sungaipenuh**, the administrative center for the park, lies in a high valley on the western fringe of Jambi. **Mt. Kerinci**, at 3806 m the tallest peak in Sumatra and a tough two-day climb for the experienced hiker, stands close to the border between Jambi and West Sumatra. But the wildest part of the reserve is further south, in the heart of the province of Bengkulu.

THE MENTAWAI ISLANDS

About 130 km from the West Sumatran coast, in what Indonesians are pleased to call the "Indonesian Ocean", lie the extraordinary **Mentawai Islands**. In the nineteenth and early twentieth centuries, the Mentawais were periodically in vogue among European explorers and writers as a stalking-ground for noble savages and tribal utopias. Ritual war and a diet of sago, tubers and the occasional banana probably made life there less than paradisical in practice, but the Mentawais are certainly a world apart. Their culture is even more singular than that of Nias, with which they form part of the same long island chain. The people of the Mentawais pose some interesting challenges to modern thought on the distant past of Indonesia. Until late colonial times, they seem to have lacked not only such technological innovations as metalwork and the blowpipe, but also basic cultural features like rice-growing, pottery and betel-chewing.

Christian missionary work began in the Mentawais in 1901, but large-scale conversions did not occur until after the Second World War, and the overall process of change is probably retarded rather than advanced by the guerilla campaign for souls being fought by the Muslims and Catholics against the Protestant pioneers. Loincloths made of stamped tree-bark may have been preached and laughed into history, but the beautiful body tattoos of the islanders are not so easily cast off. Traditional houses can still be seen at several remote villages including **Sakelot** and **Rokdok** on the northernmost and largest island, **Siberut**. But the least tangible remnants of heathendom – like beliefs in taboos, spirits and possession – may well prove the most durable of all.

GUIDEPOST WEST SUMATRA

BUKITTINGGI

INEXPENSIVE: Concentr. on Jl A Yani. **Gangga** no. 70.; Grand Hotel, no.99. **Yani**, no. 101, Tel: 22740. **Murni**, no.115. **Singgalang**, no. 130. Elsewhere: **Wisma Bukittinggi**, Jl Yos Sudarso 1A. **Mountain View**, Jl Yos Sudarso 3, Tel: 21621. **Suwarni's Guesthouse**, Jl Benteng 2. **Yogya**, Jl M Yamin 43. *MODERATE:* **Benteng**, Jl Benteng 1, Tel: 22596. **Denai**, Jl Rivai 26, Tel: 21460. **Dymen's International**, Jl Nawawi 1-5, Tel: 23781. **Lima's Hotel**, Jl Kesehatan 34, Tel: 22641. **Minang**, Jl Panorama 20, Tel: 21120.

Food

INDONESIAN (Padang): **Ria Sari**, Ngarai Sianok shopping centre, Jl Jen Sudirman 1, Tel: 21503. **Roda Group Restaurant**, Pasar Atas, blok C-155. **Selamat**, Jl A Yani 19, Tel: 22959. **Simpang Raya**, Muka Jam Gadang, Tel: 22585. *CHINESE:* **Mona Lisa**, Jl A Yani 58. *EUROPEAN:* Traditional hangout for western travelers is **The Coffee Shop**, Jl A Yani 103.

Shopping

Many craft & antique shops along Jl Minangkabau, especially near Gloria cinema: **Tiga Putra** (no.19), **Nuraini** (no.25), **H. Muchtar** (no.90). Also: **Aishachalik**, Jl Cindur Mato 94 (extension Jl Minangkabau); **Basrida**, Jl Yos Sudarso 2. Daily **Central Market** down street from clocktower.

Cultural performances

Randai dancing at zoo, Wed, Sat & Sun 12.30. *Pencak silat* at 20.00 on Wed & Sat at **Tarok Ujong Bukit**, 1 km from town.

Museums & Zoos

Taman Bundo Kanduang park contains both **Rumah Adat Baandjuang Museum** and **Bukittinggi Zoo**.

Tourist Information

Pasar Atas (main market), Tel: 22403.

Transport

ROAD: Bus station on Jl Aur Kuning, 3 km SE of town. Most bus co offices here.
INTERNAL: Horsecarts are one of Bukittinggi's trademarks.

PADANG

Accommodation

INEXPENSIVE: **Candrawasih**, Jl Pemuda 27, Tel: 22894. **Tiga Tiga**, Jl Pemuda 31, Tel: 22633. *MODERATE:* **Aldilla**, Jl Damar 2, Tel: 23962. **Grand Hotel**, Jl Pondok 84, Tel: 22088. **Hang Tuah**, Jl Pemuda, Tel: 26556. **Machudum's Hotel**, Jl Hiligoo 45, Tel: 22333. **Mariani International**, Jl Bundo Kandung 35, Tel: 22020. **Muara**, Jl Gereja 34, Tel: 25600. **Pangeran's Hotel**, Jl Dobi 3-5, Tel: 26233.

Food

INDONESIAN: **Alima**, Jl Pasar Baru 29, Tel: 21794. **Roda Baru**, Jl Pasar Raya 6, Tel: 22814. *CHINESE:* **Chan's Restaurant**, Jl Pondok 94, Tel: 22131. **King's**, Jl Pondok 86B, Tel: 21701.

Shopping

Main market (**Pasar Raya**), Jl Pasar Raya (next to city hall). *TEXTILES:* **Batik Semar**, Jl Hiligoo, Tel: 21215. **Songket Silungkang**, Jl Imam Bonjol, Tel: 23711. **Toko Batik Arjuna**, Jl Pasar Raya, Tel: 23253. *OTHER HANDICRAFTS & ANTIQUES:* **Abu Nawas**, Tabing Airport. **Mochtar**, Jl Pondok 85, Tel: 25615. **Panay**, Jl Iman Bonjol 5/IV, Tel: 21259. **Toko Sartika**, Jl Jen Sudirman 5, Tel: 22101.

Museums

Adityawarman Museum, Jl Diponegoro, Tel: 22316. Sat-Sun & Tue-Thu 8.00-18.00, Fri 8.00-11.00, Mon closed.

Cultural performances

Taman Budaya, Jl Diponegoro (opp museum): regular dancing and *pencak silat*, 9.00-14.00.

Tourist Information / Post

Tourist office for W Sumatra and Riau in **Kanwil Postel**, Jl. Khatib Sulaiman, Tel: 22118/28231. Open 7.30-14.00, except Sat 7.30-13.00. Provincial tourist office: **Dinas Pariwisata Sumatra Barat**, Jl Sudirman A3. For municipality, **Padang Tourist Office**, Jl Semudra.
Post office: Jl Brig Aziz Chan 7.

Government offices

PHPA Office (permits for Mentawais & reserves), Jl Raden Saleh 8A, Padang Baru, Tel: 24136. **Police station**, Jl M Yamin.

Transport

AIR: **Tabing Airport**, 6 km by taxi or *bis kota* from town center. *Airline offices:* **Garuda**, Jl Jen Sudirman 2, Tel: 23823. **Merpati**, Jl Pemuda 45E, Tel: 27908. **Mandala**, Jl Pemuda 29A, Tel: 22350. SEA: **Teluk Bayur** harbor, 6 km S of town center. **Pelni office**: Jl Tanjung Priok 32, Teluk Bayur, Tel: 121127. ROAD: Bus station is **Lintas Andalas**, Jl Pemuda. Frequent buses to and from Bukittinggi; long-distance services to other Sumatran towns and Jakarta. INTERNAL: *Bemo* terminal off Jl MH Yamin, between bus station and market. Main taxi stand in front of market. No *becak*, but pony carts available.

MENTAWAI ISLANDS

No hotels or homestays, but a **PHPA Guesthouse** in **Muarasiberut**. Permission from police in Padang necessary to visit Mentawais. Boats leave Padang harbor regularly; Merpati fly once a week (Mon) from Padang to **Rokot Airstrip**, Sipora island.

215

SOUTH SUMATRA

SOUTH SUMATRA

BENGKULU
LAMPUNG

BENGKULU

Bengkulu is the modern Indonesian rendition of Bencoolen, a name once famous through its association with the long British presence in what ultimately became a Dutch archipelago. In 1685, the British East India Company, expelled from the Moluccas and Java by the Dutch and their allies, set up shop in a friendly pepper-growing area on the southwest coast of Sumatra. Disease and intrigue thrived in the Bencoolen "factory", as the British called their overseas trading stations, but so, on the whole, did trade; thirty years later the company could afford to build the formidable **Fort Marlborough** a short distance along the coast from the original settlement. The modern town of Bengkulu has grown up around the fort, which still has commanding views over the market, the Chinese quarter, and the harbor it was built to guard. Indeed, it is still occupied by the modern military. Unfortunately, the army has recently seen fit to encase most of the fort's venerable walls in white concrete, giving it all the charm of a nuclear bunker. Nevertheless, the imposing main gateway, and the old gravestones in the courtyard with their interesting English inscriptions, have been preserved. The **Parr Monument**, opposite the fort, commemorates a British resident stabbed in his bed by native assassins in 1807.

The most illustrious Englishman to live in Bencoolen was that greatest of all colonizer-heroes, Thomas Stamford Raffles. A reformer and a scholar, Raffles continues to evoke admiration long after figures like Cortez, Coen, Clive and Rhodes have become distasteful. His period in shabby Bencoolen forms, however, a rather sad epilogue to his years as ruler of Java.

In 1818, after the return of Java to the Dutch at the end of the Napoleonic wars, a despondent Raffles was posted to this last remaining British colony in the archipelago. In Bencoolen he remained indefatiguable, banning slavery, introducing coffee and sugar cultivation, and opening schools; during expeditions to other parts of Sumatra, he documented new species, languages and archaeological remains, and - almost incidentally - founded Singapore. But it was a time of unhappiness and misfortune. Four of Raffles's five children died of tropical fevers, and he was tortured constantly by frustration at the greater prizes which had slipped from his grasp. In 1823, as he set sail to return to England, his ship caught

Left: A fierce-looking war-dancer from South Sumatra.

fire and sank. Raffles escaped, but lost the notes and drawings which would have enabled him to write half a dozen standard works on Southeast Asia. Two years later, imperial diplomats returned even Bencoolen to the Dutch, in exchange for the old port of Malacca on the Malay peninsula, ending the dream of British settlement in the islands. Raffles's appropriately sad monument in Bengkulu is the **British Governor's Residence**, a banyan-strangled ruin five minutes' walk from the fort. The big stonebuilt house has been uninhabited since a great earthquake in 1914.

Bengkulu town has certainly improved since Raffles described it in 1818 as "without exception the most wretched place I have ever beheld". Today it is a peaceful, friendly, not unattractive town, with the newly appreciated advantage of fine sandy beaches. But it has not lost its insular, backwater atmosphere. Ironically, it was the very marginality and irrelevance of Bengkulu which made it, in the last years before the Pacific war, the involuntary home of a second great figure of Indonesian history - Sukarno. The future president lived here in rather comfortable political exile between 1938 and 1942, in the house marked by a flag off Jl. Sukarno-Hatta.

Bengkulu is the capital of a long, narrow, sparsely populated province of the same name. Despite the fact that almost half of its perimeter is seacoast, Bengkulu is so elongated that it borders on no less than four other Sumatran provinces. The interior is just a strip of the Barisan range, entirely mountainous. Much of the north forms part of the **Kerinci-Seblat Reserve**, which also sprawls into West Sumatra, South Sumatra and Jambi. **Seblat** itself is an impressive 2383-m mountain on the eastern border of Bengkulu. Bengkulu's is the wildest section of the park, where rhinos, tigers, tapirs, clouded leopards, and sun bears are as plentiful as they get in modern Sumatra.

Outside the reserve, such spectacular game may still be shot, and Bengkulu has become a mecca for Indonesian hunters. In the center and south, one item of flora enjoys better protection than the fauna: the *Rafflesia arnoldi*, the largest flower in the world. The pungent, visceral bloom of the parasitic rafflesia can also be viewed elsewhere in Sumatra, but Bengkulu is the area most closely associated with the plant as it was here that Raffles and the naturalist Arnold became the first Europeans to discover it, in 1818. Catching a *Rafflesia* in bloom is always a tricky business, but specimens do at any rate exist in a reserve at **Tabah Penanjung**, on the road inland from Bengkulu town. Clinging to the flank of the Barisan range, Tabah Penanjung also offers superb views over the Indian Ocean.

The central interior of Bengkulu province consists essentially of a double row of peaks separated by a dramatic valley. The main settlements here are **Kepahiang** and **Curup**, on the headwaters of the Musi river, which eventually escapes from this trench into the eastern lowlands and becomes the great brown traveling sea which rolls through Palembang. The upper reaches of the Musi are the home of Bengkulu's best-known native people, the *Rejang*.

The Rejang were once accomplished miners, extracting and exporting gold from the rich deposits northwest of Curup. At the end of the nineteenth century, however, the Dutch took over themselves in a frenzied goldrush which quickly made Bengkulu the biggest gold-producing area in Indonesia. Today, an Australian company extracts gold at **Lebong Tandai**, on the **Ketaun river**.

Enggano is Bengkulu's lone link in the chain of maverick islands running parallel to Sumatra's west coast. A century ago, Enggano was an even greater anthropological curiosity than Nias or the Mentawais, lacking even weaving as well as metal, pottery and rice. But its culture was exceptionally fragile under foreign pressures, and the health of its people even more so: the native population fell from about 3000 in 1862 to 329 in 1914 and 162 in 1928. Numbers have since recovered, but immigration of Javanese, Chinese and other Sumatrans has all but submerged the island's indigenous identity. Tourist literature still displays drawings of the weird beehive-like traditional houses of Enggano, but neglects to add that the last of these disappeared before the First World War. Real adventurers who can speak Indonesian will no doubt enjoy checking out what is left, though, especially since the island is so tantalisingly inaccessible. The name "Enggano" is rather inauspicious, deriving from a Portuguese word meaning "deceit" or "disappointment"; in the sixteenth century, Portuguese ships avoiding the pirate-infested Strait of Malacca must have made landfall here on the way to Java. Enggano was also where the first Dutchman stepped ashore in Indonesia, in 1596.

LAMPUNG

The southernmost province of Sumatra is **Lampung**. Less than 30 km from Java at the closest point on the Sunda Strait, Lampung is the only part of Sumatra to have remained more strongly under Javanese than Malay influence in modern times. In a little wooden museum in the village of **Pugung**, not far from the provincial captial, **Tanjungkarang**, a Buddhist statue in East Javanese style is a reminder of the early days of the connection. With the fall of Majapahit and the rise of the coastal sultanates in the sixteenth century, Lampong, alone in Sumatra, fell within the power of Banten, just over the water in West Java. Banten exploited Lampung as a source of valuable pepper, and installed its own vassal chiefs in order to cement its authority.

After the demise of the Banten sultanate in 1809, it took the Dutch a long time to bring Lampung under their own direct control – near **Kalianda** on Lampung Bay is the ruined fort of one of the

Sunset over a South Sumatra village.

warlords of the time. Meanwhile the area became a refuge for fugitives and criminals, the landless and the lawless of desperate, *cultuurstelsel*-burdened Java. Saijah and Adinda, peasant hero and heroine of Multatuli's mid-nineteenth century political novel *Max Havelaar*, ended their stories in Lampung, on the pacifying bayonets of a colonial expedition. When, at the beginning of the twentieth century, the Dutch began to consider the increasing problem of overpopulation in Java, it seemed appropriate to formalize Lampung's long-standing function as a safety valve. The first "transmigrants" arrived in Lampung from Java in 1905, and they have kept coming ever since. While *transmigrasi* now extends to all the main outer islands of Indonesia, its effect is still most dramatic where it started, in Lampung. Half of this province's six million inhabitants speak Javanese or Sundanese; whole towns – like **Metro**, inland of Tanjungkarang – give the impression of having been transplanted virtually intact from Java.

The indigenous Lampung people have never been very numerous and still number less than a million. They and the province take their name from a legendary ancestor, who was supposedly a brother of the kings of Sunda and Majapahit, and who lived in what is now Bengkulu. Certainly Lampung culture seems closely related to that of the Rejang in Bengkulu. The Indic script used, for example, was almost identical; in Lampung, it was still universally known among young people as late as 1920, and used in the romantic and scurrilous verses exchanged between lovers during courtship. Thanks to such folk applications for writing, popular literacy in many parts of Indianized, pre-Islamic, pre-colonial Indonesia was probably higher than in the Europe of the day, and Lampung was one of the last places to lose the skill, just before the written word re-entered the culture as a European "innovation". However, Lampung script has disappeared with remarkable completeness in a short time, and specimens are now very hard to find. The area above **Krui** on the rugged west coast is one of the purest remaining Lampung areas.

The relief structure of Lampung reproduces in miniature that of the whole island of Sumatra. In the west is the tail end of the Barisan range, still a band of quite impressive mountains, including 2231-m **Mt. Pesagi**. There is even a fine mountain lake, complete with hot springs – **Lake Ranau**, on the border with South Sumatra. The remainder of Lampung is the flat green purgatory typical of eastern Sumatra, inlaid with a shining brown tracery of winding jungle rivers. The most fertile parts of the lowlands are being opened up by planters and transmigration schemes, but a large area in the remote northeast is fit only for loggers and animals and has fortunately been awarded to the animals as the **Way Kambas Wildlife Reserve**. Elephants in particular seem to thrive in this marshland, and Way Kambas is said to be the best place in Sumatra to see them.

Lampung as a whole is nevertheless the most domesticated province of Sumatra. There is even a railway from South Sumatra into Lampung; started in 1911, it is the only one in Sumatra which still carries passengers. Roads and railway converge on the twin cities of **Tanjungkarang** and **Telukbetung**, by the historic trading coast opposite broken Krakatau, which wreaked almost as much havoc here as over the water in West Java in 1883. The twin towns, sometimes known collectively as **Bandar Lampung**, have the teeming, gimcrack, half-modern atmosphere of a Javanese port; even the *war-teg* foodstalls are here with their absurdly cheap fried *tahu* and *tempe*. Beyond Telukbetung are **Panjang** and then **Bakauheni**, embarkation points for Java and Jakarta, the beating heart of the vast, beautiful Indonesian beast of which Sumatra is just one sinewy limb.

GUIDEPOST SOUTH SUMATRA

BENGKULU
INEXPENSIVE: **Penginapan Aman**, Jl Pendakian. **Wisma Kenanga**, Jl Sentosa. **Wisma Melati**, Jl Veteran 35, Tel: 31186. **Wisma Rafflesia**, Jl Jen A Yani, Tel: 31650. **Penginapan Samudera**, Jl Benteng. *MODERATE:* **Asia**, Jl Jen A Yani 922B, Tel: 31901. **Wisma Balai Buntar**, Jl Khadijah 122. **Wisma Malabero**, Jl Dr Hazairin 1, Tel: 31004. **Pantai Nala Samudra**, Jl Pantai Nala 142, Tel: 31722.

Shopping / Post
Only real local speciality buy is gold, mostly in Chinatown. **Post office:** opp Parr monument.

Transport
AIR: Airport with daily flights to Jakarta & Palembang and less frequently to Padang & Telukbetung (Lampung). *Airline offices:* **Garuda**, Jl Jen A Yani 922. **Merpati:** Jl Let Suprapto 67, Tel: 31331. **SEA:** Small vessels, incl those for Enggano island (no airstrip on Enggano), sail from Bengkulu town harbor. Larger ships, like fortnightly Pelni services to Padang & Jakarta, call at new port **Pulau Baai**, 14 km further S. **ROAD:** Most buses on trans-Sumatra route run via Lubuklinggau, Curup & Bengkulu town. Main bus station is **Terminal Lingka Timur**, 9 km from town. **INTERNAL:** *Bemo* terminal is **Pasar Minggu**.

TELUKBETUNG/TANJUNGKARANG
INEXPENSIVE: **BNW**, Jl Jen A Yani 6, Tanjungkarang, Tel: 53624. **Intan**, Jl Raden Intan 45, Tanjungkarang, Tel: 52289. **Malaya Losmen**, Jl Tongkol 25, Telukbetung, Tel: 41581. **New Jakarta**, Jl Belanak 28, Telukbetung, Tel: 41048.
MODERATE: **Marcopolo**, Jl Dr Susilo 4, Telukbetung, Tel: 41511. **Nusa Indah**, Jl Raden Intan 132, Tanjungkarang, Tel: 53029.

Transport
AIR: Branti Airport, 30 km N of Tanjungkarang; buses stop within walking distance. *Airline offices:* **Garuda**, Marcopolo Hotel, Jl Dr Susilo 4, Telukbetung. **Merpati**, Jl Simba 20, Tel: 42325. **SEA:** Ferries to and from Java (Merak) dock either at Panjang near Telukbetung or at **Bakauheni**, 2 hrs' bus ride further SE. **RAIL:** Passenger rail link to Palembang and to Lubuklinggau (for Bengkulu and western route northwards) terminates in **Panjang**, but many travelers board at station on N side of Tanjungkarang. 2 trains daily. **ROAD:** Long-distance buses await ferry passengers at **Panjang & Bakauheni**, or leave from **Terminal Rajabasa** in Tanjungkarang. Intra-province services leave from several terminals in N of Tanjungkarang.

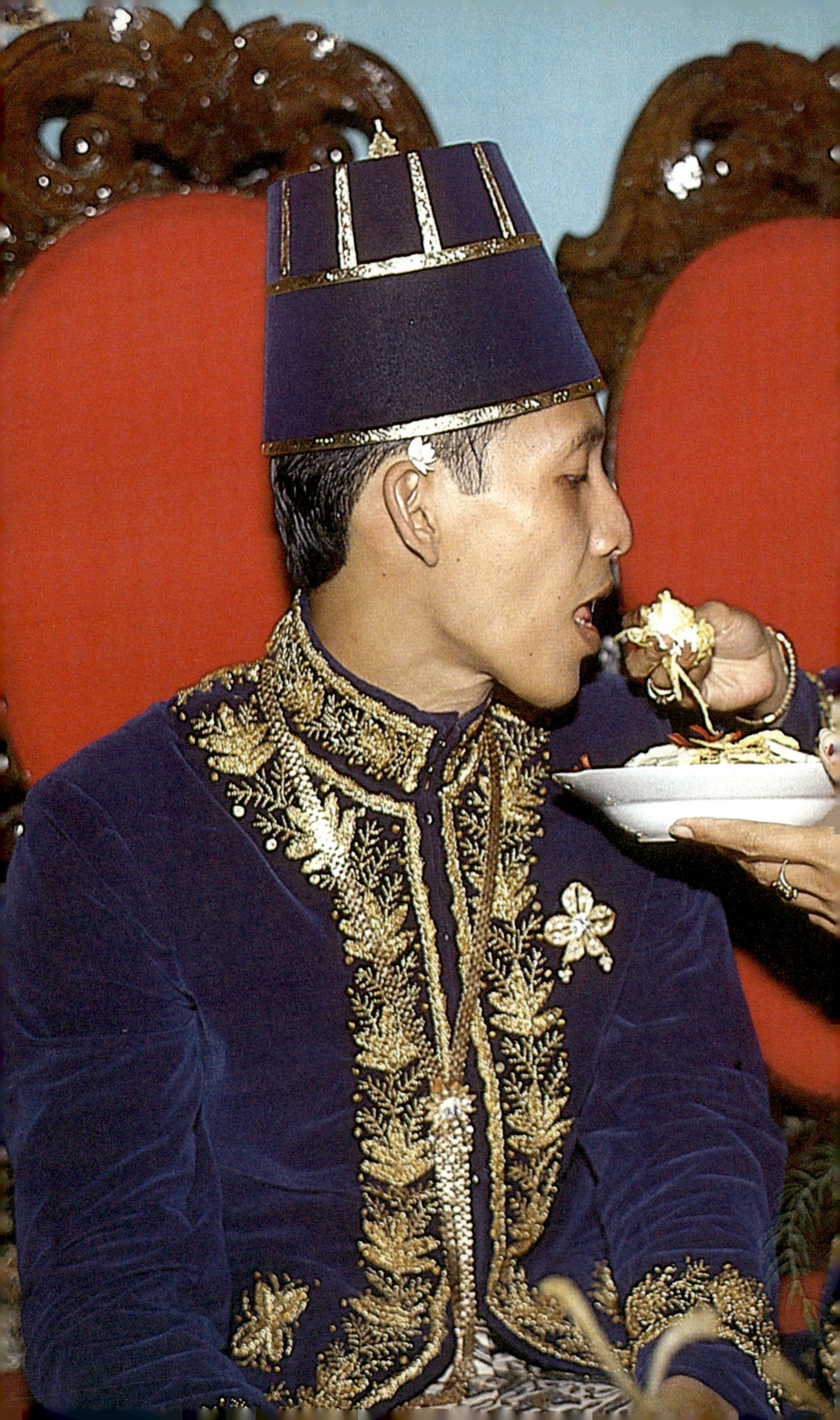

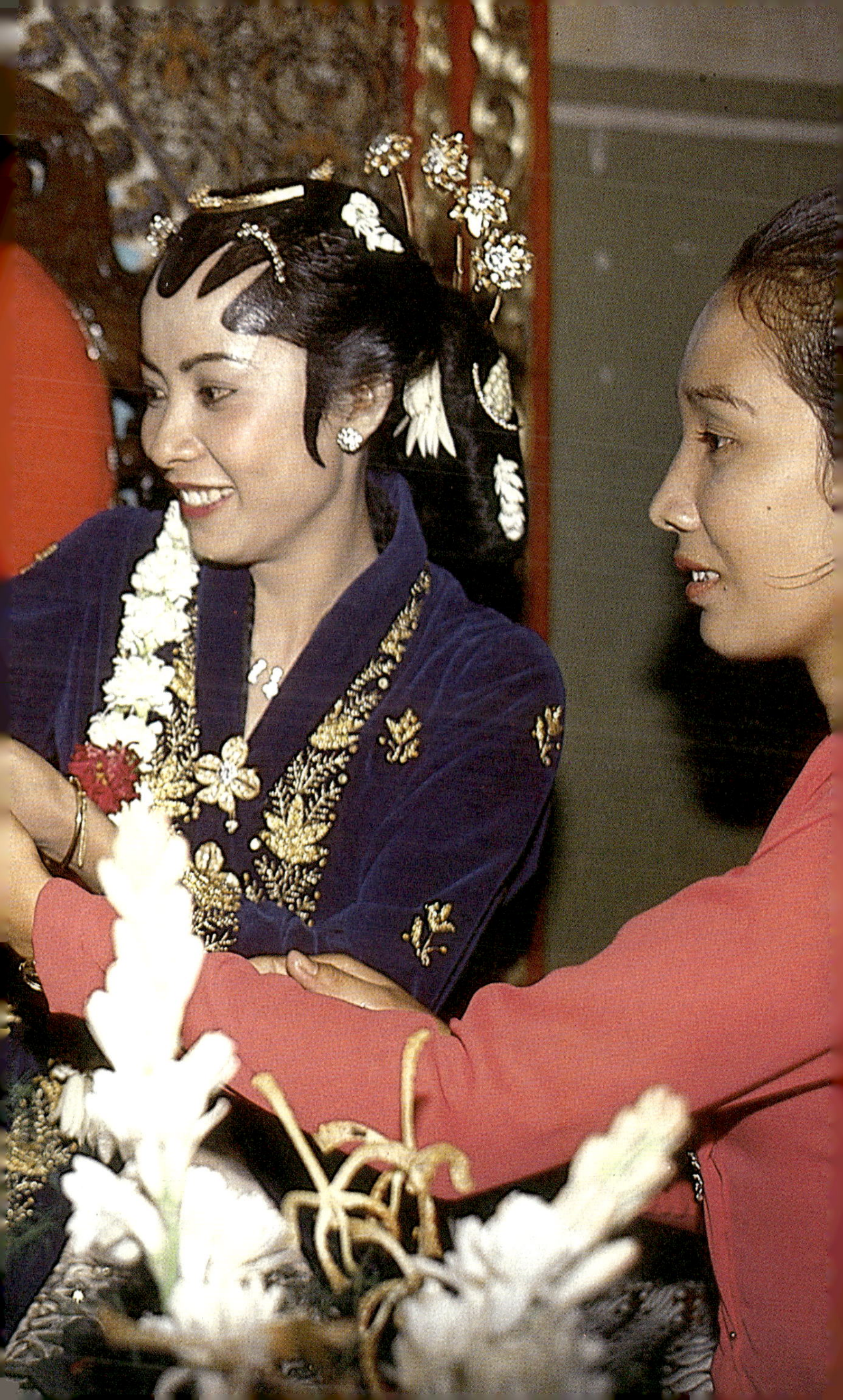

INDONESIAN CUISINE

Various styles of cooking have been blended with the gastronomic arts of traditional Indonesia. The result has been a number of culinary triumphs surprising those who enjoy fine food and greatly expanding their culinary horizons, adding new dishes to their repertoire.

While you are in Indonesia, you owe it to yourself to savor authentic Indonesian cuisine, or at least those popular dishes that are found all over Indonesia, such as *Opor Ayam*, chicken in mild creamy sauce. This dish calls for the use of chicken, coconut milk, finely ground ingredients such as candle nuts, green ginger, *laos*, coriander, cumin, garlic, onions, and oil to fry them in after they have been ground plus salam leaves, lemon grass, tamarind juice and salt to taste. This creative way of cooking the chicken in coconut milk with the exquisite blend of stir-fried spices and herbs, plus the practical know-how of an experienced cook produces magnificent flavors and

Preceding pages: Javanese wedding. Above: Selling fish in Denpasar. Right: Hot peppers and sambal paste in Sumatra.

an aroma that you never dreamt existed. *Opor Ayam* is usually accompanied by a vegetable dish such as *Sambal Goreng Buncis* (stir-fried green beans in coconut milk), *Pergedel Kentang Dengan Daging* (meat and potato croquettes), *Kerupuk* (crackers) and *Serundeng* (roasted coconut with peanuts). Each and every one of them complements the others.

Remember that Indonesian meals are not served as separate courses, and that all the dishes just mentioned are eaten with boiled white rice. The rice supplies the bulk of the meal, and its blandness is ideal for absorbing and combining the various flavors of the meat and vegetable dishes, and as the background against which to savor the contrasting tastes and textures.

Many people have the idea that dishes from Minangkabau are hot and spicy. But they are only half right. They do not real-

INDONESIAN CUISINE

ize that slow cooking reduces the pungency of chillies, and that chillies mixed with other spices and ingredients in the right proportions in a dish, can blend beautifully, and make it wonderfully appealing. If you get the measurements right you should not be able to distinguish any individual ingredient.

There are hundreds of dishes from Indonesia: hot ones, mild ones, sweet ones, sour ones, tangy ones and creamy ones, salty and bland ones. You could eat for weeks without seeing the same dish served twice. You know, of course, from reading other sections of this guide book, that there are hundreds of ethnic groups in Indonesia. All have numerous dishes of their own.

Have you ever heard of *Sate?* Beef, chicken, lamb or goat? Pieces of meat are placed on bamboo skewers, marinated in spices and grilled over a bed of charcoal fire, then served with a sauce consisting of ground peanuts mixed with chillies, garlic, onions, sugar, soy sauce, vinegar, salt, and water, or one made of soy sauce, sliced shallots, sliced chillies, crushed garlic, and the juice of lime. It is excellent to eat in or out of doors, at informal gatherings or cocktail parties. Foreigners usually take to *Sate* like ducks to water. If you are in Jakarta and want to try some *Sate* go to Jalan Sudirman to sample one of the *Sate* restaurants there. *Sate* is usually served with *Lontong* - compressed cooked rice steamed in a banana leaf - or a form of compressed rice called *Ketupat*, boiled in square bags (or other shapes) plaited from young coconut palm leaves.

Perhaps you are a vegetarian, or a semi-vegetarian. If so, then ask for a dish called *Gado-gado*, a kind of vegetable salad served with peanut sauce. This salad consists of lettuce, boiled shredded cabbage, boiled carrots (cut up into matchsticks), boiled sliced green beans, bean sprouts (scalded), quartered ripe tomatoes, and quartered hard-boiled eggs. All these ingredients are arranged attractively on a platter and before serving, peanut sauce is poured over them and fried onion flakes sprinkled on top. The peanut sauce is prepared like this: ground garlic, onion and chillies are stir-fried in a small amount of oil. Some water and ground peanuts are added, and the mixture is brought to the boil while being stirred. Sugar and vinegar are then added, with salt to taste.

Tempe is an Indonesian food much sought after by vegetarians, which is both nutritious and tasty. It is prepared from boiled soy-beans which are then fermented, a process that takes three days. The finished product is firm and compact like a cake, the beans being tightly bound together and covered evenly with a light coating of white mould, with an aroma something like that of fresh mushrooms. *Tempe* is firm enough not to crumble when sliced thinly. It is a source of high-quality protein.

It used to be a very nutritious dish in Indonesia for lower income groups because it was cheap and economical. Unlike fish, chicken, or beef, a pound of *Tempe* is a pound of *Tempe*. There are no bones, gristle or fat, in other words, no waste. But today, now that increasing numbers of educated people are turning towards vegetarian dishes, they too prefer *Tempe* to meat.

Fried *Tempe* is served with rice for breakfast, lunch and dinner in most homes in Indonesia, and in a variety of dishes at many restaurants. If you want to try it, then ask for *Tempe Goreng* (fried *Tempe*) or *Sambal Goreng Kering Tempe* (crisp deep-fried *Tempe* with seasoning), which consists of thin slices of crisp deep-fried *Tempe* with a sweet and spicy coating. The latter is also available in the market or in food shops, wrapped in shiny banana leaves or cellophane.

Yet another vegetarian food, also high in protein and entirely free of cholesterol, is *Tahu*, known in the West as soy-bean curd. Like *Tempe*, it is prepared from fermented soy-bean paste.

It originated in China about two thousand years ago, and is today an important part of the daily diet throughout East Asia and widely available in Western countries. It was first brought to Indonesia by Chinese travelers so many years ago that Indonesians regard it as belonging to their own cuisine, for they have their own ways of preparing it. For example they serve it as *Tahu Goreng* with *Gado-gado*. *Tahu* is available fresh daily in most parts of Indonesia.

If you are in Yogyakarta, you must try *Nasi Gudeg*, a dish which is specific to Central Java. It consists of pieces of chicken, and chopped young jack-fruit, cooked in coconut milk for hours, on low heat, with spices like coriander and cumin plus shrimp paste, onions, garlic, candle nuts ground into a paste, *laos*, brown sugar, and lemon grass with salt to taste. It is served with white rice.

Nasi Campur consists of a portion of white rice scooped onto a plate, on top of which is placed either fish, beef, chicken, or goat together with a mixture of vegetables, sprinkled with *Serundeng*, and topped off with a piece or two of *Krupuk*. This makes a tasty, substantial and reasonably priced meal.

Nasi Padang is so called because it is named after, and indeed characteristic of the cuisine of Padang, a port, and the capital city of West Sumatra. There are a number of Padang restaurants in Yogya. Indeed, there is hardly a city in Indonesia without its quota of Padang restaurants. Such restaurants are best known for the variety of curries and hot spicy dishes prepared from beef, chicken, goat, liver, tripe, kidneys, eggs and fish, and numerous vegetable dishes. Look out especially for the dish called *Kalio Ayam* (creamy chicken curry), and *Rendang*, a wonderfully flavored beef dish. And do not forget *Dendeng Balado*, fried seasoned sundried meat with a spicy coating. These three dishes alone make Minangkabau cuisine stand out from any other.

But food is not only served and eaten to satisfy hunger. It is a means of communication. There are special dishes to mark critical points in the life cycle. In Java, for example, a dish called *Nasi Tumpeng* is prepared when a woman has reached the seventh month of pregnancy. It consists of boiled rice pressed and shaped into a cone, 30 to 40 cm high, set in the center of a large, round bamboo platter lined with banana leaves, the cone shape symbolizing ascent and progress. It is surrounded by seven miniature cones of rice with a variety of dishes, vegetable, beef and chicken, interspersed with brightly colored sweatmeats. Relatives and neighbors are invited to share it. The serving of this dish announces to the community the happy news that the seventh month has been reached safely; it is at the same time an act of thanksgiving and a prayer for future blessings, in which all are invited to share. *Nasi Tumpeng* is also prepared to mark other occasions: a birthday, a wedding, or a wed-

INDONESIAN CUISINE

Delicious gifts from a bountiful sea.

ding anniversary. The shape of the *Nasi Tumpeng* is the same, but the meat and vegetable dishes that surround it differ according to the nature of the occasion.

Nasi Tumpeng is also prepared when a death has occurred. But in this case the cone is cut neatly from tip to base, and the two halves placed back to back, indicating that life, and with it any onward or upward movement, has come to an end.

In Bali, known as Pulau Dewata, the Isle of the Gods, food also plays a major role, not least in religious ceremonies. Bali is an island of thousands of temples, and an important part of Balinese religious devotion is expressed in taking food to these temples as offerings. The act of presenting the offerings has a deep symbolic meaning. It is above all an expression of thanks from the worshippers to *Sang Hyang Widhi*, the paramount God, for all his gifts to mankind. Everything offered to him or any of the lesser deities must be as beautiful and perfect as man, woman or child can make it.

As soon as the morning cooking is done, before anything is eaten, small offerings, consisting of a tiny mound of freshly cooked rice, a smidgin of ground chilli with salt and a stem or two of flowers are set on a small piece of banana leaf and put in a variety of places deemed important: in the household shrine, next to the hearth, by the well, and at the gate to protect the dwelling from evil spirits who are supposed to be everywhere.

Everyday meals are cooked by women. Only men, however, may prepare ceremonial meals and banquets including such specialities as *babi guling,* roast suckling pig. Bali is also known for its turtle steak and turtle Sate, delicacies not readily available anywhere else in Indonesia.

However, whether you stay in Kuta or Sanur, there are many restaurants and eating places to choose from, and you can indulge yourself in delicious foods from many parts of the world.

ARTS AND CRAFTS

Well-earned reward for skill and patience.

TRADITIONAL ARTS AND CRAFTS

Batik is undoubtedly the art form for which Indonesia is best known, although this technique of patterning textiles with wax-resist dye is almost exclusive to Java. *Batik* cloth, however, is immensely popular throughout Indonesia and in many other parts of Southeast Asia. In fact *batik* is the term used throughout the world for the wax-resist technique of patterning fabric, an acknowledgement of the supremacy of the Javanese at this art. Although widely used elsewhere, this method reached its most refined state in Java where the hot molten wax is applied to the surface of fine cotton fabric with a pen-like instrument *(canting)* that permits the application of intricate patterns of very fine dots and lines.

In addition to these elaborate *batik* techniques, during the nineteenth century a copper stamp *(cap)* was also invented in Java to provide a speedier means of applying the molten wax enabling local textile producers to counter the flood of printed cottons from the factories of industrial Europe. The *batik* textiles produced by this method *(batik cap)* are considerably cheaper than the painstaking, hand-drawn and more labor intensive *batik tulis*. In recent years, textile factories in Java have mass-produced printed cloth in batik-like patterns, known fallaciously as *"batik"* print although no wax is ever applied to these fabrics.

Batik still exhibits great regional variations in color and design, although the largest *batik* companies are now able to sell these under the one roof. The *batik* cloths of central Java *(kain panjang)* are probably the most familiar. The designs are usually based on geometric all-over patterns, and the typical colors of these cloths are blue-black and brown against a cream ground (for Solo) or a white ground (for Yogyakarta). The sombre elegance of the *batiks* of these old central

Javanese principalities is in sharp contrast to the vibrant colors of the floral and bird designs of north-coast centers such as Pekalongan. The art of coastal Java has been strongly influenced by trade: European, Chinese and Arab influences can be identified in the *batik* designs of these areas. North-coast *batik* cloth usually displays the tubular *kain sarong* design structure featuring a contrasting head-panel section, or the *pagi soré* ("morning and evening") style with different designs at each end of one cloth. Another variation of particular interest is the *batik* of the Cirebon region on the border between West and Central Java, where large frieze-like patterns or rocks, shrines, clouds and mythical monsters appear against pale plain grounds. These *batiks* are still produced in workshops at Trusmi and Plered on the outskirts of the city. Meanwhile, from the other end of Java, in the Tuban area, simple but charming village *batik* textiles are still being produced on hand-spun cotton.

More Batik

The export of *batik* cloth to regions outside Java, especially in Bali and Sumatra, has been taking place for centuries and old *batiks* are still an important part of ceremonial costume on those islands. Blue and white *batiks* from north-coast Java are especially favored in Bali and these are often embellished with gold leaf gluework *(perada)* to enhance their appearance as costume for dance-dramas and royal ceremonies. Gold leaf (or gold dust) is also applied to plain fabric by first painting or stamping glue patterns onto the cloth surface to which the costly gold substance adheres. The crisp rustling of these lustrous garments complements their dazzling impression, although many of these cloths are now made by stencilling the lotus and other floral designs in gold paint. While such textiles continue to achieve a spectacular effect at theatrical performances, close scrutiny reveals them to be far less subtle than the genuine older and more expensive *kain perada*.

The Balinese have produced many types of textiles using a multitude of decorative techniques, including tie-dye, tapestry weave, twill weave, weft *ikat* and supplementary weft brocade. At textile craft centers such as Gianyar and Batuan such textiles are made in considerable quantities for local and tourist markets. Usually in silk, the weft *ikat (endek)* is produced by tying and dyeing the weft threads into patterns before weaving them into a plain warp. The technique is sometimes combined with gold thread brocade weaving *(songket)* in which supplementary wefts of gold-wrapped thread are added to provide floating patterns, especially in borders and elaborate triangular ends. The effect is a sumptuous textile suitable for ceremonial use by the traditional aristocracy, and such fabrics, displaying designs derived from imported luxury textile heirlooms or shadow-puppet style motifs taken from the great Hindu epics, were only woven in the past for the fastidious Balinese élite.

One justly famous textile – the double ikat *geringsing* – is made only in Bali and on that island exclusively in the small village of Tenganan near Karangasem in the east. According to this complicated technique, both the warp threads and the weft threads are separately tied and dyed into patterns which the weaver combines during the weaving process to reveal the complex designs. These masterpieces of textile art are worked on the simplest of backstrap tension looms, although as they are sacred objects the support of the gods is sought by offerings throughout the various stages that are required to create them. Like many other traditional textiles, the *geringsing* are used in the various ceremonies of the religious calendar and life-cycle. The centrality of the

ARTS AND CRAFTS

geringsing in ritual and ceremony explains the great care that is taken to produce these beautiful traditional cloths.

The Sasak people who inhabit the isolated slopes of Mount Rinjani on the island of Lombok also make sacred textiles which fulfil similar important functions. Although some of the most ritually potent Sasak textiles are decorated only with simple stripes and rich natural dyes, such fabrics are often embellished with huge quantities of old Chinese coins threaded through the fringes to add to their spiritual presence.

Textiles are widely used as ceremonial gifts among the Batak peoples of northern Sumatra. At a wedding, for instance, each guest wraps the seated bridal couple in a traditional *ulos* of appropriate design and complexity, according to the giver's age, social standing and family realtionship to the bride or groom. Toba Batak textiles are clearly distinguishable from those of the Karo, the Simalungun and the Angkola Batak groups. In addition, within each of these Batak regions differ-

Wayang golek puppets. Right: Basket-weaver on Bali.

ent villages specialize in producing one or two of the district's characteristic textiles. The finest of these include the *ulos ragidup* ("cloth of life") with intricately woven black and white supplementary weft inserts depicting male and female symbols, made around Taratung, Porsea, and Muara on the shores of Lake Toba; the *ulos ragi hotang* in simple stripes but with striking wide twined end-braid made around Baligé; and the dark-blue warp *ikat ulos sibolang* made on the island of Samosir in the center of Lake Toba.

Batak textiles are always woven from cotton, and with the exception of the Angkola Batak *abit* and *parompa* which display bright tapestry-weave bands and glossy beads, the cloths are worked in sombre earth or indigo tones appropriate to the misty atmosphere of the Batak highlands. The textiles of the various Malay peoples of Sumatra, however, are

ARTS AND CRAFTS

bright and colorful, like those of the Balinese. Intricate examples of Minangkabau gold and silver thread weaving from Pandai Sikat, and Malay silk and gold brocade from Palembang are made in traditional styles using time-tested apparatus and techniques. Only the quality of the gold thread has changed, and unlike other types of the more robust traditional textiles these splendid textiles must be rolled and not folded during storage and transportation to avoid permanent creasing and damage.

As social and religious changes have occurred, other textile traditions have steadily become less important. In Aceh it is not weaving but gold-thread embroidery that has survived, and ceremonial hangings, cushions and food covers, items of regalia – even such items as mosquito-net clasps – carry decorative designs stitched to an expensive basecloth such as luxurious velvet. Sadly, however, one of the greatest textile-producing cultures in the whole of Southeast Asia, the Paminggir of southern Sumatra, no longer weave their famous shipcloths. The National Museum in Jakarta has a fine collection of these supplementary weft hangings and the splendid embroidered women's skirts that also display fanciful ships with mythical creatures and human riders. A few nineteenth-century examples are available at high prices in antique shops, and an enterprising weaver in Java is producing the Sumatran ship-cloths in considerable numbers for the tourist trade.

Other Crafts

Similar regional variations are evident in the other arts of western Indonesia. In the past, particular styles of sculpture, metalwork, basketry, leatherwork and pottery, for instance, could be identified with specific ethnic groups, and even with certain villages. Historically, the peoples of Indonesia depended upon imported glazed ceramics from China and mainland Southeast Asia. Although their own traditional low-fired pottery for water and cooking vessels is still in use, it is rapidly being replaced by plastic and metal containers, and although the traditional utensils are still found throughout Indonesia, they remain most prominent in Bali and West Lombok where clay vessels are an integral part of the paraphernalia required for religious offerings. Matting and plaiting skills are also under threat from cheap plastic manufacturers, although fine durable cane and palm-leaf objects are widely available: Lombok basketry in traditional forms is particularly attractive, and the Tasikmalaya area of West Java produces some of the best plaited objects in all of Indonesia.

Metalwork is one craft that has received an enormous boost from the tourist industry, and in Bali and Java traditional metal-smithing villages have maintained and expanded their repertoire, offering well-made products in an elaborate traditional form or a simple modern style. Metal workers continue to make ceremonial swords *(kris)* and the musical instruments that form part of the traditional percussion orchestras *(gamelan)* of Java and Bali. The smiths of Kota Gede near Yogyakarta display high quality silver-working skill. Celuk in Bali and Kota Gadang in West Sumatra are other long-standing silver-smithing centers where regional styles of jewelry are still being produced. Gold, long regarded as a safe investment against inflation, is widely available in every Indonesian town and city. Judged largely by weight, gold jewelry is usually made in a contemporary style, although in regional centers such as Banda Aceh it is still possible to seek out gold worked with particular traditional regional designs.

Wooden sculpture is also region-specific. Javanese centers such as Jepara, on the north coast, and Balinese villages such as Ubud and Mas continue to produce wood-carving in various styles for both domestic consumption and foreign tourists. Objects as large as doors, room-dividers and items of furniture and as minute as buttons and bangles are produced by these craftsmen. Sculptural mastery is now less apparent in Sumatra and it seems that the great traditional carving skills that embellished the grand ancestral dwellings, meeting houses and ricebarns of the Toba and Karo Batak, the Minangkabau and the inhabitants of the island of Nias have steadily disappeared. Replicas of smaller traditional objects are available in the form of small buffalo horn, wood and bamboo artifacts, although the spiritual qualities that imbued the magic wands, the charm containers, and sacred book covers of the village shaman and great stone sarcophagi for the bones of the ancestors are difficult to achieve in a more secular age.

Pigment painting on cloth has traditionally been of less significance in Southeast Asia than in the West, and in Indonesia it is only in Bali that traditional painting is still practiced. These paintings take a variety of forms, and include Balinese traditional calendars, scenes from the great Hindu epics and romances, and stylized panoramas of village life and ritual which have flourished in the twentieth century. Painting, however, is still important in the production of the dance masks and leather shadow-puppets required for the vital theater arts of Java and Bali. Village artisans specialize in the working of buffalo leather to produce the *wayang kulit* puppets. An intricate patterning of bright pigments and gilding of clothing and jewelry identify the various characters. Balinese shadow-puppets are more rounded and less attenuated than those used in Central Java. In West Java the puppets (known there as *wayang golek*) take a three-dimensional form and the performances take place in the round without a shadow screen.

While the most famous instances of Indonesian art are the massive stone monuments of great antiquity that dot the landscape, many of the finest objects in other less permanent media - textiles, wooden sculpture, paintings and *wayang* puppets - can still be examined in the collections on display in the national, regional and palace museums in most of the provinces of western Indonesia. These institutions are often housed in fine old buildings and are imposing examples of regional traditional architecture. With many of these art forms, the skills have been maintained over the centuries by the demands of ritual and the need to continually replace artifacts consumed by time and ceremonial use. Some of these no longer hold a place in modern Indonesia. In Bali, however, the ceremonial cycle is still of paramount importance. Yet much of that island's art is of the most transitory nature. The splendor of the great rituals is often achieved with the most temporary and fragile materials – offerings of flowers and colored rice cakes, and banners of plaited palm-leaves, cremation

ARTS AND CRAFTS

Fishing boat cruising in the Indonesian archipelago.

towers and coffins of soft woods and paper – which quickly deteriorate or are destroyed after the ceremony.

Sailing Boats and Outrigger Canoes

Nowhere in the world is there such a variety of colorful fishing villages and maritime cultures as in Indonesia; thriving, busy and open for all to see, but often just a little more isolated than the average tourist likes. Hunting the traditional sailing *prahu* (Indonesian for "boat") and haunting genuine fishing villages, usually involves discomfort for a rewarding collection of memories and photographs. To find fishing villages you must search for the *kampong nelayan*; there is often one at the edge of the coastal towns, but those on stretches of isolated coast are cleaner and more beautiful.

Prahu harbors are often located away from the port areas for powered ships, for example at Kali Baru beyond Tanjung Priok to the east of Jakarta and at Gresik just to the north of Surabaya on the straits of Madura. These are the places to see concentrations of sailing *prahu*. Ports along the north coast of Java usually have a corner for traditional sailing boats and almost every town among the eastern islands is a port on the coast.

Traditionally, communication depended on the sea, and a great variety of local styles of boats have been developed over the centuries. Today many have vanished forever, but the persistent traveler, keen on sail, can still find a rewarding variety. Not only is Indonesia a nation of islands, with few roads in pre-colonial days - the winds are kind to ships, with few cyclones. The winds blow steadily from the southeast from May to October, then reverse and blow the other way from November to April, allowing annual return trips from one end of the archipelago to the other. Rot-resistant timbers and material for sails, strings, and floats are readily available, sheltered harbors are abundant (except on the shores of the open oceans) and durable trade goods, particularly rice and cloth, metal, spices and luxury goods are unevenly distributed.

Building boats is traditionally done by the specialist craftsmen with many trade secrets. Boatbuilders have a spiritual commitment which preserves tradition; ceremonies at every stage reinforce the importance of the supernatural world. Any deviation from the ways of the ancestors is likely to be punished by the spirits which are all around.

Like any other object that is made by a skilled craftsman, the boat has a spirit of its own which is derived from the life force of its creator and locked into the hull by ceremony. The days to fell the trees, lay the keel, start a new section or launch the boat, are fixed by a priest or soothsayer. Offerings are made at each stage; in Bali, offerings are made every 210 days at the feast of Galungan to the spirit of each outrigger canoe, which is dressed up with a *sarong*. Knots in the tree have to be considered, insects in the wood are a disaster, timber must not be used twice, women may not stand on the partly constructed boat, the top and bottom of the timber may be significant, but above all, every measurement is a ratio between simple numbers carried in the master builder's head.

The size of the whole boat is fixed by a unit length, which in an outrigger canoe is the inside length of a hull, and on a planked boat is the length of the keel. The large unit length is always divided into twelve parts (equal to the number of ribs in the human body) and every dimension of the boat is a multiple or fraction of this unit.

Houses in Bali are still built on the same principles of ratios, taken from the body dimensions of the master builder.

The basic boat is the dug-out canoe, which in Indonesia has an outrigger on each side, and is almost always specialized for fishing. The double outrigger provides a stable platform, so that the occupants (often only one) can turn their attention to the fishing. Nets, lines and trawling are the usual methods. Single outrigger canoes are specialized for use with the throwing net.

A splendid place to see double outrigger canoes is the Lombok Straits where there are hundreds of Balinese *jukung* trawling for tuna.

The dug-out hull was originally built up with planks by lashing and sewing but about a thousand years ago the technique of connecting the planks edge to edge with dowels was introduced. Ribs were lashed into place and the whole structure could easily be dismantled. Ships of several hundred tons were built for trade with China and India. Western designs have been introduced slowly and patchily over the centuries, and the process is still not complete.

The principal modern types are the Bugis *prahu*, now almost entirely motorized; the Madurese *leti leti*, of which several hundred still operate, with a large triangular sail fixed between two booms; a few Madurese *janggolan* still trading along the north coast of Java, with a complicated rig that is supported by beams pushed out on each side; and the Western-style *lambo* which looks something like a modern yacht, often with gunter-lug rig and one or two jibs.

Hundreds of these boats trade in goods of all kinds between small harbors all over Indonesia. The older designs have lateral rudders; the more modern ones, often sailed by Bu-tungese, have a center rudder and a tiller. These boats are all well adapted to Indonesian waters, where they can easily run for shelter, but they are not designed for the high stresses of the fore-and-aft rig; the planks are often short, and the deckhouse is easily swept away, so that they are not suitable for a Western yachtsman looking for a cheap hull.

A friendly guide through the Sumatran jungle.

WILDLIFE AND ENVIRONMENT

Western Indonesia used to abound with wildlife of every kind, mostly rain-forest-living but some specialized to life in open woodland, mountain moorland or limestone hills. Nowadays the human population explosion, combined with the depradations caused by unrestrained logging, have seen to it that most wildlife is confined to reserves and national parks, except for those birds, rats, frogs and fish that can live in ricefields. To see more spectacular wildlife, visitors must travel to more remote areas.

National parks are an innovation in Indonesia; since about 1980 more and more have been set up, based on an already existing system of nature reserves *(cagar alam)* and wildlife reserves *(suaka margasatwa)*. Many of these reserved areas have a section where visitors are permitted to look around without restriction *(taman wisata)*; but to go into the reserve proper a permit is necessary, which is most easily obtained from the offices of the Perlindungan Hutan dan Pengewatan Alam or PHPA (Directorate of Forest Conservation and Nature Protection) at Jalan Ir. H. Juanda 9, Bogor.

The most famous of Indonesia's reserves is probably **Ujung Kulon** (now a national park), on the western tip of Java. Here lives what may be the world's only remaining viable population of a once widespread and abundant species, the Javan rhinoceros. Rhinos are still actively hunted for the supposed medicinal properties of their horns; Western mythology has it that rhino horn is "used as an aphrodisiac in China", but actually its use is as a reputedly powerful fever-reducing drug – in 1988 the horns of Asian rhinos were worth over US$ 40,000 in Taiwan! It says a great deal for the devotion of the staff, and the abilities of successive conservationists, that since the mid-1960s the number of rhinos in Ujung Kulon has risen from a couple of dozen to over 60 today, and that despite numerous attempts only one or two rhinos have been killed by poachers in a quarter of a century. Visitors have perhaps an even chance of seeing a rhino there today; they are sure of seeing deer, wild pigs, peacocks, hornbills, two or three species of monkey, and the rare *banteng (Bos javanicus)*, a species of wild cattle. Visitors to Ujung Kulon who have already been to Bali will notice that *banteng* resemble a larger, leaner, longer-horned version of typical Balinese domestic cattle, with the same white legs and white rump, and as with them, the bulls are usually black, the cows and calves golden-brown. Bali cattle are also bred in eastern Java, Madura, Lampung and Sumatra Selatan; but the true wild *banteng* are confined now to a very few areas in Java.

There are leopards in Ujung Kulon, but tigers became extinct there in the 1950s; indeed they are probably gone from the whole of Java. A reserve, **Meru Betiri**, was set up to protect the last remaining population of the distinctive Javan tiger, but it was poorly guarded and they are almost certainly now gone for ever.

Other reserves in Java which are worth visiting are **Cibodas**, a montane forest national park between Bogor and Bandung; **Pangandaran**, on the south coast of West Java, where there are *banteng* and the rare *lutung* or Javan leaf-monkey; and **Baluran**, in the far east (accessible from Surabaya), which is much more open than the more westerly reserves, and has a large population of *banteng*.

Just across the straits from Baluran lies the **Bali Barat National Park**, the last known home of the beautiful white starling or Rothschild's grackle, which is much sought after (and still sometimes obtained, illegally) by aviarists. Crab-eating or long-tailed macaque monkeys are still common in Bali (as in Java aud Sumatra too), and live protected around Hindu temples; a race of the *lutung*, different from the Javanese one, survives in the forests on Kitamini volcano.

Sumatra has a much smaller human population than Java, and is correspondingly better supplied with wildlife. In the **Gunung Leuser National Park**, in Aceh, lives the Sumatran rhinoceros, smaller than the Javan and with two horns instead of only one; though there are 130 to 200 there, they live in thick forest, mainly in the remote mountain valleys, and the visitor will be very lucky to see one (but they are still occasionally killed by poachers). Visitors will however be able to see orangutans, locally known as *mawas*, perhaps in the wild but certainly at the **Bohorok** and **Ketambe Rehabilitation Centers**, on the edges of the park, where orangutans confiscated from illegal captivity are taught forest skills and eventually persuaded to return to the wild. There are also elephants, wild pig, *serow,* tigers, sun bears, gibbons, and several species of monkeys. The Bohorok center is easily accessible from Medan; Ketambe is north of Kutacane, on the Alas River, further inland.

Gunung Kerinci, Sumatras's highest mountain, is partly covered by a national park (**Kerinci Seblat**); here, too, the Sumatran rhinoceros lives (perhaps even a couple of hundred of them), as well as its smaller relative, the curious black-and-white Malay tapir. **Bukit Barisan Selatan** is another national park, in far southwestern Sumatra, which has both rhinos and tapirs, as well as the bizarre bearded pig, and among birds the beautiful argus pheasant. Tigers occur, if sparsely, in all these reserves; the Sumatran tiger is slightly different from the Javan, but seems to be headed for the same fate unless it can be better protected than at present. Oddly, there are no leopards in Sumatra; but there is the slightly smaller clouded leopard, which can sometimes be seen up in the trees. Finally in Sumatra the **Way Kambas Reserve** should be mentioned; the Javan rhinoceros used to occur here, but was apparently exterminated single-handed by a Dutch hunter in the 1930s.

The Mentawai Islands, west of Sumatra, have a very unusual fauna, including a species of gibbon and three species of monkeys, found nowhere else; these are best seen in the **Tettei Batti Reserve** .

The Environment

Typical of the western half of Indonesia is tropical rain-forest; mostly lowland forest, but of the lower, more open types known as montane and moss forest along the Barisan Range in Sumatra and the central mountain spine of Java; wide areas of swamp forest along the east coast of Sumatra; mangroves along the tidal zones themselves; and patches of specialized forest elsewhere, such the distinct forest type of the limestone hills and peat forest. What makes these forests unusual among the world's rain forests is the

WILDLIFE AND ENVIRONMENT

Baby Sumatra crocodiles.

dominance of a single plant family, *Dipterocarpaceae*, a valuable timber tree. Many of the lowland forests of Sumatra have now been clear-felled; only in mountainous regions are there still substantial stands of the original rain forest.

As one travels east through Java, the climate becomes drier, and the flora changes from rain-forest to monsoon forest and open country. As the flora changes, so does the fauna: gibbons, for example, are not found east of Gunung Slamet in Central Java nor (in the days of their abundance) were rhinos, whereas ecologically tougher species like wild pigs and *banteng* lived all over the island.

Bali, small though it is, is as diverse as Java in its environment. The whole of the western side is dry, almost scrubby forest; it is the wetter, hence more fertile, eastern side that is densely populated and so denuded of its natural vegetation.

In the past, forest clearance – especially rain forest logging – was almost unregulated; government control over logging and other forms of clearance is now much tighter, but illegal activities still go on, and control of illegal settlement and wood-cutting in wildlife reserves is less than perfect, although the laws have been passed. Forest destruction used to be attributed to slash-and-burn agriculture, and the notion that planned commercial activities could be the real culprit has, for rather obvious reasons, taken some time to become accepted!

The laws controlling the killing and exploitation of wildlife are tough; they are, of course, difficult to police, and many people do not even know about them. A species that is strictly protected in this way is the Sumatran rhinoceros. Its habitat is dense and difficult to control, but poachers, if caught by competent and uncorrupt authorities are severely dealt with. Yet the Torgamba forest, where the species was known to live was scheduled for clear-cutting in the early 1980s. This seems to make a mockery of the strict preservation laws.

Islam goes modern in the Jakarta mosque.

ISLAM

Few sounds are more evocative than the *azan,* the Islamic call to prayer which drifts over Indonesia's ricefields and rooftops five times daily, from the first glimmer of dawn to the evening dark. For the Indonesian Muslim, it is the sound of a certainty and continuity which most of the West has lost forever. He knows that it has echoed down thirteen centuries, and that the same Arabic chants can be heard from Morocco to the Philippines.

But the timelessness is deceptive. The *azan* now comes from an amplified cassette, and celebrates a fragmented and fast-changing faith. Change is nothing new to Islam: intrinsically the most puritanical of the great religions, it seems to have spent most of its history in a constant state of reformation. But in Indonesia at least, the current changes are crucial because they are determining the relationship between Islam and the new gods of progress, development and modernity.

Not that Indonesian Islam is under threat: quite the reverse. In a country already 87 per cent Muslim on paper, it gains ground daily as ever more "identity card Muslims" *(Muslim KTP)* are persuaded to take the tenets and duties of their faith more seriously. Men whose Islam went no deeper than their excised foreskins are on the floor at every *azan;* pagan and Hindu beliefs which for centuries dove-tailed perfectly with Muslim practice are being confronted at last. In the cities, signs of the revival are everywhere: Islamic bookshops and publishing are booming; new mosques and religious schools are going up; government offices, stations and airports, now provide special prayer rooms for the devout.

Why the new-found zeal? Partly it is a conservative reaction against rapid social change and against an urban immorality perceived as an import from the godless West. At another level, it might be seen as

Giggling Muslim girls in Banten, West Java.

a symptom of progress itself, as a developing people trades its rural superstition and hocus-pocus for a more consistent, analytic faith, valid outside the insular society of the village and strong enough to sustain its adherents through the shocks of urban life. There is, however, another important element in the reaction: opposition to the current political order. The government rides the Islamic tide where it can, funding schools and mosques and striving to attract religious politicians into its fold. But it cannot direct the current, beneath which runs a strong undertow of criticism and protest.

In more than a thousand Islamic discussion groups, earnest young men and women debate not only the interpretation of the Koran but also inequality, public morality, corruption, the relationship between Islam and politics, and the idea of an Islamic state. Since the slaughter of the left in 1965, the social and moral prescriptions of Islam have attracted many discontented young people who, in a different time or place, would probably have been socialists. And somewhere in the murky wings, there are also a few men of religious violence. Muslim terrorists hijacked a Garuda airliner in 1984, and the Indonesian army exterminated an extremist cell in Lampung in 1989. Suharto and other powerful figures want Javanese mysticism recognized and sponsored as an approved religion to challenge the growing momentum of Islam, but have been unable even to get such a bill past their own tame parliament. There was bitter opposition even to the 1985 law obliging all political organizations to accept the principle of religious tolerance embodied in the official state philosophy. The New Order hopes to forge the traditional religious tolerance and theological vagueness of Java into a sort of pseudo-secularism appropriate to a modern industrial society. But the social ferment of development may instead distil a dangerously heady religious brew.

IMPRINT

Nelles Maps ...the maps, that get you going.

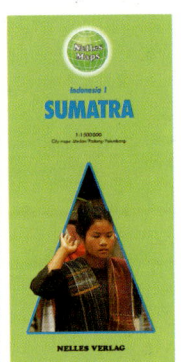

Nelles Map Series:

- Afghanistan
- Australia
- Burma
- Caribbean Islands 1 / Bermuda, Bahamas, Greater Antilles
- Caribbean Islands 2 / Lesser Antilles
- China 1 / North-Eastern China
- China 2 / Northern China
- Crete
- Hawaiian Islands
- Hawaiian Islands 1 / Kauai
- Hawaiian Islands 2 / Honolulu, Oahu
- Hawaiian Islands 3 / Maui, Molokai, Lanai
- Hawaiian Islands 4 / Hawaii
- Himalaya
- Hong Kong
- Indian Subcontinent
- India 1 / Northern India
- India 2 / Western India
- India 3 / Eastern India
- India 4 / Southern India
- India 5 / North-Eastern India
- Indonesia
- Indonesia 1 / Sumatra
- Indonesia 2 / Java + Nusa Tenggara
- Indonesia 3 / Bali
- Indonesia 4 / Kalimantan
- Indonesia 5 / Java + Bali
- Indonesia 6 / Sulawesi
- Indonesia 7 / Irian Jaya + Maluku
- Jakarta
- Japan
- Kenya
- Korea
- Malaysia
- West Malaysia
- Nepal
- New Zealand
- Pakistan
- Philippines
- Singapore
- South East Asia
- Sri Lanka
- Taiwan
- Thailand
- Vietnam, Laos Kampuchea

INDONESIA WEST
©Nelles Verlag GmbH, München 45
All rights reserved
ISBN 3-88618-367-X

First Edition 1990
Co-publisher for U.K.:
Robertson McCarta, London
ISBN 1-85365-235-0 (for U.K.)

Publisher:	Günter Nelles	**DTP-Exposure:**	Schimann, Pfaffenhofen
Chief Editor:	Dr. Heinz Vestner	**Color**	
Project Editor:	David E. F. Henley	**Separation:**	Priegnitz, München
Cartography:	Nelles Verlag GmbH, Dipl. Ing. C. Heydeck	**Printed by:**	Gorenjski Tisk, Kranj, Yugoslavia

No part of this book, not even excerpts, may be reproduced without prior permission of Nelles Verlag

- 01 -

TABLE OF CONTENTS

Preparation 242
   Climate 242
   Visas 242
   Money 242
   Health 242

Travel to Indonesia 243

Domestic Travel 244
   Guided Tours 246
   National Parks 246

Practical Tips 246
   Accommodation 246
   Business Hours 247
   Crime 247
   Customs 247
   Eating and Drinking 247
   Electricity 247
   Etiquette 248
   Holidays 248
   Liquor 248
   Photography 248
   Post and Telecommunication 248
   Time 249
   Weights and Measures 249

Addresses 249
   Embassies/Consulates 249
   Tourist Offices Outside Indonesia 249

Indonesian Language 250

Authors 251

Photographers 251

PREPARATION

Climate

Indonesia has a very hot, wet climate. In coastal cities, daytime temperature hovers around 28°, and air humidity around 80 per cent, throughout the year. In the wet season, usually November till April, it will rain hard every afternoon. Wear light, loose, quick-drying cotton clothes. Take hints from the way the locals behave. Learn to walk slowly, without tension, as they do; to seek shade at all times; to nap indoors if you can during the early afternoon; to take a cooling *mandi* three times a day. Temperatures fall rapidly with altitude, however, and a windy mountain pass in Java can be downright cold, especially at night, so bring one sweater. Wear sandals unless visiting or hiking - but remember to bring them with you if you have big feet, because Indonesians laugh if you ask to buy a pair of size elevens.

Visas

Citizens of Australia, New Zealand, Canada, the USA, Japan, South Korea, Thailand, Malaysia, Singapore, the Philippines, and all western European nations except Portugal are not required to obtain tourist visas before arrival. Provided they carry a passport valid for at least six months after entry, and have onward or return tickets or proof of purchase of such, they are issued a **two-month tourist pass** upon arrival. Other nationalities must apply at an Indonesian embassy or consulate abroad. Israelis and South Africans may not enter Indonesia on their passports. With the 2-month tourist pass no extension whatsoever is possible - you must leave Indonesia when your time is up. If you want to stay longer you must leave the country, normally for Singapore, and re-enter.

Other types of visa, available only by prior application to an Indonesian embassy, include the **Visitor Visa**, issued initially for 5 weeks but extendable by increments to 6 months at **Imigrasi** offices, and the **Business Visa**, issued for 30 days and extendable to 3 months. But both of these require letters of sponsorship.

Money

US dollars are the most useful foreign currency in Indonesia, and travelers' cheques (preferably American Express) should always be in dollars. Take proof of purchase with you. Change money and cheques at banks if you can, not in airports or hotels. You will always be asked for your passport. Rates are much poorer in out-of-the-way towns than in Jakarta or Bali. There is no black market in foreign currencies. Credit cards are useless except in the very plushest hotels.

There is a chronic shortage of change - though not as chronic as pocket-groping taxi-drivers would have you believe. Get cash in small denominations and plenty of coinage from a bank for bus fares, telephone calls and so on.

Although travel tickets, prepared food and some of the more expensive urban shops have fixed prices, bargaining is the norm in many everyday transactions. Indonesian participants usually have a rather accurate idea of the outcome before they start, but insist on reaching it through a protracted struggle in which both exorbitantly high and insultingly low figures are named. This conflict, necessary and even enjoyable for the local, may be highly stressful for the uninitiated foreigner. Shop around first, ask advice, take along an Indonesian friend if you can. Be patient, smile, play down your interest, but never make a bid you do not mean. As a last resort, try the old walk-away trick - but be warned, the grubbiest stallholder can be an awfully good judge of intent.

Health

Always remember that Indonesia has a tropical climate to which your Western body will have to get accustomed and in part be innoculated against. There are standard vaccinations: against **typhoid**, **hepatitis A** (no guarantee but better than nothing); **hepatitis B** (the latter to be administered at least six months before departure); and **cholera**, which exist in Indonesia, but outbreaks are rare.

Consult an experienced, up-to-date doctor on prevention of **malaria,** the tropics' most dangerous disease. Make sure you do this in time for your trip! Recommended practices are constantly changing with the evolution of resistant strains. Use of insect repellent is a helpful additional precaution.

Water should always be boiled for at least ten minutes before drinking, which is why you might ask the street vendors not to cool your soft drink with crushed ice. Raw foods, cold cooked meats, even ice creams possibly made with unpasteurized milk should be avoided. Try to peel fruit yourself.

If you wish to enjoy your stay in Indonesia and get a taste of local culture however you will have to learn to avoid what seems obviously silly and take the rest on trust. As your body adjusts you may get a mild gripe and the runs. This is normal and any commercial antidiarrhoeal will take care of the problem.

Fungal infections can be battled with **Canesten** – keep on applying it long after the battle is apparently won. Bring an antiseptic soap (for example **Sapoderm**) as a prophylaxis against skin infections. Avoid walking barefoot as some parasites enter the body through the sole of the foot. Antiseptics can help especially if you aim to travel far from any urban center, for example **Betadine**, for small cuts; **Cicatrin** is a topical antibiotic. You might even want to carry for safety, an oral antibiotic suitable for killing sepsis even in a deep wound, alongside a broad-spectrum one such as **Bactrin** for gut and lung infections. Many of these are available in Indonesia itself even in street barrows of Jakarta if you know exactly what you are looking for, and manage to avoid dangerous fakes. Finally: bring some 15+ blocking lotion and drink beyond your thirst to prevent heat stroke.

Indonesia has a fair number of provincial hospitals and doctors with varying competence. If you need major treatment try to get to a big city, preferably Jakarta. Ask your consulate, embassy or expatriot residents to recommend a doctor. The Pertamina Hospital (Jl Kyai Maja, Kebayoran Baru, Tel. 707-214) is most often used by foreigners in Jakarta. In case of an emergency you will want to leave the country: Make sure that your travel or medical insurance covers such things as air ambulance.

TRAVEL TO INDONESIA

By air: Indonesia's main international air gateways are **Cengkareng (Soekarno-Hatta) Airport**, Jakarta, and **Ngurah Rai Airport**, Denpasar. Many airlines serve these increasingly important termini from the major cities of Southeast and East Asia, Western Europe, and the west coast USA, with less frequent flights from some South Asian and Middle Eastern airports.

Medan's **Polonia Airport** is also a long-standing international air destination, with cheap hops to Penang and Singapore. The air travel situation is becoming more complex and less rigid all the time, with **Padang**, **Palembang** and **Surakarta** now receiving direct international flights from Singapore. For through travelers, there are also a few international flights in and out of eastern Indonesia: Pontianak to Singapore and Kucing, Tarakan to Tawau, Kupang to Darwin. But for the average, long-distance, short-stay non-Asian visitor, the choice is usually Jakarta, Denpasar, or the short connections from Singapore and west Malaysia. There is no space here for the lore of the ticket jungle, but remem-

GUIDELINES

ber that it is always more informative and cheaper to go to a reputable "cheapie" agent than to deal direct with an airline.

By ship: Incredibly, it is difficult to enter this island nation by sea. The only regular international passenger services are the ferries between Singapore (**Finger Pier**) and Batam island (with onward boat connections to Pekanbaru, Jakarta and elsewhere once inside Indonesian territory), and between Penang and Medan.

DOMESTIC TRAVEL

The **domestic passenger shipping** network which once tied the archipelago together is in a skeletal state today, but what there is is safer and more reliable than a decade ago. Since re-eqipping with modern German-built liners, the state shipping concern **Pelni** has become a competitive alternative for those with sufficiently loose timetables.

Several Pelni ships ply the ports of East Sumatra and North Java on long, scheduled circuits; one, the *Kerinci*, also serves the west coast of Sumatra as far north as Sibolga. Pelni tickets can be bought only at Pelni offices – see the local information sections. Many smaller shipping operations exist; one to avoid if possible is the "pioneer" line **Perintis**, active in insular Riau, whose ships are as bad as Pelni's used to be. On smaller and cruddier vessels, you will probably be moved to hire the upper-deck cabin which some enterprising crewman will offer you, thus eliminating any price advantage of going by sea.

Domestic air travel in Indonesia is highly developed. Thanks to the squadrons of Fokker Fellowships, DC-9s and Airbuses on its internal routes, **Garuda**, the national carrier, has the largest air fleet in the southern hemisphere. If you have your ticket in your hand, there should be no problem with Garuda. Indonesia's second airline is **Merpati**, a Garuda subsidiary flying mainly turboprop machines and serving a more complete network, including airstrips too small for Garuda's jets. Where Merpati duplicates Garuda routes, it is slightly cheaper, but Merpati is not as adept at ticketing and you should check in early. Also cheaper are the private airlines, the biggest of which are **Bouraq** and **Mandala**, both operating mostly on outer island routes. Luckily their ageing British turboprops were sturdily built. Airline offices, and headquarters in Jakarta, are given in the local information sections. Passengers flying Garuda into Indonesia can often claim discounts on pre-booked internal flights.

Only Java and Sumatra have **railways**, and of the three unconnected networks in Sumatra, only the southern one (Tanjungkarang to Palembang and Lubuklinggau) carries passengers. But Java, which once had perhaps the densest rail network in the colonial world, still boasts quite an impressive system despite closures. All of the major cities are served, as are the ferry terminals at Merak and Banyuwangi. Exhaustive class gradations both between and within trains cater for every pocket, and you pay for what you get. The cheapest *(Langsam, Cepat, Gaya Baru, Senja)* are like traveling Javanese villages, complete with livestock, hawkers and thieves.

At the opposite extreme are the *Bima* and *Mutiara Utara* air-conditioned express sleepers, linking Jakarta to Surabaya via Yogya and Semarang respectively. Somewhere in between are the Jakarta-Bandung *Parahyangan* express and the Jakarta-Yogya *Senja Utama* night train. On long hauls, trains can be far safer and more comfortable than buses, if slower. They also deliver you to the city center, whereas long-distance bus terminals are usually peripheral. On the other hand, buying train tickets can be a problem in itself. In Jakarta there are travel agents which can book them in advance, but in most places you must turn up and queue on the day of departure, the earlier the better. Trains generally leave on time, but usually arrive late.

The length of asphalted **road** in Indonesia has quadrupled since 1970, and the roads of parts of rural Java would not now shame rural England. Unfortunately, driving standards and practices have not yet adjusted to the new situation, and drivers belt gratefully down every good stretch, making traffic more lethal than ever before. You may even be thankful to the ever-mounting congestion for cramping the style of suicidal drivers. At least the express **buses** *(bis)* which are now displacing the trains as standard long-distance people-carriers in Java have the advantage of size in any violent encounter. The best new-generation night buses *(bis malam)* have reservable airline-type seats, air conditioning, onboard toilets, videos (for a mixed blessing of blaring midnight melodrama), and meals included in the ticket price. Daytime and local buses, and the full-size *bis kota* ('town buses') found in some of the largest cities, are less salubrious, but still more comfortable for the clumsy western frame than the tiny **colts** (pronounced 'kol') and *bemo* which now dominate short-haul and intra-urban routes. A colt is a Japanese minibus, a *bemo* a covered pickup truck fitted with plank seats. Pick the seat you want – always an aisle seat in a colt – and do not be shifted. Have appropriate coins ready, plus an extra one for knocking on the coachwork to signal when you want to get off. Marvel at the casual, gritty efficiency of the driver/conductor team. Such vehicles are always plentiful and cheap, but seldom leave a terminal until they are full, so do not get on an empty one if you can help it.

Immense distances and poor roads make overland travel in **Sumatra** a far tougher option than in Java or Bali. The euphemistically-named 'Trans-Sumatran Highway', running the whole length of the island from Lampung to Medan and Aceh, is always passable with patience, but you might need a lot of it, as well as an iron constitution, especially in the wet season (any time from October to April). The short wheelbase Mercedes and high-chassis, thick-tyred Japanese buses used are up to the job as earlier vehicles were not, but they have not abolished the misery of interminable cramp, motion-sickness, window leaks and Indonesian pop at distorting amplification. Under ideal conditions the Tanjungkarang – Medan trip takes 4 days, but few would have the stomach for such a sustained assault. Away from the highway, things can be worse still.

If you have enough guts and an international driving licence, you can hire motorcycles and self-drive cars in Bali and sometimes in Java. One car hire office in Java is in front of Adisucipto Airport, Yogya. On Bali you will still need to get a special local licence, available from Denpasar police after a facile test and a hefty charge. Indonesia drives on the left – more or less.

Most so-called **taxis** in Indonesia are actually chauffeur-driven hire cars, available by the hour for a minimum of one hour, and usually expensive. Metered taxis exist on a large scale only in Jakarta, where they are a boon. Never use one whose driver says his meter is *mati* ('dead'). The bottom line in motorised passenger transport is the *bajaj* (pronounced 'bajai'), an Indian-designed motorised tricycle contraption. Found mainly in Jakarta, the nimble *bajaj* can occasionally reach the parts other vehicles cannot reach, but not very fast, and unless you are a good bargainer it might well cost as much as a metered taxi.

Muscle power is not yet obsolete, even in urban Indonesia. **Horsecarts** *(andong, bendi, dokar)* are found in the smaller towns; they have an old world charm, but animal lovers might rather not watch the underfed, cowed beasts terrified by

GUIDELINES

screaming *bemo*. On the other hand, it is a revelation to observe how quickly enlightened westerners reconcile themselves to that very symbol of indignity, the *becak* or tricycle-pedicab. Though excluded from certain arterial roads, scores of these pretty, practical vehicles wait with their human engines at stations and junctions to ferry haughty passengers off through the maze of backstreets and alleys. Foreigners usually overpay *becak* drivers, but then, they probably should.

Guided Tours

Do not be too quick to spurn local guided tours; some of these can show you and teach you things you would not discover on your own, or at least do it faster and cheaper. Mainstream internal tour organisers include **Vayatours** and **Natrabu**, but there are hundreds of small and off-beat operators; see big hotels and local tourist offices for details.

National Parks

A permit from an office of the Directorate of Forest Protection and Nature Conservation (**PHPA**) is required to enter any national park or reserve, except for the pass-free enclaves called **Taman Wisata** (Tourist Parks) within some of them. The PHPA headquarters is at Jl Ir. H. Juanda 9, Bogor. For local branch offices, see the main travel text.

PRACTICAL TIPS

Accommodation

There is a huge range of types and standards of accommodation available, and the cheap end tends to offer the more unusual and rewarding experiences, if you are up to its challenges. Prices vary geographically, being lowest in Bali and small-town Java and highest in urban Sumatra. In general, rooms in the **budget** category, which in this book means less than Rp 12,000 (about US$ 7) per night, are found in *losmen*. In some areas, particularly in Sumatra, these are known by the Malay term *penginapan*. Rooms are individual – dormitories are rare in Indonesia – but in other respects the *losmen* is hostel-like, with thin walls, short beds, dicey wiring, possibly no fans and certainly no air conditioning. Bring a 100 W bulb if you want to read - those supplied are usually impossibly dim. Toilets are of the squat type - you soon get used to them, but they are no place to read the paper. You bathe *(mandi)* by means of an open concrete water tank *(bak)* and a plastic scoop *(gayung)*. Do not climb in the tank! And do not scream for the manager if there are fish in it - they eat the larvae of dangerous mosquitos. Hygiene standards in *losmen* vary hugely, but few are cockroach-free. Noise can also be a problem, especially from the TV set which is usually left on at full volume all evening; the only mercy is that transmission ceases at midnight.

After this catalogue of potential woes, it must be said that many *losmen* have a major redeeming feature other than low cost: they are prime places to learn about Indonesian lives, loves and languages. In some places, however, foreigners are beginning to expropriate and transform *losmen* culture. On Bali and in Yogyakarta, many *losmen* cater to European foibles, providing toast or porridge breakfasts and a higher than usual standard of toilet hygiene. Some are even explicitly closed to Indonesians!

A step above the ordinary *losmen* in price and comfort, **medium range** (Rp 12,000-45,000 or US$ 7-27) accommodation in Indonesia includes a motley variety of dowdy old colonial hotels, spartan new business hotels, and souped-up *losmen* and guesthouses, often grandiloquently calling themselves *wisma*. All three can be very good value, but shop around. Medium range places may afford greater cleanliness, security and privacy than budget ones; many have western toilets, air conditioning and their own restaurants. Above Rp 45,000 or so are **first class** rooms with (more or less) all modern conveniences – although you will have to pay a lot more than that for the night clubs and gymnasia of the top Jakarta hotels. One attraction of better hotels can be some worthwhile free cultural entertainment.

Business Hours

Sunday is a day of rest, but Friday afternoon is also free in honor of the Muslim sabbath; Saturday, on the other hand, is a half day. Government offices work 8.00-15.00 Monday to Thursday, 8.00-11.00 Friday, and 8.00-14.00 Saturday. In practice, nothing much gets done on Friday or Saturday, making Indonesia much more the "land of the long weekend" than Australia.

Commercial offices and banks, on the other hand, work a more familiar Monday-Friday week with a half-day on Saturday, though they tend to open (usually at 8.00) and close (15.00-17.00) earlier than in the west. In the more energetic retailing world, shops often stay open as late as 22.00, including Saturday, although they may close for an afternoon siesta.

Any note on time in Indonesia must conclude with a mention of *jam karet*, 'rubber time'. This phrase is used with a grin whenever something does not occur when it was supposed to.

Crime

Violent crime is now probably rarer in Indonesia than in most western countries. But **theft** – from rooms, vehicles, bags and pockets – is a constant danger, especially for the foreigner, considered rich by definition. Leave as little as possible unattended, be alert, and avoid crowds. Where hotels are concerned, security generally correlates with price.

Drugs are fairly widespread among Indonesian urban youth. But possession and purchase – even of cannabis – is much more dangerous for the conspicuous and vulnerable foreigner.

Customs

Customs can confiscate pornographic and 'subversive' literature – definitions of which may not correspond with yours. Video films are subject to lengthy inspection and best avoided. Any writing in Chinese characters is forbidden. 200 cigarets and 2 litres of alcohol are duty-free.

Eating and Drinking

Eating is a major part of the magic of Indonesia. Not just the food itself, which is always an adventure and can be superlatively good, but also the whole experience of the public eating places, especially the ramshackle *warung* or canvas foodstalls which line so many city streets. Often the most persistent memory of Indonesia is not a great work of nature or man, but simple food amid gaslight and *kretek* smoke and unfamiliar cooking smells on a hot tropical night.

Proper restaurants, despite their often spartan appearance and blaring TVs, also have a special atmosphere of their own. Jot down your order on the pad provided, but do not set too much store by the printed menu, which except in very expensive places is probably very hypothetical. The bill is called *rekening;* tips are not customary. Chinese food in Indonesia is a little-known world, but the pioneer will not be disappointed.

Electricity

Both 110 V/50 Hz and 220 V/50 Hz electricity supplies are in use, the intent being to convert entirely to the latter in the long term. Check which you are looking at before plugging in any foreign appliance. Blackouts occur occasionally even in big cities, and wild current fluctuations are commonplace – a hi-fi or computer will need a surge protector. Poor or remote villages have electricity only from dusk to midnight, or not at all.

Etiquette

The following are some specific rules of formal etiquette, which will help even if you cannot manage the deeper adjustments. Dress should be modest and clean. Shorts, singlets and strapless tops are suitable only for the beach. The demands of 'formality' are not high – jackets and ties, for instance, are almost never worn – so there is little excuse for not meeting them, at least for house and office visits. Talk quietly and with good humour, even in disputes, and try never to show anger, which is regarded as weakness.

Certain gestures are taboo. Never stand with hands on hips, which is aggressive. To beckon or point with the forefinger is insulting; point with the thumb or pursed lips, beckon with the whole hand, palm downwards. Never give or receive with the left hand; it is used with water to clean the anus. This one will become second nature after you have used Indonesian toilets for a time, unless you are the toilet-roll carrying type. If provided with food or drink in an Indonesian house, let it stand until the host explicitly invites you to start. If you empty your plate completely, it is usually taken to mean you are still hungry. Second helpings are customary, so do not overload first time round. Always eat something to avoid insult to the host. Small gifts such as flowers or sweets are regularly given to hosts, but do not offer to share the cost of anything done for you. Indonesians will sometimes honor you by stooping as they pass your chair, keeping their head below yours; if you take this up yourself you will impress conservatives, but be aware that some Indonesians, especially Christians, are actively against this 'feudal' practice.

Bear in mind that the above guidelines refer to those Indonesians belonging to fairly traditional households, and although these are still in the vast majority, students and some urban families may be different.

Holidays

One spin-off of Indonesia's religious diversity is a unique array of **national holidays**, including no less than three New Year's Days – Islamic, Christian and Hindu. Islam contributes the most, but the dates of the Moslem holidays are not predictable without reference to the special lunar calendar. Avoid travelling during *Idul Fitri,* at the end of the Moslem fasting month, when millions of Indonesians hit the road to visit relatives.

Liquor

Alcohol does not play an important part in this mainly islamic society, but there are no severe restrictions for tourists. Imported liquor and beer are usually available only at the bigger hotels and supermarkets and tend to be rather expensive.

Photography

There are only the usual restrictions such as defense installations and bridges. It is important to respect the privacy of individuals, especially in temples. If buying films check date of expiry, even in large stores.

Post and Telecommunications

Despite recent improvements, the **postal service** is still something of a lottery. If everything goes right, it is fast and efficient. But theft is a huge problem. It is particularly risky to send anything vaguely attractive-looking into Indonesia from abroad – even magazines tend to get filched. And to post a letter inside the country, you must first know your way round the obstacle course of an Indonesian post office. Lots of people, but no queues as we know them. Anything short of assault is acceptable manners, but keep things impersonal by never catching the eyes of the people you elbow and jostle. Notice that Indonesians never trust the excuse for gum on the back of their stamps, always re-glueing them from vile pots provided – they know what they are doing. Try to watch the stamps being franked yourself, otherwise some lucky sub-postmaster may supplement his meagre earnings by re-selling them, and your letter goes nowhere. Always use the *Kilat* or *Kilat Khusus* express services, and register anything of value. Poste restante services are widely available. Only bigger post offices can send parcels.

Though still under tremendous pressure, the **telephone system** is now remarkably good by third world standards. Even public booths usually work. Most cities of western Indonesia now have international direct dialing, but it is still much cheaper to use the local telephone office than your hotel phone.

Time

Indonesia spans no less than three time zones, but with the exception of Lombok, the whole of the area covered in this book falls within the western zone, which is 7 hours ahead of Greenwich Mean Time. Lombok is 8 hours ahead of GMT.

Weights and Measures

Indonesia follows the metric system in both weights and measures.

ADDRESSES

Embassies / Consulates

Australia. *Jakarta:* 15 Jl. M.H. Thamrin, Tel: 323109. *Denpasar:* 146 Jl. Raya Sanur, P.O.Box 243, Tanjung Bungkak, Tel: 25997/8. **Austria.** *Jakarta:* 44 Jl. Diponegoro, Tel: 338090, 338101. *Bandung:* 2 A Jl. Prabu Dimuntur, P.O.Box 150, Tel: 439505. **Belgium.** *Jakarta:* Wisma BCA, 15th floor, 22/23 Jl. Jend. Sudirman, Tel: 5780510. *Medan:* 459 Jl. Pattimura, P.O.Box 286, Tel: 520559, 527991. **Canada.** *Jakarta:* Wisma Metropolitan I, 5th floor, Jl. Jend. Sudirman Kav 29, P.O.Box 52 JKT, Tel: 510709. **France.** *Jakarta:* 20 Jl. M.H. Thamrin, Tel: 332807, 332383. *Bandung:* 32 Jl. Purnawarman, Tel: 52864. *Yogyakarta:* 1/I Jl. Sagan, Tel: 4109. *Surabaya:* 10 Jl. Darmokali, Tel: 52864. *Balikpapan:* P.O.Box 6, Tel: 22010/14. **Federal Republic of Germany.** *Jakarta:* 11 Jl. M.H. Thamrin, Tel: 323908, 324292. *Medan:* 271 Jl. S. Parman, Tel: 324073, 327071. *Denpasar:* 17 Jl. Pantai Karang, Sanur, Tel: 8535. **Great Britain.** *Jakarta:* 75 Jl. M.H. Thamrin, Tel: 330904. *Medan:* P.O.Box 163, Tel: 518699. *Surabaya:* 150 Jl. Janur Sari, P.O.Box 310. **Ireland.** *Jakarta:* 11 Jl. Gedung Hijau I, Pondok Indah, Tel: 7690070. **Netherlands.** *Jakarta:* Jl. H.R. Rasuna Said Kav. S-3, 12950, Tel: 511515. *Bandung:* Hotel Savoy Homann, 112 Jl. Asia Afrika, Tel: 439482. *Medan:* 27 Jl. Rivai, Tel: 519025. *Surabaya:* 79 Jl. Sumatra, Tel: 45202. **New Zealand.** *Jakarta:* 41 Jl. Diponegoro, Tel: 330552, 330680. **Philippines.** *Jakarta:* 6-8 Jl. Imam Bonjol, Tel: 348917, 3100345. *Manado:* Jl. Toar, Tel: 2404. **Singapore.** *Jakarta:* Blok X/4, Kav, 2 Jl. H.R. Rasuna Said, Tel: 5201489/90/91/92. *Medan:* 3 Jl. Teuku Umar, Tel: 23356, 513134. **Switzerland.** *Jakarta:* Blok X/3/2, Jl. H.R. Rasuna Said, Kuningan, Tel: 516061, 517451. **United States of America.** *Jakarta:* 5 Jl. Merdeka Selatan, Tel: 360360. *Medan:* 13 Jl. Imam Bonjol, Tel: 322200. *Surabaya:* 33 Jl. Raya Sutomo, Tel: 69287.

Tourist Offices
Outside Indonesia

ASEAN and Hong Kong: 15-07 Ocean Building, 10 Collyer Quay, Singapore, Tel: 5342837, 5341795. **Australia:** Garuda Indonesia Office, 4 Bligh Street, P.O.Box 3836, Sydney 2000. **Europe:** Wiesenhüttenplatz 17, 6000 Frankfurt/Main 1, Tel: 069/233677. **Japan:** Asia Trans Co., 2nd floor, Sankaido Building, 1-9-13 Akasaka, Minato-ku, Tokyo, Tel: 5853588, 5821331. **North America:** 3457 Wilshire Boulevard, Los Angeles, CA 90010, Tel: 0231/387-2078.

GUIDELINES

INDONESIAN LANGUAGE

Hallo	salam
Good morning	selamat pagi
Good day	selamat siang
Good evening	selamat sore
Good-bye	sampai bertemu lagi
What's your name(he)?	apa nama tuan?
What's your name(she)?	apa nama nyonya?
My name is...	nama saya ...
I live in...	saya tinggal di...
Where is the...?	(di)mana...?
How far is it from ...to...?	berapa jauh?
How do I get to...?	bagamaina saya ke...?
How much is it?	berapa harga?
May I have the menu?	saya mau lihat daftar makanan
I would like to have something to drink	saya mau minum
The bill, please!	saya mau bayar
I stay here...days	saya tinggal disini...hari
What's that?	apa ini? / apa itu?
What time is it?	jam berapa?
I	saya
you	kamu
we	kami / kita
okay	baik
yes	ya
no	tidak
big	besar
small	kecil
today	sekarang
afternoon	siang
evening	sore
night	malam
week	minggu
month	bulan
year	tahun
clean	bersih
dirty	kotor
hot	panas
cold	dingin
please	silahkan
thank you	terima kasih
less	kurang
more	lebih banyak
to come	datang
to go	pergi
price	harga
shop	toko
medicineo	obat
market	pasar
room	kamar
vegetable	sayuran
water	air
tee	teh
milk	susu
rice (cooked)	nasi
rice (uncooked)	beras
sugar	gula
salt	garam
butter	mentega
meal	makanan
breakfast	makanan pagi
one	satu
two	dua
three	tiga
four	empat
five	lima
six	enam
seven	tujuh
eight	delapan
nine	sembilan
ten	sepuluh
eleven	sebelas
twelve	duabelas
twenty	duapuluh
thirty	tigapuluh
forty	empatpuluh
fifty	limapuluh
sixty	enampuluh
seventy	tujuhpuluh
eighty	delapanpuluh
ninety	sembilanpuluh
one hundred	seratus
one thousand	seribu
ten thousand	sepuluhribu

Pronunciation:

j . . . . as dj (jet-set)
y . . . . as j (bei ja)
c . . . . pronounced as tj or z.
h pronounced also at the end of a word

CREDITS

AUTHORS

David E. F. Henley is a geographer whose addiction to travel in Indonesia led ultimately to a doctoral thesis on the country's colonial past.

James J. Fox is a noted anthropologist who has written extensively on several Indonesian regional cultures and is now fascinated above all by Java, where his involvement in development projects takes him regularly.

Putu Davies is a historican who combines her academic knowledge with the practical insights of a decade spent living in her beloved Bali.

Anthony J. S. Reid is professor of southeast Asian history at the Australian National University. His work includes classic books on the Indonesian national revolution and the history of northern Sumatra.

Yohanni Johns is a lecturer in Indonesian language and literature and also an expert cook who has produced a number of books on the cuisine of her native Indonesia.

Robyn Maxwell is an acknowledged expert on Indonesian arts and handicrafts. She has traveled to the remotest corners of the archipelago collecting textiles for the Australian National Gallery.

G. Adrian Horridge is a leading authority on Indonesian sailing craft, which he pursues indefatigably during breaks from his work as a research biologist.

Colin P. Groves is a naturalist whose research on southeast Asian mammals led him to a deep interest in ecological and conservation issues in Indonesia.

PHOTOGRAPHERS

Gunderson, Nick 45, 159

Höbel, Robert 8/9, 10/11, 35, 38, 40, 59, 80, 141 L, 155, 160, 194, 227, 228

Kohl, Günter 73, 90, 224, 235

Kunert, Rainer E. 1, 2, 12, 14, 16, 44, 50, 52, 54, 58, 74/75, 94, 116, 130, 135, 139, 164, 174

Maeritz, Kai 110, 152, 173, 191, 238

Müller, Kai Ulrich 62, 184, 213

Muller, Kal cover, 15, 18, 19 R, 21, 24, 26, 27, 28, 31, 32, 36, 42, 48, 53, 60, 63, 65, 66, 67, 69, 70, 71, 82, 86, 91, 96, 97, 106, 111, 122, 127, 129, 132, 137, 138, 141 R, 144, 168, 172, 175, 177, 181, 182, 183, 185, 187 R, 188, 189, 203, 206, 210, 216, 220, 222/223, 225, 230, 231, 233, 237, 239

Oey, Eric 202

Schwarz, Berthold 154, 187 L

Steinhardt, Jochen 19 L, 23, 41, 46, 56, 76/77, 100, 105, 107, 131, 140, 149, 150, 156, 157

Vestner, Rainer 199

INDEX

A

Aceh 72, **169-175**, 176
Aceh Sultanate **64-65**
Adat 58, 59
Adat houses 186
Adityavarman Stones 207
Adityavarman, King 62
Agma Tirtha, religion 55
Agung 107
Agung, Sultan 28, 128, 140
Airlangga, King 132
Ala'ad-din al-Kahar, Sultan 64
Alas River 176
Alas, culture 175
Ali Mughayat Syah, Sultan 64
Alisjabana, Takdir 70
Amangkurat I, Sultan 43
Ambarawa 118
Ambarita 186
Amlapura 167
Ampenan 163
Anai Valley 212
Angklung 91
Angkola 187
Anyer 98
Anyer Kidul 89
Arasbaya 129
Arif Muhammad 95
Arjuna-Butak-Kelud 131
Arjuna-Kawi-Kelud 22
Arjunawiwaha, epic 127
Arjuno-Lalijiwo Reserve 130
Asahan Project 182
Asahan River 181
Asokan, empire 22
Austronesia **37-38**, 49
Austronesians **19-21**, 51

B

Babad, traditional histories 56
Badui, people 92
Badung 58
Bagelen 40
Bakara 187
Bakauheni 221
Bakso 44
Balaikota 97, 97
Bali **48-59**, 237
Bali Barat National Park 236
Bali-Aga, villages 55
Balige 186
Balinese, language 38, 50
Baluran 143
Baluran National Park 141, 236
Banda Aceh 72, **169-172**
Bandar Lampung 221
Bandung 44, **93-95**, 98
  Institute of Technology 93
  Gedung Merdeka 94

Gedung Sate 93
Geological Museum 93
Savoy Homann Hotel 94
Bandungan 102
Bangli 155
Banjar Padangtegal 166
Bantam 89
Banten 40, 89, 98
Banten, language 38
Banyumas 40
Banyuwangi 140
Banyuwangi Selatan Reserve 141
Barong 56
Barong Landung, dance drama 57
Barumun River 188
Barus 62
Batak 70, 182
Bataklands **182-186**
Bataks 64
Batam Island 198, 205
Batang Hari River 204
Batang Palupuh 212
Batavia (Jakarta) 27, 29, 39, 40
Batik 108, 113, 130, **228-231**
Batuan 154
Batubulan 150
Batur 157, 167
Batusangkar 207, 209
Batutulis Ciampea 90
Bawomataluwo 190, 191
Bayan 162
Bayat, tomb 42
Becak 35, 79
Bedono 102
Bedulu 55
Bedulu-Pejeng 56, 57
Belahan 132
Belawan 173
Bengkulu **217-219**, 221
Benteng Ambarawa 103
Besakih 158
Besakih, temples 51
Bharatayuddha, epos 127
Bhatara, goddess 55
Bhatari Dewi Danu 57
Bhatari Durga, goddess 55
Bintan 198
Blambangan 40, 143
Blitar 137
Blora 117
Bogor 87, 90, 98
  Bogor Botanical Garden 90
  Bogor Zoological Museum 91
  Istana Bogor 90
  Kebun Raya 90, 91
  Museum Herbarium Bogoriensis 90
Bohorok 181
Bohorok Rehab. Center 236
Bojonegoro 123

Bondowoso 140
Bonjoi 212
Borobudur **103-105**
Brahma, god 21, 55, 105
Brantas River 134
Brantas Valley 135-136
Brastagi 184, 193
Bratan Lake 157
British 67, 68, 70, 71, 115, 127, 217
Buddhism 21, 55, 57, 104
Budi Utomo 29
Bukit Barisan Selatan Nat.P. 236
Bukit Barisan, mountains 61
Bukit Dharma Durga 151
Bukit Kubu 184
Bukit Peninsula 148
Bukittinggi **209-211**, 214, 215
Buleleng, kingdom 159

C

Cakranegara 163
Candi Belahan 132
Candi Bima 101
Candi Ceto, temple area 114
Candi Dasa 167
Candi Jago, temple 133
Candi Jalatunda 132
Candi Jawi, temple 133
Candi Kalasan, temple 105
Candi Kidal, temple 133
Candi Mendut 104
Candi Pawon 104
Candi Plaosan, temple 105
Candi Prambanan, temple 105
Candi Sari, temple 105
Candi Sewu, temple 105
Candi Singosari 133
Candi Sukuh, temple 113
Candidasa 167
Candra Wilwatikta 132
Carita 89, 98
Celebes (Sulawesi) 15
Celuk 153
Celukanbawang 159
Ceribon, language 38
Chinese 22, 32, 56, 68, 70, 117, 126, 134, 135
Ciater 94
Cibodas Botanical Garden 92
Cibodas National Park 236
Cilegon 98
Ciliwung River 80
Cimahi 94
Cipanas 92
Cirebon 95, 99
  Balaikota 96
  Klenteng Thiaw Kak Sie 96
  Kraton Kanoman 96
  Kraton Kesepuhan 96

252

INDEX

Linggarjati 96
Mesjid Agung 96
Taman Sunyaragi 96
Tomb of Gunungjati 95
Citanduy River 95
Ciwidey 95
Clampea 90
Cremation 51, 52
Cultuurstelsel 29
Cupak 212
Curup 218

D

Dabo 199
Daendals, Herman Willem 28
Daerah Istimewa Yogyakarta 104
Damar Wulan, epic 127
Dated Temple 137
Demak 116
Demak, kingdom 25
Denpasar 144-145, 165
  Abian Kapas Arts Centre 145
  Bali Museum 145
  Main Square 145
  Natour Bali Hotel 145
  Pura Jagatnata 145
  Pura Maospahit 145
  Puri Pemecutan 145
Dewi Danu 57
Dewi Sri, goddess 55
Dieng 101, 118
Dieng Plateau 22
Diponegoro 29, 111
Dokar 35
Dong-Son, culture 56
Dumai 200
Dutch 13, **26-34**, 39, 58, 64, 66, 67, 68, 70, 81, 111, 124, 125, 159
Dutch East India Company 26-30, 39, 40, 80

E

East Java 122-143
Eka Dasa Rudra, ceremony 158
Elephant Cave 55, 151
Enggano 218

F

Florida Beach 89, 98
Fort Marlborough 217

G

Gamelan 14, 16, 91, 101, 108, 110, 113, 134, 154, 155, 164, 211, 232

Gajah Mada 150
Galungang, festival 57
Garebeg Maulud 110
Garebeg, festivals 110
Garut 95
Gayo, people 64, 175
Gede Agung Sukawati 153
Gede Pangrango National Park 92
Gedong 118
Gedong Kirtya 59
Gedong Songo 101
Gedung Cendrawasih 143
Geumpang 176
Gianyar 155
Gili Air 164
Gili Meno 164
Gili Trawangan 164
Gilimanuk 52, 56
Goa Gajah 55, 151
Goa Selamangleng, cave 136
Goa Semar 101
Great Post Road 93, 94, 95
Gresik 123
Gunugsitoli 190
Gunung Agung, mountain 55
Gunung Kawi 55, 152
Gunung Leuser Nat. Park 236
Gunung Penanggungan 131
Gunungsitoli 191
Gunungtua 187

H

Harau Canyon 212
Hatta, Mohammad 70
Hayam Wuruk, King 22
Hinduism 21, 23, 53, 55, 57, 104, 105, 133, 146

I

IPTN Aircraft-Project 93
Ibn Battuta 63
Ijen Plateau 140
Imogiri 108
Indianization 21-24, 54
Indramayu 97
Iskandar Muda, Sultan 65, 170
Iskandar, Nur 70
Islam 23-26, 53, 57, **62-69**, 209, 238-239
Isvara, god 55

J

Jaipongan, dance 91
Jakarta 40, 44, **78-85**
  Bahari Museum 80
  Chicken Market drawbridge 81

  City Hall 80
  Company Wharf 80
  Dabo-Gong 82
  Department of Finance 81
  Dharma Jaya 82
  Gedung Kesenian 81
  Gedung Pancasila 81
  Glodok 82
  Historical Museum 80
  Hotel Indonesia 83
  Irian Jaya Liberation Memorial 83
  Istana Merdeka Palace 81
  Istana Negara (State Palace) 81
  Istiqlal, mosque 79
  Jinde Yuan 82
  Kemayoran 83
  Kota 80
  Lapangan Banteng 81
  Manteng 83
  Merdeka Square 81
  Mesjid Alanwar 83
  Monas 83
  National Archives Building 81
  National Cathedral 79
  National Monument 83
  National Museum 81
  Pasar Ikan 80
  Pasar Seni 79
  Portuguese Church 82
  Senayan Sports Complex 83
  Si Jagur 81
  Statue of Welcome 83
  Sunda Kelapa Harbour 80
  Supreme Court 81
  Taman Fatahillah 80
  Taman Ismail Marzuki 79
  Taman Mini Indonesia Indah 83
  Youth Statue 83
Jambi 62, 195, 204
Japanese 13, 30, 45, 71, 81, 127, 180
Jatiluhur Reservoir 94
Java 22, 27, **36-47**
Javanese, language 45
Jayapangu 57
Jepara 117, 121
Johor, dynasty 197
Jong, ship 27

K

Kabanjahe 183
Kadilangu 116
Kalianda 219
Kalitengah 97
Kaliurang 103
Kaliwuri 97
Kampar River 200
Kampung 35, 79

253

INDEX

Karangasem **160-161**
Karangpandan 114
Karo Batak 183
Kartasura 112
Kawah Ijen, volcano 141
Kawah Talagabodas 95
Kawitan, temple 51
Kebun Raya Rurwodadi 134
Kecak 153
Kecapi 91
Kediri 136
Kemaro Island 202
Kepahiang 218
Kerinci-Seblat National Park 236
Kerinci-Seblat Reserve 214, 218
Kerta Gosa 154
Kertanegara, King 133
Ketambe Rehab. Center 236
Ketaun River 218
Ketembe 176
Ki Pandhan Arang, Sultan 42
Klenteng Thiaw Kak Sie 97
Klungkung 154
Kokar 146, 165
Kopeng 103
Kota 81
Kota Gede 107
Krakatau, volcano 17, 61, **88-89**
Kraton Hadiningrat 112
Kraton Kanoman 96
Kraton Kesepuhan 96
Kraton 108, 123
Kris 65
Kretek 35
Kroncong, music 35
Krui 221
Krupuk 130
Kubu-culture 204
Kubutambahan 160
Kudus 116, 121
Kuta **147-149**, 164, 165
Kutacane 176

L

Labuan 42
Labuhan 89, 98
Labuhan Lombok 164
Ladang agriculture 162
Lagundi Bay 191
Lahat 203
Lake Cangkuang 95
Lake Maninjau 212
Lake Ranau 221
Lake Rawapening 102
Lake Singkarak 212
Lake Tawar 176
Lake Toba 61, 69, 183, 186, 193

Lalang River 204
Lambo 234
Lamno 169
Lampung **219-221**
Langsa 174
Lawang 134
Lebak 93
Lebong Tandai 218
Legian 147, 165
Lembang 94
Lembar 163
Lhokseumawe 174, 175
Limakaum 207
Lingga 199
Linggajati 97
Lombok **161-164**
Loro Jonggrang Theatre 107
Lovina Beach 167
Ludruk, drama 128
Lusi river valley 117

M

Maclaine Pont 93
Madura **128-130**, 143
Madurese, language 38
Magelang 103, 111, 118
Mahabharata, epos 23, 35, 91, 112
Mahameru, mountain 55
Majapahit 34, 107, 108, **135-136**, 143
  Bajang Ratu 136
  Candi Brahu 136
  Candi Surowono 136
  Candi Tegowangi 136
  Candi Tikus 136
  Mojokerto 136
  Pendopo Agung 136
  Purbakala Mojokerto Museum 136
  Purbakala Tirtoyoso Museum 136
  Purbakala Trowulan Museum 136
  Tralaya 136
Majapahit, King 25
Majapahit, kingdom 22, 42
Makam Maulana Malik Ibrahim 124
Makam Proklamator, tomb 138
Makam Suharto 114
Malacca 26, 28
Malang **133-134**, 143
Malay, language 30, 38, 39, 61
Malays **195-205**
Maligai Stupa 200
Malik Ibrahim of Gresik 125
Malik as-Salih Tombstone 174
Maluku 26, 27

Mancanegara, kingdom 40
Mandailing 186
Mandailing Batak 187
Mandailing, culture 187
Mangkunegaran 113
Mantingan 117
Manuaba 56
Maribaya 94
Mas 154
Mataram 34, 40, **162-164**, 167
Medan 63, 70, 72, **179-182**
  Buitenzorg Botanical Gardens 181
  Chong Ah Tie 181
  Grand Mosque 180
  Hotel Dharma Deli 180
  Immanuel Church 180
  Jl. A. Yani 180
  Jl. Jen. Sudirman 180
  Maimun Palace 180
  Merdeka Square 180
  Pulau Brayan Cemetery 181
  Vihara Gunung Timur 181
Melayu, kingdom 204
Mengwi 155
Mentawai Islands 214, 215, 236
Merak 89
Merapi 112
Merapi, volcano 103, 207
Merauke 172
Merbabu, volcano 103
Meru Betiri 143, 236
Meru Betiri Reserve 141, 236
Mesjid Agung 96
Metro 220
Minangkabau 68
Minangkabau Highlands **207-215**
Minangkabau, kingdom 62, 67
Mohammad Hatta 211
Moluccas (Maluku) 15, 31
Monkey Dance 153
Monkey Forest 156
Monsoon 16
Moon of Pejeng 56
Mt. Agung 158, 160
Mt. Arjuna 130, 131
Mt. Batukau 157
Mt. Batur 55, 56
Mt. Bromo 139, 143
Mt. Galunggung 95
Mt. Halimun Reserve 92
Mt. Kelud 132, 137
Mt. Kerinci 214
Mt. Lawu 113
Mt. Leuser 176
Mt. Merapi 211
Mt. Meru 131
Mt. Papandayan 95
Mt. Pengsong 164
Mt. Pesagi 221

INDEX

Mt. Rinjani 162, 167
Mt. Ungaran 101
Muara Takus 205
Mughal, dynasty 25
Muhammad, Arif 95
Muis, Abdul 70
Multatuli 93
Museum Grobogan 117
Museum Kereta Api 102
Musi River 201

N

Nahdatul Ulama 39
Nasi Campur 226
Nasi Gudeg, food 226
Nasi Padang, food 226
Nasi Tumpeng, food 226, 227
Negara 157
Negara Agung 40
Negarakrtagama, 164
Ngarai Sianok Gorge 210
Nias 193
Nias Island **189-191**
North Chalk Hills 123
Nusa Dua 148, 165

O

Oncer, dances 164
Oosthoek 138, 140, 141
Opor Ayam, food 224
Ottomans 64

P

Padang **212-214**, 215
Padang Lawas 193
Padang Lawas, temple areas **187-189**
Padangpanjang 211
Padangsidempuan 187
Padangtegal-Kecak 166
Padri 68
Padri Movement 209
Padris 67
Pagaruyung 208, 209
Pajajaran, kingdom 87
Pajang 41
Pajaran, kingdom 80
Pajeng 150
Pajeng Moon 150
Pajeng-Bedulu 52
Pakerisan, river 150
Palembang 22, 61, 68, **201-203**, 205
Pamakesan 130
Pandaan 132
Pangandaran 95, 99, 236
Pangkalan Brandan 182
Panguruan 186
Panjang 221

Panji, 127
Parangtritis 107
Pararruyung 67
Pare 136
Pariaman 213
Parvati 55
Pasai 63
Pasemah megaliths 203
Pasisir 40
Pedang 70
Pejeng 56, 150
Pejeng Giant 151
Pekalongan 114, 120
Pekanbaru 199, 205
Pelabuhan Ratu 93, 98
Peliatan 154
Pepper 63, 66, 89
Pemalang 44
Pematang Purba 184
Pematang Siantar 182, 193
Penang 66
Penataran **136-138**
Penestanan 153
Pengalengan 95
Penulisan 157
Penyenget 198
Perindungan Hutan dan... 235
Pesantren 39
Petanu, river 150
Peureulak 174
Portuguese 25, 27, 29, 39, 64, 117, 123, 136, 197
Prahu 128, 233, 234
Prambanan 104
Prambanan, temples 22
Prapat 185, 193
Priangan, volcano 88
Prinangan 40
Pulau Laut 199
Pulau Seribu 80, 85
Puncak 92
Puncak Area 98
Pura Dasar, temple 154
Pura Kebo Edan, temple 151
Pura Kehen 155
Pura Kehen, temples 51
Pura Luhur 157
Pura Meru 163
Pura Penataran Sasih 56, 151
Pura Penulisan, temples 51
Pura puseh, temple 51
Pura Sakenan 148
Pura Tegeh Koripan 157
Pura Ulun Danu, temple 157
Puri Dalem 155
Puri Lukisan Museum 59
Purnavarman, King 38
Purwodadi 121
Pusering Jagat, temple 151

R

Raden Ajeng Kartini 117
Raden Mas Pekik, prince 41
Raden Saleh 108
Raffles, Thomas Stamford 28, 29, 35, 104, 111, 128, 197, 217, 218
Rain forest 237
Ramayana, 23, 35, 91, 107, 112, 127
Randai, dance 211
Rangda 53, 56
Ratu Loro Kidul 107
Rebab 25
Rejang, culture 218
Rembang 117, 121
Reog Ponorogo, dance 128
Reog, dance 128
Rhineland Missionary Society 184, 190
Riau 195, **197-201**
Rimba Panti Reserve 212
Rokan River 200
Rudat, dances 164
Rusli, Marah 70

S

Sabang 172
Sagarmatha **17-18**
Sailendra, dynasty 103
Sakai, culture 200, 204
Samosir 183, 186, 193
Samosir Island 184
Sang Hyang Widhi Wasa 55
Sangeh Monkey Forest 237
Sangiran 114
Sanjayas, dynasty 103
Sanskrit, language 21, 23, 25, 39
Sanur **147-149**, 165
Sarangan 114
Sasak 163
Sasak, people 164, 230
Saté, food 44, 225, 227
Sawahlunto 214
Seblat 218
Segura Anak, lake 162
Selecta 134
Selo 103
Seluk Tambanglaras 37
Semarang 44, 114, 120
Sembiran 55
Sembiran, temples 50
Senaro 162
Sendangduwur Mosque 123
Sendratari, dance 112
Senopati 107
Senopati, Sultan 41
Serangan Island 148
Serat Caentithini 37

255

INDEX

Serayu, river 101
Shadow plays 14, 23, 25, 46
Shiva, god 21, 55, 101
Siak River 199, 200
Sibayuk, volcano 184
Siberut 214
Sibolga 62, 193
Sidoarjo 130
Sigalegale, puppet dances 185
Silindung 69
Simalungun Batak 184
Simanindo 186
Sindok, King 107
Singamanaraja, epos 186
Singaraja 59, 159, 167
Singosari, dynasty 22, 133-135
Sipisopiso Waterfall 184
Situbondo 140
Siwa 105
Sjahrir, Soetan 70
Sjarifuddin, Amir 70
Solo 112-114, 119
Solok 209
Songket, dress 211
Sosok, culture **162-163**
South Sumatra 195
Spice Islands 15
Spices 24, 26
Spies, Walter 153, 155
Sri Adi Jayapangus, King 56
Srivijaya 61-62, 201, 203, 204
Srivijaya, dynasty 57
Srivijaya, kingdom 22
Strait of Malacca 195, 219
Subak 149
Sufi Movement 39
Suharto 33, 90, 113
Suharto Sumatran 72
Sukarare 162
Sukarno 31, 33, 34, 83, 90, 93, 94, 152, 181, 210, 218
Sukawati 154
Suling 91
Sumatra 22, **61-73**
Sunan Agung, Sultan **40-43**, 42, 43
Sunan Giri 124, 128
Sundalands 40, **90-93**
Sundanese, language 37
Sungaipenuh 214
Sungsang 201
Surabaya 40, 44, **125-128**, 142
  Bangunrejo 128
  Candra Wilwatikta Theatre 128
  Grahadi 126
  Gubeng Station 126
  Hotel Majapahit 126
  Jarak 128
  Jl. Pemuda 126
  Joko Dolog 126
  Kampong Ngampel 125
  Museum Angkatan 127
  Red Bridge 125
  Tanjung Perak 126
  Tugu Pahlawan 127
Surakarta 112
Surau, prayer hall 67
Surya, god 55
Sutan Sjahrir 211

T

Tabah Penanjung 218
Tabanan 155, 156
Tabut Festival 213
Tahu, food 226
Takengon 176
Taman Sunyaragi 97
Tampaksiring 55, 152
Tanah Datar 207
Tanah Sebarang Wetan 40, 138
Tangse 176
Tanjung Pinang 198, 205
Tanjungbumi 130
Tanjungkarang 219, 221, 221
Tarikat 67
Taruma, kingdom 38
Tarumanegara, kingdom 22, 87
Tarutung 187
Tasikmalaya 95
Tatar Sunda 91
Tattei Batti Reserve 237
Tawangmangu 114
Tegal 114
Tegaltamu 150
Teluk Dalam 190
Telukbetung 221
Tembayat, tomb 42, 43
Tempe, food 225, 226
Tenganan 55, 161
Tengger 139
Toba Batak 70, 184
Tomas Dias 208
Tomb of Gunungjati 95
Tome Pires 123
Tomok 185
Tongging 184
Topeng masks 113
Toya Bungkan 158
Trowulan 135
Trunyan 55, 158
Trusmi 97
Tuban 123
Tuktuk Peninsula 185
Tulungagung 137

U

Ubud 152, 166
Ujung Kulon National Park 89, 98, 235
Ulama 69
Ulee-balang 66
Ulu Watu, temple 146

V

Varna 55, 58
VOC (Dutch East India Co.) 28, 82, 92, 110, 140, 171, 212
Viet Nam 56
Vishnu, god 21, 55, 105

W

Waktu Lima 162
Waktu Telu 162, 164
Wali Songo, saints 39, 95
Wallace Line 161, 235
Warung 53
Way Kambas Wildlife Reserve 221, 236
Wayang gedog 127
Wayang golek 91
Wayang kulit 14, 112, 113, 133, 154, 232
We 172
Weru 97
West Bali National Park 157
West Java 86-89
Wilwatikta Open Air Theatre 142

Y

Yawadwipa, epos 38
Yeh Pulu, rock 151
Yogyakarta 104-112, 108, 118
  Affandi Museum 112
  Alun-alun Lor 110
  Benteng Vredenburg 110
  Gajah Mada 110
  Gedung Negara 111
  Jl. Tirtodipuran 112
  Kraton Yogyakarta 109
  Loro Jonggrang Theatre 112
  Mesjid Ageng (Grand Mosque) 110
  Monument Diponegoro 111
  Ngasem, bird market 110
  Paku Alaman Palace 111
  Sasmitaloka Jenderal Soedirman 111
  Sonobudoyo Museum 111
  Taman Sari 112
  Taman Sari (Fragrant Garden) 110
  Water Castle 110
Young Sumatran League 70